DEPARTMENT OF THE ENVIRONMENT

Restoration of Damaged Peatlands

with particular reference to lowland raised bogs affected by peat extraction

B. D. Wheeler and S. C. Shaw

University of Sheffield

LONDON: HMSO

ISBN 0 11 752978 8

Enquiries relating to this publication should be addressed to:

Minerals Division
Department of the Environment
2 Marsham Street
London
SW1P 3EB

or

Environmental Consultancy, University of Sheffield (ECUS)
343 Fulwood Road
Sheffield
S10 3BQ

Main cover photograph: Solway Moss (Cumbria). [Air Images, Haltwistle, Northumberland
(Tel: 034-320798), courtesy of B. Henderson & I. Richardson]
Back cover, insets: Milled peat harvesting and revegetating block-peat cuttings at Thorne Waste
(S. Yorkshire) [P.C. Roworth, ARPS]

Photographs and figures presented in the report are by B.D. Wheeler or S.C. Shaw, unless otherwise indicated.

Acknowledgements

This report has been prepared by B.D. Wheeler (Department of Animal and Plant Sciences, University of Sheffield (APS)) and S.C. Shaw (Environmental Consultancy, University of Sheffield (ECUS)), based partly on contributions from:

T.R. Birkhead	(APS)	R.P. Money	(APS)
P. Bradley	(ECUS)	D.L.J. Quicke	(Imperial College, London)
G. Foster	(Balfour-Browne Club)	C. Routh	(ECUS) (Nominated Officer)
A.L. Heathwaite	(Department of Geography, University of Sheffield)	R. Tratt	(APS)

With further assistance from: H. Morris, R. Houghton and J Clay (ECUS); R. Walker (Academic Computing Services, University of Sheffield); S.Ball (Department of Law, University of Sheffield).

The research was funded by the Department of the Environment (Minerals Division). We would particularly like to thank the nominated officer for this project, Dr Tom Simpson and Miss Ann Ward (Chair of the Steering Committee) for considerable guidance and helpful comments throughout the duration of this project.

We would like to express our thanks to all those people who have facilitated the progress of the project, in particular members of the project steering committee for helpful comments and advice on the draft project reports:

Miss A. Ward	(Minerals Division, DoE)	Dr M. Meharg	(Countryside and Wildlife Branch, DoE (NI))
Dr T. Simpson	(Minerals Division, DoE)		
Mr R. Sykes	(Secretary) (DoE)	Dr J. Miles	(The Scottish Office)
Mr C. Bain	(Royal Society for the Protection of Birds)	Dr T. Parr	(Directorate of Rural Affairs)
		Mr R.A. Robertson	(Consultant to Peat Producers Association)
Miss L. Binnie	(Cumbria County Council)		
Mr D.M. Ellis	(Doncaster Metropolitan Borough Council)	Dr J. Smart	(Plantlife)
		Mr R. Stockdale	(Peat Producers Association)
Dr W. Fojt	(English Nature)	Dr A. Stott	(Directorate of Rural Affairs)
Mr P. Gordon	(Cumbria County Council)	Mr D. Stroud	(Joint Nature Conservation Committee)
Mr S. Gorman	(Cumbria County Council)		
Mrs J. Heap	(English Nature)	Mr S.F. Shorthose	(Humberside County Council)
Mr P. Immirzi	(Scottish Natural Heritage)	Dr A.R.D. Taylor	(Somerset County Council)
Mr R.A. Lindsay	(Scottish Natural Heritage)	Dr C.P. Turner	(Sinclair Horticulture & Leisure Ltd)

We are grateful to the staff of the Joint Nature Conservation Committee, English Nature, Countryside Council for Wales, Scottish Natural Heritage, Countryside and Wildlife Branch of DOE-NI, and local Wildlife Trusts for willingly providing information for the project and allowing access to unpublished details of sites, and especially to those who gave up their time to show us round sites and discuss the issues involved in restoration initiatives.

We would like to thank all those who have found the time to comment on the draft reports, answer queries and provide informative discussion and advice. We particularly thank J. Blackie, J. Bromley and M. Robinson (Institute of Hydrology), M. Cox (Gifford & Partners), H.A.P. Ingram (University of Dundee), M.C.F. Proctor (University of Exeter), I. Richardson (Richardson's Moss Litter Company), C.E. Wright (DoE), D. Wynne (Bord na Mona).

We would like to thank colleagues in The Netherlands and Germany, who gave up their time to show us restoration sites and stimulated much thought and discussion; in particular, J. Schouwenaars, J. Blankenburg, H. Kuntze, B. Bölscher and D. Maas. We are similarly grateful to J. Feehan, G. O'Donovan, D. Wynne, J. Ryan and C. Douglas for providing information and showing us around sites in Ireland.

We are particularly grateful to Dr Jos Schouwenaars (University of Groningen) and Dr Hans Joosten (State University of Utrecht) for many valuable insights and comments on the draft project documents.

We would also like to thank all those who kindly provided photographs for inclusion in the report.

Contents

List of Figures

List of Tables

List of Boxes

List of Plates

Note that details of most of the sites illustrated are given in Appendix 6.

Summary

S1 Background and introduction

Peatlands are wetland ecosystems in which the substratum is composed largely or entirely of peat. Peat is an organic soil formed primarily from the remains of plants that have accumulated *in situ*. Peat accumulates in wetland habitats, largely because waterlogging and associated anoxia retards the decomposition of plant material. Peatlands can be divided into two main types: *ombrotrophic* peatlands are mires irrigated directly and more-or-less exclusively by precipitation inputs (rain, snow, fog *etc.*); *minerotrophic* peatlands are additionally irrigated by groundwater. This report is concerned largely with ombrotrophic peatlands, and particularly with those known as 'raised bogs' (the peatlands currently most utilised by the UK peat industry), although some consideration is also given to restoration of fen peat workings.

In Britain, as in much of north-west Europe, peatlands were once very extensive and until recently, some of these areas were largely regarded as unproductive wasteland. In consequence, in Britain as widely elsewhere, a substantial proportion of former raised bogs have been claimed for agriculture and forestry. Others have been heavily damaged by commercial or domestic peat extraction, or by drainage or repeated burning. The area of bog that has retained much of its (presumed) original character is undoubtedly small: figures collated for the National Peatland Resource Inventory (NPRI) suggest that in Britain the proportion of 'near-natural primary raised bog' which remains is only about 6 % of the original extent of raised bog of some 70,000 ha (although any such estimated figures have to be treated with some caution, not least because the concept and compass of the category called 'lowland raised bog' is itself open to debate).

In recent years there has been a growing recognition of the importance of lowland raised bogs for natural history, science and conservation. Important features include:

- visual character of the peatland landscape;

- peat archive (archaeology, palaeoecology);

- biological resource (communities and species of flora and fauna).

It is recognised that many UK peatlands, including lowland peat bogs, are amongst the country's most important nature conservation habitats. However, the peat industry also has a legitimate interest in some of these peatlands through mineral extraction activities carried out under valid planning consents. Many of the consents lacked planning conditions controlling methods of working, restoration and aftercare.

This report, prepared for the Department of the Environment, provides guidance on the potential for the restoration of worked-out or damaged bogs to regenerate, maintain or increase their nature conservation value and on the possible approaches, practicality, and requirements that may be appropriate to facilitate this process. It provides background information and scientific advice for formulating and implementing restoration strategies for the after-use of currently worked or abandoned cut-over bogs. It is intended for use by all parties with an interest in peatland restoration, including central and local government, the peat industry and conservation bodies. The report addresses two rather different issues: (i) restoration of the abandoned peat fields; and (ii) the maintenance (if needed, restoration) of vegetated peat remnants.

A separate report contains the results of a wide-ranging collation and review of relevant published and unpublished data, supplemented by consultation with appropriate individuals and organisations, and site visits in the UK, Ireland, The Netherlands and Germany.

This summary should be used in conjunction with the main reports, which provide background information and the context and elaborate on the points made here.

Two broad caveats underlie all of the information and observations presented here:

(1) Once any site has been damaged, be it a bog or other habitat, it is never possible to return it *exactly* to its former condition. However, in the case of a bog damaged by peat extraction, it may be possible to repair or regenerate a bog by restoring conditions similar to those under which it originally developed and hence to encourage the return of typical raised-bog species, both flora and fauna. In some instances this may even offer a 'value-added' approach in terms of wildlife conservation, as in those sites which have long-since been damaged by drainage, partial agricultural conversion and burning as well as peat extraction. However, effective restoration is likely to be a slow process, measured in terms of decades;

moreover, given the present 'state of the art' it is not possible to *guarantee* that a peat-accumulating system will subsequently redevelop. These guidelines and observations should not be used to provide a justification for peat extraction on little-damaged bog sites.

(2) Not all of the techniques outlined in this document are well 'tried and tested', as bog restoration is a relatively new activity. There are strong reasons to suppose that they have a good chance of success, but to help enhance knowledge and understanding of effective restoration practices, it is suggested that all attempts at the restoration of damaged peatlands should be regarded as experimental, and the projects carefully recorded and monitored. There is still much to learn. The advice given here is based upon current experience, knowledge and thought, but the guidelines may need to be amended or updated as new techniques and results from existing studies become available.

With respect to the main subject of this report, *i.e.* bog *restoration*, the terminology proposed by R. Eggelsmann and co-workers has been followed in which:

rewetting   is the re-establishment of surface-wet conditions;

renaturation   is the redevelopment of an appropriate vegetation;

regeneration is the renewed accumulation of peat.

These concepts are here grouped under the generic head of *restoration*, but they are by no means discrete and separate: indeed, the redevelopment or regeneration of a bog follows a continuum; there are no abrupt divisions or thresholds between each phase. Successful bog regeneration must seek ultimately to re-establish the self-regulatory mechanisms that ensure that permanently wet conditions are maintained.

S2 The raised-bog habitat

S2.1 Introduction

Hydrologically, raised bogs can be considered as two layered (*diplotelmic*) systems comprised of an uppermost 'active layer' (or *acrotelm)* and a lower so-called 'inert layer'[1] (or *catotelm)* [*Figure 1.2*]. The acrotelm is usually thin (< 50 cm), is largely aerobic, and forms the main functional horizon for plant growth, comprising the living plant cover, especially *Sphagnum* species, passing downwards into recently-dead plant material and thence to fresh peat. Water moves readily through the acrotelm, which both contains and regulates the water-level fluctuations (caused by variations in water inputs and outputs) and forms the main conduit of water discharge from the bog.

The catotelm is defined as the zone of permanent saturation, is largely anaerobic, and usually comprises the bulk of the peat of a raised bog. It is built from acrotelm peat which becomes incorporated into the catotelm as the bog grows upwards. The catotelm peat is typically more consolidated and more-humified than the acrotelm, within which water moves exceedingly slowly.

Raised bogs may originate and develop by a variety of pathways. The 'classic' developmental sequence shows initiation of ombrotrophic peat from within minerotrophic swamp or fen, which has developed over a pool or lake as part of a *hydroseral* or *terrestrialisation* process; however, raised bogs may also develop over once relatively dry land, by *paludification*. Starting points for raised-bog development include such diverse habitats as reedswamp, floating vegetation mats, herbaceous fen, fen carr, woodland and saltmarsh. The ombrotrophic peat may overlie a layer of fen peat or rest more-or-less directly on a mineral substratum. In the past, raised bogs have developed spontaneously in many parts of Britain. They are thought to represent climax ecosystems.

Raised bogs provide an acidic, waterlogged, low fertility environment, associated with the development of a characteristically species-poor flora and fauna.

S2.2 The vegetation of UK raised bogs

The vegetation of ombrotrophic bogs in Britain is rather species-poor and comparatively uniform. Most plant species 'characteristic' of little-damaged raised bogs also occur quite widely in some other habitats. However, although the vegetation may be confined to a limited range of species, some combinations of plant species are apparently unique to bogs. The *Erica tetralix–Sphagnum papillosum* raised and blanket mire community (*NVC*: M18) may be regarded as the 'natural' core community-type of many lowland raised bogs, and hence its recreation can be seen as the main focus of the restoration of damaged raised bogs.

The vegetation cover, in particular the abundance of some *Sphagnum* species, is of critical importance to the development of the bog. This is because they provide much of the physical basis of the bog itself and of some of its environmental conditions. In large measure the vegetation defines the habitat. This is because:

*   plant growth provides the basis for peat formation, water storage and impeded drainage;
*   plant growth provides the basis for much of the microtopography of the site and thus creates small-scale water gradients;
*   the growth of *Sphagnum* species helps to create the strongly acidic conditions of ombrotrophic peat and water.

---

[1] The catotelm is not, strictly speaking, 'inert'.

Within raised bogs, plant species show some micro-habitat 'preferences', particularly associated with the heterogeneous microtopography of the surfaces, which is induced primarily by plant growth. Certain plant species tend to occupy fairly distinct zones with respect to water level, either as part of the small-scale mosaic of a patterned bog surface [*see Figure 1.10*] or as part of a wider change in water level from the wet centre to the drier margins of a bog. It is possible to recognise a broad pattern of vegetation zonation across the surface of at least some little-damaged raised bogs, from the central complex of shallow pools and hummocks to the drier rand.

Examination of some of the main characteristics of typical bog plant species enable the following general points to be made:

- they are mostly of geographic wide distribution;
- they are not specific to ombrotrophic bogs;
- most are long-lived perennials;
- there is little evidence that seeds and spores are generally important in maintaining populations in undisturbed bogs;
- seeds of most species are light and may be readily dispersed;
- they typically have slow relative growth rates;
- they are apparently efficient at scavenging nutrients from dilute solutions;
- most have efficient internal conservation of nutrients;
- ombrotrophic conditions seem generally sub-optimal for growth.

A few species are uncommon or rare, and especially in damaged sites, for example *Andromeda polifolia*, *Drosera anglica*, *D. intermedia*, *Rhynchospora fusca*, *Dicranum undulatum*, *Sphagnum fuscum*, *S. imbricatum* and *S. pulchrum*. Of these, *Andromeda polifolia* and *Dicranum undulatum* are largely specific to raised bogs in Britain.

S2.3 The invertebrates of raised bogs

Invertebrates form an important part of the animal life of peatlands, living in and on the water and plants. In general there are few bog 'specialists', perhaps reflecting the waterlogged, oxygen-poor, acidic environment with 'poor-quality' food sources. However, raised bog sites support populations of a high proportion of notable and rare insect and spider species both within the UK and on mainland Europe, and a number of species can be identified for which raised bogs appear to have particular conservation importance. These include the beetles *Bembidion humerale* and *Curimopsis nigrita*, both known thus far only from the Humberhead Levels in the UK.

Areas which have revegetated following hand-cutting or similar block-cutting peat-removal regimes may offer a wider range of invertebrate habitats than little-damaged raised bogs, and consequently, may support a wider species range than the latter, although the species concerned are not necessarily characteristic of bogs. The extensive, bare surfaces created by modern extraction methods may be far less amenable to recolonisation than the small-scale hand peat cuttings.

S2.4 The birds of raised bogs

Open areas of little-damaged bogs typically have low bird density and low species richness, and very few bird species are considered to be particularly characteristic of raised bogs. The lack of trees and shrubs make such bogs largely unsuitable for passerines, other than at the margins, as these birds require perching posts and nesting sites above ground level. The vascular plants of bogs offer a limited food supply to birds and some of the species which do breed are common and widespread breeding species elsewhere in Britain. Species composition can be strongly influenced by the relative degree of flooding or desiccation and vegetation-types (*e.g.* scrub) developed on damaged sites. Both species richness and density may be greater on partly-damaged sites, largely owing to the increased variety of available habitats.

Birds of particular conservation value which occur on lowland raised bogs in Britain include significant populations of breeding teal, red grouse, black grouse, dunlin, curlew, redshank, nightjar and twite, and wintering populations of pink-footed geese, Greenland white-fronted geese, greylag geese, hen harrier and merlin.

S3 Archaeology, palaeoecology and restoration

Peatlands are important for archaeology and palaeoecology as they have the potential to provide detailed evidence of post-glacial vegetational history, environmental change and human occupation in specific areas (both for the site itself and its surroundings), through preservation within the peat layers of organic and inorganic artefacts, as well as pollen and plant and animal macrofossil remains. Peat cutting is also considered to be part of the 'industrial heritage' and abandoned areas may have positive value as a derelict industrial landscape. Archaeological aspects should therefore be considered in proposed restoration schemes and there is a need for close co-operation between conservationists and archaeologists, to arrive at the optimum solutions for site restoration.

S4 Characteristics of cut-over raised bogs

S4.1 Introduction

Peat extraction directly removes both the peat and the living surface from those areas where it occurs. It may also affect adjoining areas of uncut peat, particularly through indirect drainage and fragmentation.

Natural revegetation of cut-over bogs depends critically on the hydrological regime maintained after cessation of operations and the nature of the substratum exposed, as these will affect the physical and chemical conditions presented for plant re-establishment. Some sites affected by peat extraction have lost virtually all bog species; others retain undisturbed areas of vegetation that support typical bog species. In yet others, once-dug areas, which have since recolonised provide refugia for some bog species. Indeed, all of the vegetation-types and most of the plant species recorded from uncut bog surfaces have been recorded also in revegetated workings (although often in fragmentary form). Revegetated workings may also support various additional community-types, most notably when fen peat has been exposed. The protection of 'refugia' during peat extraction is important to ensure a source of recolonist species.

S4.2 Main methods of peat cutting

The surface configuration of cut-over bogs depends largely on the method and duration of the peat extraction and the extent of drainage. Three main types of peat extraction have been practised in the UK: block cutting (by hand or commercially), milling and extrusion, although local and regional variations may also occur. Certain procedures are common to most of these operations: drainage; removal of surface vegetation; drying of the excavated peat on the surface and the provision of trackways for access, passage of vehicles, trains *etc*. For extraction by milling and extrusion, the fields are often also cambered to increase surface water run-off.

All peat extraction creates disturbance and destroys the immediate habitat for plants and animals. The capacity of much of the bog flora and fauna to survive peat operations on-site will depend upon the availability of proximate, less-disturbed habitats. Large-scale commercial peat extraction inevitably reduces the opportunities for such survival compared to smaller hand-digging operations.

Block cutting

Machine block cutting is essentially a mechanised version of the traditional hand cutting method. Blocks of peat are cut from a vertical face, and stacked on baulks alongside to dry. Commercial block cutting usually produces a regular system of baulks, flats and trenches, but extensive cutting can produce a largely flat surface. Trenches may sometimes retain water and even support a (usually limited) flora of, for example, a few *Sphagnum* species.

When carried out on a small scale, the peat cutting by hand can produce a fairly haphazard surface topography, although 'organised' hand cutting could be as extensive as machine cutting. One of the main 'benefits' of hand cutting (for subsequent restoration) was that the surface vegetation was (apparently) often thrown back into the trenches, with some potential to survive and act as an inoculum once operations ceased. The typically slower speed of extraction also permitted the bog species (plants and invertebrates) in the trenches to become established between successive cuts. This 'shoeing' may be of great importance in determining the course and time of recolonisation [*Chapter 4*].

Milling (or rotavation)

Milled peat production involves the iterative removal (by scraping or vacuum) of a thin layer of peat (15–50 mm) from the surface of drained, usually cambered, peat fields (from which the surface vegetation has been removed). The harvesting cycle takes about three days, but depends on weather conditions (*e.g.* to air-dry the peat). Some 8–12 harvests may be taken each season. The surfaces remaining after milling ceases are bare and dry, and usually cover large areas. The residual peat may also be compressed, partly as a result of drainage, but also from the repeated passage of the harvesting machinery.

Milled fields are generally less well suited to *spontaneous* re-establishment of bog species than are *some* block-cut areas as they do not have closed hollows which can naturally accumulate water as is the case with some block-cutting complexes. They may also have various other features which may influence the development of restoration strategies:

- individual fields are usually large (usually of maximum possible length);

- large areas must be worked simultaneously to be economic (*e.g.* for efficient use of personnel and equipment when climatic conditions are suitable for harvesting);

- a phased program of exploitation followed by restoration may be difficult to achieve.

Extrusion ('Sausage') peat production

This technique is mostly used for production of fuel peat, and is used on both raised and blanket bogs, either on a small or commercial scale. A rotating blade extracts peat from below the surface, before it is extruded as 'sausages' through nozzles onto the ground to dry. Where the vegetation has first been removed, the surface remaining after extraction is similar to that left by milling, but there will be more sub-surface drainage channels. Even where the vegetation is not removed, considerable damage to the surface vegetation and microtopography still occurs. The technique is akin to mole-draining and often leads to surface-dry conditions.

S4.3 Starting conditions for restoration

The starting conditions for restoration that are presented by cut-over bogs may thus vary considerably. Table S1 summarises some typical starting features of cut-over sites.

S5 General aims and principles for restoration

S5.1 Aims of restoration

Raised-bog sites that have been damaged by peat extraction or other land-uses have various possible after-uses. In the past, these have often included afforestation, conversion to agriculture, use as refuse tips *etc.* However, changing attitudes and circumstances, coupled with a recognition of the conservation value of some peatlands and their potential for regeneration have led to the view amongst conservationists and others that the after-use presumption for many, if not all, peat-cutting sites should be for nature conservation. There is accordingly a need for proper planning controls over workings which will include a requirement on the peat industry to restore their sites, possibly to enable raised-bog conditions to re-establish.

Table S1. Summary of possible starting conditions on cut-over bogs.

Topography

Topography may be very variable across an abandoned peat extraction complex, depending on the method and extent of peat extraction. Two situations can be distinguished, at several scales [2.1]:

Massifs	blocks with an overall *convex* or *water shedding* profile.
Depressions	hollows with an overall *concave* or *water holding* profile.
	Note that *depressions* may occur within *massifs*.

Block cutting often produces a regular system of baulks, flats and trenches, but can sometimes result in a largely flat surface.

Milling often produces a series of long peat fields, usually as cambered beds.

Peat workings are often lower than adjoining refugium areas (which may be uncut remnants or revegetating cuttings).

Water conditions

Peat extraction and drainage modify or destroy typical bog vegetation and the charcterisitc bog acrotelm. They also typically induce dry conditions in cut-over areas and may also affect adjoining upstanding remnants either directly or indirectly [*Chapter* 2]. In consequence:

- water levels are generally too low for growth of peat-building *Sphagnum* species (except perhaps in some hollows);
- water levels tend to fluctuate to a greater extent than in 'intact' bog;
- water storage capacity of the peat is typically lower than in 'intact' bog;
- water loss may be exacerbated if the mineral subsoil is exposed.

Physical and chemical conditions

The peat surface of a little-damaged bog is typically acidic and nutrient-poor. Peat extraction and drainage may lead to changes in the physical and chemical characteristics of the peat available for recolonisation [*Chapter* 2]. For example:

- rewetting dried peat may lead to release of nutrients;
- rewetting dried peat may lead to further acidification;
- peat extraction may expose fen peat or mineral ground;
- bare, dry peat provides an inhospitable physical environment for vegetation establishment.

Vegetation

The vegetation of remnant peat surfaces and of abandoned peat workings can be extremely variable, depending upon such constraints as degree of damage, depth of extraction, topography, base status, nutrient status, water level (and source) and length of time since last worked [*Chapter* 4]. Areas to be restored may thus include the following [*Box 3.1*]:

- bog-*Sphagnum* vegetation
- *para*-bog-*Sphagnum* vegetation
- 'dry' bog vegetation
- fen vegetation
- non-wetland vegetation
- completely bare surfaces
- open water

In addition to their potential for exploitation, the perceived 'values' of raised-bog sites include:

- plant and animal species and communities;
- habitat-types;
- mire system;
- archaeological and palaeoecological archive;
- 'peatland landscape'.

Conservation priorities and restoration preferences for raised bogs will be influenced by the perceived importance of these various foci. The requirements for the preservation or, where appropriate, restoration of these features are not identical. For example, it may be possible to preserve some of the features of a 'bog landscape', or the archival value of a raised-bog peat deposit, without necessarily retaining, or redeveloping, all of the characteristic biota of such an ecosystem. Conversely, in an extensively cut-over site it may be possible to regenerate a typical bog surface, with characteristic biota, but the peat archive cannot be replaced and the redevelopment of a 'bog landscape', whilst possible, is likely to be long-term and outwith the foreseeable future. A further complication of choice arises in those raised-bog sites which have been badly damaged but where the replacement habitat has itself developed a high conservation value centred on species and habitat conditions that are essentially atypical of raised bogs. There is also a need to consider the current condition of a site when determining most appropriate after-use. It is recommended that the appropriate options for specific sites are discussed with nature conservation advisers, in the light of the information contained in this report [in particular *Chapters 4, 6 and 7*].

The following objectives are currently adopted in the conservation management of some raised-bog sites in the UK:

- *the maintenance or re-establishment of wildlife interest not pertaining to bogs*
  This may include: heath (wet and dry); rough grass; birch scrub and woodland; open water; reedbeds; herbaceous fen; fen meadow; fen woodland.

- *the maintenance or re-establishment of viable populations of typical bog species*
  This may include bog species-populations maintained on badly-damaged bog surfaces or redeveloped within peat workings *etc.* Such sites may support, and be valued for, a range of species (some uncommon) other than bog species, including both flora and fauna.

- *the maintenance or re-establishment of a regenerating, self-sustaining bog ecosystem*
  This includes the maintenance of the on-going development of an existing little-damaged bog; the regeneration of a damaged peat massif; and initiation of 'new' raised bogs in peat workings. In

vegetation terms, such sites have, or, it is hoped will redevelop, vegetation referable to the M18 bog community over all or part of their surface.

There are thus at least two rather different approaches to the conservation and restoration of damaged raised bogs. One is essentially species-centred and aims to maintain or re-establish viable populations of typical bog (or other) species. The other is mire-centred, to maintain or recreate a developing raised-bog ecosystem (with associated bog species). These two approaches are not necessarily mutually exclusive.

It is possible to maintain or re-establish populations of many bog species on damaged bog surfaces (providing they do not dry excessively). Such artificial situations may maintain numbers of typical bog species as effectively as on a little-damaged or regenerating bog (although species will not necessarily be present in the characteristic proportions, or with the typical micro-topography). Biodiversity may be increased relative to a little-damaged bog by the occurrence of supple-mentary species on damaged sites with increased diversity of habitats (including those produced by past peat extraction activities and those atypical of bogs).

In principle the regeneration of a *Sphagnum* bog may be expected to occur spontaneously in a variety of situations. However, some starting conditions are more immediately suitable for raised-bog redevelopment than are others; and where the object of restoration initiatives is to regenerate an ombrotrophic ecosystem within the foreseeable future, it is likely to be desirable to consider active procedures that will optimise and facilitate such a process, rather than to adopt a *laissez faire* approach in which natural processes of mire development are just left to sort themselves out.

Where parts of cut-over raised-bog sites have considerable existing conservation interest, there is often an understandable desire amongst conservation-ists to maintain or enhance the *status quo*. By contrast, there may be scope for a wider choice of objectives for current workings where the existing biological interest is minimal, but even in current peat workings the restoration opportunities may be constrained by practicalities. For example, in some sites there may be little option but to accept that wet restoration will, at least in the first instance, be to a minerotrophic habitat (or, or course, some form of alternative 'dryland' habitat). However, even this does not necessarily preclude the development of raised bog in the long term.

S5.2 Principles of raised-bog restoration

As different species and restoration objectives may have markedly different environmental requirements, the creation of appropriate habitat conditions can only be considered in terms of the specified objectives. The purpose of rewetting damaged peatlands is not just to make them wet, but to provide conditions appropriate for the desired renaturation and regeneration object-ives. The development of restoration strategies needs to consider the conditions required to realise the specified objectives, whilst recognising, for example, that the conditions needed to *re-establish* desired types of vegetation may differ from those required to *maintain* existing examples.

Two broad approaches to peatland restoration can be distinguished: *repair* and *rebuilding*. *Repair* usually entails relatively minor restorative operations (ditch-blocking *etc.*) and aims at *direct reinstatement* of the desired objectives. It is particularly appropriate for sites with limited damage. *Rebuilding* involves the *redevelopment* of the peatland and implies that the desired endpoint cannot be produced directly but requires phased construction, with a starting point often rather different from the final product. In some cases, further 'damage' may be required to produce a secure foundation for rebuilding. Depending on the restoration objective, the restoration of bogs extensively damaged by commercial peat extraction will usually require rebuilding rather than repair.

The aim of restoring cut-over peatlands to raised bog may be achieved following four different paths:
- direct colonisation of bog peat by plants associated with typical bog vegetation (M18);
- colonisation of ombrotrophic water by plants and mosses associated with bog pools followed by successional invasion of other bog species;
- colonisation of fen peat (or wet mineral soils) by fen plants followed by successional development to bog;
- hydroseral colonisation of minerotrophic water to form fen and thence bog.

Restoration initiatives must endeavour to create environmental conditions which are conducive to the development of acid mire vegetation and peat accumulation, and re-instatement of an acrotelm with properties comparable to that of a little-damaged bog, with the intention of leading to the development of a self-sustaining, ombrotrophic system. To halt or reverse hydrological effects of peat cutting and drainage and their impacts on the flora and fauna, two main objectives must be realised:
- establishment and maintenance of consistently wet surface conditions, maintained primarily by rainfall;
- development of a suitable peat-forming vegetation-type, dominated by *Sphagnum* species.

In practice, these may be brought about by the following measures:
- increase in appropriate retention of nutrient-poor precipitation input;
- prevention or reduction of water inputs from other sources;
- facilitation of waterlogging;
- facilitation of colonisation by bog species, in particular, *Sphagnum* species;
- reduction of water-level fluctuations.

These aims will be mainly realised by on-site management, but with careful regard to activities within the surrounding catchment which may affect the site [*Chapters 5 & 8*].

A summary of the main factors affecting restoration options is given in Table S2 [*see also Chapters 3 & 4*].

S6 Planning a restoration strategy

S6.1 Introduction

There are at least three broad approaches to peatland restoration: *unplanned*, *empirical* and *measured*. Although several important conservation sites are largely a product of unplanned restoration, this cannot be commended as a reliable approach to realise a specific restoration goal. The 'empirical approach' is one in which restoration is substantially based upon an intuitive appraisal of the requirements for habitat manipulation, rather than upon the data acquisition and prediction, which forms the basis of a 'measured approach'. Both of these approaches have merits and limitations [*see Chapter 7*], and in practice, many restoration schemes will rely on a sensitive interaction between them. In most cases, empirical procedures require some 'hard' data to help ensure (and monitor) their success, but equally, the empirical approach may provide the only realist option when data acquisition is inadequate or of limited predictive reliability. To yield maximum benefits for restoration, data acquisition should be: (a) focused upon answering specific, defined questions that are critical to particular aspects of restoration; (b) sufficiently well resourced to ensure that reliable and useable data are collected; and (c) performed by experienced practitioners who are aware of the inherent problems and likely limitations of their studies. Emphasis must be placed on the need for collection of relevant and reliable data and for a considered appraisal, at the outset of planning a restoration strategy, of the salient questions and data that are likely to be required to answer them.

Thus, in most damaged peatland sites, particularly those subject to extensive commercial peat extraction, some form of plan will be required to optimise restoration, particularly where it is desired to restore

Table S2. Summary of main factors affecting restoration options

---

Legal considerations

National, regional and local planning legislation and policies	*Will affect decisions on most appropriate after-use (particularly with respect to planning conditions and costs)*
International and national conservation legislation (including wildlife, archaeology, palaeoecology *etc.*)	*Will affect decisions on most appropriate after-use and methods by which it can be achieved*
Legislation relating to water resources (*e.g.* water impoundment, abstraction, discharge)	*May affect methods by which a particular after-use can be achieved*
Obligations to neighbouring land-owners *etc.*	*May constrain possibilities for after-use and methods by which they can be achieved*
Miscellaneous legal constraints (rights of way, grazing rights, public utilities *etc.*)	*May constrain possibilities for after-use and methods by which they can be achieved*

Practical considerations

Topography (within site and in relation to surrounding landscape) (includes size and shape of site, and disposition of surface)	*Determines the feasibility of retaining water on site, preventing minerotrophic inputs etc. and methods by which these can be achieved*
Hydrology	*It is important to establish causes of dryness, degree of drainage, water inputs and outputs, interactions with water in surrounding 'catchment' etc.; affects feasibility of potential options; provision of appropriate hydrological conditions determines recolonist species and type of succession*
Peat depths and types (or mineral substratum)	*Hydrological, physical and chemical implications*
Climate	*Affects feasibility of potential options for water retention, and timescales for phasing of work*
Flora and fauna	*Preservation of existing interest; availability of recolonist species (especially Sphagna); availability or provision of appropriate hydrological and chemical conditions for individual species; possible conflicting conservation demands*
Archaeology / Palaeoecology	*Preservation of existing interest; monitoring during extraction*
Chemistry	*Base and nutrient status of substratum (peat or mineral) and irrigating water determines recolonist species, and rates of recolonisation; air pollution may influence recolonisation, especially by Sphagna*
Access by machinery	*May affect feasibility of different management operations, particularly in relation to phasing of work*
Practical assistance	*Possibilities may affect management options (includes machinery, survey, monitoring, management etc.)*

Financial considerations

Financial considerations	*May affect management and monitoring options (possibilities for compensation and grant-aid etc.; costs of surveys, feasibility studies, management operations, on-going maintenance etc.)*

---

the raised-bog habitat. A plan is required to ensure that, *inter alia*:

- areas of existing natural history interest that will not be subject to further peat extraction are safeguarded;
- peat workings are left in a condition optimal for restoration;
- restoration practices and objectives for specific areas are well phased and integrated with one another;
- techniques appropriate to achieve specific restoration objectives are identified.

Formulation of such a restoration plan for a raised-bog site requires the acquisition of some information about the site in question. Information (environmental and biological) is particularly required (i) to help select appropriate restoration options; (ii) to identify the constraints upon the chosen options and to enable informed decisions to be made on the most appropriate ways to achieve specific objectives; and (iii) to provide base-line data for monitoring purposes. Consultation with various statutory and non-statutory bodies will form an important part of the planning stage. These include the local mineral planning authority, heritage, conservation and water resources bodies. It is also likely to be necessary to involve specialists in order, for example, to carry out survey work; interpret the results; assist in the preparation of an appropriate restoration scheme with detailed specifications and perhaps occasionally to provide legal advice.

The variability of starting conditions amongst damaged lowland peatlands means that a universal statement of 'information required' cannot be made, although it is possible to identify some of the main types of information that may be required.

Assessments will be based on information derived from (a) a preliminary 'desk study' by collation of existing information and (b) from on-site investigations. The latter, together with interpretation of the information, may require the expertise of specialists from several different disciplines. Collection of superfluous information should be minimised by careful scoping of the site assessment programme (an example of the potential scope of a feasibility study is given in Table 7.1).

S6.2 Potential legal and land-use constraints on development

The relevant legislation (local, national and international) which may affect development [*Appendix 2*] should be investigated and its implications for restoration options identified. The most important areas to be considered concern legislation relating to planning, conservation and water resources. Consultations with the local planning authority, conservation bodies and water resources bodies are therefore of particular importance. Searches should also be made for possible constraints such as common land, rights of turbary, rights of way, riparian rights, mineral rights, shooting rights, grazing rights, location of public utilities such as gas pipes, electricity pylons *etc.* The implications of any such constraints for the project should be assessed.

S6.3 Financial considerations

Unless funding for restoration work has been agreed in advance, the feasibility of restoration options may depend on financial limitations, as well as practical and legal constraints, and the potential for financial or practical assistance from statutory and non-statutory bodies should be assessed.

S6.4 Field investigations

The aim of the field investigations is to build on the information gathered in the preliminary desk-study, enabling all the relevant options to be considered in the formulation of an appropriate restoration strategy. Site surveys must necessarily gather information on a wide range of inter-related topics (topography, hydrology, peat depths *etc.*), so it is desirable to co-ordinate efforts from interested parties. Particular care should be taken to ensure that data acquisition is well focused, sufficiently well resourced and performed by experienced

practitioners who, when appropriate, are aware of the likely limitations of their studies.

Site physical characteristics

A broad survey of the topography and physical characteristics of the site should be carried out to obtain information on the following factors, if not already available in sufficient detail from existing documentation:

- general size and shape; extent of site in relation to whole peat body;
- surface and subsurface topography; peat depths;
- geology and soils underlying and surrounding the site;
- access for machinery and equipment;
- location of existing tracks, pathways, boundaries, buildings and other structures; location of potential hazards (*e.g.* rubbish tips).

Hydrology

The major problem for the restoration of most damaged bog sites is the lack of sufficient water of appropriate quality at or near the surface of the bog to sustain the growth of peat-building Sphagna. It is essential to identify the causes of dehydration and the main water inputs and outputs in different areas of the bog. Useful information may be obtained while peat extraction is on-going, for example incorporating pump tests to gain information on water gradients and flows.

It is recommended that expert hydrological advice is sought on the level of detail required for an adequate hydrological assessment of a site in relation to the proposed restoration objectives. Information which may be required could include the following (at least those items marked * are likely to be needed):

- climatic information*;
- details of water courses* (type, distribution, slope, degree of functioning);
- water outputs*;
- topographical disposition of peat fields* and remnants*; peat depths* and sub-surface contours;
- peat hydraulic conductivity;
- vegetation characteristics;
- distribution and stability of open water*;
- potential for water supply;
- local and regional context of the site.

Substratum characteristics and water quality

The chemical properties of water and peat will have a profound influence on the plants that will colonise a given area of peatland, and on the likely course of subsequent succession [*Chapters 1, 2 & 4*]. They may also affect the long-term preservation of some archaeological structures. Thus some basic chemical data may be needed to make decisions on the most appropriate strategies and outcomes.

Knowledge of the type of peat present is very important in assessing the potential and options for restoration. One of the most important factors is whether the peat is ombrotrophic (bog) peat or minerotrophic (fen) peat. Simple assessment of the degree of decomposition of the peat (humification value) may also give insights into likely water storage capabilities and permeability of the peat, and its suitability for use in the construction of water-retaining structures.

Biological interest

A survey and assessment of the existing biological interest of a site is an important component in the formulation of a restoration strategy. Where possible, field survey should build on the information collated during the initial desk study [7.4]. The aims of the survey should ideally include the following:

- identification and assessment of any areas with existing biological interest;
- identification of any species or communities with special conservation status (*e.g.* statutory protection) either present on, or using the site; for the less common species, some assessment of population size should be assessed;
- identification of any potential conflicts between existing conservation interest and aims of restoration strategy;
- assessment of the potential for 'natural' and 'assisted' recolonisation of damaged or rewetted areas (*i.e.* the availability of inoculum *etc.*);
- identification of areas with 'undesirable' species or communities (*e.g.* scrub *etc.*);
- identification of potential 'threats' to the existing flora and fauna;
- provision of base-line data for monitoring.

Archaeological and palaeoecological interest

A search should be undertaken for existing documentation or records and professional advice sought on the potential archaeological interest of the site. In addition to the palaeoecological record and artefacts, the historical and industrial landscape and buildings on a cut-over site may be of interest, and may warrant recording before remedial action is undertaken. Specific points which should be considered during an archaeological investigation include:

- the 'value' of the site both in terms of the individual structures and artefacts and the site as a whole;
- the importance of the site in the context of others in the area;
- the historical and industrial landscape;
- the palaeoecological record contained in the peat;
- the conservation needs of any finds and potential for conflict with wildlife conservation aims (and restoration methods).

Additional assessments

Assessments should also be made of:

- land use on and around the site;
- potential for the control of fire (identification and assessment of access routes for vehicles carrying fire-fighting equipment, potential water sources and firebreaks *etc.*);
- engineering assessment, particularly on sites where restoration involves construction of bunds, movement of considerable amounts of peat *etc.*, considering the nature and properties of the materials available on site, the existing topography, the condition of structures, the potential for building water-retaining constructs, the potential for access by machinery and the movement of water through the site;
- safety assessment – *e.g.* consideration of physical and chemical hazards, and health and safety legislation;
- assessment of potential implications of rewetting for nearby inhabitants – *e.g.* increase in biting insects.

S7 Options and procedures for restoration

S7.1 Introduction

Practical experience of wetland restoration and creation suggests that chances of success are likely to be improved by defining clear objectives [*Chapters 4 & 6*] and identifying appropriate management strategies for their achievement [*Chapters 5 & 8–10*]. In most situations, the procedures adopted and associated outcomes of raised-bog restoration are likely to be a combination of desirability modified by feasibility. The feasibility of specific objectives will be determined primarily by the starting conditions available for restoration, *viz.* the environmental context of the site and the particular conditions created by peat extraction or other forms of damage [see Table S1]. Tables summarising the likely outcomes of restoration procedures from a contrasting range of starting conditions are given in *Chapter 6* [*Table 6.1*]. It is recommended that these tables are used as the basis for discussions between regulatory and planning professionals and professional ecological advisors when identifying options to follow for individual sites.

S7.2 Restoration options for ombrotrophic peat surfaces

In a little-damaged bog, the character, integrity and on-going growth of the system is in large measure maintained by the functional characteristics of the acrotelm (see above). In a damaged bog, where there is no acrotelm (in its full, functional sense), the surface is essentially characterised by relative instability of various environmental variables, especially water level.

The essential problem of restoration of bog vegetation on a damaged surface is one of 'kicking' the system from the 'damaged surface' stable state to a 'bog-acrotelm-based' stable state. The difficulty of this is that the conditions required to redevelop an acrotelm with the properties typical of little-damaged bog surface are in considerable measure provided by this sort of acrotelm itself. A solution to this problem is to try to construct devices that mimic some of the properties of the original acrotelm and which permit its redevelopment by sustaining the growth of typical bog species. Many of the different approaches to bog restoration essentially represent different ways of attempting to solve this problem.

The re-instatement of a *Sphagnum*-based vegetation on a damaged ombrotrophic surface is widely regarded as a most desirable aim of raised-bog restoration [*Chapter 3*]. It requires the establishment and maintenance of consistently wet surface conditions. The extent to which this is possible will be influenced by the prevailing climatic conditions and regulated by the main water-balance terms of each bog, *viz.* rate of precipitation input, rate of water loss (lateral and vertical discharge and evapotranspiration) and water storage at the peat surface.

Rewetting problems may be greater on massifs (which have a propensity to shed water) than in depressions (which are typically water-holding areas) [*see Chapter 2*]. Various approaches can be used to rewet massifs [*Chapter 5*; *Table 6.1a*], but particular difficulties can be found with badly damaged remnants. Likewise, a series of upstanding blocks, at different levels, which are found in some (usually abandoned) peat extraction complexes can present particularly intractable problems for restoration. In some situations it may have to be accepted that effective rewetting is not feasible, in which case the remnants may be left to support some replacement habitat – which may include some bog species – though they are ultimately likely to be wasting assets.

Because of their situation, effective rewetting of peat fields [*Chapter 5*; *Table 6.1b*) may be technically less difficult to achieve than rewetting of massifs. In many cases it will be necessary to have structures to impound water against lateral flow and to increase storage, though this will depend upon the topography and disposition of the abandoned surfaces and the climatic context. The flat or gently sloping surfaces of modern commercial peat fields are often well suited to rewetting over extensive areas. Nonetheless, the rewetting of peat fields cannot be divorced from that of peat massifs, particularly if the aim is to regenerate a bog across the whole site, integrating both peat fields and the massifs (see below).

S7.3 Restoration options for minerotrophic peat surfaces

The type of vegetation that develops in abandoned peat workings in fen peat is primarily a function of water depth (and stability), water quality (particularly base-richness and nutrient-richness) and management regime (if any). Peat workings within fen peat can provide a variety of habitats, which are valued for conservation for various reasons and in some cases are managed to maintain or redevelop these interests:

- *open water*   (interest often mainly ornithological and entomological);
- *reedbeds*   (interest often mainly ornithological and entomological);
- *herbaceous fen* (various types);
- *fen woodland*;
- *fen meadow*;
- Sphagnum *bog.*

Prospects for restoration of minerotrophic surfaces will depend critically upon the topography of the site, the water level that can be maintained and the quality of the water used to achieve this (*Table 6.1c*). In some cases revegetation within flooded peat workings has produced some of the most important areas of fen currently extant within the UK. Such hydroseral situations are also susceptible to *Sphagnum* establishment and in some locations considerable thicknesses of *Sphagnum* peat have accumulated (up to 1 m depth in *c.* 100–150 years) and an ombrotrophic surface has re-established. By contrast, *Sphagnum* re-establishment on solid fen-peat surfaces is generally much more limited (except in high rainfall regions), probably on account of periodic dryness and irrigation with base-rich water.

The formulation of desirable restoration options for fen peat sites is often more difficult than for sites based on bog peat as there is often more scope for habitat manipulation and of renaturation outcome. A primary decision is whether to focus upon the recreation of bog or fen, though these options are not mutually exclusive, as some forms of fen can give rise to bog vegetation. With the fen option, the choice then becomes the type of fen desired, as this can be influenced by determining water sources and water levels. The choice of objectives is likely to be determined by topography, availability (and quality) of minerotrophic water sources and implications for on-going management and maintenance as well as by conservational desirability.

Procedures adopted for rewetting fen peat will depend strongly on the surrounding topography of the peat workings. In general, rewetting can be achieved most readily where the workings form a closed depression (within bog peat, fen peat or mineral soil) or where they have been deliberately bunded. In this situation it may be possible to inundate the depressions. In other situations cut-over fen surfaces are flat and located at about the same level as, or even higher than, surrounding farmland. In this case attempts to maintain a permanently high water table on the peat surface with minerotrophic water may be difficult without causing (at least temporary) waterlogging of adjoining land. Bunding may be used to help hold water on the site, both to prevent flooding of adjoining land and to maintain a high water level in the fen peats. In some situations, it may be necessary to provide a drain to carry away water from the agricultural land, to help prevent the bund from drying out, and occasionally to provide 'top-up' water to the fen in dry summers.

S7.4   Restoration options for mineral substrata

In some sites peat has been extracted to expose large areas of the underlying mineral substrata. Specification of restoration options for this situation may be subject to the same problems as for fen peat with respect to variation in the character of water sources and sinks. It is further complicated by the great variability of physico–chemical characteristics of the substrata, which, for example, may vary from very acidic gravels to base-rich clays. Growth of Sphagna and other bog species may be just as good (if not better) on acidic, nutrient-poor mineral substrata as it is on ombrotrophic peats and may provide the basis for the development of bog in the long term.

S7.5   Integration of the restoration of remnant massifs and commercial peat fields

In some situations the restoration of damaged peatlands can be approached piecemeal. This approach is likely to be most satisfactory when it is possible to provide independent hydrological control of particular land parcels. For example, in the fen peat basins of individual holdings in the Somerset Levels it may often be possible to renature each working independently of the others. Similarly, some sealed depressions within ombrotrophic peat may be rewetted independently of their surroundings; indeed, such an approach may be the only practical possibility in some sites where cut-over surfaces have been left at widely differing levels. This approach may be very effective in maintaining populations of bog species within the landscape (*i.e.* production of a series of 'bog-gardens') but it is less suited to the co-ordinated regeneration of an entire mire [*see Chapter 5*], for which a more holistic approach to water management is likely to be desirable.

The options for the water management of composite sites, where the aim is to restore (or maintain) bog conditions in both the peat fields and the massif, are essentially:

a) to treat the massifs and peat fields largely as separate objects; this approach involves the artificial maintenance of high water levels in the massif and does not attempt to restore the bog as a single entity. The possibility of future integration, as accumulating peat over the peat fields coalesces with that on the massif, is not precluded but is unlikely to occur rapidly;

b) to unify the massif and the extraction fields by encouraging or engineering a common water mound appropriate to maintain, or recreate, wet conditions in the massif. The possibilities for this will depend upon the salient characteristics of the water mound associated with the remnant massif. Approaches which have been suggested are (i) to reduce the height of the massif to the level of a sustainable water mound; (ii) to elevate the water levels (over the peat fields) around the remnant massif; (iii) grading of the peat surface up to the massif.

In some situations it may be necessary to treat the peat fields and massifs separately in the short or medium term, while aiming for integration as a whole in the long term. It is important to avoid the situation where treating areas separately could lead to a conflict of conservation interests.

In many instances, restoration of a raised bog does not *demand* the rewetting of adjoining land, even in those cases where it once formed part of the original peatland area. However, in some instances localised rewetting could enhance the coherence of the bog or effective rewetting of a bog may only be possible by some manipulation of the drainage in the surrounding land. This is likely to be the case where land-drainage systems directly (a) drain the mire or (b) indirectly drain it, in situations where the water table in fen peat or an underlying aquifer would otherwise form the impermeable base to the water mound. Rewetting of peat workings in fen peat may have greater repercussions upon the adjoining land as often the ability to rewet the workings may depend upon water supply and retention that is determined, directly or indirectly, by adjoining land drainage systems.

S7.6   Optimisation of peat working practices and starting conditions for restoration

It is not possible to set out universal guidelines on desirable working practices, as these will partly depend upon site-specific features, including:

•   conservation objectives;

•   character of the existing biological resource;

•   character and configuration of the remaining peat deposit (especially topography and peat properties);

- environmental context (especially climate, but also characteristics and use of the adjoining landscape);
- existing or future planning constraints.

However, it is possible to identify some of the underlying principles and suggest working practices which should facilitate the restoration process, and which should be taken into account, particularly if planning permissions and conditions are under review. General requirements include:

- a scientific assessment of the character of the site, possibly by independent scientists, with particular regard to features important in determining desirable and feasible restoration options, based on factors identified in *Chapter 7*;
- a restoration strategy should be devised and agreed for the site, based on the scientific assessment and conservation objectives [*Chapter 3*];
- where feasible, peat extractors should optimise and phase working operations to facilitate the agreed restoration strategy;
- working practices should aim to minimise further damage to abandoned areas and refugia, and, where feasible, enable restoration work to commence on some working areas as soon as possible;
- at cessation of operations (in parts or all of the site), peat fields should be configured into an (agreed) condition that will optimise restoration (*i.e.* to maximise use of *in situ* machinery, operators and infrastructure) [*Chapters 5 & 8*].

The following principles should be taken into consideration, and implemented where possible:

- Important refugia (which may include little-damaged areas of bog, as well as revegetated cuttings or damaged areas with an important biological resource) should be identified and steps taken to preserve or enhance their existing conservation interest.

- If feasible and necessary a buffer zone [*Chapter 8*] should be designated around the core part of any refugium areas, which should also remain uncut.

- Work should start on the restoration of abandoned areas and maintenance of refugia as soon as possible, so that dehydration is minimised.

- Peat should be extracted in such a way as to leave upstanding baulks to a specified eventual height at agreed intervals.

- If feasible, operations should be phased such that:
  (i) Contiguous areas should be completed in sequence.
  (ii) Areas closest to refugia should be abandoned first, leaving agreed depths of peat.

- If the aim is to regenerate ombrotrophic bog directly, it is recommended that *as a general rule* a minimum of 50 cm of *ombrotrophic* peat be left *in situ*. Sufficient peat should also be left to allow for constructs to impound water (bunds or a scalloped surface).

- Drains should not be dug into mineral subsoil (unless this is impermeable and unlikely to lead to downward water loss). [Where minerotrophic conditions are produced, fen

vegetation will result. It is quite possible that ombrotrophic bog may develop from this, by natural successional processes, but this may take longer than when ombrotrophic conditions are retained *in situ*.]

- Where possible, 'nursery' pools for the 'farming' of *Sphagnum* should be initiated, to provide an inoculum for abandoned areas [*Chapter 9*].

- Drainage operations should be assessed, and where possible redesigned to minimise impacts on remnants and areas undergoing restoration. In low rainfall areas it may be desirable to pump drainage water into abandoned peat workings *etc.*, although this will partly depend on the quality of the pumped water [*Chapter 5*].

S7.7 Rewetting and revegetation

Once an area has been brought out of production, further operations should start as soon as practicable to facilitate the creation of optimum conditions for rewetting and revegetation, including the building of constructs, such as bunds where necessary [*Chapters 5, 8 and 10*], though this should be planned to ensure that rewetting initiatives do not preclude subsequent access or actions elsewhere on the site. In sites where peat extraction is ongoing in adjoining areas, it will usually be most cost-effective to make use of the machinery available on site for restoration work. Some of the main constraints to be overcome and potential solutions are identified in Table S3.

Rewetting

Approaches considered for minimising hydrological change within upstanding peat remnants and for rewetting cut-over sites include:

- elevation of the water level by ditch-blocking;
- natural subsidence of peat to the position of the perched water mound;
- sculpting of the peat surface to the position of the perched water mound;
- elevation of the water level by containment within bunds;
- elevation of the water level by increasing water levels in the surrounding area;
- inundation using bunds;
- reduction of the level of the peat surface to form lagoons;
- provision of supplementary water.

The potential applications and limitations of these procedures in different situations are considered in *Chapter 5* and practical approaches in *Chapter 8*. In most situations, it will be necessary to utilise more than one technique to optimise rewetting. Where possible, use should be made of the existing network of embankments *etc.*, raising levels where necessary, although the permeability of the baulks should first be determined to assess their efficacy. On milled surfaces, it may be necessary to subdivide large peat fields to create lagoons to facilitate rewetting and renaturation. Conversely, on block-cut surfaces, depending on the

Table S3. Practical constraints and possible solutions in the restoration of cut-over bogs

Constraint	Possible solution
Sloping surfaces and cutting fields at different levels	Reconform surface to create more level conditions; create lagoons, as a series of 'paddy-fields' where necessary
Uneven topography	Reconform surface to create more level conditions; lower the height of some baulks
Loss of bog basal area, with steepened hydrological gradients	Peripheral bunding; raise water levels in claimed areas surrounding site; provide supplementary water; create lagoons; remove peat
Water losses through drainage	Block all ditches and outfalls where possible; ditches cut through to mineral soil should be sealed along the whole length unless shown to be water-tight
Lack of water storage	Provide permanent inundation; consider use of mulch (e.g. bunkerde[1]) if available.
Widely fluctuating water levels	Increase control of water levels and increase water storage
Water loss through base of bog	Investigate nature of sub-peat mineral material and connectivity with regional water levels – remedy if possible (a greater depth of residual peat may help to reduce the amount of downward seepage)
Input of water of 'undesirable' quality	Block or re-route sources if possible
Lack of recolonist bog species, especially Sphagna	Inoculation from elsewhere on site (or further afield); Sphagnum 'farming' and inoculation
Presence of 'undesirable' plant species (e.g. birch and Molinia)	Removal of vegetation, followed by raising of water levels to keep in check. May need to consider chemical treatment
Dry, bare surfaces	Raise water levels (inundate if necessary); inoculate with plant material; consider use of mulch (e.g. bunkerde) if available
Shallow depth of ombrotrophic peat	Consider using mineral material for bunding
Ombrotrophic peat cut away to expose fen peat or mineral substratum	Consider alternative habitats as such or as precursor to bog development
Very low base- or nutrient-status	Consider use of lime or fertiliser

Positive features

Baulks and trackways	Use to retain water, if possible, (check functioning first), although may be necessary to reduce height of baulks to encourage rewetting; use for access and firebreaks
Localised depressions or trenches	Use to identify where water naturally collects as a basis for developing rewetting strategy; use for Sphagnum 'farming'
Existing conservation interest	Preserve and enhance where possible; use as 'core'
Presence of Sphagnum species	Use as sources of inoculum (where abundant) or as nuclei from which to spread

configuration remaining, it may be desirable to flatten baulks to achieve a more level area for rewetting, (though keeping some of them to help retain water). It should be possible to use some of the material from the 'redundant' baulks to fill the ditches. However, procedures involving the movement of peat and altering the configuration of the abandoned peat cutting may require consultation with the statutory conservation and archaeological bodies.

Because the rewetting necessary to regenerate raised bogs can only be achieved by retaining the incoming precipitation, all drains, trenches and outfalls must be dammed where possible. However, any measures used for reduction in outflow from the bog must have the capacity to deliver peak discharges from the bog, otherwise erosion of the regenerating peat surface, or damage to the dams, bunds or recolonist vegetation may occur.

[1] see glossary

After-care and vegetation management

Certain practices are used widely in the management of vegetation of damaged bogs and bog remnants, from which some common principles can be identified [*Chapters 3, 9 & 10*]:

- vegetation management is necessary to reduce the invasion and spread of 'undesirable' species, which are normally checked by high water levels;
- scrub invasion and its control can be a major problem;
- there are few circumstances in which mowing or grazing are likely to be appropriate techniques if attempts are being made to restore raised bog, except as an interim measure;
- it may be necessary to consider the use of herbicides to control 'undesirable' species;
- it may be necessary to consider encouraging revegetation by 'desirable' species, through inoculation of diaspores or whole plants, in particular, *Sphagnum* species;
- adequate provision for control of fire is essential;
- ongoing maintenance of bunds and dams may be required.

Consideration should be given to implementing practical management procedures as soon as production ceases, both to reduce the establishment of 'undesirable' plant species, especially if it is not possible to raise water levels within a short time, and to start encouraging establishment of 'desirable' plant species. Where 'abandoned' fields lie within the zone of ongoing peat extraction, and cannot be rewetted in the near future, it may be possible to achieve the former by running rotavating machinery over the surface each year. Where this has not been done, it may be necessary to remove some vegetation (*e.g.* birch and *Molinia*) from abandoned areas prior to rewetting (although small amounts of vegetation may be useful in acting as 'nurse' species for *Sphagnum* inoculum).

Full renaturation and regeneration of rewetted peat fields is likely to be slow, partly on account of the 'difficult' nature of the ombrotrophic environment (and the intrinsically low relative growth rates of bog plants). As the cut-over areas regenerate into bog they may be expected to become increasingly self-sustaining. However, some degree of maintenance may be needed in the early stages of rewetting and renaturation, such as removal of scrub from dry sites within the peat fields. The condition of the peat bunds, especially the outer ones, will also require periodic inspection and, if needed, some maintenance. The expected intrinsically-slow renaturation of the peat fields is likely to mean that some (intermittent) maintenance may be required for much longer than an after-care period of 5 years. The restoration scheme should be designed to minimise on-going management requirements[1] but also to make it practicable for them to take place, if needed.

Natural recolonisation of cut-over bogs by plants may take place quite readily where there are local refugia of typical bog species. However, where these do not exist, or have a sparse range of species, or where sites are particularly large, it may be necessary to consider the merits of 'inoculating' the damaged sites with selected species either by transplantation of plant material or seeding. Plans for inoculation of rewetted areas must be considered carefully with respect to the phasing of restoration operations, as the practicable options will depend critically on the planned hydrological regime. Clearly, provision of the optimum water regime, both in terms of quality and quantity, for the desired vegetation-type will be an important basic consideration [*see Chapters 4 and 5*]. Conversely, the restoration scheme developed should take into account the

availability of plant inoculum. Legislation concerning uprooting of plants and transplantations must be taken into consideration [*Chapter 9*].

The main feature of the vegetation of an undamaged raised bog is the extent of the *Sphagnum* cover, which, besides being characteristic, plays various important rôles in the functioning of the bog [*Chapter 1*]. Thus, one of the most important factors in the restoration of a damaged bog is the question of how to regain the *Sphagnum* cover, particularly in sites which possess few refugia with conditions suitable for the survival of *Sphagnum* species. A lack of appropriate, available propagules may hinder recolonisation, and it may be desirable to consider inoculation with plant material. Clearly, it will be necessary to wait for hydrological conditions to stabilise following any rewetting measures before undertaking any inoculation or transplantation work. For large-scale restoration, removal of *Sphagnum* from donor sites is likely to be considered unsatisfactory, and the possibility of increasing the availability of propagules by farming *Sphagnum* could be considered. This could be started in abandoned areas well in advance of complete cessation of extraction to provide an ongoing source of inoculum.

It may also be appropriate to consider inoculation with suitable vascular plants. Where possible, it is recommended that planting should be carried out in the autumn or early spring so that maximum establishment can be achieved before possible summer dry periods. Material should be transplanted as soon as possible after collection (preferably the same day), and drying out in transit must be avoided. It should be apparent after only one growing season whether transplanted material is likely to become established. Reasons for failure should be investigated and remedied where possible.

It may be possible to encourage rafting of vegetation in certain situations. For example, there is evidence that the establishment and spread of *Sphagnum* within embryonic bogs can be facilitated by the presence of 'nurse species' such as *Molinia caerulea*, *Eriophorum vaginatum* and *Juncus effusus*, or the provision of 'artificial' constructs within the water such as birch brashings. Rafting may also be encouraged by loose peat fragments or particles floating in the pools, either washed in from the sides, or detached and lifted from the base of the cuttings.

S8 Recording and monitoring

Procedures and progress of monitoring schemes should be monitored, for the following reasons:

- all schemes must be regarded as essentially experimental, and therefore recording is important in increasing the knowledge of techniques *etc;*

---

[1] For example, by ensuring that the floors of lagoons can be kept inundated, to minimise opportunities for establishment of undesirable species; a strongly undulating, or sloping, surface may create periodically dry areas that are susceptible to birch encroachment *etc.*

- provision of 'base-line' data so that progress can be assessed and the restoration programme revised where necessary;
- provision of 'hard' data so that current and future managers (and other interested parties) know the starting conditions, exactly what has been done and can continue to assess the degree of success, in order to formulate appropriate further management strategies;
- provision of information that can be used to assess the applicability and potential of similar schemes at other sites.

As recolonisation may be rather slow, monitoring may need to be long-term, and projects should be devised accordingly.

Monitoring procedures need to be set up with clearly-defined objectives and with identified yardsticks by which the direction and extent of change can be measured. It may be difficult to carry out and interpret in a meaningful way. It is recommended that a monitoring programme should be set up taking the following aspects into account:

- management operations (present and future);
- base-line data on flora, fauna and water levels (based on reconnaissance surveys, but with additional detail if possible) will allow identification of selected species or priority areas (e.g. those identified as refugia), plus species of special conservation status for regular monitoring checks to assess response to management operations;
- the hydrological and biological response within a representative selection of cut-over areas should be regularly monitored;
- annual review of results to allow assessment of any changes needed to the management programme.

It may be desirable to involve specialists in detailed monitoring periodically in order to assess progress in detail, but it is possible to make some simple records and measurements which will provide useful information and give a good insight into progress [Table S4].

Some hydrological measurements should be made

before deciding on the optimum surface configurations (*e.g.* where to put the bunds for lagoons), particularly where water-table fluctuations are known to be erratic or there is a possibility of vertical water loss. Similarly, once the lagoons are constructed, a further period of at least a year should elapse to ensure that water levels will stabilise before making decisions on planting operations, so that appropriate areas can be targeted, plant material is not wasted and any adjustments can be made without fear of damage to the vegetation.

As each restoration initiative should be regarded as 'experimental', it is desirable that the details and outcome should be disseminated through publications or accessible reports.

S9 Prospects and costs

There are numerous examples of spontaneous revegetation of (mostly) small-scale peat workings and on some damaged mires revegetated peat cuttings provide the 'best' examples of bog or fen habitat. Most such workings on raised bogs are relatively old (*i.e.* abandoned some 60–80 years ago) so, whilst it is possible to fix an upper time limit for effective revegetation, the absence of younger workings that have been kept appropriately wet since abandonment prevent specification of the lower time threshold. [It can, of course, also be argued that recolonisation of these workings has been favoured by special circumstances, such as their (usually) small size and possible 'shoeing' of the cuttings.]

Restoration initiatives on large commercial cut-over raised bogs are mostly still in their infancy, *i.e.* have been attempted for less than 10 years or so; moreover some of them have been in sites where problems of water management have been exacerbated by several unusually dry summers and by vertical loss of water into a permeable subsoil. They have also mostly been carried out as post-extraction procedures, rather than as

Table S4. Factors which can be simply recorded, measured or monitored

These include:

- careful recording of management operations undertaken (including time taken and costs);
- water level depth and stability (using data from dipwells, WALRAG's and stage boards);
- recolonisation of rewetted areas (and others), especially by *Sphagnum* species;
- birch death;
- *Molinia* death;
- photographic record, including:
  - 'fixed point' photographic records, including 'before' and 'after' -type pictures and regularly thereafter;
  - management operations (such as bund and dam construction);
- regular checks to be made on any water control structures (dams, bunds *etc.*) and remedial action taken as necessary;
- records should be made of events beyond the control of site managers (*e.g.* heavy storms, fires, vandalism *etc.*) which may influence the future interpretation of 'success' of the project.

an integrated programme of extraction and restoration. It is nonetheless evident (a) that a wide range of bog plant species can invade commercially-cut-over surfaces (where there is a proximate inoculum source); and (b) that it is possible to rewet the peat fields to the extent that (c) carpets of aquatic Sphagna can rapidly colonise large areas. Some of the rewetting initiatives in NW Germany have shown a massive expansion of *Sphagnum cuspidatum* over extensive areas. This event provides much optimism for regeneration prospects as in both the natural development of bogs and that of recolonised peat workings, a wet *Sphagnum cuspidatum* phase has provided a basis for spontaneous successional development of a more diverse vegetation composed of more important bog-building species such as *Sphagnum papillosum* and *S. magellanicum*. It is difficult to see why this process should not be repeated on rewetted commercially-cut over sites, provided that two conditions are satisfied: (i) that the site is accessible to potential recolonist species (if it is not, then re-introduction of species will need to be considered); and (ii) that the chemical composition of precipitation inputs will support the growth of recolonist species. [It is possible (but by no means certain) that the growth of some bog species, especially some species of *Sphagnum*, may be considerably constrained in some regions by atmospheric contaminants, particularly NO_x and NH_4 [*Chapter 1*].] However, if such conditions are not limiting, it seems likely that commercially-cut peat fields will redevelop a characteristic bog vegetation and that peat accumulation will recommence in time. It is difficult to specify the likely time-scale involved, but known rates of spread and establishment of bog vegetation suggest that, depending on the starting conditions, effective revegetation may often be possible within the upper threshold of 70 years known from the spontaneous revegetation referred to above, and perhaps considerably more quickly than this, especially if it is possible to discover, by further research, the conditions needed to optimise the establishment of the bog-building Sphagna upon the lawns of *Sphagnum cuspidatum*.

Effective renaturation does, of course, require effective rewetting. It is important to note that sustained rewetting of relatively flat, cut-over surfaces may sometimes be achieved more easily and effectively than that of residual massifs. These may show a tendency to remain 'high and dry', unless provided with substantial bunds to help retain water. Moreover, the long-term stability of peripheral bunds is not known. Such considerations are of great importance in terms both of the optimal surface configuration required at the cessation of peat extraction and of the possibility of premature termination of peat extraction. The desirability of creating comparatively flat, uniform surfaces for initiation of wide-scale bog redevelopment must, of course, be balanced against the need to retain some residual massifs on account of their existing biological value, which may be important not only in its own right, but also as an inoculum source for the rewetted, cut-over surfaces.

The costs of restoration are likely to depend strongly upon starting conditions and restoration objectives. They must be split between capital costs (such as land purchase), surface preparation costs and maintenance costs. Typical costs incurred in some projects are summarised in *Chapter 7*. These show considerable variation, reflecting specific site circumstances and, probably, the 'one-off' nature of may initiatives. Some of the most reliable guides to costing come from NW Germany, where a number of bogs have now been prepared for restoration. These suggest that preparation costs of cut-over surfaces are in the region of £200 – 400 ha^{-1} when appropriate equipment exists on site and £800 – 1250 ha^{-1} when it has to be brought in.

Background

Peat and peat extraction

Peatlands are wetland ecosystems in which the substratum is composed largely or entirely of peat. Peat is an organic soil formed mainly from the remains of plants that have accumulated *in situ*. Peat accumulates in wetland habitats, primarily because waterlogging and associated anoxia retards the decomposition of plant material.

Globally, peatlands are very widespread and extensive, occurring in all but the drier regions of the world, from the tropics to the tundra (Gore, 1983a, b; Lugo, Brinson & Brown, 1990). Estimates of the global peatland resource vary considerably and none are probably very accurate. Values of over 40 million hectares of the land area are sometimes suggested (Bather & Miller, 1991).

The waterlogged conditions required for peat accumulation are provided by two broad circumstances. The first is in situations where more-or-less permanent saturation is provided by telluric water (*i.e.* water derived from the ground and which has had some contact with mineral substrata, such as those that surround or underly the peatland). Amongst other factors, this may be because of a high regional groundwater table, groundwater discharge or impeded drainage of various water sources (such as land-drainage or river floodwater). But in all such cases, the wetness of the wetland is a product, at least in part, of water that has had some residence within, or contact with, mineral soils and substrata. Peatlands that develop under the influence of telluric water are referred to as *minerotrophic* peatlands, to which the term *fen* is often applied as a synonym.

In some climatic regions peat is also able to accumulate because relatively high and consistent precipitation, coupled to comparatively low rates of evapotranspiration, permit the maintenance of permanently wet conditions perched above the level of the mineral ground and groundwater table. Such conditions lead to the formation of a peat deposit that is raised above the original ground level and which is fed and formed directly and more-or-less exclusively by precipitation. Such peatlands are known as *ombrotrophic* or *ombrogenous* peatlands and the word *bog* is often applied as a synonym. In many instances they have developed from fen.

In Britain, as in much of north-west Europe, both minerotrophic and ombrotrophic peatlands were once very extensive. The total area of fen in Britain, past or present, has not been quantified, but was undoubtedly once great. The largest fen complex (The Fenland of East Anglia) was once a huge wetland basin, covering an area of more than 1200 km^2 (a total which includes some ombrotrophic peatland). Ombrotrophic peatlands occupy extremely large areas (*e.g.* some 1.5 million ha in the British Isles) but some lowland bogs were also large, the biggest being Thorne Waste (S Yorkshire) with an original area of over 2500 ha. On the opposite side of the North Sea, in The Netherlands and Lower Saxony, much greater lowland bogs once occurred. The biggest had an estimated area in excess of 1000 km^2 (Barkman, 1992) (*i.e.* about 1½ times the area of the island of Anglesey).

Although some peatlands have long and intricate history of interaction with human societies (Coles, 1990), given their once-huge area it is scarcely surprising that over the last few centuries much of the focus of human activity in peatlands has been to drain and claim them for a more remunerative use. Some minerotrophic peatlands have been particularly amenable to agricultural conversion, their derivative soils often being both base-rich and nutrient-rich. The peats of the Fenland basin of East Anglia have been almost entirely converted to productive farmland (Darby, 1983). By contrast, bog peat is typically acidic and nutrient-poor. Nonetheless, large areas have been drained and claimed for agriculture or forestry. Various methods have been found to reduce the acidity and enrich the bog peat. Some have involved the application of lime and fertiliser, sometimes using 'night-soil' (sewage) as a source of nutrients; others have entailed physical removal of the peat. At Thorne Waste (S. Yorks.), the primary stimulus to drainage and peat removal in the nineteenth century seems to have been a desire to lower the altitude of the bog surface so that it could be 'warped' – that is, covered with silt by inundation with estuarine water at high tides (Smart, Wheeler & Willis, 1986). In the Forth valley of Central Scotland, Cadell (1913) reports how large areas of peat were stripped to expose the underlying carse clays for agriculture. The unwanted peat was jettisoned into the river to such an extent that fish stocks were damaged. Such profligacy with the peat resource suggests that it was not at all in short supply, as peat is likely to have been of some value to the inhabitants of the Forth valley as a fuel.

Peat has a number of properties that make it a valued resource and it has found a very wide range of uses. In Britain, its principal usage has been for fuel, litter (bedding material for animals) and as a growing medium for plants. Its use as a domestic fuel is of long standing. Records indicate that various peatlands have been dug for fuel since Medieval times and, in some cases, probably long before. Most of the accessible lowland peat deposits, and various upland ones, show signs of former domestic peat cutting, especially around their margins. The effects of these 'domestic' activities should not be underestimated. In the early nineteenth century, peat was removed from up to 90% of the surface of some fens in the Norfolk Broadland (Giller & Wheeler, 1986; J. Parmenter, *unpublished data*), mainly to provide fuel for the parish poor. Some individual pits were more than 11 ha in area. Elsewhere in East Anglia, at the about the same time, estimated peat extraction rates in Parish Fuel Allotments approximate to the equivalent of removal of 1m depth of peat from an area of 1 ha every 50 years (Wheeler & Shaw, 1995). At Thorne Waste, eighteenth century peat extraction was considerable and led to the agricultural conversion of a sizeable portion of the south-west part of the bog, apparently starting in the seventeenth century (Limbert, 1987). However, more systematic attempts to drain and exploit peatlands, for fuel or litter, generally date from the nineteenth century onwards.

In Britain, peat is no longer harvested for litter, but domestic extraction for fuel persists in some areas, mainly in the north-west of Britain, and there is a small amount of commercial fuel peat production. Elsewhere the fortunes of the peat industry may well have flagged had it not been for the widespread adoption of peat by the horticultural industry as a base for growing media. Peat has long been an important ingredient of various soil-based composts, such as the John Innes composts developed in the 1930s, but it was not until the 1960s that the potential benefits of composts based largely, or entirely, on peat were recognised and promoted, revitalising peat extraction.

The properties of peat are largely a product of the plant species that produced it and the conditions under which it accumulated. Both fen peats ('sedge peat') and bog peats ('moss peat') are harvested in Britain but the *Sphagnum*-rich moss peats are of particular value to horticulture, because of their structure, waterholding capacity, low fertility, sterility and consistent character. Most moss peats are extracted from lowland bogs, primarily from sites which contain thick deposits of suitable peat, which are in comparatively dry regions (to facilitate drying of the material) and which are relatively close to the main markets. Most of these sites are sometimes referred to as 'lowland raised bogs'.

In Britain as widely elsewhere, a substantial proportion

of former raised bogs have been claimed for agriculture and forestry; others have been heavily damaged by commercial or domestic peat extraction; by drainage or repeated burning. Figures collated for the National Peatland Resource Inventory (NPRI; Lindsay *et al*, in prep.) suggest that in Britain the proportion of 'primary near-natural' raised-bog vegetation cover which remains is only about 5 – 6 % of the original extent of raised bog of some 70,000 ha.

All of these estimated figures have to be treated with some caution, not least because the concept and compass of the category called 'lowland raised bog' is itself open to debate. Nonetheless, it is clear that in England, Wales, southern and central Scotland the area of lowland bog that has retained much of its (presumed) undamaged character is undoubtedly small.

The 'peat debate'

In recent years there has been a growing recognition of the importance of lowland bogs for natural history, science and conservation. Features which are perceived to be important include:

- visual character of the peatland landscape;
- peat archive (archaeology, palaeoecology);
- biological resource.

The importance of lowland bogs as a biological resource is most obviously expressed in terms of their populations of typical 'bog species'. However, they also have importance in supporting populations of species of wider habitat-range in landscapes from which other semi-natural habitats have largely disappeared. Some of these species may persist in parts of bogs that have been partly damaged. Damaged sites may also support populations of some uncommon species which are not really typical of lowland bogs but which have established upon them in response to changes in habitat conditions, such as those induced by drainage and peat extraction.

The recognition of the importance of some lowland bogs for wildlife *etc*. has led to some concern with regard to their continued exploitation. As, today, peat extraction is the principal form of on-going utilisation, there has been some suggestion that the operations of the peat industry should be curtailed or reduced.

The response of the British Government to the debate on peat in the House of Lords on 9 May 1990 was to recognise that many UK peatlands, including lowland bogs, are amongst the country's most important nature conservation habitats. The response also recognised that the peat industry had legitimate interests in some of these peatlands through mineral extraction activities carried out under valid planning permissions. However, it was also recognised that many of those permissions were granted in the early years after the passing of the first Town and Country Planning Act in 1947. This was before the nature conservation importance of peat areas had been fully appreciated. Many of the permissions lacked planning conditions controlling methods of working, restoration and aftercare. The Government concluded that there was a need for a full assessment of all the relevant issues which had been raised.

Scope of the report

This report is the outcome of a project commissioned by the Department of the Environment (Minerals Division) in 1992. The main aims of this were to assess the potential for and limitations of restoring worked-out and damaged lowland peat bogs in the UK and to provide the basis for guidance and options for appropriate working practices and methods to restore these bogs, the main focus being on nature conservation requirements.

The study has proceeded through two phases:

(i) A collation and review of relevant published and unpublished data, supplemented by consultation with appropriate individuals and organisations, and site visits in the UK, Ireland, The Netherlands and Germany. A working document was prepared for consideration by a Steering Group of the project and a revised version of this is available from the Environmental Consultancy, University of Sheffield.

(ii) The information and experience collated for the initial working document has been utilised to prepare this present document, which provides background information and scientific advice on the practice of restoration of cut-over lowland peatlands. It is intended for use by any parties with an interest in peatland restoration, including central and local government, the peat industry, conservation bodies *etc.*, in particular with regard to formulating restoration strategies for the after-use of currently worked or abandoned sites.

This report is concerned with the restoration of peatlands that have been damaged by peat extraction, with particular regard to lowland bogs. It gives a wide-ranging review of much of the available information and experience relating to the science and art of restoration of peatlands subject to peat extraction, based on practical experience and current understanding of salient ecological processes which operate within peatlands; it identifies some of the potential opportunities provided by restoration initiatives, and associated difficulties; it examines various approaches to restoration that may be used and considers the requirements appropriate to successful restoration.

The study has focused on lowland bogs, as these are the peatlands currently most utilised by the peat industry. The dwindling resource of lowland raised bogs with conservation interest, makes it important that efforts are made to *actively* preserve extant areas to prevent further degradation and, where possible, to restore damaged areas and attempt to recreate the habitat conditions suitable for the development of the characteristic flora and fauna of raised bogs.

Cut-over peatlands can be broadly divided into two structural components: the peat cutting fields and uncut bog remnants. The 'remnants' sometimes retain considerable biological interest, even when adjacent to on-going peat extraction. This report thus addresses two rather different, but related, main issues:

(i) restoration of the abandoned peat fields; and

(ii) the maintenance (and, if needed, restoration) of vegetated peat remnants, both during and after peat extraction of adjoining areas.

This document is intended to be used for the formulation of future planning policy with regard to peat workings and restoration, but it is *not* itself a policy document. Similarly, it is intended for use as a guide to best practices in the restoration of worked out or damaged peatlands, but is *not* intended to provide a prescriptive 'management handbook'.

Structure

The material presented in this document falls fairly readily into three main parts. The first part considers various aspects of peatland ecology relevant to restoration and with particular reference to some effects of peat extraction upon the characteristics of peatland sites. The second part builds on this to outline some of the objectives of peatland restoration and examines relevant principles and information to assess possible approaches to restoration and some of the constraints upon them. The final part is concerned more with various practical aspects of restoration, such as identifying the sort of information that may be required to undertake a restoration programme or some of the possible methods of facilitating the process. However, the overall focus of this report is *not* to provide detailed technical guidance. Nor is it to prescribe universal restoration formulas for lowland peatlands. This is not least because the permutations of possible restoration objectives and site-specific conditions in which restoration takes place prevent any simple recitation of a 'recipe' for restoration. Rather, an attempt has been made to identify the salient issues involved in peatland restoration initiatives and provide an overall factual and conceptual basis which it is hoped will enable informed decisions to be made and strategies developed that are applicable to the peculiar circumstances of individual peatland sites.

Citations

This volume is a much condensed version of the original working document [see above]. Although it contains numerous references to the sources of information upon which it is based, it is not practicable to include all relevant citations, nor the details of other pieces of evidence (field observations, discussions *etc.*) which have contributed to various comments and conclusions. Comprehensive citations and other details can be found in the working document.

Scope for restoration

One important component of this review was an evaluation of the potential for the restoration of worked-out or damaged bogs to regenerate, maintain or increase their nature conservation value; and to provide guidance on the practicality of such procedures. This is because peat extraction does not *of necessity* destroy, or irreversibly change, the salient environmental conditions and circumstances that permit the growth and reproduction of many typical bog species and the formation of bog peat. In principle, the effect of peat extraction is to remove some of the accumulated peat and to cut the surface of the bog back to an earlier stage in its development so that, depending upon the condition and conformation of the 'new' surfaces, it may be possible to encourage the regeneration of 'new' raised bogs within the worked-out ramparts of the 'old' ones. That potential exists for the redevelopment of bog vegetation is illustrated by the spontaneous recolonisation of some abandoned peat workings and by some experimental attempts to regenerate bog vegetation. Nonetheless, many current commercial operations are on a much larger scale than those of the early workings which have spontaneously revegetated and this may present some additional constraints to restoration. Moreover, it must also be recognised that, in cutting the peat back to a lower level, peat extraction also removes any existing living surface, together with incidental peat contents, such as the pollen grains *etc.* that preserve a palaeoecological record. The palaeo-ecological record cannot be restored and whilst recolonisation by plants and animals typical of bogs may be possible in the long-term, it will not only require the redevelopment of conditions appropriate for their growth but may also depend upon the survival of these species in a refuge adjoining, or near to, the peat workings whilst extraction is taking place.

Two broad caveats underly all of the information and observations presented here:

(i) Once any site has been damaged, be it a bog or other habitat, it is never possible to return it *exactly* to its former condition. However, in the case of a bog damaged by peat extraction, it may be possible to repair or regenerate a bog by restoring conditions similar to those under which it originally developed and hence to encourage the return of typical raised-bog species, both flora and fauna. In some instances this may even offer a 'value-added' approach in terms of wildlife conservation, as in those sites which have long-since been damaged by drainage, partial agricultural conversion and burning as well as peat extraction. However, effective restoration is likely to be a slow process, measured in terms of decades; moreover, given the present 'state of the art' it is not possible to *guarantee* that a peat-accumulating system will subsequently redevelop. It is therefore suggested that these guidelines and observations should not be used to provide a justification for peat extraction on little-damaged bog sites.

(ii) Not all of the techniques outlined in this document are well 'tried and tested', as bog restoration is a relatively new activity. There are strong reasons to suppose that they have a good chance of success, but to help enhance knowledge and understanding of effective restoration practices, it is suggested that all attempts at the restoration of damaged peatlands should be regarded as experimental, and the projects carefully recorded and monitored. There is still much to learn. The advice given here is based upon current experience, knowledge and thought, but the guidelines may need to be amended or updated as new techniques and results from existing studies become available.

Terminology

A deliberate attempt has been made to reduce the number of technical terms in this publication, using commonplace or colloquial words and expressions to convey the appropriate idiom, where possible. However, for both brevity and clarity it has been necessary to use some technical words. Some terms are defined in the text and a glossary (Appendix 1) is also provided. With respect to the main subject of this report, *i.e.* bog *restoration*, the terminology proposed by R. Eggelsmann and co-workers has been followed, in which:

rewetting	is the re-establishment of surface-wet conditions;
renaturation	is the redevelopment of an appropriate vegetation;
regeneration	is the renewed accumulation of peat.

These concepts are here grouped under the generic head of *restoration*. However, note that they are by no means discrete and separate: indeed, the redevelopment or regeneration of a bog follows a continuum; there are no abrupt divisions or thresholds between each phase. Successful bog regeneration must seek ultimately to re-establish the self-regulatory mechanisms that ensure that permanently wet conditions are maintained.

PART I

Ecological Characteristics of Lowland Peatlands

used for Peat Extraction

Chapter 1

Lowland peatlands

1.1 Peatlands: fens and bogs

Different types of peatland can be recognised based on various characteristics (Gore, 1983a). One of the most widely-used distinguishing features is the nature of the water supply. Von Post & Granlund (1926) subdivided peatlands into three main types – *ombrogenous*, *topogenous* and *soligenous* examples – reflecting the different primary causes of surface wetness and peat accumulation. This classification is still widely used. *Ombrogenous* peatlands are those where surface waterlogging is maintained primarily by precipitation; *topogenous* peatlands occur in basins, flood-plains *etc.*, where water accumulates on account of the topography of the landscape; whilst *soligenous* examples are those where laterally mobile water maintains wet conditions, most typically on sloping sites (Sjörs, 1950).

Although both topogenous and soligenous peatlands are partly fed by precipitation, they also receive inputs of *telluric* water (*i.e.* water derived from the ground and which has had some contact with mineral substrata, such as those that surround or underly the peatland) and they are often referred to as *minerotrophic* ('rock-fed') peatlands (or *fens*). By contrast, ombrogenous ('rain-made') peatlands (or *bogs*) are exclusively *ombrotrophic* ('rain-fed'), with the supply of water to their surface being derived directly and exclusively from precipitation. Various broad differences can be observed [Table 1.1] but, nonetheless, certain types of

fen can be very similar to bogs in many of their characteristics and it is difficult to provide a simple, universal specification of how the two types can, in practice, be consistently distinguished (Wheeler, 1993).

Whilst (as in this account) ecologists often use the word 'bog' to refer to ombrotrophic peatlands and 'fen' to mean minerotrophic examples, such usage is by no means universal. Some wetlands that are often called 'bogs' are actually fens in that they are minerotrophic in character. For example, most of the *Sphagnum* 'bogs' of the New Forest (Hampshire) are strictly-speaking 'poor fens', as they receive substantial inputs of groundwater (and this is reflected in their vegetation composition). Similarly, entire peatland sites are sometimes loosely called 'bogs' or 'fens', even though they support (or once supported) both ombrotrophic and minerotrophic components. Here, the term 'bog' is used to refer specifically to the ombrogenous component of a peatland site.

The term 'mire' has received a variety of usage (*e.g.* Ratcliffe, 1964; Gore, 1983a,b). It is often used as a synonym for *peatland* (Gore, 1983a), but some workers also include some mineral-based wet land within the compass of 'mire'.

In Britain, peat extraction currently takes place both in fens and bogs, but commercial extraction of bog peat is much more widespread than is that of fen peat (which is confined to the Somerset Levels). In consequence, most attention in this report is focused upon bogs.

Table 1.1 Some distinguishing features of fens and bogs

	Fen	Bog
Water source	Precipitation plus telluric water (*minerotrophic*)	Exclusively from precipitation (*ombrotrophic*)
Nutrient status	Nutrient-poor to nutrient-rich (may be supplemented by enrichment of water supply from agriculture *etc.*)	Nutrient-poor (nitrogen may be supplemented by atmospherically-derived enrichment)
Character of substratum	Usually peat but may have varying mineral content; some mineral soils	Peat
Peat types	Typically various mixtures of sedges, grasses, herbs, woody species, mosses *etc.*	Typically *Sphagnum* mosses with some sedges, herbs and woody (ericaceous) species
Peat pH	Typically *c.* 4.0 – 6.0 (*poor fen*) and *c.* 5.0 – 8.0 (*rich fen*)	Typically < 4.5
Species diversity of vegetation	Low to high (largely dependent on nutrient supply, pH and management)	Typically low (unless damaged)

1.2 Origin and development of peatlands

The origin and development of peatlands, both as individual sites and as part of the broader landscape, is often complex and is beyond the scope of this volume (see, for example, Kulczynski, 1949; Heinselman, 1963; Walker, 1970; Casparie, 1972; Tallis, 1983; Pons, 1992). In very broad terms peatlands form by two main mechanisms – by the infilling of open water and by the waterlogging of once-dry land.

The process by which water becomes wetland is often referred to as *terrestrialisation* or *hydroseral succession* (Weber, 1908; Tansley, 1939). It occurs around lakes and pools and can lead to the complete replacement of once open water by peatland. The details of terrestrialisation processes can be complex (Walker, 1970), but they usually proceed by one of two main routes – *rooting* or *rafting*. Rooting (or *littoral*) successions occur when water bodies gradually accumulate deposits of silts, muds and peats. The shallowing water becomes subject to centripetal invasion by plants of swamp and fen, rooting on the accumulating sediments. By contrast, in the rafting process, vegetation grows across the surface of open water to form a floating mat, composed of peat and plants. In its early stages, this raft of precocious peatland is often thin, unstable and quaking and well-deserves the name of *schwingmoor* ('floating mire') which is sometimes given to it. But later, it may become so thick and consolidated that the former existence of a floating raft can only be deduced by peat stratigraphical studies. *Rafting* successions are particularly characteristic of small, sheltered and often deep water bodies, and have occurred quite frequently in kettle-holes and similar basins.

The processes associated with terrestrialisation have had a pervasive influence upon the conceptual development of paludology, to the extent that the term 'hydrosere' is sometimes used loosely (and incorrectly) for all forms of developmental change in wetlands. However, many peatlands have not developed by the terrestrialisation of open water but by the swamping, or *paludification*, of once relatively-dry land (Cajander, 1913). It is often not clear, just on superficial inspection, which mechanism has been instrumental in the development of a particular peatland and, in consequence, the past occurrence of the two processes in Britain is not really known. Nonetheless, there can be little doubt that, in terms of the total area of peatland, paludification has been a far more important process than has terrestrialisation. For example, the extensive peatlands (fens and bogs) that occupy, or once occupied, the flood-plains of many lowland rivers (such as The Fenland of East Anglia) have largely formed by paludification. So have the huge areas of bog peat that blanket many upland landscapes. Such contrasting situations as these point to a variety of causes of paludification, including climatic change, land–sea level change and deforestation.

The initial type of peatland that develops by terrestrialisation of open water is usually a form of fen, but in suitable climatic regions [1.3], ombrogenous peat may subsequently develop within and upon this as impeded drainage of precipitation permits the gradual accumulation of layers of ombrotrophic peat above the level of mineral soil water influence. Paludification of dry land also often leads, first of all, to the formation of minerotrophic mire, which again may sometimes be subject to progressive ombrotrophication. However, in some circumstances paludification can result in a more-or-less direct development of ombrotrophic peat, without a significant intervening minerotrophic phase.

Ombrogenous bogs are thought to be climax ecosystems, which have developed spontaneously from a variety of starting points and which are believed to be stable, at least when undamaged.

1.3 Types of fens and bogs

Minerotrophic peatlands occur in a very wide variety of situations, wherever the water table is sufficiently and consistently high to sustain peat accumulation. The distribution and occurrence of fens is largely determined by an interaction between landscape topography and local or regional hydrology. Likewise, the gross morphology of a fen is often largely a reflection of the features of the landscape in which it occurs. Deep accumulations of fen peat are most characteristic of topogenous sites, *e.g.* ground hollows, basins and river flood-plains. Various classifications of fens based on their situation, shape and water supply have been proposed (*e.g.* Succow & Lange, 1984). Schemes suggested for Britain (*e.g.* Ratcliffe, 1977; Wheeler, 1984) require clarification and revision (Wheeler, 1993).

Ombrogenous peatlands occur over a similar range of topographical situations to minerotrophic examples but both their geographical distribution and the range of topographical situations in which they can form is strongly constrained by climate. This is because their development requires a sufficiently high rate of precipitation input (often coupled with low rates of evapotranspiration) to permit peat to accumulate above the level of the mineral ground or the influence of telluric water. Within suitable regions, ombrogenous peatlands may be far more extensive than are fens (Goodwillie, 1980), but globally they have a more restricted distribution. The exact climatic conditions required for bog development have yet to be established, but examples occur from the tropics to the

Plate 1.1 Aerial view of the west bog, Cors Caron (Dyfed). The drier margins of the raised bog are picked out by the lighter colour of the vegetation, with the River Teifi forming the 'lagg' on one side of the bog. [Photo: J. Davis]

boreal regions. In temperate Eurasia, most ombrotrophic mires occur between the latitudes 50–70° N (Proctor, 1995).

By their nature, ombrogenous mires form as a peat deposit raised above the level of the regional water table, the underlying minerotrophic peat and mineral soil. The shape and dimensions of bog-peat deposits vary very considerably, depending primarily upon their age, the underlying landforms and the climatic regime in which they have developed. In the drier regions of Britain, bog formation has been restricted to flattish surfaces or very gentle slopes, whereas in the wetter, cooler regions of the north and west, it has also been able to occur upon quite steeply sloping terrain. This difference has provided the basis for the recognition of two, rather ill-defined, main categories of bog in Britain – 'raised bog' and 'blanket bog' [BOX 1.1].

Raised bogs: These are primarily (but not exclusively) lowland peatlands which, in Britain, mostly occupy the bottoms of broad, flat valleys, the heads of estuaries or shallow basins [Plate 1.1]. In their most distinctive development they form shallow domes of ombrogenous peat delimited usually by mineral ground, fen or watercourses. They sometimes form large complexes in which tracts of bog are separated by watercourses or fen. In Britain, sites that are usually called raised

bogs typically occur in regions with an annual precipitation range of *c.* 800–1200 mm a^{-1} and with 140–180 wet days a^{-1} (Rodwell, 1991), though the full range is wider than this [BOX 1.2]. [See also 1.5]

Blanket bogs: These are ombrotrophic peatlands that 'blanket' large areas of variable topography. Unlike raised bogs, they can form on quite strongly sloping ground (slopes typically up to *c.* 10° (Tansley, 1939), but sometimes steeper (Moore & Bellamy (1974) suggest 25°). This reflects the particularly wet, cool conditions in which they occur, with an annual precipitation typically in excess of *c.* 1200 mm a^{-1} and more than 160 wet days a^{-1} (Ratcliffe, 1977). In much of England and Wales they are restricted to the higher altitudes (above *c.* 400m) but in western and northern parts of Scotland and Ireland they descend to near sea level. The capacity of blanket bogs to form on slopes means that they often form much larger tracts of continuous ombrogenous peat than is the case with raised bogs. They are most usually delimited by a transition to mineral soil (often a peaty podsol). and sometimes form very large complexes in which areas of bog peat are separated by watercourses or fen. The term *blanket mire* can be used to refer to blanket peat ecosystems in aggregate (*i.e.* including both ombrogenous and minerotrophic components), restricting

BOX 1.1 *Hydromorphological types of bog in Britain: the concept of 'raised bog'*

Two types of ombrogenous bog have been generally recognised in Britain: *raised bog* and *blanket bog* (*e.g.* Tansley, 1939). Some workers have suggested that these are linked by an intermediate type, such as 'ridge-raised mire' (Moore & Bellamy, 1974). However, the characteristics of these bog 'types' have not been critically or rigorously defined and the terms have been applied loosely to sites, sometimes without examination of their actual features.

'Classic' raised bog in Britain, as described by Tansley (1939), reflected the observations of Weber (1908). It occupied a discrete lowland site; it had developed by hydroseral succession from open water (open water → swamp → fen → bog); and it formed a shallow dome of ombrogenous peat, with a quite strongly sloping marginal rand leading down into a peripheral moat-like, minerotrophic lagg. However, many raised bogs in Britain do not conform to this 'classic' model, for example, in mode of origin, gross morphology or altitude.

In the 'classic' raised bog, ombrogenous peat, developed upon a flat surface of fen, formed a dome independent of the underlying base. Such 'independent doming' is sometimes regarded as part of the character of a raised bog, but examination of stratigraphical sections reveals that the characteristics of domes of ombrogenous peat in sites that are normally considered to be raised bogs can show much variability. The degree of 'doming' appears to be a product of age, topographical situation, basal area and climate. It is often most evident in small bogs; larger examples often do not appear strongly domed, but may form an extensive plateau of peat with steep edges (Ratcliffe, 1964). The surface of the bog peat may sometimes be strongly related to the underlying topography, as when the summit of the dome reflects an underlying mineral ridge. Such sites may have developed by the coalescence of separate ombrogenous mires that originated in and spread out from adjoining basins and are thus referable to the 'ridge-raised mires' recognised by Moore & Bellamy (1974). However, it is far from certain that this represents a useful point of distinction as many of the sites that are normally called 'raised bogs' in the British Isles and on the European mainland have developed by expansion across ridges of mineral ground (for example, most of the Lancashire mosses (C.E. Wells, *unpublished data*).

The range of hydromorphology of those British sites that are often referred to as being raised bogs can be illustrated by four sections [Figure 1.1]. Cors Caron [Plate 1.1] comes close to being a 'classic' raised bog, with a clear 'independent' dome and a flat base, having originated by autogenic succession from preceding phases of fen and open water. The stratigraphy of Bowness Common–Glasson Moss points to a site where peat initially developed, hydroserally, in depressions, but grew out of these to coalesce across substantial ridges. Flanders Moss West seems to have developed largely by paludification. Its section illustrates the manner in which the 'doming' of some British raised bogs reflects the contours of the underlying mineral ground. The section of Coalburn Moss points to a gently sloping site without a clear dome; moreover, undulations in its surface show some parallel with the underlying relief. Such systems have strong hydromorphological affinities with some examples of blanket bog, and the actual point of distinction is far from clear – a confusion exacerbated by the occurrence within some blanket bog landscapes of mires with strong affinities to many 'lowland raised bogs' (see below).

Raised bogs may be surrounded by a minerotrophic lagg, which is sometimes considered to form part of the concept of raised bog. The actual character of the lagg of many British bogs is difficult to assess, as it has frequently been destroyed, but a well-developed, or complete lagg, may not have been a feature of all examples (Ratcliffe, 1964) except in the sense that, as with all ombrogenous peats, their lateral limits must have been marked by a transition into some form of minerotrophic fen or mineral soil. Distinctive, moat-like laggs are

often most evident in basins where the lateral expansion of the bog has been constrained topographically. In other cases, as where a dome of ombrogenous peat has extended beyond the former limits of a basin, the lagg, if present, may largely be a product of the growth of the bog. Elsewhere, minerotrophic mires adjoining or surrounding a raised bog may predate the bog and be substantially independent of it. In yet other sites the 'lagg ' has effectively been imposed upon the bog, as where water courses and regular flooding has prevented further lateral expansion of ombrotrophic peat (Ratcliffe, 1964). Such considerations suggest that it may be best to exclude the lagg from any general concept of raised bog and to restrict this specifically to the deposit of ombrogenous peat.

It is more difficult to identify a 'classic' concept of blanket bog – it is often informally considered to be ombrogenous peatland with a more upland and north-western distribution than raised bog, which blankets large tracts of land, conformed by the topography and restricted only by the steeper slopes and other obstructions. There is a tendency to regard all ombrogenous peatlands within 'blanket bog regions' as blanket bog, irrespective of their actual character, and even to consider their great extent, across a wide variety of relief, as a diagnostic feature. However, location is not a hydromorphological attribute and size alone seems a specious basis for a distinction of bog types – especially as, elsewhere in Europe, lowland 'raised bogs' once covered areas of comparable magnitude to some tracts of blanket bog [1.4]. The key distinguishing feature of blanket bog is the occurrence of ombrogenous peat on hillslopes and it is far from clear that the ombrogenous peatlands of the basins, flats and gentle slopes of 'blanket bog regions' are necessarily fundamentally different – in terms of their origin, gross form and stratigraphy – from the 'raised bogs' of drier climates. Indeed, various stratigraphical sections suggest that some units of bog embedded within a 'blanket bog landscape' have greater similarity with 'raised bogs' elsewhere than they do with the blanket peats on adjoining slopes (*e.g.* Department of Agriculture and Fisheries for Scotland, 1962–8). If such units are included within a broad concept of 'blanket bog', they expand this to encompass much of the hydromorphological range of raised bogs elsewhere, thus eroding any 'real' distinctions that there may be between the two types. It seems probable that the most distinctive hydromorphological subdivision within ombrogenous peatlands is that between sites in topogenous situations and those on hill slopes, as has been recognised in the categories of *hill bog* and *topogenous bog* used by the Scottish Peat Survey. On this basis, the 'blanket peatlands' of oceanic regions can be seen as a mosaic of hill bog, topogenous bog and various types of fen, whilst 'lowland raised bogs' of drier regions are referable to topogenous bog.

The variability of ombrogenous mires in Britain undoubtedly makes it difficult to formulate a clear and coherent concept of 'raised bog'. We suggest the following tentative, working definition of 'raised bog' in the UK: "Ombrogenous mires in which much of the vegetation is typically referable to, or closely allied with, or derivative from (*e.g.* as a result of damage), *Erica tetralix–Sphagnum papillosum* mire (Rodwell, 1991); they may exhibit a dome (or domes) of peat independent of the underlying subsoil contours, but this is not always the case; some (usually older) examples contain deep (sometimes > 5m) bog peat, which is frequently little-humified in the upper layers." Mires thus identified typically occur in topogenous situations – in basins or on surfaces which are, in aggregate, more-or-less flat or very gently sloping (the surface may have undulations or depressions and ridges, over which the bog has developed); in some instances they have developed by coalescence of adjoining mires (sometimes originating in separate basins). Such sites may be surrounded by mineral ground, fen or an ombrotrophic 'hill peat'. Using this definition, most sites of commercial peat extraction in Britain are (sometimes former) raised-bog sites.

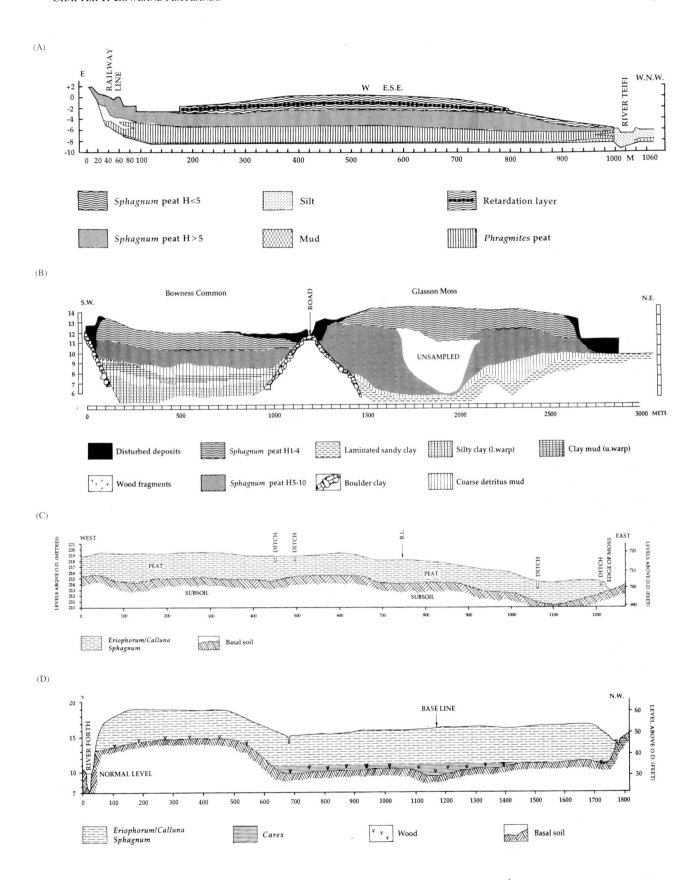

Figure 1.1 Stratigraphical sections across (A) Cors Caron (Godwin & Mitchell, 1938)[1], (B) Bowness Common and Glasson Moss (Walker, 1966)[2], (C) Coalburn Moss[3] and (D) Flanders Moss West[3].

[1] Reproduced by permission of the New Phytologist Trust; [2] Reproduced by permission of the Royal Society and Professor D. Walker; [3] 2nd report of Scottish Peat Committee and Archives of the Scottish Peat Surveys, DAFS (1962–8).

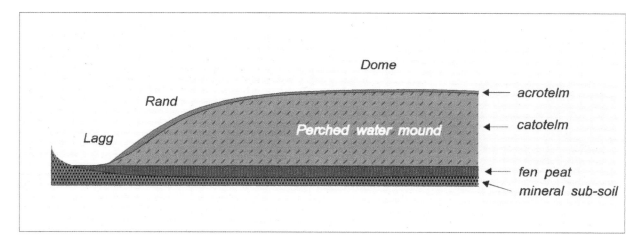

Figure 1.2 Diagrammatic profile across a raised bog, illustrating some of the terms used in the text.

blanket **bog** specifically to refer to the ombrogenous elements of this.

In Britain, most commercial peat extraction concerns lowland raised bogs and these are the focus of this account.

1.4 Some features of raised bogs

On casual inspection, little-damaged raised bogs frequently appear to be rather featureless, uniform tracts of waterlogged ground, sometimes with a wind-swept desolation that may be perceived variously as dismal or delightful. They vary very considerable in their size. In Britain, embryonic 'raised bogs' (*e.g.* areas of ombrogenous peat within fens) may cover just a few square metres, whilst the largest raised bogs are in excess of 1000 ha, although the majority are quite small (< 30 ha). Extremely large examples once occurred on the European mainland, the biggest complex having an estimated area in excess of 1000 km^2 (Barkman, 1992). The depth of peat in raised bogs is

very variable and depends particularly upon the age of the deposit. Thicknesses of bog peat reported from Britain typically range between about 1 and 5 m.

The overall topography of little-damaged raised bogs varies considerably. Some (usually rather small) examples have a quite strongly domed appearance in which the profile of the bog peat deposit approximates to a half-ellipse. In others, the peat deposit is more like a plateau, dipping sharply around its margins [Box 1.1]. In both cases the margins are usually steeper than the main bog expanse and are sometimes referred to as the *rand*. In some situations the interface of the bog margins with the adjoining mineral ground is marked by a moat-like *lagg*, normally supporting fen vegetation. [A diagrammatic profile across a raised bog is shown in Figure 1.2]. However, the natural morphology of many raised bogs, especially the natural state of the margins, is not really known, as peat extraction and agricultural conversion has altered the topography of most sites. Commercial peat extraction usually alters the configuration of the entire bog whilst domestic extraction, or agricultural improvement,

---

Box 1.2 *Climate and the occurrence of raised bogs*

The formation of a deposit of ombrotrophic peat, and to some extent its dimensions, is dependent upon the climatic regime in which it occurs, especially the ratio of precipitation to evaporation [see Box 1.5], but the precise range of climatic circumstances in which bog formation can occur is not well understood, partly because some water balance terms have received but limited study. Water supply to bogs is frequently specified just in terms of precipitation input, but this has to be balanced against potential losses by evapotranspiration. (The amount of evapotranspiration is influenced by such factors as solar radiation, air and surface temperatures, wind speed and relative humidity. Vegetation-type and mulching effect of the moss or litter layer also affect it.) Moreover, the annual mean values that are usually provided for these variables may not be as significant to the development and maintenance of bogs as are seasonal values, though the importance of these latter has been little-quantified. Factors such as the frequency of rainfall (proportion of rain-days, *i.e.* days with 1 mm or more of precipitation), number of days with sunshine, relative humidities, temperature, exposure *etc.* may be of considerable importance in maintaining some ombrotrophic systems. In regions with smaller rates of evapotranspiration, raised bogs can form with lower precipitation input. Various notional figures have been suggested as a minimum precipitation thresholds for the development of raised bogs (*e.g.* 460 mm, S Sweden; 600–700 mm, N Germany). In the UK, peatlands that are usually called raised bogs occupy a wide range of mean annual precipitation: Thorne Waste (S. Yorks.): *c.* 570 mm; south Solway Mosses (Cumbria): *c.* 800 mm; Cors Caron (Dyfed): *c.* 1275 mm; Moine Mhor (Argyll): *c.* 2,000 mm. Such differences are likely to affect both the feasibility of restoration of damaged sites and the nature of the restoration procedures that can be used.

Plate 1.2 Distinctive microtopographical patterning of the bog surface (hummocks, lawns and bog pools), illustrated at Claish Moss, Argyll (*left*) and Mongan Bog, Ireland (*right*).

around the margins has obliterated the natural transition to drier ground (or fen). In consequence, the original character of presumed features such as the rand and lagg is often not known. In some cases, by sharpening the edges, marginal damage may have accentuated the domed appearance of peat deposit. Direct and indirect drainage may also have caused some changes in the topography of many sites, including little-damaged examples, but the nature and extent of this can scarcely even be guessed.

In Britain, as in other regions of the Atlantic sea-board, little-damaged raised bogs are generally treeless; where trees do occur this seems mainly to be in response to some surface damage (such as drainage). In this respect the oceanic bogs differ from their counterparts in more continental regions of the European mainland, where conifer species can be important components of at least the landward zones of bogs. It is possible that, even in Britain, trees may once have been natural components of bog vegetation, at least towards the margins, and perhaps more widely in extended dry periods (*cf.* Casparie, 1972), and that the role of grazing and burning in preventing natural scrub encroachment has been underestimated (H. Ingram, *pers. comm.*).

The vegetation of little-damaged bogs forms a mire surface with a characteristic appearance, based upon its main constituents of sub-shrubs, 'sedge-like' plants and bog mosses (*Sphagnum* species) [see Plates 1.4 and 1.5]. The sub-shrubs are mostly members of the Ericacea (*e.g.* heather (*Calluna vulgaris*) and cross-leaved heath (*Erica tetralix*)) together with similar plants from related families, such as crowberry (*Empetrum nigrum*). 'Sedge-like' plants (*i.e.* members of the Cyperaceae) include the cotton grasses *Eriophorum angustifolium* and *E. vaginatum*. Sphagna are often key components of the vegetation, in terms of their cover and their contribution to the surface processes and peat

formation of the bog [1.7; 1.8; 1.9]. The vegetation of little-damaged raised bogs and blanket bogs has a generally similar overall appearance, but there are some broad differences between them in terms of their species composition (Rodwell, 1991).

Some parts of the surface of a little-damaged bog may show a distinctive patterning (microtopographical heterogeneity), in which various components can be recognised (hummocks, lawns, hollows, pools *etc.*) [Plate 1.2]. Often 'pools' are just shallow-flooded hollows with aquatic species of *Sphagnum*, but larger, deeper and more permanent areas of open water also occur in some bogs. These may range greatly in size, from a few metres to several tens of metres across. Larger examples are variously known as 'bog lakes', 'moor eyes', 'wells' and 'dubh lochans', the latter reflecting the appearance of their black, peat-stained, water. Some are sufficiently large to be marked even on quite small-scale (1:50,000) maps and may even have acquired individual names. Despite a quite large amount of research, the causes of surface patterning are not at all well understood, neither for the 'hummock-hollow' pattern nor the more permanent pools.

The surface of a little-damaged raised bog is typically waterlogged, despite its elevation above the adjoining land. The highest, more central, parts of the bog are often the wettest and typically show the most pronounced development of surface patterning and pool systems, whereas the rand is better drained. The wet conditions are created (in most cases) by an accumulation of rainfall [1.7] and the chemical characteristics of the bog water reflect the composition of the rainfall, modified by processes within the peat and by the growth of plants. The water of raised bogs can be described simply as being 'acidic and nutrient poor' [1.9.4].

1.5 Occurrence of raised bogs

Raised bogs occur widely in temperate and boreal regions of Eurasia and North America. They are (or were) important features throughout much of northern Europe, being particularly widespread and extensive in Britain and Ireland, the Netherlands and north west Germany, southern Sweden and Finland and in the Baltic States. Examples also occur, somewhat separated from the main range, in the foothills and valleys of the Alps. There is a tendency for raised bogs in different regions to show some differences in gross morphology, particularly with respect to the concentricity of their domes and areal extent (Moore & Bellamy, 1974).

In Britain, although many examples have been damaged or destroyed, lowland raised bogs still have a wide distribution. They are especially widespread in the cooler, wetter regions of the north and west (north-west England and southern and central Scotland), but examples also occur (or once occurred) in a number of southern and eastern localities, including sites in S. Yorkshire, Lincolnshire, Cambridgeshire, Somerset and Sussex. It is possible that raised bogs were once even more widespread in these drier regions than is currently recognised, as in some situations agricultural conversion and ancient peat-cutting may have removed most traces of former ombrotrophic peat. Figure 1.5 shows the distribution of peat soils that are regarded by the National Peatland Resource Inventory (Lindsay *et al*, in prep) as being associated with raised bogs in England, Scotland and Wales.

Raised bogs are particularly characteristic of lowland regions of Britain, where they occur in basins, along flood-plains, at the heads of estuaries *etc*. However, examples have been described also from more upland situations, such as Tarn Moss, Malham (W. Yorks.) and Dun Moss (Perths.) which are both at about 350 m altitude.

Raised bogs have developed both by terrestrialisation and paludification processes and sometimes by a combination of the two mechanisms. Although they are mainly initiated in depressions or on flat surfaces, continued upward accumulation of bog peat has permitted some examples to spread onto adjoining, once-dry, slopes and to coalesce across ridges of mineral ground [BOX 1.3].

BOX 1.3 *Origins and development of raised bogs*

Raised bogs may originate and develop by a variety of pathways. The 'classic' developmental sequence (Weber, 1908) [Figure 1.3] shows initiation of ombrotrophic peat from within minerotrophic swamp or fen, which has developed over a pool or lake as part of a *hydroseral* or *terrestrialisation* process. However, it has long been recognised that raised bogs have also developed by the swamping of ground that was once relatively dry, either more-or-less directly or, more usually, through an intervening (sometimes short-lived) phase of fen (Cajander, 1913). This process is known as *paludification*. Thus starting points for raised bog development include such diverse habitats as reedswamp, floating vegetation mats, herbaceous fen, fen carr, woodland and saltmarsh [Figure 1.4]. Common to all of these developments is the progressive upward growth of peat above the level of influence of groundwater, leading to a surface irrigated almost entirely by precipitation inputs. The character of this is, in large measure, independent of its starting conditions. The time taken for the development of bog peats from a preceding phase is also variable – it has been suggested that the transition between fen vegetation and bog vegetation may take from between just a few years to about five centuries.

Some examples of raised bog have developed initially in a basin, often as a late phase of hydroseral succession, but have subsequently expanded over adjoining 'dry' land. This process can lead to the fusion of adjoining raised bogs to produce a larger unit. The very extensive raised bogs of The Netherlands and Germany are thought to have formed in this way, as have some UK examples (*e.g.* Bowness Common / Glasson Moss – Figure 1.1). In some cases the gradual 'spilling' of ombrotrophic peat out of the original basin onto adjoining mineral ground produces, at least initially, a thin humified peat-type that, both in character and situation, is reminiscent of some types of blanket bog peat. This has been little documented in Britain but is probably quite widespread. Examples are thought to occur at Wedholme Flow and Walton Moss (Cumbria).

In some mires the development of bog peat has been so complete as to cover most traces of former fen. However, more usually the apparent present-day dominance of some peatland sites by bog reflects the drainage and agricultural conversion of once-adjoining fen. This may be the case, for example, in situations where some, or all, of the bog peat has been left unclaimed on account of the greater difficulties of converting it into productive agricultural land. Deep peat excavation sometimes exposes underlying fen peat and provides the possibility for the re-establishment of fen vegetation.

The initiation of ombrotrophic peat implies impeded drainage of precipitation inputs. This may be produced in various ways. Where the bog peat has developed from fen and swamp, then the low-permeability bottom of the bog is fixed either by the fen water table itself, or by the surface of low-permeability fen and wood peats. Where bogs have developed by paludification, the basis for the establishment of permanently wet conditions may be provided by a variety of low-permeability horizons. These including crystalline bedrocks, glacial and estuarine clays *etc*. Nonetheless, paludification can also occur upon more permeable substrata (*e.g.* sands and gravels). In this situation waterlogging may be possible either because of a high groundwater table within the porous medium (as in zones of groundwater discharge) or because of the development of low permeability pans of iron or organic material, in some cases possibly related to 'fossil' indurated, cemented layers formed in periglacial conditions.

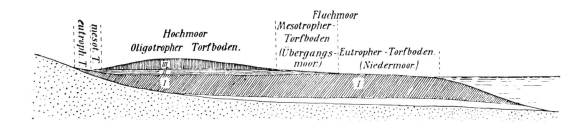

Figure 1.3 "Classic" topographical development of raised bog (Weber, 1908), showing the horizontal and vertical sequence of peat types in a mire-landscape which has progressed to the formation of a raised bog. On the right of the diagram is the lake on whose shore the mire has developed. Marl ('lake-chalk') is shown between peat type I and the underlying mineral substratum (stippled). I - eutrophic; II - mesotrophic; III - oligotrophic peat types [Torfboden]. [Hochmoor - raised bog; Flachmoor - mire; Übergangsmoor - transition mire; Niedermoor - fen]

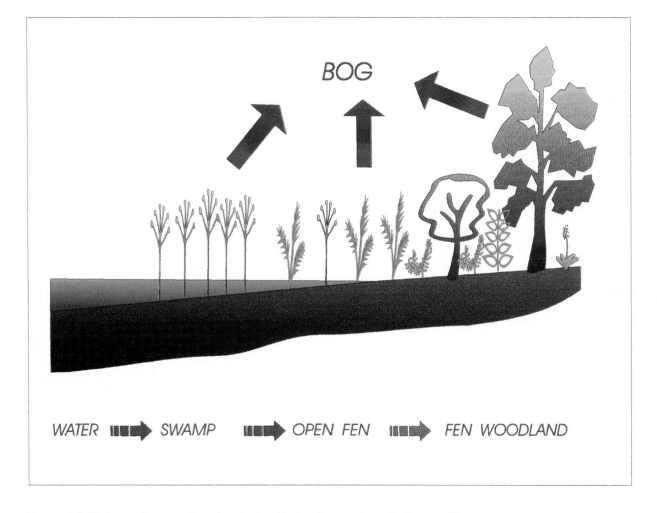

Figure 1.4 Hydroseral succession of ombrotrophic bog from various starting conditions.

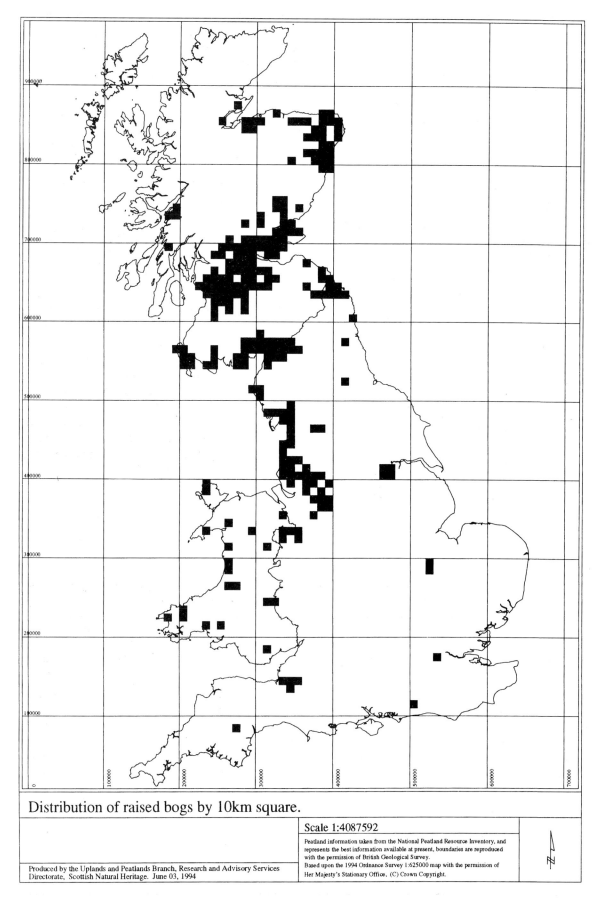

Distribution of raised bogs by 10km square.

Scale 1:4087592

Peatland information taken from the National Peatland Resource Inventory, and
represents the best information available at present, boundaries are reproduced
with the permission of British Geological Survey.
Based upon the 1994 Ordnance Survey 1:625000 map with the permission of
Her Majesty's Stationary Office, (C) Crown Copyright.

Produced by the Uplands and Peatlands Branch, Research and Advisory Services
Directorate, Scottish Natural Heritage. June 03, 1994

Figure 1.5   Distribution of soils identified by the National Peatland Resource Inventory as associated with raised
bogs in England, Scotland and Wales, by 10 km square. [Diagram provided by Scottish Natural Heritage].

1.6 Current condition of British raised bogs

Scottish Natural Heritage are preparing an inventory of the extent and condition of raised bogs in Great Britain (Lindsay *et al.*; *in prep.*), on behalf of the three country statutory nature conservation agencies. Summary statistics from the draft inventory are presented in Table 1.2, although the data are still subject to verification and review. Categories given are for the *major* land-cover classes of raised bogs and the 'best' land cover classes identified for each site.

The category of 'closed-canopy woodland' includes both forestry plantations and sites that have become spontaneously wooded, although the majority is commercial plantation. Thus, wooded bogs, together with the agriculture and urban categories, account for some 48% of the original raised-bog area. These areas may retain some general wildlife 'interest' and, in some instances, are probably amenable for restoration to bog. If, however, they are considered to be areas effectively 'lost' from the raised-bog resource, then the residue represents some 36,000 ha of raised-bog sites in variable condition. Only a small proportion of this is regarded as being more-or-less 'natural' (little-damaged). The biological condition of the remainder is not specified, but it cannot be assumed that it has no conservation value, even in terms of bog species. This is not least because the areas given are based on the major land-use class for each site: partly-damaged bogs

and revegetating peat cuttings can still provide a rich repository of bog species. For example, Wedholme Flow, which retains some of the finest examples of little-damaged *Sphagnum*-rich raised-bog vegetation in England, is categorised under its major land-use class of 'secondary – revegetating'. Likewise, it should be noted also that the area of bog designated as 'secondary – active commercial peat extraction' contains some large expanses of vegetated (sometimes revegetated) bog peat, as well as active peat fields.

There can be little doubt that the total area of 'good-quality raised bog' remaining in Britain is small, nor about the identity of some of the main causes of damage. However, the loss of 'quality' in bogs may not just be a product of direct damage of the type identified in Table 1.2. In various lowland mires, once-diverse *Sphagnum* communities have been replaced by lawns dominated by one species, *Sphagnum recurvum* (Tallis, 1973). The explanation of this is not known: past sulphur pollution, enrichment with atmospheric nitrogen sources, especially perhaps ammonia, or some other form of enrichment from agricultural sources, are all candidate hypotheses. Such considerations make it difficult to be confident about the full measure of impact and significance of the more direct forms of damage identified in Table 1.2. It cannot be assumed that former raised bogs would necessarily still support 'good-quality' vegetation had they not been subject to direct drainage or destruction.

Table 1.2 The major land cover classes* on raised bogs in Britain, as identified by the National Peatland Resource Inventory (Lindsay *et al*, in prep). Source: Department of the Environment (1994).

Condition class	England		Scotland		Wales	
	Number of bogs	Area (ha)	Number of bogs	Area (ha)	Number of bogs	Area (ha)
Primary – near-natural	1	8	49	2673	5	2694
Primary – degraded (burnt / moribund)	9	1699	83	3148	2	136
Primary – drained	13	562	20	1192	5	35
Primary – open canopy scrub or woodland	14	427	5	176	1	6
Primary – closed canopy woodland	41	1734	193	9780	0	0
Secondary – revegetating	15	1163	39	2881	3	790
Secondary – active commercial peat extraction*	15	14498	12	2284	1	4
Archaic – agriculture	92	16972	238	3048	3	247
Archaic – built (urban / waste disposal *etc.*)	7	350	26	890	1	174
Unknown	0	0	144	1818	0	0
Total	207	37413	809	27890	21	4086

* Note that these figures are based on assessment of the dominant land cover class on each site. Thus, for example, the figures for active commercial peat cutting include more than just the area either permitted for, or actually affected by peat extraction (see text).

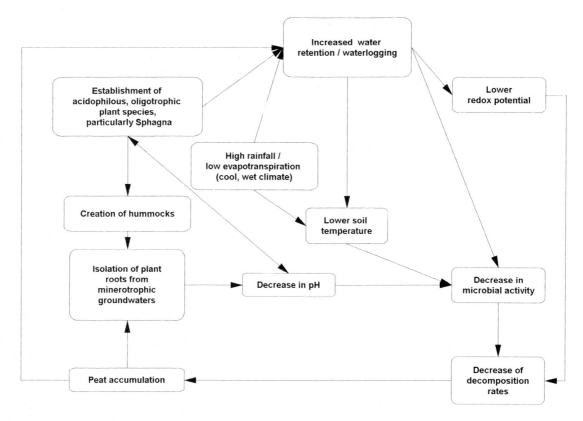

Figure 1.6 Main mechanisms leading to accumulation of peat and bog succession.

1.7 Hydrology and morphology of raised bogs

1.7.1 Introduction

In any wetland ecosystem, hydrological processes help determine the character of various environmental features, such as water chemistry, nutrient availability and degree of soil aeration. These in turn influence the identity of the flora and fauna of the mire. In ombrotrophic peatlands hydrological processes and vegetation are linked through a positive feed-back mechanism whereby the accumulation of the dead plant remains as peat also helps to determine some of the hydrological processes [see Figure 1.6].

1.7.2 The diplotelmic mire

Hydrologically, raised bogs can be considered as two layered (*diplotelmic*) systems comprised of an uppermost 'active layer' (or *acrotelm)* and a lower so-called 'inert layer'[1] (or *catotelm)* [Figure 1.2]. The catotelm is defined as the zone of permanent saturation but, in a little-damaged bog, various additional features help to distinguish the acrotelm from the catotelm. The acrotelm forms the main functional horizon for plant

growth. It is composed of the living vegetation cover together with underlying, recently-dead plant material and fresh peat. The acrotelm is usually thin (< 50 cm) because the peat that forms within it gradually becomes incorporated into the catotelm below, as the upper level of the permanent water table is elevated and the bog grows upwards. Water moves quite readily through the upper layers of the acrotelm, which both contains and helps to regulate water-level fluctuations caused by variation in water inputs and outputs. It forms the main conduit of water discharge from the bog. The acrotelm has high permeability to water near to the surface, but becomes more impermeable with depth as the peat becomes more consolidated and decomposed (humified). Water movement and fluctuations mean that conditions in the acrotelm remain largely aerobic and it is here that microbial activity is strongest.

The acrotelm of a little-damaged bog can be regarded as an integrated combination of plants (especially *Sphagnum* species), peat and water. Plant growth contributes to the formation of a structure which has some capacity for hydrological self-regulation and which helps to maintain conditions suitable for the continued growth and survival of the plants. Such feedbacks help to maintain the growth and character of the bog surface [Figure 1.6], and the acrotelm is critical to the normal development and functioning of a raised bog [BOX 1.4] (see also Joosten, 1993).

---

[1] The catotelm is not, strictly speaking, 'inert'.

Box 1.4 *The acrotelm layer of raised bogs in relation to restoration*

In a little-damaged bog, the acrotelm layer functions essentially (a) to support the growth of bog plants; (b) to produce the raw organic material which subsequently accumulates in the catotelm as peat; and (c) to feed the catotelm with water to maintain and, as the bog grows, to increase the zone of permanent saturation. Perhaps the most remarkable feature of the acrotelm of a growing raised bog is that it provides a structure which can accommodate considerable fluctuation of water level whilst sustaining the continued growth (or at least survival) of the bog plants that ultimately contribute to the accumulating peat mass.

The acrotelm layer of a little-damaged bog may be readily modified or destroyed by various operations. Peat extraction often leads to its complete and direct removal. (A possible exception occurs in some hand-cutting operations, where the living surface turves are immediately placed upon the floor of the cutting, thus providing direct re-instatement of the surface layer.) Other processes, such as drainage, dehydration, repeated and deep burning, can also much modify its properties. The primary objective of restoration of damaged bog surfaces must be to recreate an acrotelm with properties similar to those of the original. The primary problem of such initiatives is that some of the properties that are provided by the original bog acrotelm (most notably its capacity for hydrological self-regulation) are themselves required to regenerate a new surface with a comparable functional rôle. The 'trick' of much bog restoration is therefore to contrive to mimic on the exposed peat surface some of the functional properties of the original acrotelm until a 'new' acrotelm has developed.

It is possible to envisage situations (*e.g.* when a bog first begins to form) where an acrotelm layer can occur without an associated catotelm. It is sometimes also suggested that when the acrotelm has been removed from a bog, as by peat extraction, the resulting structure then becomes one-layered (*haplotelmic*), *i.e.* comprised only of a catotelm. However, such a residual peat body is unlikely ever to be truly haplotelmic (*sensu stricto*). This is because, after the acrotelm has been removed, the newly exposed catotelm surface is likely to dry out occasionally, because of periodic lack of precipitation input coupled with on-going evapotranspiration. Hence the surface of the zone of *permanent* saturation will sink, leading once more to a diplotelmic structure. This new surface layer will serve to feed the catotelm with recharge water, thus providing one of the functions of the original acrotelm, but it lacks some of the other characteristics of the acrotelm as found on little-damaged bogs. This circumstance is frequent in many bog sites that have been damaged by peat extraction (and other operations) and where, for various reasons, the zone of permanent saturation (*i.e.* the upper surface of the catotelm) [see Box 1.5] has fallen to a lower level in the peat mass. In this situation the peat below the new level of permanent saturation can still be regarded as a legitimate 'catotelm', but the original catotelm peat above it does not possess all the functional characteristics of the original acrotelm. Such considerations suggest that it is important to distinguish between an acrotelm defined just as the upper layer lacking permanent saturation and an acrotelm as a structure possessing the properties characteristic of a little-damaged bog surface. However, such a terminological distinction has not yet been made, leading to corresponding confusion in usage. In this report, unless qualified, the term 'acrotelm' is restricted to refer to the 'fully-functional' surface layers such as characterise little-damaged bogs.

The lower layer of the bog (the *catotelm*) usually comprises the bulk of the peat in a raised bog. It is built up from former acrotelm peat which has become incorporated into the catotelm. By contrast with the acrotelm, catotelm peat is typically well-consolidated and often strongly-humified. It has a much lower permeability than the acrotelm and correspondingly much slower rates of water movement within it. By definition, the catotelm is permanently saturated with water. It provides a water-saturated, anaerobic base to the acrotelm and the impeded drainage thereby produced gives the hydrological basis to development and growth of the raised bog. [This is additional to the impeded drainage in the underlying substratum or minerotrophic peat which permitted the initiation of an ombrotrophic nucleus.] Although most microbial activity occurs within the acrotelm, there is also some activity of anaerobic microbes within the catotelm.

1.7.3 The water balance of a raised bog

In an ombrotrophic peatland, the only source of water to the surface is from precipitation (rainfall, snow, fog *etc.*). Some of this is returned to the atmosphere through surface evaporation and plant transpiration (together termed *evapotranspiration*), while the remainder gradually seeps laterally towards the edges of the bog, mainly through the surface layers (*acrotelm*) or vertically to become stored within the lower layers (*catotelm*) [see Figure 1.7]. Vertical loss of water downwards through the base of the bog *via* the catotelm is generally assumed to be negligible, although this may not always be the case [see Chapter 2]. Although a raised bog develops because of an overall precipitation surplus, during some parts of the year, especially summer, evapotranspirative losses may temporarily exceed precipitation inputs. On such occasions, the perched water level will fall, as water is removed from storage. Subsequent precipitation will replenish the storage water, before seepage towards the margins is increased as the water table rises again.

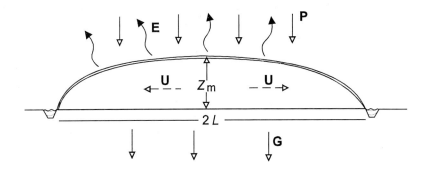

The water budget of a mire can be represented as: $P - E - U - G - \Delta W = 0$

where P = precipitation; E = evapotranspiration; U = flux density with which water enters the catotelm; G = leakage through the base of the mire (generally very small); ΔW = increase in storage.

For a raised mire of approximately circular plan, the maximum height of the 'groundwater mound' (Z_m) can be estimated from the equation:

$$U / K = 2 Z_m^2 / L^2$$

where K = hydraulic conductivity of the peat; L = radius of the mire.

Figure 1.7 Water budget of a raised bog and terms used in hydrological modelling of the 'groundwater mound' (after Ingram, 1987)[1].

1.7.4 The shape and size of raised bogs

The formation of a dome of ombrotrophic peat and, to some extent, its ultimate shape and height, is dependent upon the climatic regime in which the peatland occurs and most notably on the ratio of precipitation to evaporation [see Box 1.5]. A clear understanding of the hydrodynamics of raised-bog systems has emerged only in the last twenty years, with the recognition that the waterlogged conditions which permit ombrotrophic peat to accumulate above the level of the regional water table (or impermeable substratum) are produced by impeded drainage of rainwater through the peat mass (Ingram, 1982). This has lead to the formulation of models to predict the size and shape of raised bogs, based on standard groundwater hydrology and soil physics [Box 1.5].

A major limitation of all models which attempt to explain the shape and size of raised bogs just in terms of hydrodynamics is the likelihood that the dimensions and profile are actually determined by several inter-acting influences. These include the constraints of the topography of the landscape in which the bog occurs, the degree of slope upon which it is developed, the age and mode of development of the bog (*i.e.* by spreading from a single nucleus or by multiple nucleation) and the rate of peat decay. Clymo (1991) has pointed out that the calculated 'hydrological limit' of a bog may be

very much greater than its measured height on account of ongoing peat decomposition. Disparities will be greatest in bogs of large basal area and the hydrological limit may only be reached in rather small sites. A consequence of this is that, within a given region, strongly-domed bogs may be primarily a feature of small sites whereas bigger bogs may be more flat-topped. Thus, in Britain, the two main 'types' of raised bog which some workers have identified, *plateau raised bog* and *concentric domed bog*, may more reflect the basal area of the peat deposit than fundamental differences.

1.8 Peat profiles and types of peat

In very broad terms, the stratigraphy of a little-damaged raised bog can be summarised as:

living plants + *loose* acrotelm *peat*

ombrotrophic catotelm *peat*

minerotrophic peat[2]

The acrotelm is usually some $10 - 40$ cm deep, but the other layers can show much variation in thickness, depending on the age, situation and development of the bog.

The ombrotrophic catotelm peat (which, in most cases,

---

[1] Reproduced from Ingram (1987) by permission of the Royal Society of Edinburgh and H.A.P. Ingram.

[2] This may be extremely thin in some examples that have developed by paludification.

is the focus of interest of the peat industry) often shows substantial variation in character, between sites and within sites and both laterally and vertically [see Figure 1.8]. The character, and stratigraphy, of bog peat is determined by the vegetation that produced it, the conditions in which it formed (which affect the rate of accumulation) and post-depositional changes. The lower peat layers of bogs are often darker, more humified and more solid (greater bulk density) than the upper layers. This is due in part to the effects of compression and decomposition coupled, but may also reflect differences in the composition of the peat-forming vegetation and the circumstances of accumulation. In some peatlands, the catotelm peat is quite sharply divided into two distinct layers [see Plate 1.3]. This can be observed clearly, for example, in some bogs in north-west Germany (Weber, 1908) where there is often a sharp boundary between the lower 'black peat' (decomposition degree usually H6 to H8 or H9) and the overlying 'white peat' (usually H2 to H5). ['H' values refer to the von-Post scale of

decomposition (humification), see Table 1.3]. Similar layers can be found in some British bogs and the terms *black peat* and *white peat* have also been applied to these. However, such terms are often used as loose, ill-defined categories of variable compass and it cannot be assumed that the black peat found at the base of some UK bogs is necessarily equivalent with the 'true' black peat of continental bogs. For example, some British bogs (mainly rather young examples) consist almost entirely of 'white peat' (*sensu* Weber, 1908), but nonetheless the lower peats are usually more humified and compacted than are the upper ones and they are often referred to as 'black peat'. In addition, in the Somerset Levels, the 'true' sedge peat is also sometimes referred to as 'best black peat'. Thus, terms such as *black peat* and *white peat* should be treated with some considerable circumspection. They are good examples of terms that receive quite widespread use without agreement upon their exact meaning and compass.

Box 1.5 *The 'Groundwater' Mound hypothesis*

In an important contribution to understanding the hydrology, development and shape of raised bogs, Ingram (1982) pointed out: (a) that water and peat accumulates to form a raised bog on account of impeded drainage of rainwater; (b) that this gives rise to a characteristic near-hemi-elliptical mound of water perched above its surroundings and supported by the growing mass of vegetation and peat that has developed because of its presence; and (c) that the surface of this mound determines the surface of the catotelm (the zone of permanent saturation) and hence the shape and dimensions of the bog (because the unsaturated zone is thin and is moulded around the catotelm). This suggestion, and its implications, have come to be known as the 'Groundwater Mound hypothesis'.

The concepts and title of the 'Groundwater mound hypothesis' are based on standard groundwater hydrology and soil physics. They recognise that the surface of the zone of permanent saturation of a raised bog is analogous to the groundwater table between ditches in a drained field (that is, highest midway between the ditches and declining towards them). Thus this hypothesis is not specific to peat soils or to ombrogenous bogs – indeed, its importance is particularly in its recognition that the behaviour of the water table in bogs *can* be understood and described in terms of 'normal' soil hydrology and physics, with regard to the impeded drainage of rainfall – and not, as some previous workers had supposed, in terms of capillary rise of water up through the peat mass. Nonetheless, the title 'Groundwater Mound hypothesis', whilst accurately reflecting its lineage, is perhaps rather unfortunate with respect to ombrotrophic bogs, as it suggests precisely the opposite to what it means: the water that accumulates to form the 'groundwater' mound is derived from meteoric sources and is thus not what hydrologists most usually understand by groundwater, *i.e.* water derived from telluric sources. To help avoid confusion, in this report reference is made to a 'groundwater' mound or a 'perched water mound'.

'Groundwater' Mound theory indicates that the profile and dimensions of the catotelm are a function of (i) the shape and size of the basal plan of the bog; (ii) the net recharge to the catotelm; and (iii) the overall permeability of the accumulating

catotelm peat [see Figure 1.7]. The relationship thus infers that taller groundwater mounds are associated with higher rates of water input or slower seepage and with greater basal area (Bragg, 1989). Support for the model has been derived from a quite close correspondence between observed and predicted profiles of some Scottish bog sites (Dun Moss and Ellergower Moss).

The 'Groundwater' Mound hypothesis undoubtedly provides a very useful conceptual basis for understanding the development and shape of raised bogs. It also helps to demonstrate some of the hydrological repercussions of damage to bogs. For example, an important consequence of the model is that operations which serve to reduce the basal area of a bog (such as extensive drainage and conversion for agriculture or peat extraction around its margins) may lead to a concomitant reduction in the height of the water mound in the remnant of bog and hence a drying-out of some, or all, of its surface.

The 'simple' 'Groundwater' Mound model does, however, have some limitations. It is a static rather than a dynamic model (Schouwenaars, 1995); it assumes a single value of hydraulic conductivity for the catotelm, whereas actual conductivities may show very considerable spatial variation (Kneale, 1987); it assumes a flat base and is most readily solved for peatlands of relatively simple plan. Some of these limitations (*e.g.* difficulties of obtaining a meaningful estimate of catotelm permeability) are common to all models; others may be resolved by more sophisticated developments (*e.g.* of finite element models).

Some further practical limitations of 'groundwater' mound models rest upon the possibility that, in some sites, 'true' groundwater may help to maintain, or even contribute to, the water mound. 'Fen windows' are known in various bogs and some raised bogs have developed over zones of groundwater discharge. A model, accurately but confusingly, known as the 'groundwater' model (Glaser, 1987; Glaser, Janssens & Siegel, 1990) has recently been developed to describe this type of situation. It is not known to what extent this may be applicable to British bogs.

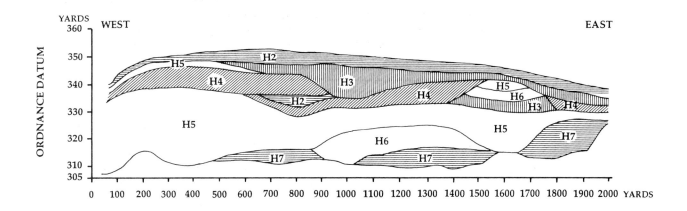

Figure 1.8 Stratigraphical section across Raheenmore Bog (Ireland) [Reproduced by permission of Bord na Mona.] H values indicate the humification degree of the peat (von Post scale) [see Table 1.3]

Plate 1.3 Section through raised bog peat (Solway Moss, Cumbria) showing the division between the upper weakly-humified peat ('white peat') and lower strongly-humified peat ('black peat'). [Photo: I. Richardson]

Differences occur between different types of peat in such attributes as bulk density, porosity and water storage capacity. This can affect the use of peat as a horticultural medium and its suitability as a substratum for restoration [2.3]. Peat-based composts are often made by blending different peat types from differing locations in a bog.

Weakly-humified light peats are particularly valuable for horticulture because of their loose structure and high porosity. They are generally less desirable than darker peats as a fuel.

Strongly-humified dark peats have been much-prized as fuel peats but have been generally of less value to the horticultural industry. Nonetheless, they are widely used blended with light peats in some peat-based composts and can also be used by themselves. Their importance to horticulture may be expected to increase as reserves of the upper, lighter peats become depleted.

Table 1.3 Modified version of the von Post Scale for assessing the degree of decomposition of peat (from Burton & Hodgson, 1987). [Reproduced by permission of the Soil Survey and Land Research Centre]

Degree of decomposition	Nature of liquid expressed on squeezing	Proportion of peat extruded between fingers	Nature of plant residues	Description
H1	Clear, colourless	None	Plant structure unaltered; fibrous, elastic	Undecomposed
H2	Almost clear, yellow–brown	None	Plant structure distinct; almost unaltered	Almost undecomposed
H3	Slightly turbid, brown	None	Plant structure distinct; most remains easily identifiable	Very weakly decomposed
H4	Strongly turbid, brown	None	Plant structure distinct; most remains identifiable	Weakly decomposed
H5	Strongly turbid, contains a little peat in suspension	Very little	Plant structure clear but becoming indistinct; most remains difficult to identify	Moderately decomposed
H6	Muddy, much peat in suspension	One-third	Plant structure indistinct but clearer in the squeezed residue than in the undisturbed peat; most remains unidentifiable	Well decomposed
H7	Strongly muddy	One-half	Plant structure indistinct but recognisable; few remains identifiable	Strongly decomposed
H8	Thick mud, little free water	Two thirds	Plant structure very indistinct; only resistant remains such as root fibres and wood identifiable	Very strongly decomposed
H9	No free water	Nearly all	Plant structure almost unrecognisable; practically no identifiable remains	Almost completely decomposed
H10	No free water	All	Plant structure unrecognisable; completely amorphous	Completely decomposed

1.9 The vegetation of British raised bogs

1.9.1 Plant species and vegetation-types

The vegetation of ombrotrophic mires is of great importance, not just in its own right but because it provides the physical basis of the mire itself and helps to define some of its characteristics and conditions. This is because:

- plant growth provides the basis for peat formation, water storage and impeded drainage;

- plant growth provides the basis for much of the microtopography of the site and creates small-scale water gradients;

- the growth of *Sphagnum* species helps to create and regulate some characteristics of the bog surface environment.

Although a range of vascular plants are found in bogs, some of the most characteristic and important plant species of bog vegetation are the bog mosses of the genus *Sphagnum* [Plates 1.4 and 1.5]. Some ten species are common components of lowland bogs in Britain. They grow in pools, lawns and hummocks and contribute to the formation of these structures. Sphagna possess neither roots nor specialised conductive tissues

for internal water transport. They do, however have some capacity for external transport of water, by movement between the stems, branches and leaves. The leaves of *Sphagnum* contain two types of cells: narrow, sinuous photosynthetic cells and large water-filled *hyaline* cells. These latter cells allow even dead remains of *Sphagnum* to store a great deal of water and *Sphagnum* plants are reported to contain up to 40 times their dry weight as water (Romanov, 1968). Sphagna are of great importance to the development of many bogs. They are often the major peat-producing species, they help create the characteristically-low pH environment of bogs and they can store large volumes of water. They contribute to regulation of the water balance of a bog's surface, through the storage of water, a 'mulching' effect during dry periods and a capacity for 'bleaching' when drought-stressed (which helps to reflect solar radiation).

The vegetation of ombrotrophic bogs is typically rather species-poor and comparatively uniform, probably reflecting the specialised nature of the habitat. Many bog species have a wide global distribution and some (for example *Sphagnum magellanicum*) occur in both southern and northern hemispheres. Over 130 plant species have been recorded from UK bogs (Wheeler, 1993), but only some 50 of these are particularly characteristic of little-damaged raised-bog sites [Appendix 4]. Most of these also occur, some widely, in a

Sphagnum capillifolium[†]

Sphagnum magellanicum[†]

Sphagnum cuspidatum[†]

Sphagnum papillosum[†]

Sphagnum fuscum

Sphagnum recurvum[‡]

Plate 1.4 Some characteristic species of *Sphagnum* found on ombrotrophic bogs.
[Photos: [†]M.C.F. Proctor; [‡] P.C. Roworth (ARPS)]

Drosera anglica

Eriophorum angustifolium[‡]

Drosera rotundifolia on *Sphagnum fimbriatum*[‡]

Eriophorum vaginatum[‡]

Andromeda polifolia[‡]

Vaccinium oxycoccos[‡]

Plate 1.5 Some characteristic vascular plant species found on ombrotrophic bogs. [[‡]Photos: P.C. Roworth (ARPS)]

variety of other waterlogged habitats and some are abundant also in drier environments. A few are uncommon or rare, such as *Andromeda polifolia, Drosera anglica, D. intermedia, Rhynchospora fusca, Dicranum undulatum, Sphagnum fuscum, S. imbricatum* and *S. pulchrum*. Of these, *A. polifolia* and *D. undulatum* are largely specific to raised bogs in Britain; most of the others occur in poor fen as well as in bogs. When growing in the ombrotrophic habitat some of these species, such as *D. anglica*, are

particularly associated with north-western bogs in Britain. It is not known to what extent this represents a natural oceanic distribution or reflects their loss from more south-eastern bogs, perhaps because of damage or atmospheric pollution.

Although bog vegetation contains a limited range of plant species, certain species combinations appear to be unique to bogs [Table 1.4]. In a little-damaged raised bog, small pools are typically occupied by vegetation of the *Sphagnum cuspidatum–S. recurvum* bog pool

Table 1.4 The main plant community-types of ombrogenous mires in Britain, as identified by the National Vegetation Classification (Rodwell, 1991). The principal community-types of little-damaged raised bog are shown in bold type. For further details of community types of cut-over bogs, see Box 2.1.

COMMUNITY-TYPES LARGELY CONFINED TO OMBROTROPHIC MIRES

    M17 *Scirpus cespitosus– Eriophorum vaginatum* blanket mire
        (a) *Drosera rotundifolia–Sphagnum* sub-community
        (b) *Cladonia* sub-community
        (c) *Juncus squarrosus–Rhytidiadelphus loreus* sub-community

    M18 *Erica tetralix–Sphagnum papillosum* raised and blanket mire
        (a) *Sphagnum magellanicum–Andromeda* sub-community
        (b) *Empetrum nigrum–Cladonia* sub-community

    M19 *Calluna vulgaris–Eriophorum vaginatum* blanket mire
        (a) *Erica tetralix* sub-community
        (b) *Empetrum nigrum* sub-community
        (c) *Vaccinium vitis-idaea–Hylocomium splendens* sub-community

    M20 *Eriophorum vaginatum* blanket and raised mire
        (a) species-poor sub-community
        (b) *Calluna vulgaris–Cladonia* sub-community

COMMUNITY-TYPES ALSO FOUND CHARACTERISTICALLY IN OTHER HABITATS (MAINLY POOR FEN AND WET HEATH)

    M1 *Sphagnum auriculatum* bog pool community

    M2 *Sphagnum cuspidatum / S. recurvum* bog pool community
        (a) *Rhynchospora alba* sub-community
        (b) *Sphagnum recurvum* sub-community

    M3 *Eriophorum angustifolium* bog pool community

    M15 *Scirpus cespitosus– Erica tetralix* wet heath
        [(a) *Carex panicea* sub-community – *not strictly ombrotrophic*]
        (b) typical sub-community
        (c) *Cladonia* sub-community
        (d) *Vaccinium myrtillus* sub-community

COMMUNITY-TYPES CHARACTERISTIC OF NON-OMBROTROPHIC HABITATS BUT PRESENT ON (USUALLY DAMAGED) OMBROTROPHIC BOGS.

These include:

    M25 *Molinia caerulea–Potentilla erecta* mire
        (a) *Erica tetralix* sub-community
        (b) *Anthoxanthum odoratum* sub-community

    W4 *Betula pubescens–Molinia caerulea* woodland
        (a) *Dryopteris dilatata* sub-community
        (c) *Sphagnum* sub-community

    H9 *Calluna vulgaris–Deschampsia flexuosa* heath
      Pteridium aquilinum stands

    Various fen community-types may occur in laggs

community (M2) whilst much of the rest of the surface is referable to just one community-type, the *Erica tetralix–Sphagnum papillosum* community (M18), which is largely specific to raised-bog systems. This community is split into two sub-units. One of these (the *Sphagnum magellanicum–Andromeda polifolia sub-community,* M18a) essentially refers to wet *Sphagnum* lawns and hummock-hollow complexes, that may be intermingled with, or occur peripheral, to the pool systems, most typically in the central, wettest part of the bog. The other (the *Empetrum nigrum–Cladonia* sub-community, M18b) represents vegetation with a greater prominence of ericoid plants and usually occupies rather drier conditions, such as may occur further from the centre of the bog. Near the edge of the bog, the drier rand may sometimes also support an *Erica tetralix–S. papillosum* (M18) community, but often has examples of a more heathy vegetation (*e.g. Scirpus cespitosus–Erica tetralix* wet heath, M15) or even *Molinia* grassland or birch scrub.

A broad zonation can be recognised across the surface of at least some little-damaged raised bogs, from the central complex of shallow pools and hummocks to the drier rand and thence to a minerotrophic lagg [Figure 1.9]. In many sites, the natural character of a presumed lagg is not known, as marginal areas have often been damaged or removed by drainage, agricultural conversion or peat cutting. Very often, even in little damaged bogs, the rand may also have been subject to some modification (improved drainage *etc.*) and again it is difficult to be certain of its natural character. It is often assumed that the rand is naturally drier than much of the bog and that it is naturally treeless but, given the current propensity for tree invasion of slightly-dried surfaces in little-damaged bogs, it would be of interest to know why trees were naturally absent from a drier rand, if indeed they were.

It can also be difficult to specify the presumed 'natural' condition of the main expanse of little-damaged bogs. This is partly because even little-damaged sites have often been subject to some disturbance (including, in some cases, deposition of atmospheric contaminants) but it is also because the vegetation of even an undisturbed bog is not completely stable. Peat stratigraphical evidence points to both abrupt and gradual changes in the past vegetation composition, with a shifting tendency for dominance of bog surfaces by 'hummock species' *versus* 'hollow species', probably mainly in relation to changing conditions of surface wetness, such as may sometimes reflect climatic shifts (Aaby, 1976; Barber, 1981). Dry phases may show an abundance of ericoid species with Sphagna suppressed and, sometimes, even localised tree invasion (Casparie, 1972).

The causes for some major changes in the composition of bog vegetation are not really known. For example, in many bogs in Britain (and elsewhere), *Sphagnum imbricatum* was replaced by *S. magellanicum* as a main peat-forming species, at about the Middle Ages (Barber, Dumayne & Stoneman, 1993). The reasons for this have yet to be established, but the consequence is that a once-dominant bog-building species in now rare in raised bogs. Such changes make it difficult to specify the 'natural' character of bog vegetation – and the desired objective of bog restoration initiatives. However, the *E. tetralix–S. papillosum* community is often considered to be the 'natural' core community-

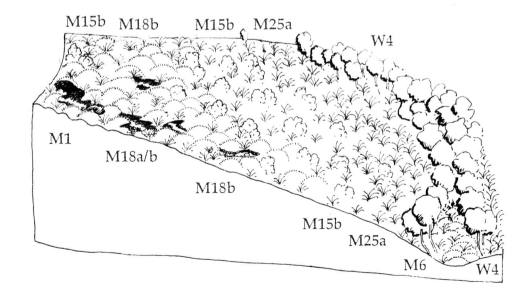

Figure 1.9 Typical zonation of plant communities across a raised bog (after Rodwell, 1991). [see Table 1.4 for identity of communities] [Reproduced by permission of Cambridge University Press.]

type of many lowland raised bogs, and its recreation forms a focus of the restoration of damaged raised bogs [see Chapter 3].

The vegetation of bogs can also be broadly categorised by its physiognomic characteristics and the habitat conditions in which it occurs. A broad, informal classification is suggested in Table 1.5.

1.9.2 Reproduction and spread of bog plant species

Some plant species of bogs are long-lived perennials (*e.g.* plants of *Eriophorum vaginatum* may live for more than 100 years) and, for these, recruitment of new individuals may be of limited importance to species survival in undisturbed bogs. However, other species (*e.g. Drosera* spp.) are short-lived and have a greater dependence upon seed production to maintain their populations.

Diaspore production and dissemination is important for all bog species in the context of restoration of damaged bogs because the ability of plant species to recolonise fresh peat surfaces, or to re-establish on 'old' ones, depends largely upon their reproductive capacity and the dispersal and survival of their propagules. The dispersal agents of the seeds of some bog species are not well known. The seeds of many species are small (< 4 mm length) and light, leading to a presumption that wind dispersal may be of particular importance and that the seeds may be able to travel over wide areas

from one isolated raised bog to another (Moore, 1990). However, some studies suggest rather limited dispersability of certain species (Poschlod, 1995). Seeds of some bog species can be dispersed by water or trampling, but the general significance of this in bogs in not well established.

Some bog species form *diaspore banks* – *i.e.* their seeds or spores can retain viability for long periods (years or decades, but not in perpetuity), but there is considerable variation in this capacity (Poschlod, 1988, 1989, 1995) (Appendix 3). Considerations of diaspore banks are substantially irrelevant to many cut-over peatlands, as the lower peats exposed by extraction do not contain viable seeds (Curran & MacNaeidhe, 1986; Salonen, 1987a). They may, however, be of greater importance to the rewetting of uncut bog surfaces.

Most wetland plants have some mechanism for vegetative expansion, which can sometimes lead to the development of large clonal patches of particular individuals. This may be important for the maintenance of populations *in situ* but is likely to provide rather slow rates of recolonisation on abandoned, bare peat surfaces.

Wetland plants generally have a good capacity to regenerate from fragments but the actual significance of this for spontaneous recolonisation of cut-over peat surfaces by bog species is not known. It does, however, facilitate the propagation and planting of bog species, should this be seen as desirable. In particular, *Sphagnum* species can be readily propagated from

---

Table 1.5 Informal physiognomic-habitat categories of raised-bog vegetation in Britain. [*NVC* – see Table 1.4]

'Bog-Sphagnum' vegetation

Accommodates vegetation in which *Sphagnum* species typical of bogs are prominent, often dominant, components. It includes the *NVC* mire-expanse community M18 and the bog-pool communities M2 and M3. These latter may occur as a mosaic with M18 vegetation, forming the so-called 'regeneration complex'. This vegetation is particularly characteristic of the surface of little-damaged raised bogs.

'Para-bog-Sphagnum' vegetation

Refers to vegetation with broad similarities to 'bog-*Sphagnum*' vegetation, but which differs either in not containing all of the species typical of the latter, or in having them but not with the same proportions or structure. Ericaceous species or *Eriophorum vaginatum* typically dominate (rarely *Molinia caerulea*). *Sphagnum* species are often sparse or represented mainly by taxa characteristic of the drier microsites within bogs (*e.g. S. capillifolium*), but in some (richer) examples it is possible to find most of the characteristic species of 'bog-*Sphagnum*' vegetation scattered sparsely. Various additional species, particularly taxa associated with drier conditions may also occur. This category includes some examples of *NVC* communities M15, M20, M25a. Such vegetation may be indicative of partial damage to a bog surface (*e.g.* burning or drainage) but it may possibly also be a natural constituent of some little-damaged bogs, as on the drier slopes of a rand or as part of a 'still-stand' condition.

'Dry bog' vegetation

Includes a range of vegetation-types which usually contain few typical bog species. Those that do occur are usually the more drought-tolerant taxa such as *Eriophorum vaginatum*. Some examples are not readily referred to *NVC* vegetation-types. Where identifiable, the vegetation-types of this category include:

> *wet heath* (some examples referable to M15)
>
> *dry heath* (*e.g.* H9)
>
> Molinia *grassland* (richer examples = M25; others are near-monocultures of *Molinia*)
>
> *bracken-dominated vegetation*
>
> *birch scrub* ((some examples referable to W4)

'Dry bog' vegetation-types are almost always associated with some form of damage to raised-bog sites, most typically drainage.

small fragments. The significance of these factors for the revegetation of cut-over bogs is discussed further in Chapter 4.

1.9.3 Characteristics of bog plant species

Examination of some of the main characteristics of typical bog plant species enable the following generalisations to be made:

- mostly of geographic wide distribution;
- not specific to ombrotrophic bogs;
- most are long-lived perennials;
- seeds and spores may have little importance in maintaining populations of some species in undisturbed bogs;
- seeds of most species are light and *may* be readily dispersed;
- typically have slow relative growth rates;
- apparently efficient at scavenging nutrients from dilute solutions;
- often efficient internal conservation of nutrients;
- ombrotrophic conditions seem generally sub-optimal for growth.

The main characteristics of some of the typical species found on raised bogs in Britain are given in Appendix 3.

1.9.4 Habitat conditions and vegetation of raised bogs

The environment of raised bogs is not well-suited to the growth of many plant species. The low pH values and limited availability of nutrients makes the ombrotrophic habitat 'difficult' even for the growth of species tolerant of high water levels. Those that do occur may grow more slowly than in some other habitats.

Microtopography and water levels

Within raised bogs, plant species show various micro-habitat 'preferences'. Certain plant species often occupy rather distinct positions with respect to water level, either as part of the small-scale microtopographical mosaic of a patterned bog surface (*e.g.* Ratcliffe & Walker, 1958; see Figure 1.10) or as part of a wider change in water level from the wet centre to the drier margins of a bog. Species of the genus *Sphagnum* often show clear and well-documented distribution patterns with respect to water levels (Ratcliffe & Walker, 1958; Vitt, Crum & Snider, 1975, Andrus, Wagner & Titus, 1983; Wallén, Falkengren-Grerup & Malmer, 1988). Experimental studies suggest that with low water tables the hummock species appear better

able to transport water up the stem and maintain water content at the top of the stem (capitulum) than can hollow or lawn species and they are thus better able to grow in relatively dry conditions. Their exclusion from pools and lawns may not be because such conditions are intrinsically unsuitable for them but because pool species grow more rapidly (Clymo & Reddaway, 1971; Pedersen, 1975; Clymo & Hayward, 1982; Hayward & Clymo, 1983; Luken, 1985)

pH and base-richness

The ombrotrophic waters of raised bogs are characterised by having hydrogen (H^+) as the dominant cation and sulphate (SO_4^{2-}) as the main cation (Sjörs, 1950; Bellamy, 1967; Proctor, 1992). The high concentration of hydrogen ions (pH values are often below 4) is partly a product of acidification induced by the growth of species of *Sphagnum* (Clymo, 1963; Clymo & Hayward, 1982; Andrus, 1986), whilst the small concentrations of other solutes reflect the meteoric water source. Characteristics such as a high cation exchange capacity confer upon *Sphagnum* some ability to acidify its environment and, where *Sphagnum* species have colonised minerotrophic systems an increase in hydrogen-ion activity by some three or more orders of magnitude has been reported (Bellamy & Rieley, 1967; Karlin & Bliss, 1984; Giller & Wheeler, 1988).

The ionic composition of bog water shows quite strong geographical variation, reflecting variation in solute concentrations in rainfall. There is a gradient of chemical conditions in bogs across both Britain and the European mainland (Bellamy, 1967; Proctor, 1992). In British bogs, concentrations of several ions, especially sodium, are greater than in more continental examples, reflecting maritime influence. [Some ranges of chemical concentrations are given in Table 2.1].

Plants typical of ombrotrophic peatlands are not necessarily confined to low pH environments. Most also grow in poor fens (pH < *c.* 5.5) and some grow in rich fens (pH > *c.* 5.5). In Britain, the *Sphagnum* species that are typical of bogs also grow in many poor fen sites, but are usually absent from rich fens, except where there are acidified microsites. Nonetheless, some (*e.g. Sphagnum papillosum, S. magellanicum*) have been recorded from sites with water pH values of *c.* 6.5 (Andrus, 1986; Lindholm & Vasander, 1990; Shaw & Wheeler, 1991). Several plant species that are characteristic constituents of bog vegetation in Britain are confined to fens in more continental parts of their range (*e.g. Eriophorum angustifolium, Narthecium ossifragum, Sphagnum papillosum*). This phenomenon has long been recognised (Aletsee, 1967; Müller, 1976; Malmer, 1986), but its explanation is not really known.

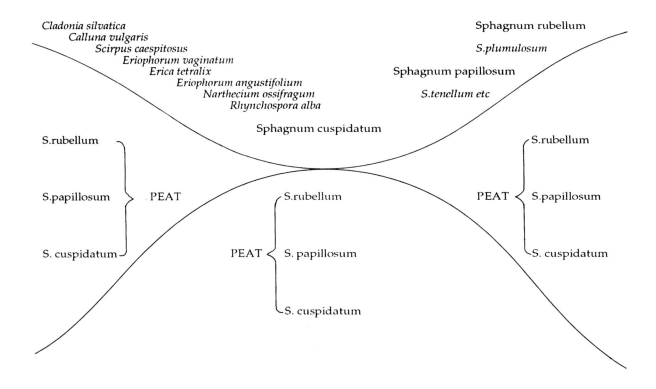

Figure 1.10a   Diagram of the succession of species forming the peat in a typical "hollow-hummock cycle (regeneration complex) (Tansley, 1939) [Reproduced by permission of Cambridge University Press].

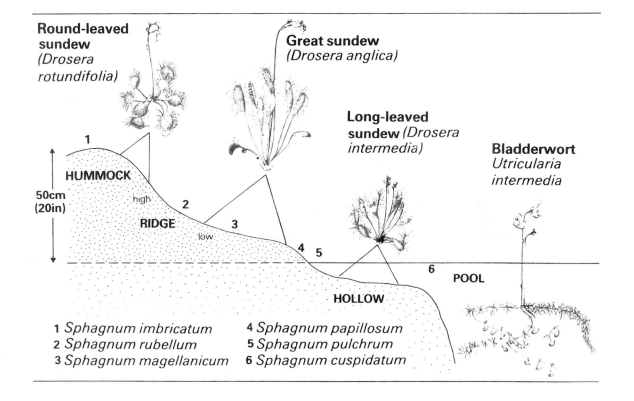

Figure 1.10b   Niche zonation within the micro-topography of a bog (Lindsay *et al* ., 1988).
[Reproduced by permission of JNCC and SNH]

It may partly relate to the higher pH values and greater solute concentrations measured in more oceanic situations (Bellamy & Bellamy, 1966; Sparling, 1967; Boatman, Hulme & Tomlinson, 1975; Proctor, 1992), which makes the chemical environment of such sites approach that of weakly minerotrophic fens (Shaw & Wheeler, 1991; Proctor, 1992). However, it is far from clear that this is a sufficient explanation (Malmer, 1986).

The response of typical bog species to very low pH environments (< 3.0) has been rather little studied, but there is evidence that growth of some species is impaired at such levels (Austin & Wieder, 1987; Richards, Wheeler & Willis, 1995; Money, 1994).

Sphagnum colonisation of rich fens in Britain is usually pioneered by a small range of species (*e.g. S. squarrosum, S. fimbriatum, S. palustre* and *S. recurvum*; Shaw & Wheeler, 1991) which are particularly tolerant of high pH or high calcium concentrations (Clymo, 1973). They form an acidic layer separate from the base-rich water (Giller & Wheeler, 1988) upon which less base-tolerant species such as *S. magellanicum* and *S. papillosum* can become established.

Productivity and nutrient availability

Raised bogs are generally regarded as being 'unproductive' and infertile ecosystems. Estimates of vegetation production rates are hampered by the difficulties of obtaining meaningful measures of *Sphagnum* productivity (Clymo, 1970), but estimates of above-ground net production of ombrotrophic vegetation are typically in the range of 300–700 g m^{-2} (Doyle, 1973, Clymo & Reddaway, 1974; Forrest & Smith, 1975). It is notable that, whilst quite small, such rates are comparable with, or even greater than, those reported from various types of fen (Wheeler & Shaw, 1991).

Low availability of nitrogen or phosphorus is likely to be a major constraint upon primary production in bogs. Fertilisation of bog peats usually increases the production rates of vascular plants and may even enhance the growth of *Sphagnum*, at least in the short-term (Tamm, 1954; Reinikainen, Vasander & Lindholm, 1984; Baker & Boatman, 1989; Aerts, Wallén & Malmer, 1992). It is less clear which nutrient is naturally growth-limiting in bogs, not least because present-day N concentrations may be artificially-elevated by deposition from atmospheric sources (Aerts *et al.*, 1992). The low availability of nutrients has led some, probably most, bog species to be well adapted to scavenge solutes from dilute solutions, a trait seen clearly in *Sphagnum* species (Malmer, 1988). Generally, bog plants may show a 'tight' redistribution of nutrients, so that scarce resources are not lost from senescing leaves *etc*. *Rhynchospora alba* seems to be

an exception to this general rule (Ohlson & Malmer, 1990) and there is some variation in nutrient retention efficiencies amongst some other species. For example, whilst *Eriophorum vaginatum* is particularly well able to retranslocate and accumulate nutrients (Goodman & Perkins, 1959; Jonasson & Chapin, 1985), *Molinia caerulea* appears to have a smaller capacity for this (Markert *et al.*, 1990).

Growth of *Sphagnum* species in water may also be constrained by availability of carbon (as CO_2) (Baker & Boatman, 1985; Baker & Macklon, 1987). This may help to explain the poor growth of aquatic species (*e.g. Sphagnum cuspidatum*) that is sometimes observed in deep water (Boatman, 1983; Paffen & Roelofs, 1991).

Atmospheric pollution

As raised bogs are irrigated directly and more-or-less exclusively by precipitation inputs, and as their component plant species may be well adapted to 'scavenge' solutes from dilute solutions, they may be particularly susceptible to atmospheric contaminants. Those most likely to affect plants growing on raised bogs are the main constituents of 'acid rain' [*i.e.* sulphur dioxide and derivatives, especially bisulphite; nitrogen oxides (NO_x) and derivatives, especially nitrate; and ammonia]. There is very little direct information on deposition of contaminants into British bogs, but interpolated maps provide estimates of emissions and possible rates of deposition (UKRGAR, 1990).

Various experiments have demonstrated that *Sphagnum* species are differentially sensitive to SO_2 and derivatives (HSO_3^-), but at concentrations considerably greater than current ambient values (Ferguson, Lee & Bell, 1978; Ferguson & Lee, 1980). Total SO_2 emissions in the UK have decreased by some 40% from national peak values at around 1970 (Gilham, Leech & Eggleston, 1992) and, whilst high concentrations of SO_2 may have led to the disappearance of some *Sphagnum* species in the past, present concentrations are unlikely to be so acutely injurious to *Sphagnum* growth that the plants will be unable to survive (Ferguson & Lee, 1982; Press, Woodin & Lee, 1986).

The importance of atmospheric sources of nitrogen (NO_x and ammonia) to the growth of bog species is not well understood. There is a quite widespread suspicion that deposition of nitrogen may be responsible for the loss of some *Sphagnum* species from bogs and an expansion of *Molinia caerulea* and perhaps even of birch, but critical evidence for this is lacking. N deposition can act as a fertiliser for vascular plants and under certain circumstances is thought to encourage the growth of *Molinia* in wet heath ecosystems (Heil & Bruggink, 1987; Aerts & Berendse, 1988). Nonetheless its effects in bogs are obscure. Various experimental investigations have examined the relationship between *Sphagnum* growth and N supply, in the field and laboratory, but have not reached consistent conclusions – both growth inhibition and stimulation has been reported, probably due partly to variation in experimental and other conditions (Clymo, 1987; Press *et al.* 1986, Rudolph & Voight, 1986; Bayley *et al.*, 1987; Baker & Boatman, 1990; Woodin, Parsons & McKenzie, 1991; Aerts *et al.*, 1992). Especially little is known about the effects of dry deposition of ammonia upon bog plants, though UKRGAR (1990) suggest that "over much of the country ammonia dry deposition is believed to dominate total nitrogen deposition."

1.10 The invertebrates of raised bogs

Invertebrates form an important part of the animal life of peatlands, living in and on the water and plants, but until recently they have received relatively little systematic attention. This is perhaps not surprising since there are so many species (even within different invertebrate groups) that even on peat bogs in the UK to attempt species-level identification of them all would require the time and expertise of many individual specialists. The information reviewed for the present reports was thus mainly derived from a large body of mostly fragmentary evidence and *ad hoc* records, as most studies have concentrated on particular invertebrate groups and have collectively been conducted with a wide range of aims. In general, invertebrate studies of raised bogs appear to have been strongly biased towards insects and arachnids (spiders and harvestmen).

Invertebrate species found on bogs may be herbivores, carnivores or detritivores, but in general there are few bog 'specialists', perhaps reflecting the waterlogged, oxygen-deficient, acidic environment with 'poor-quality' food sources. However, several invertebrate surveys to date have suggested that raised-bog sites support populations of a high proportion of notable and rare insect and spider species both within the UK and on mainland Europe. Lowland raised bogs in the UK appear to have particular conservation importance for a number of species [Table 1.6], including the beetles *Bembidion humerale* and *Curimopsis nigrita*, both known thus far only from the Humberhead Levels in the UK. However, there are very few true indicator species for lowland raised bogs. Most species that show a 'preference' for this habitat are also sometimes found in other situations (although interpretation of data is often hampered by lack of detailed habitat information). Many species also show marked differences in their degree of specificity to raised bogs in different parts of their geographical range. The

British Isles are on the edge of the natural range for many species.

Several major insect groups appear to have no, or very few, species that are specifically associated with raised (or other) bogs within the UK, and certainly no notable or rare ones. The Hymenoptera (sawflies, parasitic wasps, gall wasps, bees wasps and ants) is the largest Order of insects within the UK with more than 6,000 known species. However, most of the more familiar stinging species (the aculeate wasps, bees and ants) are largely associated with dry habitats, and those that may be caught within raised-bog sites include many that are either transient or nest or forage outside of the bog habitat (von der Heide, 1991). Only one species, the ant *Formica transkaucasica*, is typically associated with *Sphagnum* bogs, though its nest sites are in drier grassy tussocks. In other groups, it is often the case that only a very few species are associated with bogs and these are seldom restricted to lowland raised bogs. Nevertheless, there is a general consensus that of the Hymenoptera species associated with peat bogs, a high proportion are of conservation interest. For example, Kirby (1992) suggests that "[t]here are relatively few Heteroptera associated specifically with bogs, but a large proportion of them are local or rare". This probably largely reflects the scarcity of the bog habitat.

Herbivorous insects are often oligophagous (occasionally monophagous)[1] and may be limited in their distribution by the availability of suitable foodplants. Thus, the great majority of species with conservation interest are likely to occur in habitats which include the greatest diversities of potential foodplant species with limited distributions. The limited herbivorous insect fauna of raised bogs may therefore reflect the floristic poverty of raised bogs.

Bogs that have been subjected to hand-cutting or similar peat-removal regimes and which have since revegetated may offer a wider range of invertebrate habitats than little-damaged raised bogs and consequently, may support a wider range of species. Many taxa seem to have either a preference or requirement for the range of micro-habitat conditions that are created by certain peat-cutting regimes (*i.e.* limited hand cutting) and such species may be scarce or absent in little-damaged bogs. For many species regarded as having great conservation interest in lowland raised bogs, it is the mix of microhabitats present in areas that have been subjected to traditional hand-cutting over a period of time that seems to be important in their continued survival. In some sites, hand cuttings may also offer wet refugia for some species when much of the remainder of the site surface

---

[1] Oligophagous: restricted to a small number of food plants; monophagous: restricted to one species or variety of food plant.

has become damaged and dry. However, an increase in habitat and species diversity due to disturbance is not considered by the conservation agencies to provide an increase in conservational 'value' over the naturalness of an undamaged bog. The extensive, bare surfaces created by modern extraction methods may be far less amenable to recolonisation than the small-scale hand peat cuttings.

There have been few studies of the behavioural or physiological selection processes that lead to peatland species being found in a particular habitat, but the habitat requirements of many invertebrate species will be governed by both the requirements of the adult and the juvenile stages (larva, pupa, etc.). These may be rather different, necessitating the presence of two or more different and perhaps even spatially separated features. Natural *Sphagnum* hummocks and hollows serve in part to provide this sort of microtopographical heterogeneity. However, in general, high water tables, ensuring that *Sphagnum* remains saturated, appear to be essential for the continued existence of many

'desirable' species in raised-bog sites, even though many of them [see Table 1.6] seem to require an 'interface' situation between *Sphagnum* and/or bare peat and drier zones.

Dragonflies are often top predators in bog pools, which, due to their acidity, lack fish. Many dragonflies are able to tolerate highly acidic conditions as larvae, favouring pools with *Sphagnum* (*e.g.* Soeffing & Kazda, 1993). Different species may favour pools of different sizes. In general, dragonflies benefit from some protection from the wind and are favoured by sites with peat walls, adjacent scrub or at the edges of raised bogs where woodland may act as a windbreak (R.G. Kemp, *pers. comm*).

Most species of carabid beetle display a considerable degree of latitude in their habitat preferences and are not restricted to a single vegetation or soil type. Rather, it is thought that physical factors "...such as soil water content, ...vegetation height and temperature..." may be important (Butterfield & Coulson, 1983). Thus few carabids are likely to be entirely restricted to a single

Table 1.6 Invertebrate species for which raised bogs are considered to have particular conservation importance in the UK.

Species	Order	RDB[1] status	Notes
Heliophanus dampfi	Aranae	RDB	Associated with peat in Europe, and in the UK known only from Cors Fochno (Dyfed) and Flanders Moss (Stirling).
Coenagrion mercuriale	Odonata	RDB 3	Paradoxically associated with basic seepages in UK oligotrophic mires, though also found in heathlands
Somatochlora arctica	Odonata	RDB 3	
Hagenella (=*Oligotricha*) *clathrata*	Trichoptera	RDB 1	Specifically associated with raised peat bogs; probably favoured by old hand peat cuttings
Acilius canaliculatus	Coleoptera	RDB 3	Associated with old, exposed peat cuttings
Bembidion humerale	Coleoptera	RDB 1	Favoured by bare wet peat as found in old peat cuttings (Key, 1991)
Curimopsis nigrita	Coleoptera	RDB 1	Associated with the interface between wet peat and damp litter where there is heather growing, therefore probably favoured by old hand peat cuttings.
Hydrochara caraboides	Coleoptera	RDB 2	Occurs in a range of aquatic habitats in Europe, though in the UK its distribution is very limited.
Eilema sericea	Lepidoptera	RDB 3	Although found on 'mosses' its larvae feed on algae growing on heathers *etc.*, and therefore it will be absent from *Sphagnum* carpets
Eugraphe subrosea	Lepidoptera	RDB 1	In UK for some years only found known from Cors Fochno (Dyfed) though previously found in other bogs and fens; it has now been recorded from a number of other raised bogs in mid Wales.
Hercostomus angustifrons	Diptera	RDB 2	
Limnophila heterogyna	Diptera	RDB 1	Likely to be associated with disturbed bog sites; (so far known only from canal lagg at Whixall Moss)
Phaonia jaroschewskii (=*crinipes*)	Diptera	RDB 2	Not restricted to lowland raised bogs; sensitive to falls in water table
Prionocera pubescens	Diptera	RDB 2	
Tipula grisescens	Diptera	RDB 3	More typically an upland bog species
Pachybrachius luridus	Hemiptera	RDB 3	Requires grassy tussocks
Formica transkaucasica	Hymenoptera	RDB 1	Associated with lowland bogs with *Molinia*

[1] Red Data Book (Shirt, 1987); see also Bratton (1990) and Falk (1991 a, b) for definitions.

habitat type, such as lowland raised bogs, at least throughout all of their range.

Many invertebrate species, including dragonflies, benefit from areas of open water and would be disadvantaged by loss of pools induced through drainage or successional overgrowth, though some open pools in bogs, particularly the large examples, may be permanent. Management which restores the open-water habitat may benefit these species. For virtually all threatened invertebrates, two factors appear to be of critical importance: (i) the maintenance of high water tables and (ii) the presence of a moderate diversity of habitat types with elements of bare peat, open water of various sizes, *Sphagnum* hummocks, some grass, sedge and/or heather clumps and some rather drier banks.

1.11 The birds of raised bogs

Raised bogs in Britain have been modified and fragmented to such an extent that an assessment of the 'typical' ornithological resource of 'intact' raised bogs in Britain is difficult, and must rely heavily upon historical records and on data from the few remaining extensive bogs in Britain. Available information suggests that no bird species is exclusive to raised bogs in Britain, although certain birds are considered to be characteristic of the habitat.

There is a paucity of detailed site-specific ornithological data from raised bogs in Britain. Available data indicate low bird density and low species richness on open areas of little-damaged bogs. The lack of trees and shrubs make them largely unsuitable for passerines that require perching posts and nesting sites above ground level. The vascular plants of bogs offer a limited food supply to birds and some of the species which do breed are common and widespread breeding species elsewhere in Britain.

The naturally low density and species richness of bird populations on raised bogs does not imply lack of conservation interest. Birds of particular conservation value (see Batten *et al*, 1990) which occur on lowland raised bogs in Britain include significant populations of breeding teal[1], red grouse, black grouse, dunlin, curlew, redshank, nightjar and twite, and wintering populations of pink-footed geese, Greenland white-fronted geese, greylag geese, hen harrier and merlin.

The number of bird species breeding on the open surface of an unmodified raised bog is small and breeding densities are generally low. Meadow pipit and skylark are the two most characteristic species of raised

bogs (Stroud, 1989), with mallard, curlew, snipe and cuckoo also typically present, with the local addition of other species. Red grouse occur on some northern and Irish raised bogs. Of the rarer species, merlin and hen harrier may occasionally breed on extensive raised bogs in Scotland, northern England and Ireland.

Several species, including golden plover and dunlin, seem to have declined in numbers or have ceased to breed on lowland bogs during the last century, although they have continued to breed in the uplands and on blanket bogs. Others, such as black-tailed godwit, ruff, and Montagu's harrier have not bred on raised bogs for at least 50 years. Twite were once widely distributed on the Lancashire and Cheshire mosses and have since disappeared (Orford, 1973). Gull colonies are also thought to have become more localised than in the past (Ratcliffe, 1977). The decline of these breeding species of little-damaged lowland bogs has received little attention. It is clearly a relatively recent phenomenon which may possibly be attributed to habitat fragmentation and lowering of water levels.

Some of the more extensive raised bogs are important as wintering sites for grazing wildfowl species. Of these, the Greenland race of white-fronted geese has received much attention. A significant proportion of the world population of this distinctive race winter in the British Isles (Batten *et al.*, 1990), historically returning each year to certain lowland bogs. Although traditionally associated with these bogs many of the 'Greenland white-fronts' have abandoned raised-bog wintering sites in Britain and Ireland in favour of alternative habitats (Pollard & Walters-Davies, 1968; Ruttledge & Ogilvie, 1979; Fox & Stroud, 1986; Madden, 1987; Foss, 1991; Warren *et al.*, 1992). The reasons for this behavioural change may include increased disturbance and habitat loss, together with establishment of wildfowl refuges in other areas.

Modification of raised bogs has introduced a new mosaic of habitats which has increased the diversity of the bird species occurring on the former open areas, although many of the additional species are those which naturally occupy the bog margins. The response of bird communities to peat cutting and associated changes is complex because of the diverse nature of the changes that can be induced by these activities. Depending on the degree of damage, such changes may have a more marked effect on spatial distributions and relative abundances of species rather than increasing species diversity in a particular site. Many species which occur on 'intact' bogs also occur on modified sites, provided that sufficiently large areas of their 'preferred' habitat remain. However, if trees extensively invade damaged bog surfaces, such species are eventually replaced by woodland birds.

---

[1] Latin names of bird species mentioned in the text are given in Appendix 5.

Species richness and bird density generally increases with the development of scrub or occurrence of fen. Although the early stages of succession benefit certain important species, such as nightjar (Fuller, 1982), an incipient climax community dominated by generalist passerine species seems likely on such sites. However, species composition can be dramatically affected by the relative degree of flooding, desiccation and scrub clearance on damaged sites. Bog restoration initiatives which involve impoundment of surface water may suffer from the effects of pioneer bird colonists, such as wintering gulls, for example through guano-trophication and physical damage.

1.12 Non-avian vertebrates of raised bogs

Non-avian vertebrates (mammals, amphibians, reptiles) usually form a relatively minor part of the conservation interest of raised-bog sites but records from raised-bog sites have included such species as otter, mountain hare, deer and adder. Bogs may also constitute important feeding areas for bats, especially around marginal habitats.

1.13 Archaeology, palaeo-ecology and restoration

Peatlands are important for archaeology and palaeoecology. They preserve remains of many of the plants that once formed their living surface and of some of the animals (especially Coleoptera) that inhabited this. The pollen rain, produced from the bog's surface and from the surrounding landscape, is often preserved exceptionally well. These, and other features, provide a valuable palaeoecological archive. This can be used, for example, to reconstruct, the character of past post-glacial environments, climatic change and flooding episodes, vegetational history, human occupation and management history.

Some peatlands (especially fens) have been a focus of past human activity and a rich range of artefacts may be preserved in the peat. Peat excavation has often helped to reveal some artefacts, for example the head of a cow found at Solway Moss, Cumbria (Middleton, 1992) [Plate 1.6], and 'Lindow Man' at Lindow Moss, Cheshire (Stead, Bourke & Brothwell, 1986), but it has doubtless destroyed others. The peatlands of the Somerset Levels have provided particularly great archaeological interest (*e.g.* Coles & Coles, 1986;

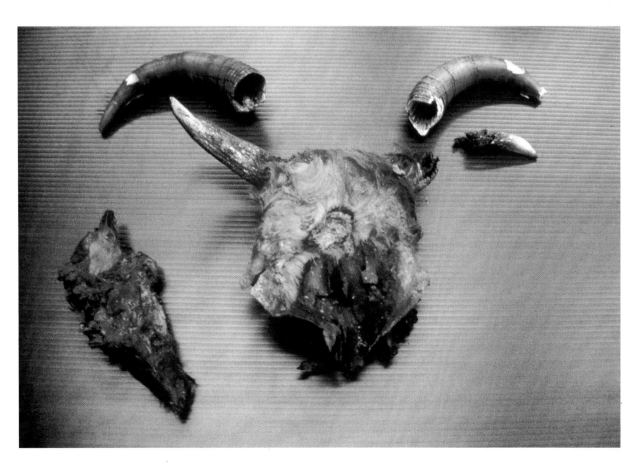

Plate 1.6 Remains of a cow [*c.* 800–900 AD] found during peat extraction operations at Solway Moss (Cumbria). [Photo: North West Wetland Survey, © Lancaster University Archaeology Unit]

Plate 1.7 The Sweet Track – built in 3806 BC across a *Phragmites* reed swamp in the Somerset Levels. Excavated by the Somerset Levels Project (funded by English Heritage and the Universities of Cambridge and Exeter). [Photo: Somerset Levels Project].

Somerset Levels Papers, 1-15, (1975–1989), as exemplified by the Sweet Track [Plate 1.7]. By contrast, some of the raised-bog sites investigated by the North-West Wetland Survey have, as yet, yielded few artefacts (Middleton, 1990–1992).

Peatland restoration schemes may need to consider the requirements for preservation of archaeological and palaeoecological interests and in some cases they may require close co-operation between conservationists and archaeologists, to arrive at the optimum solutions for site restoration. Nonetheless, it must be recognised that if the object of raised-bog restoration is to regenerate a new raised bog, at the very least this will require effective rewetting of the peatland. The following factors merit consideration [see also Chapter 7]:

- the removal or disturbance of peat will also remove the historic and industrial landscape, the immediate palaeo-environmental record and any artefacts.

- survey of the landscape and of archaeological features could form part of field investigations prior to initiation of a restoration scheme [Chapter 7].

- raised water levels can lead to erosion where they adjoin upstanding blocks of peat, thus destroying both the palaeo-environmental record and surviving structures. It may be necessary, both to minimise erosion and to encourage revegetation, to construct breakwaters in large areas of open water.

- the potential for damage to *in situ* artefacts, sites and the palaeo-environmental record by the roots or rhizomes of such species as *Phragmites* should be considered in both the deliberate encouragement and potential for colonisation by such species (although such species are unlikely to provide much of a problem in ombrotrophic systems).

- in some cases, it will be desirable to preserve peat deposits and archaeological structures *in situ*. Schemes designed specifically for nature conservation should also consider the *in situ* conservation of archaeological deposits.

Peat extraction is also part of the 'industrial heritage' of Britain and abandoned, cut-over bogs form a 'derelict industrial landscape'. Even drainage schemes and methods used can have historical interest. If such topics and artefacts are perceived as legitimate areas of interest, their preservation may impose its own constraints upon restoration procedures and objectives for damaged bogs. Conservation and restoration schemes can also be seen as yet another stage in the history of human intervention in peatland ecosystems, and, perhaps in the future, constructs associated with restoration may be valued as much as artefacts of 'conservation archaeology' as for their ecological effects.

Chapter 2

Characteristics of cut-over raised bogs

2.1 Introduction

Peat extraction directly removes both the peat and the living surface from those areas of bog where it occurs. It may also affect adjoining areas of uncut peat, particularly through indirect drainage. Thus it is important to consider not only the direct effects of peat extraction, and their implications for restoration, but also its influence (or that of other reclamation measures) on bog remnants. The various techniques of peat extraction used may influence restoration options, as the conditions remaining when the sites are abandoned differ. Approaches to the rewetting of sites cut-over by different methods and the preservation of bog remnants are considered in Chapter 5.

Where any substantial peat extraction has taken place it is likely to have much modified the topography of the original bog and the resulting conformation will be an important determinant of rewetting approaches. Two broad, but not exact, topographical situations can be recognised, depending on whether the area in question tends to shed or hold water. These situations will be referred to respectively as *massifs* and *depressions* [Figure 2.1].

A *massif* can include:
- the entire mire, in relation to the topography of the surrounding landscape;
- a remnant of the original ombrotrophic dome;
- a surface that has been cut-over but which is proud of surrounding cut-over areas;

At each particular scale the structure tends to have an overall *convex* or *water shedding* profile.

Depressions effectively refer to areas that have been cut for peat and which form hollows or flat surfaces *in relation to adjoining blocks.* They tend to have an overall *concave* or *water holding* profile.

Note that this terminology is relative – for example, an individual baulk may form a 'massif' in relation to the adjacent peat cutting, but lie within a mire which is in a depression relative to the surrounding land. Similarly, a peat cutting or field may form a depression within a mire remnant which is itself a 'massif' as the general surface lies above the level of the surrounding land.

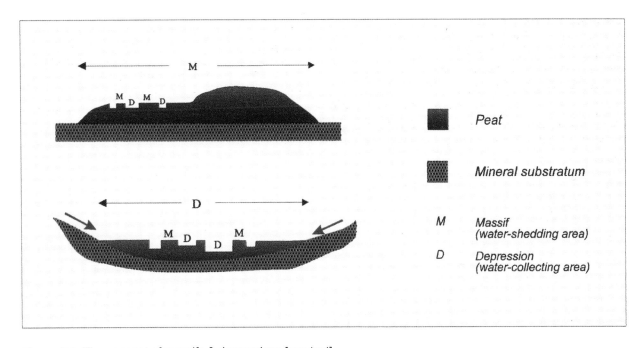

Figure 2.1 The concept of massifs & depressions [see text].

2.2 Effects of peat extraction on bog remnants and refugia

2.2.1 Introduction

Some sites affected by peat extraction retain undisturbed areas of vegetation that support typical bog species. In others, recolonised, formerly-disturbed areas may provide refugia. In both cases, they may sustain an important biological resource and their protection may be important both in terms of an overall programme of mire conservation and as a means of conserving plants and animals adjacent to areas of on-going peat extraction as sources of recolonist species [see Chapter 4]. The preservation of undisturbed areas should be an important part of a restoration strategy. Management and maintenance of such refugia needs to be carried out alongside ongoing peat extraction and not left until extraction has ceased [Chapter 6].

In gross terms, marginal damage, including peat extraction, can be considered to have two major effects on bog remnants:

a) hydrological – disruption of the hydrological integrity of the 'groundwater' mound; increase in the hydraulic gradient between the remnant and its surroundings;

b) fragmentation of habitat.

These effects are considered below.

2.2.2 Hydrological effects

Introduction

The surface of bog massifs can be dry for various reasons, of which drainage is one of the most direct and obvious. However, even without direct drainage of the massif, water conditions may be considerably influenced by other factors, for example, extraction of surrounding peat, since one of the features of the 'groundwater mound' concept is that the height of the water mound may be considerably influenced by its effective basal area [Chapter 1].

Surface drying may thus be promoted by various agents, depending on the situation [see Figure 2.2]. These include:

• direct drainage of the peat body;

• indirect drainage through loss of basal area of the peat body, by agricultural conversion or peat extraction;

• indirect drainage through lowering of adjacent water courses, or regional groundwater tables (this will depend on the permeability of the underlying mineral ground);

• reduced water storage capacity of the dehydrating peat or peat layers remaining after extraction;

• reduction in depth of peat may be associated with decreased resistance to vertical seepage through the bottom of the bog. [The importance of this will depend on such factors as the nature of the underlying mineral substratum].

• increase in evapotranspirative losses through the growth of 'undesirable' vegetation (*e.g. Molinia*, birch). [This will be particularly important in relation to water conditions in summer.]

Most damaged sites are likely to be affected by one or more of these factors, although the first two are perhaps the most common causes of dehydration. The factors leading to dehydration are perhaps the greatest threat to the ecohydrology of mires because by lowering the water table and accelerating the rate of

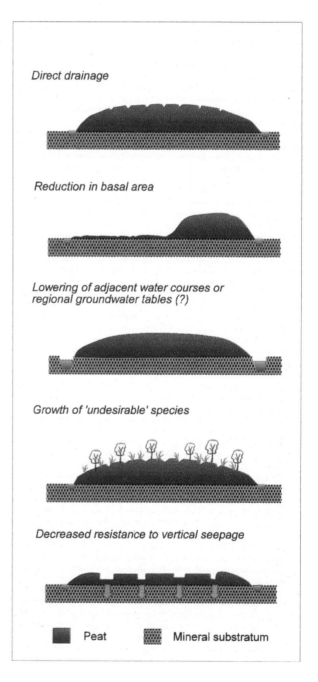

Figure 2.2 Potential causes of dehydration of a raised bog massif (see text).

decomposition of the peat, changes in the physical properties of the peat, and the hydrology, morphology and ecology of a mire are likely to take place, some of which may be irreversible. Although any assessment of the effects of drainage on the physical properties of peat have to qualified by reference to peat types, the following responses are some of those which have been suggested as typical following drainage of peatland (see *e.g.* Clausen & Brooks, 1980):

increase in: subsidence;

                  bulk density;

                  amplitude of water fluctuation;

decrease in: active porosity;

                  water content;

                  water storage coefficient;

                  permeability.

Thus, for example, drainage results in primary consolidation followed by shrinkage, secondary compression and finally wastage of the upper layers of the bog (Hobbs, 1986), and can lead to considerable reduction in the height of the peat surface. Observations at the Holme Post (Hutchinson, 1980) provide graphic evidence of the effects of drainage and agriculture in the progressive lowering of a peat

Plate 2.1 Vertical peat face between cut-over area and 'remnant' uncut peat block (Breitenmoos, S. Germany).

surface, even without peat extraction. Over a period of 130 years, the surface has fallen by nearly 4 m. In the early stages of drainage of a virgin bog, the peat shrinkage could be as much as 0.2 m per year., although the rate of peat loss may decrease with time. Ivanov (1981) suggests that an average rate of collapse after drying over a period of 40–50 years varies widely from 1–2 to 8 cm per year, and cites the formula given by Maslov (1970) for calculating rates of peat shrinkage.

Many, perhaps most, British bogs have been affected by drainage to some degree. This can range from extensive drainage in preparation for peat extraction, which was subsequently abandoned (*e.g.* Roudsea Moss, Cumbria) to the digging of one or more boundary drains across the bog, marking ownership (*e.g.* Wedholme Flow, Cumbria), and to the gross effects of adjacent peat extraction and conversion for agriculture. In most cases it is difficult to separate the effects of peat extraction upon adjacent bog remnants from other causes of damage such as drainage, as bogs have often been subject to various forms of damage. However, it seems likely that effects are often synergistic. For example, lowering of the surrounding ground surface often produces a sharp boundary [Plate 2.1], and will increase the hydraulic gradient between this and the uncut surface, thereby increasing the efficiency of any drains. As the basal area is reduced as a result of peat extraction, a new perched water mound is formed within the peat remnant. The shape and position of the new water mound will be determined by site-specific conditions. In some examples it may no longer reach the surface of the bog, which is correspondingly dry [Figure 2.3]; in others, where the drop of water level has not been great, or where the amount of marginal damage is small in proportion to the residual area of bog (or possibly where a change in the permeability of the peat has lead to a reduction in water runoff) the water level may still reach the surface of the bog peat, at least in the more central areas.

Interpreting the impact of drainage on bog systems is complicated by their 'diplotelmic' or two-layered structure and its role in maintaining the hydrological stability of the bog; in undisturbed bogs the acrotelm buffers the catotelm from some external influences [1.7]. Where drains are cut into a well-developed *Sphagnum*-rich acrotelm, the hydrological and ecological impact of drainage may be expected to be widespread on the bog surface because of the high transmissivity of the acrotelm (Ingram & Bragg, 1984; van der Schaaf *et al*, 1992). The plant species (particularly *Sphagnum* mosses) that are particularly characteristic of little-damaged acrotelms may be especially susceptible to any induced periods of dehydration and there may be an interaction between changes in the character of the bog vegetation and

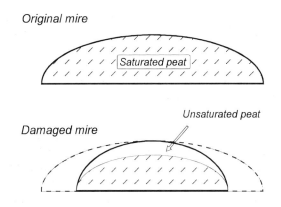

Figure 2.3 Conceptual illustration of the potential water drawdown of the perched water mound in a raised bog as a result of marginal damage.

hydrological functioning of the bog as a result of drainage. For example, drainage may lead to a bog surface from which former hollows and pools have been lost, thus affecting factors such as water storage and run-off (Ivanov, 1981) (see below), and reduce the capacity of the acrotelm to consistently 'feed' the catotelm with water and maintain a relatively stable water regime. The small hydraulic conductivity of the catotelm means that the effect of an individual drainage ditch upon the water table in the catotelm may be confined to a few metres either side of the drainage ditch. This is recognised in the preparation and maintenance of bogs for peat extraction, where ditch spacings of *c.* 10–20 m are needed to provide effective drainage of the upper layers of peat. Shrinkage as a result of loss of water from these layers usually means that drains have to be deepened each year, and it may take up to ten years for a newly drained bog to be in a suitable condition for extraction to commence.

Effects of drainage upon chemical characteristics

Besides causing physical loss, drying of peat is likely to induce biochemical oxidation, mineralisation and release of hydrogen ions and nutrients. Even on little-damaged bogs, seasonally low water levels may substantially increase acidity, and subsequent rewetting can lead to the release of various ions on the rising water table (*e.g.* Braekke, 1981). In damaged sites, with frequent or protracted dry episodes, these processes may be accentuated. It is likely that the oxidation of reduced sulphur compounds during dry periods may be an important mechanism of (temporary) acidification. In some circumstances, concentrations of SO_4^{2-} may reach potentially toxic (but not lethal) levels for *Sphagnum* (Ferguson and Lee, 1982–3). pH values may fall below 3.0, to values that may be suboptimal for growth of *Sphagnum* and some other typical bog species. Mineralisation of the

drying peat may also contribute to nutrient release and such effects may be exacerbated by water table instability and recurrent dry periods. Certainly, increased concentrations of various solutes have been measured in water draining cut-over bogs compared with little-damaged bogs (*e.g.* Clausen & Brooks, 1983a, b). However, the permanence of these effects, or their significance to revegetation prospects is not known.

Effects of drainage on bog vegetation

As a result of the close relationship between water levels and the distribution of plant species on bogs, it is clear that drainage will affect the vegetation, as well as the peat of raised bogs. The definition of bog communities is likely to become 'blurred' under the impact of drainage, leading to impoverished types. The magnitude of the effect will depend on the degree of water table change. A small, but sustained reduction in water level in a bog is likely to cause a shift in species composition towards 'para-bog-*Sphagnum* vegetation', *i.e.* away from the natural hummock-hollow complex, towards those species normally associated with hummocks, with overgrowth of the hollows, an increase in species such as *Calluna* and *Molinia* and, possibly, invasion of woody species, particularly birches (*e.g.* Eigner & Schmatzler, 1980; Bolte, Flügger & Cordes, 1985; Montag, 1989) [Plates 2.2, 2.3, 2.4]. A large sustained reduction of water levels is likely to lead to an eventual loss of bog species together with loss of the original acrotelm and aeration of the upper catotelm peat, leading to cessation of peat deposition and bog growth.

In many sites damage (from whatever source) has caused significant drying-out of the uncut surfaces such that the only remaining bog flora survives in the wetter conditions of abandoned workings. In other cases, bog remnants have survived alongside peat extraction,

Plate 2.2 *Molinia*-dominated surface of raised-bog 'remnant'; Holcroft Moss (Cheshire).

Plate 2.3 *Calluna*-dominated vegetation on drained raised-bog surface at Moine-Mhor (Argyll).

Plate 2.4 Birch and *Rhododendron* invasion on raised-bog 'remnant'; Wreaks Moss (Cumbria). [see also Plate 10.1]

Plate 2.5 *Sphagnum*-dominated bog vegetation confined to cut-out pools, surrounded by *Calluna*-dominated dry bog surface; Bankhead Moss (Fife).

apparently still retaining reasonably wet conditions at the surface despite removal of adjacent peat. Examples include Wedholme Flow (Cumbria), where much of the uncut dome appears to retain high water levels with typical bog vegetation, despite continued adjacent peat extraction. However, the long-term effects of this are not known.

The effects of drainage on the bog vegetation can be seen in microcosm in many damaged sites and peat-extraction complexes, where the cuttings may support Sphagna and other bog species while the baulks or upstanding remnants have lost such taxa and have become dominated by species such as *Calluna*, *Molinia* and birch (*e.g.* Thorne Waste, S. Yorkshire; Crowle Moors, Lincolnshire; Risley Moss, Cheshire; Bankhead Moss, Fife [Plate 2.5]). In general, plant species changes concomitant on drainage of bog surfaces are usually regarded as undesirable: the taxa that replace typical bog species have less intrinsic conservation 'value'.

Effects of drainage on bog invertebrates and birds

The changes in the hydrology and vegetation of a bog outlined above will affect the bog fauna through changes in habitat and concomitant changes in vegetation structure and food sources *etc.* (for example, loss of open water or wet, *Sphagnum*-dominated areas, increase in heathy-bog or scrub). These may lead to changes in population size and species composition.

In general, high water tables which ensure that areas of *Sphagnum* remain saturated appear to be essential for the continued existence of some 'desirable' invertebrate species in raised-bog sites, though some of them may also require an 'interface' between *Sphagnum* and bare peat or drier zones. For example, drying appears to have had deleterious effects on populations of the RDB 2 category muscid fly, *Phaonia jaroschewskii* (= *crinipes*), at Thorne Waste (Skidmore, 1991). The rare beetle *Bembidion humerale* may also be favoured by the maintenance of high water tables so that the peat surface is kept moist (Hyman, 1992 rev; Shirt, 1987). High water levels are also cited as an important criterion for a number of mire-associated bugs, for example, *Micrantha marginalis* and *Pachybrachius luridus* (Kirby, 1992a). Many dragonfly species benefit from the maintenance of areas of open water (*e.g.* *Sphagnum* pools of various sizes) and may be expected to suffer if these disappear, either through drainage or by them becoming choked with vegetation. Studies of the effects of raising water tables in bogs that had previously been partially drained have generally shown what have been interpreted as favourable responses of invertebrate populations (*e.g.* Fox, 1986b), particularly where this has led to an increase in open water habitats.

An increase in heathland vegetation and progressive encroachment of birch scrub as a result of drying provides a mosaic of different habitats which may favour various non-mire invertebrate species, some of which may be uncommon, for example, the bog bush cricket, *Metrioptera brachyptera* (Shirt, 1987), the clouded buff moth, *Diacrisia sannio* and the cranefly, *Pilaria meridiana*. It usually leads also to an increase in the number of breeding bird species compared with those typical of open bog. For example, the drier conditions in combination with the provision of song posts, in the form of birch scrub, undoubtedly favour the spread of such species as tree pipit, whinchat and stonechat on certain sites. Light scrub, characterised by scattered pioneer birch and Scots pine, can favour the colonisation of bogs by nightjar. Nightjars usually nest at the base of saplings and also require trees from which to proclaim their territories and as roosting sites; for these reasons nightjars do not usually nest beyond the edges of 'intact' treeless bogs, although the bogs are important feeding areas. Nonetheless, as tree invasion continues, the habitat structure will eventually become less suitable for nightjars – light scrub is essentially a transitional habitat on damaged bogs, and the development of denser scrub encourages an essentially woodland bird community to develop (RSPB, 1983; Fuller, 1982).

2.2.3 Habitat fragmentation

Introduction

Utilisation of bogs for agriculture and forestry has lead to a large loss of former raised-bog sites and to habitat fragmentation (Lindsay, 1993); burning, drainage and peat extraction (domestic and commercial) has contributed further damage to remaining sites. Fragmentation has increased the distances between sites supporting typical bog flora and fauna, which may have implications for the recolonisation of peat workings. Changes in the size and shape of the remnant bogs may have various repercussions. As well as possible effects upon the hydrologic stability of the remnants, it may also affect their capacity to sustain communities or independent populations of particular species (in which case it may be impossible to maintain them).

Size of remnants

There is considerable interest amongst conservationists in the relative merits of several small, versus single large reserves in the conservation of biodiversity of threatened habitats. May (1975) pointed out that, as a rough rule, a ten fold decrease in area would lead to a halving of the equilibrium number of species present and concluded that several small areas would support less species than a large area of equivalent size.

However the general conclusion of most of the studies concerning the single large or several small (S.L.O.S.S.) debate was that several smaller reserves contain more species than a single large reserve of equivalent total area. However, the advantage of conserving a number of small sites rather than a single large reserve will also depend on such factors as the overlap of species present in the small sites (Higgs, 1981), the stability of the sites, and geographical distribution and requirements of the species.

The importance of critical minimal areas for conservation of plant communities has not been widely studied, mainly because area usually accounts for only a small amount of the variation in species richness in different sites and ultimately sites and species may need to be considered individually for conservation purposes. However, typical bog vegetation occurs in some tiny sites (< 2 ha), when habitat conditions are appropriate.

For animal populations the importance of the size of the site relates to such factors as habitat specificity and territoriality, together with reliability and availability of food source. Fragmentation of habitat is particularly important in those species with low dispersal abilities and high habitat specificity. Thus it has been suggested that species composition within a site may change with a reduction in available habitat, and that species specific to a particular habitat would suffer greater losses than more generalist species and need larger areas for their preservation (*e.g.* Humphreys & Kitchener, 1982). The same principle is likely to apply to plant populations and species, and there are clearly problems in trying to define critical minimum areas for protection of both plant and animal populations in bogs (*e.g.* Kuntze & Eggelsmann, 1981).

Invertebrates

For invertebrates, assuming a species in which all individuals contribute to the future generation, a rough rule-of-thumb for a genetically viable population would be about 500 individuals. Kirby (1992a) suggests that small insects such as the bug *Micranthia marginalis* require only a few square feet of bare or sparsely vegetated ground for a viable population. For some species (for example, the dragonflies *Somatochlora alpestris* and *S. arctica*) only extremely small pools are needed for larval survival (Sternberg, 1982), though for the maintenance of viable populations a number of such pools may be required. In addition, suitable areas need to be present for the adults to catch their prey, hold territories and conduct courtship. The area required by a species depends partly on the distribution and density of its food supply. Thus, predators might be expected to be more abundant in areas where there is an abundance of their prey.

In the case of dragonflies, which are amongst the largest insects inhabiting raised bogs, some measures of male territory size suggest that the minimum size of refugium would seem to be 50 ha. However, large dragonflies may not be a good example on which to base this calculation because they probably have effective dispersal and the gene pool of the population in the refugium may be supplemented by immigrants from time to time. It is likely therefore that genetically sensible raised-bog refugia, even for large dragonflies, could be significantly smaller than 50 ha. In general, however, it should be expected that larger species will require larger areas of habitat for maintenance of a viable population than smaller ones. Hence, for the vast majority of insects and arachnids inhabiting lowland raised bogs, nearly all of which are significantly smaller than dragonflies, the minimum effective area for a refugium is likely to be far smaller.

It should be noted that maintenance of minimum areas for conservation of any particular species presupposes that conditions within such refugia can be maintained in the same condition as they would have had when the area was surrounded by larger areas of bog. Further, it remains an unresolved problem to know whether efforts aimed at maintaining populations of any given single species would also ensure survival of the community of invertebrates as a whole.

Birds

There have been very few studies relating to the spatial requirements of birds occurring on raised bogs. In Sweden, Boström and Nilsson (1983) observed that breeding-bird species richness increased strongly with bog area and that the density of most waders was higher on larger (>50 ha) than smaller bogs. These authors considered that, from a conservation point of view, one large bog is on average more valuable than several small bogs with the same area. Certain species also have specific requirements within the bog habitat (Bölscher, 1995) which are likely to determine the minimum areas of refugium for those species. It must also be recognised that the requirements of certain species may also include adjacent (or nearby) habitats, thus further complicating the application of the refugia concept to birds on bog habitats.

Examination of notification documentation for Sites of Special Scientific Interest containing raised bog[1], has found records of six taxa which have only been recorded from sites greater than 100 ha. These include five very rare breeding species on raised bogs (merlin, hen harrier, Montagu's harrier, dunlin, golden plover) and one wintering subspecies (Greenland white-fronted

goose). These species have only occasionally nested on raised bogs in the British Isles over the last hundred years, and several may now be extinct on this habitat. Breeding teal, black-headed gull, short-eared owl, grasshopper warbler and reed bunting, and wintering merlin and hen harrier seem to be associated with sites of between 50–100 ha in Britain. Black grouse and twite have only rarely bred on raised bogs of this size. Birds also found on smaller raised-bog sites in Britain (<50 ha) include breeding mallard, red grouse, curlew, snipe, redshank, nightjar, cuckoo, meadow pipit, whinchat and skylark, plus wintering short-eared owl.

Shape of remnants

The shape of a habitat remnant has been considered to be important in the minimisation of edge effects [see Glossary] and it has been suggested that circular sites, with the smallest edge : area ratio, are most suitable as reserves for species conservation, minimising the risk of invasion by uncharacteristic species and input of agro-chemicals *etc.* which may lead to eutrophication, mineral-enrichment *etc.* The effect of shape may be obscured by other unidentified sources of variation.

Although shape itself is probably not of major concern in the general preservation of nature reserves, for raised-bog remnants the importance of shape is more likely to relate to the preservation of a favourable water balance, than preservation of species *per se* – a bog remnant of 'simple' plan shape is likely to be easier to restore hydrologically than one with a complex margin. The provision of buffer zones to reduce edge effects is perceived to be one practical solution to the protection of particularly susceptible sites [8.3].

2.3 Peat extraction methods and habitat conditions

2.3.1 Peat extraction and residual topography

The surface configuration of the cut-over areas remaining after peat extraction has stopped depends largely on the method and duration of the peat extraction and the extent of drainage, both through direct alterations in topography and indirect effects such as slumping of the peat.

There are three main methods of peat extraction in the UK: block cutting (by hand or commercially), surface milling and extrusion. Locally other methods are used, for example open-cast harvesting and wet mining. Certain procedures are common to most of these operations: drainage; removal of surface vegetation; drying of the excavated peat on the surface to achieve a suitable moisture content (typically *c.* 50%); provision

---

[1] Many of these include habitat other than raised bog, or derived habitats, which represents a significant limitation of the data source.

of trackways for access, passage of vehicles, trains *etc.*
Main baulks are often left at intervals for passage of
machinery, or, in the larger operations, upon which a
light railway can be laid, to remove the peat either to
collection points or directly to the peat works [see Plate
2.9]. This infrastructure can be useful in restoration
after peat extraction both in providing a means of
transporting equipment and materials across a site, and
also acting as bunds[1] to retain water in the peat
workings[2].

The main extraction techniques are described below, in
relation to the conditions remaining on the site when
the extraction ceases.

Block cutting

Blocks of peat are cut out from a vertical face and
stacked on baulks alongside to dry. Drying of the peat
is thus more dependent on winter climatic conditions
than is the case for milled peat production.

Block cutting can create a range of surface
topographies, dependent upon the exact procedures
used. The method often produces a regular system of
baulks, flats and trenches which are usually dry, damp
and wet (respectively) when cutting ceases. However,
when carried to its conclusion it can also produce a
very extensive, largely flat surface. In some
circumstances, following block cutting, other methods
may be used to extract the lower peats. Trenches
sometimes retain water and may even support a usually
limited flora, of, for example, a few *Sphagnum* species.
The character of the surface is important in considering
restoration options. It may often be possible to use
existing baulks and tramways to increase water
retention; in other cases, as where there are numerous
narrow ridges, it may be desirable to level the surfaces
and fill in some of the trenches by bulldozing the
baulks into them.

Traditional hand cutting

When carried out on a small scale, the results of peat
cutting by hand can be a fairly haphazard disposition of
the surface topography [Plate 2.6]. However,
'organised' (± commercial) hand cutting could be as
extensive as machine block-cutting, sometimes leaving
large areas denuded of peat and vegetation and with a
similar regular topography of baulks and cuttings [as in
Plate 2.7]. In some cases however, hand cutting may
produce a relatively level area, as, for example at Cors

Plate 2.6 Small-scale hand peat cutting at Glasson
Moss (Cumbria) (top; centre) and Montiaghs Moss
(Antrim) (bottom).

---

[1] The term 'bund' is used here to mean an embankment used to
pond back water over a large area. By contrast, use of the term dam
has been restricted to refer to structures built to block linear water
courses [see Chapter 8].

[2] The efficacy of the baulks as bunds will depend on their size,
intactness and degree of dehydration of the peat.

Plate 2.7 *Left:* Block cutting at Solway Moss, Cumbria [Photo: A. Lynn] *Right:* Block-cut peat fields in the Somerset Levels. [See also Plates 4.1, 5.3, 5.4, 5.5]

Caron (Dyfed) where the peat was stripped to the lowest water level attainable by drainage.

One of the main 'advantages' of hand cutting (for subsequent restoration) is that the surface vegetation was sometimes thrown back into the trenches, and may provide inoculum for revegetation. The slow speed of extraction also allows the bog species (plants and invertebrates) in the trenches to become established between successive cuts. This 'shoeing' is probably of great importance in determining the course and time of recolonisation [Chapter 4]. Revegetation of such areas depends critically on the hydrological regime that has been maintained after the cessation of operations. Where the cuttings have been kept sufficiently wet, they have often developed some 'good' examples of bog vegetation.

Machine block-cutting

Machine block cutting is essentially a mechanised version of the traditional hand cutting method, but can be carried out on a larger scale with greater speed and each cut is usually deeper [Plate 2.7]. The ground is usually prepared by drainage (both open drains and slit or mole drains), removal of trees and scrub and levelling of the surface. The 'topsoil' is removed from the area to be cut, and either spread alongside or pushed into the trenches. Cuts are typically *c.* 50' apart, 3' deep[1] x 2'4" wide (*c.* 15 x 1 x 0.7 m). The peat is cut into blocks, and stacked alongside the trenches. The peat may take up to 9–12 months to dry sufficiently for collection and use. A complete cut can take 5–7 years, which can sometimes allow some recolonisation by bog species in the trenches if the water table is not too low. Some species may also survive on (or recolonise)

the baulks, but in many cases they may be too dry, or covered by drying peat blocks, to support more than a few ruderal, non-wetland species.

The presence of the slit drains has proved a particular problem for rewetting block-cut areas at Glasson and Wedholme Mosses (Cumbria) because they can be difficult to locate and block. Practical problems for rewetting may also be created where cuttings exist at substantially different levels, or where there is a big height difference between the top of baulks and the floor of cuttings.

Milling (or rotavation)

Milled peat production involves scraping or vacuuming off a thin layer of peat (15–50 mm) from the surface of bare peat fields. The surface of the moss is first prepared for peat extraction by drainage at *c.* 15–20 m intervals and stripping off the surface vegetation with a screw leveller some 5–10 years before extraction can begin[2] . This reduces the water content of the peat and increases the load-bearing capacity to facilitate harvest by machinery. The vegetation may be removed, or is pushed into the middle of the extraction fields and compressed by peat-extraction machinery. It gradually rots and can be further worked to provide a camber to the bed to improve the surface drainage. In bogs containing a high proportion of highly humified peats, surface runoff to drainage ditches may account for a relatively high proportion of the rainfall input; in weakly-humified peat, rainfall is largely absorbed by the peat and little free drainage occurs.

After the initial reduction in water content by deep drains, a system of under-drainage by mole drains may be installed [Plate 2.8]. Drainage reduces the water

---

[1] The effective depth of each cut is usually less than 3' as there is some wastage.

[2] The time taken will depend on the permeability of the peat, the hydraulic gradient and the recharge.

content to *c.* 85–90%, and this is further reduced to *c.* 55–65% by the milling and harrowing operations prior to collection of the peat. In general, the harvesting cycle takes about three days, but this depends on dry weather to air-dry the peat. Some 8–12 harvests may be taken each season.

The milled surfaces remaining after peat extraction ceases are bare and dry, and usually cover large areas [Plate 2.9]. The remaining peat is likely to be compressed, partly as a result of drainage, but also from the repeated passage of the harvesting machinery. These bare surfaces are prone to invasion by 'weed' species unless rewetting procedures are adopted.

Milled fields are generally much less well suited to the *spontaneous* re-establishment of bog species than are *some* block-cut areas as they usually do not have closed hollows which naturally accumulate water as is the case with some traditional block-cutting complexes.

They may also have various other features which may influence the development of restoration strategies. For example, large areas must be worked simultaneously to be economic (*e.g.* for efficient use of personnel and equipment when climatic conditions are suitable for harvesting) such that an integrated, phased program of extraction followed by restoration may be difficult to achieve [6.5].

Extrusion ('Sausage') peat production

This technique is mostly used for production of fuel peat, and is used on both raised and blanket bogs. It is used both on a small scale, for example by crofters in Scotland and Ireland, and commercially. The rotating blade of the cutter extracts peat from up to about 1 m below the surface, before extruding it as 'sausages' through nozzles onto the ground to dry [Plate 2.10]. Thus there is a minimum depth of peat that can be worked, although when this is reached, it would be possible to continue extraction by surface milling.

As for all methods, the peat deposit must be drained prior to extraction. The fields are also cambered to increase surface run-off and avoid puddles *etc.* Intensive drainage is not always considered necessary as increased energy would be needed to extrude the peat if it was too dry.

Plate 2.8 Mole drains in milled peat field.

Plate 2.9 Milled-peat fields, with temporary rail-track for removal of peat stockpiles; Bolton Fell (Cumbria). [See also cover photograph of milling at Thorne Waste]

Plate 2.10 Peat extracted by the extrusion method; Montiaghs Moss (Antrim).

The surface vegetation is sometimes removed to facilitate collection of the peat 'sausages' by machine rather than by hand. In this case, the residual surface is similar to that left by milling. However, the method of extraction means that there are usually more sub-surface drainage channels, (although the slots are usually cut at an angle to encourage closure). Even

where the vegetation is not removed, considerable damage to the plants and microtopography still occurs, mainly through cutting of the roots and fibrous layer, compaction due to the passage of machinery and personnel and deposition of peat on the surface (Bayfield et al., 1991; Meharg, Montgomery & McFerran, 1992; I Miller, pers. comm.). Bayfield et al. (1991) consider in detail the impacts of extrusion cutting on the vegetation of and runoff from blanket peats .

Other production methods

Peat may be won by methods other than those described above. For example, fuel peat is sometimes extracted from deep trenches, whereby the soft peat is extruded onto a conveyor belt and then cut into blocks before being laid on the ground to dry. This leaves deep, wet trenches and may sometimes create 'islands' of peat [Plate 2.11], both of which may provide a suitable habitat for recolonisation, particularly if surface vegetation were to be returned directly, although further examination of such sites is required.

In Somerset, small-scale peat extraction is often carried out by rotavating the peat and forming into ridges to dry [Plate 2.12], before removal to stockpiles.

Plate 2.11 Large-scale extraction of 'fuel-peat' (top), leaves trenches and 'islands'; Solway Moss (Cumbria).

2.3.2 The hydrological environment of cut-over bogs

Peatlands have to be drained for efficient peat extraction. The degree to which sites are drained depends upon individual site characteristics and the peat extraction technique used. Drainage is primarily needed for permitting access by machinery but it is also a prerequisite for some drying of the peat, especially in surface milled sites. However, it is not the aim of drainage to remove as much water as possible, as too much drainage would allow the lower layers of peat to oxidise and waste. The drains are therefore deepened as necessary, usually annually.

Few data are available on the hydrology of raised bogs during peat extraction, but it is evident, for example, that whilst removal of vegetation may reduce water losses by evapotranspiration, the dense network of drains (which may be linked to a pumping system) ensures that the rate of water loss through runoff will be higher than that of undrained bogs. In cut-over bogs it must be accepted that drainage will cause alterations to some of the characteristics of the original bog, for example, changes to some of the hydrophysical attributes, such as water storage capacity and peat permeability, some of which may be irreversible [2.2].

The water level that develops, spontaneously or by engineering, within an abandoned extraction complex

Plate 2.12 Peat extraction by the rotavating and ridging method (Somerset Levels).

is of crucial importance to the subsequent revegetation. In large measure, it will be a product of the topography of the abandoned peat workings (see above), climate and functioning of the drainage system. The water table of cut-over bogs is often characterised by a greater degree of fluctuation than that found in intact systems (Meade, 1992; Money, 1994, 1995). This may partly be a reflection of the existence of drains, but also because the exposed peat surface lacks the hydro-regulatory properties of an intact bog surface [1.7]. Hence, cut-over surfaces may be very wet, or flooded during the winter, but dry and dusty during the summer.

Water storage characteristics of residual peats

The lower peats that are left following peat extraction may differ in various properties from the peats above them, either in consequence of changes induced by drainage (Hobbs, 1986) or because of their intrinsic character [1.8]. This may influence their suitability for restoration. It is widely considered that variation in capacity for water storage may be important in this respect. Even deep catotelm peat may have high total porosity (Reynolds *et al.*, 1992), but the ratio of macropores (> 50 μm) to micropores is thought to be of more importance to water storage capacity (Schouwenaars, 1982; Blankenburg & Kuntze, 1986); the structure of strongly-humified peat gives it a higher ratio of small to large pores than weakly-humified peat, and thus although the former may in fact lose *less* water than the latter on drainage, it contains a lower percentage of 'free' water (the loose *Sphagnum* peat of a typical bog acrotelm can contain some 85% of 'free' water compared with only some 8% in strongly-humified peat (Streefkerk & Casparie, 1989)). This leads to higher water table fluctuations, as for the same amount of water lost ↓hrough evapotranspiration, the water table will fall further in a strongly-humified peat than a weakly-humified peat (Schouwenaars & Vink, 1992).

Although there is a clear difference between the water storage coefficients of the acrotelm and the catotelm peats, trends are less readily apparent within the catotelm peat. Porosity and bulk density may vary both within and between peat types and the broad categories of 'light' and 'dark' peat do not necessarily have different water storage coefficients (Streefkerk & Casparie, 1989; Schouwenaars & Vink, 1992).

Peat thickness and vertical water loss

The perched water table in a raised bog is often regarded as being independent of the behaviour of groundwater in the fen peat or subsoil aquifers below it. Indeed, the 'groundwater mound' hypothesis [1.7] effectively assumes an impermeable base to the water mound. These conditions may well be satisfied in many

UK raised bogs. Nonetheless, it is clear that the perched water mound may, in some situations, show connectivity to underlying ground-water tables, which may even make a positive contribution to its water balance. This situation occurs in The Netherlands and NW Germany where the bogs overlie fluvio-glacial sands and where, due to falling regional water tables, there is now thought to be an unsaturated layer in the mineral ground beneath the base of the peat (Joosten & Bakker, 1987; Blankenburg & Kuntze, 1987; Schouwenaars, 1992, 1993). It is not known to what extent this situation exists in the UK, although it has been suggested that this could be the case at Thorne and Hatfield Moors – work is in progress to investigate this. Even where sites seem to overlie an impermeable substratum (*e.g.* clay) the possibility that there may be permeable windows within these cannot be discounted.

The importance of residual peat thickness to rewetting and revegetation prospects is discussed in section 4.3.5.

2.3.3 The chemical environment of cut-over bogs

The ombrotrophic waters of raised bogs are characterised by hydrogen (H^+) as the principle cation with sulphate (SO_4^{2-}) as the main anion (Sjörs, 1950). Nutrients such as N, P and K are usually in short supply (Waughman, 1980). A bog surface is typically of low fertility and supports low rates of primary production. The chemical characteristics of raised-bog waters vary temporally and spatially. Typical values are summarised in Table 2.1. A major control on the pattern of variation is rainfall quantity and quality, itself controlled by factors such as proximity to the sea and degree of atmospheric pollution. Coastal raised bogs are generally richer in solutes (see for example, Boatman *et al.*, 1975; Sparling, 1967) and the chemical environment may approach that of weakly minerotrophic fens (Wheeler, 1988; Shaw & Wheeler, 1991).

There has been little detailed work on the effect of peat extraction on the chemical environment of raised bogs, but there is some empirical evidence to point to some degree of chemical enrichment (*e.g.* Clausen & Brooks, 1980). This may be as a result of:

i. chemical changes caused by drainage (*e.g.* acidification and mineralisation + nutrient release from the aerated peat layers);

ii. exposure of the underlying fen peat or mineral sub-soil;

iii. nutrient runoff from the surrounding catchment.

Few chemical data exist for peat extraction complexes in the UK, but a number of samples have been taken from parts of Thorne Waste (Smart, Wheeler & Willis, 1989; Money, 1994) and from Danes Moss, Cheshire (Meade, 1992). In general the concentration of most ions is higher in the samples from peat extraction sites than in little-disturbed sites, and in some cases resembles the chemical characteristics of poor fen rather than ombrotrophic bog (Tallis, 1973) (Table 2.1). It is not always evident why such chemical differences occur: for example, the high concentrations of NH_4 recorded from the milling fields at Thorne Waste, in comparison with vegetated cuttings, may be because it is released in consequence of peat operations or because it is derived from other sources (e.g. atmospheric inputs) but lack of vegetation cover means that it is not assimilated by plants. At these concentrations of NH_4 some degree of toxicity to *Sphagnum magellanicum* (Rudolph & Voight, 1986) and *S. cuspidatum* (Press *et al*, 1986) may occur, though evidence of the response of *Sphagnum* species to N enrichment is inconsistent.

Mineralisation

Mineralisation of drying peat [2.2] may contribute to release of solutes and increase availability of plant nutrients (Gorham, 1956; Braekke, 1981). It has been suggested that in block-cut sites mineralisation may lead to some movement of nutrients from the drier peat in the baulks into the wet cuttings (Smart *et al*, 1986; Beckelman & Burghardt, 1990; Nilsson, Famous & Spencer, 1990), but this needs further evidence to be substantiated. The amount of recolonist vegetation present able to take up the released nutrients is also likely to affect the measured concentrations.

Peat mineralisation and oxidation may produce changes in the chemical environment which could conceivably affect the growth of *Sphagnum* and other vascular plants. For example, extremely low pH values (< 3.0) may be detrimental to the growth of some bog species, including some species of *Sphagnum* (Austin & Wieder, 1987; Richards *et al.* 1995; Money, 1994). Very high concentrations of nitrogen may be damaging

to some *Sphagnum* species (Press *et al.*, 1986; Twenhöven, 1992), though evidence for this is not clear-cut (Rudolf & Voight, 1986; Baker & Boatman, 1990; Aerts *et al.*, 1992), nor is the likely effects of very high concentrations of SO_4^{2-} (Ferguson *et al.*, 1978; Ferguson & Lee, 1982–3; Austin & Wieder, 1987; Rochefort, Vitt & Bayley, 1990). The significance of this to restoration is not known, though as recolonisation by bog species has occurred in numerous cut-over situations it seems unlikely to present an insuperable, or universal, problem, especially when cuttings have been effectively rewetted. Moreover, modest enrichment of some elements (e.g. phosphorus) may enhance the growth of some bog species including some Sphagna (Baker & Boatman, 1992; Money, 1994, 1995).

Exposure of fen peat or underlying mineral ground

The domes of ombrotrophic peat which form raised bog have often developed over fen peat, which usually has greater base-richness than the former. This is readily shown in chemical profiles. For example, samples from Striber's Moss (Roudsea Mosses, Cumbria; Gorham, 1949) showed the trend of increasing pH (and conductivity) with depth, from the surface *Sphagnum* peat (pH 3.8) through to fen peat (pH 4.8) and basal clay (pH 6.1). Thus where peat extraction has exposed fen peat, the chemical environment is likely to be more conducive to the establishment of fen rather than bog vegetation (White, 1930; Poschlod, 1989, 1992). Even where fen peat is not directly exposed, a shallow layer of residual peat may be penetrated by some fen plants rooting in the underlying mineral ground. As well as modifying the floristic composition of the revegetating cut-over, such plants may conceivably serve as chemical pumps,

Table 2.1 Some chemical conditions in waters sampled from little-disturbed bogs compared with peat extraction sites. [Concentrations are mg l^{-1}; blank cells indicate no data; nd = not detected].

	Natural bog waters (UK & Ireland)*	Danes Moss, (Cheshire) vegetated block-cuttings (Meade, 1992)	Thorne Waste, (S. Yorks.) vegetated block-cuttings (Smart et al., 1989)	Thorne Waste, (S. Yorks.) milled-peat field (Money, 1994)
pH	3.2 – 4.5	3.0 – 3.7	3.8 – > 5.0	3.2 – 3.6
Ca	0.2 – 3.0	3.2 – 11.4	3.8 – 6.2	5.1 – 18.2
Mg	0.1 – 2.5	1.7 – 2.9	1.8 – 4.5	
K	0.04 – 2.0	0.5 – 0.8	0.6 – 2.1	2.1 – 6.6
Na	2.3 – 23.0		4.6 – 6.3	
Fe	< 1.0			0.6 – 2.2
SO$_4$	2.4 – 18.0	18.6 – 32.9	6.2 – 13.8	30.0 – 42.0
NO$_3$	0.1 – 0.3	1.3 – 2.2	0.04 – 0.20	1.8 – 6.2
NH$_4$		0.4 – 0.7	0.0 – 0.3	9.2 – 29.0
SRP**	nd / 0.05	0.0 – 0.3	0.0 – 0.08	0.0 – 0.06

* Sources: Clausen & Brooks (1980); Proctor (1992); Bellamy & Bellamy (1966). ** Soluble reactive phosphorus

enriching the ombrotrophic surface with nutrients from deeper layers.

Exposure of underlying mineral material may also lead to base-enrichment, but this effect will much depend on the chemical characteristics of the sub-soil. In some sites (*e.g.* parts of Thorne and Hatfield Moors), underlying sands and gravels are themselves of low pH and base status (pH 3 – 4) (B.D. Wheeler, *unpublished data*). There have also been reports of low pH values associated with some basal clays.

Where the exposed substrata are very base rich (for example, exposure of marl at Turraun Bog, Ireland) [Plate 2.13], rich-fen vegetation is likely to redevelop. Most typical raised-bog species do not occur in such situations and redevelopment of raised bog will depend on a slow build-up of peat and acidification (*e.g.* Giller & Wheeler, 1988). By contrast, most bog species can grow in base-poor fen conditions, though they will normally be accompanied by a range of poor-fen plant species.

Runoff from the surrounding catchment

In areas where peat has been extracted to below the level of the regional ground water table or to a position where the surface may receive run-off from the surrounding catchment, there is a possibility that groundwater may be able to run onto some or all of the site, and cause nutrient or base enrichment (Pigott & Pigott, 1959; Meade, 1992). The potential for a general ingress of groundwater will depend on the topography of the site. It may be particularly likely to occur in sites in basins; where areas of fen, which buffered the raised bog against ingress of groundwater have been destroyed; or where ditches draining adjoining land have been deliberately introduced into the bog. Examples of the latter include Danes Moss (Cheshire),

Plate 2.13 White marl deposit underlying peat, exposed in a drainage channel through cut-over bog; Turraun Bog (Offaly, Ireland).

Brackagh Bog (Co. Down), Fenns & Whixall Moss (Shropshire / Clywd).

Where enrichment from the surrounding catchment is seen as a particular problem, it will be necessary to take this into account in development of an appropriate restoration strategy, as it may severely limit the potential options for after-use, if remedial action is not feasible.

2.3.4 The physical environment of cut-over bogs

Peat extraction leaves a bare peat surface, which is usually dry, at least in summer. Bare peat is also prone to erosion by wind or water, particularly where sloping, and if dark, is likely to absorb heat; increased temperature will exacerbate moisture loss. The surface may be physically unstable and show considerable temperature fluctuations (Tallis & Yalden, 1983; Heikurainen & Seppälä, 1963; Salonen, 1992) and thus provide an inhospitable environment for establishment of plant propagules and animal colonists. [see also 4.4.2]

2.3.5 The vegetation of cut-over bogs

The vegetation of remnant peat surfaces and of abandoned peat workings can be extremely variable, depending upon such constraints as degree of damage, depth of extraction, topography, base status, nutrient status, water level (and source) and length of time since last worked. Money (1994) has surveyed the vegetation of peat cuttings in a range of British bogs – all of the vegetation-types recorded from uncut bog surfaces have also been recorded from cut-over areas (although usually in fragmentary form); cuttings may also support various additional community-types, most notably where they have exposed fen peat [Box 2.1]. Similarly, most of the species characteristic of raised-bog vegetation on uncut surfaces have also been recorded from cut-over areas [Appendix 4].

A few bog species are sometimes more abundant in revegetated peat cuttings than they are on uncut surfaces (*e.g. Rhynchospora alba*). Moreover, in numerous raised-bog sites, revegetated cuttings provide the main reservoir for some bog species, as the uncut surfaces are too dry to support any but the more tolerant bog taxa [Plate 2.14 and 2.15]. There is a broad relationship between the commonness of species on uncut surfaces of British raised bogs and their occurrence within peat cuttings. The rarer bog species are rare also in peat cuttings or have not been recorded at all from them. Some species (*e.g. Sphagnum imbricatum* and *S. fuscum*) which have not been recorded from peat cuttings in Britain have been found in peat cuttings elsewhere (van Wirdum, *pers. comm.*).

It can be concluded that peat cuttings are not intrinsically unsuitable for the growth of most, or all, of typical bog species (including rare species). However,

Plate 2.14 *Eriophorum angustifolium* growing in excavated peat pit, surrounded by *Molinia*-dominated vegetation on drained bog surface; Astley Moss (Lancashire). [see also Plate 2.5]

Plate 2.15 Wet hand-peat cutting colonised by such species as *Sphagnum cuspidatum, S. papilllosum, Eriophorum angustifolium* and *Narthecium ossifragum*, surrounded by *Calluna-dominated* vegetation on dry cut-over bog surface; Killaun Bog (Ireland).

many of the cuttings that support a rich variety of typical bog species are relatively small scale, domestic excavations (some are old commercial excavations, as at Thorne Waste). This is not least because such workings are the only ones that have been abandoned (and kept wet) for sufficiently long for 'good' revegetation to have occurred, but at some sites this may also relate to a former greater availability of propagules.

The main factors influencing the natural, spontaneous revegetation of cut-over bogs are discussed further in Chapter 4.

2.3.6 The fauna of cut-over bogs

Peat extraction creates disturbance and destroys the immediate habitat for animals, removing important structural features as well as food sources so that the capacity of much of the bog fauna to survive peat operations will depend upon the availability of proximate little-disturbed habitats, or of abandoned workings that are suitable for recolonisation. Large-scale commercial peat extraction inevitably reduces the opportunities for such survival compared to smaller hand-digging operations.

Once revegetated, bogs that have been subjected to hand-cutting or similar peat-removal regimes, often offer a wider range of habitats for birds and invertebrates than do undamaged raised bogs and may support a wider range of species, or at least, a change in relative abundances (*e.g.* Ball, 1992; Andreessen, 1993). Such an increase in habitat and species diversity due to disturbance does not necessarily increase the perceived conservational 'value' of such sites over the naturalness of an undamaged bog, particularly where generalist species replace specialists. However, some of the species that are prevalent on damaged bogs are themselves uncommon.

Invertebrates

Some abandoned peat workings are rich in invertebrate species. A number of 'conservationally-desirable' taxa seem to have either a preference or requirement for the range of micro-habitat conditions that are created by certain peat-cutting regimes (*i.e.* limited hand cutting) and such species may be scarce or absent in undamaged bogs, although such conditions may be provided locally (Kirby, 1992a). An example of such an insect is the caddisfly *Hagenella clathrata* (Wallace, 1991). For many species that are cited as being of great conservation interest in lowland raised bogs, it is the mix of microhabitats present in areas that have revegetated over a period of time following traditional hand-cutting that seem to be important in their continued survival. Thus, for example, both the RDB 1

Box 2.1 *Main vegetation-types occurring in cut-over bogs in the United Kingdom* [*nomenclature follows the National Vegetation Classification (Rodwell, 1991; in prep.) – see also Table 1.4*].

The vegetation of cut-over bogs is extremely variable, depending upon such constraints as depth of extraction, topography, nutrient status, water level and age (*i.e.* length of time since last worked). In some examples, cuttings have recolonised to produce clearly identifiable examples of specific NVC community-types [see Table 1.4] (which in some cases may be absent from the rest of the site), although these may not have developed the full associated typical microtopographical structure of hummocks and hollows. In other cases, the vegetation may be an atypical species mix, either because of some extraneous influence (*e.g.* nutrient input), extreme environmental heterogeneity within the cuttings or the vagaries of the recolonisation process. In the latter case it is possible that the vegetation may develop towards a recognisable NVC community-type in time.

(i)   **'Bog-Sphagnum' vegetation:** *Sphagnum*-based vegetation such as is characteristic of little-damaged raised bogs in the UK (M18) and bog pool communities (M2, M3) occur within peat workings, though they vary in the degree to which they conform to *NVC* vegetation-types. Examples have been noted at Bankhead Moss (Fife), Cors Caron and Cors Fochno (Dyfed), Glasson Moss (Cumbria), Moss of Achnacree (Argyll), Thorne & Crowle Moors (S. Yorks. / Lincs.). In some sites, such communities are better developed in peat cuttings than on the 'intact' peat.

(ii) **'Para-bog-Sphagnum' vegetation:** Many peat workings support examples of this vegetation category, which includes surfaces that may support a wide variety of typical bog species, though not in the same proportions, or with the same vegetation structure, as is characteristic of bog-*Sphagnum* vegetation. Typical dominants are *Calluna vulgaris, Erica tetralix, Eriophorum vaginatum* and, sometimes, *Molinia caerulea*. Some examples are referable to *NVC* communities M15, M20 and M25a but others are not obviously referable to any *NVC* communities. Examples have been noted at Danes Moss (Cheshire), Peatlands Park (Armagh) and Thorne & Crowle Moors.

(iii) *'Dry bog' vegetation:* Drier peat workings support a range of vegetation types with few, if any, bog species. They include the physiognomic categories of wet heath, dry heath, *Molinia* grassland, birch scrub, bracken *etc.* Some examples are impoverished versions of M15, M19, M25 and W4 communities, but many are not clearly referable to any *NVC* vegetation-type. There are numerous examples of these vegetation-types, including Astley Moss (Lancashire), Cors Caron, Danes Moss, Fenns & Whixall Moss (Shropshire / Clwyd), Glasson Moss, Holcroft Moss (Cheshire) [Plate 2.2], Moss Moran (Dunfermline), Peatlands Park, Roudsea Moss (Cumbria), Somerset Levels and Thorne & Crowle Moors.

(iv) **Fen vegetation:** A few fen species may occur in peat cuttings on ombrotrophic peat, when there is some degree of enrichment (*e.g.* Thorne Waste: Smart *et al.*, 1986). However, where underlying fen peat has been exposed by extraction, or where there is substantial ingress of minerotrophic water, true fen vegetation may occur. A large range of fen vegetation-types have been recorded from cut-over bogs, the variety reflecting differences in water quality (base status and nutrient status), depth and vegetation management. Examples include a number of mires at which little, if any, raised bog now remains[1]; sites which are more obviously raised-bog sites include Brackagh Bog (Armagh), Cors Caron, Cors Fochno, Tarn Moss (Malham) and the Somerset Levels.

Fen community-types recorded from cut-over bogs include: *Common physiognomic or habitat descriptors*

M4	*Carex rostrata–Sphagnum recurvum* mire	poor fen / fen
M5	*Carex rostrata–Sphagnum squarrosum* mire	poor fen / fen
M6	*Carex echinata–Sphagnum recurvum/Sphagnum auriculatum* mire	poor fen / fen
M9	*Carex rostrata–Calliergon cuspidatum* mire	poor fen / rich fen / fen
M22	*Juncus subnodulosus–Cirsium palustre* fen meadow	fen meadow
M23	*Juncus effusus/acutiflorus–Galium palustre* rush pasture	fen meadow
M24	*Molinia caerulea–Cirsium dissectum* fen meadow	fen meadow
M25	*Molinia caerulea–Potentilla erecta* mire	poor fen / fen meadow
S1	*Carex elata* swamp	sedge swamp
S3	*Carex paniculata* swamp	sedge swamp
S4	*Phragmites australis* swamp & reed beds	reedbed
S9	*Carex rostrata* swamp	sedge swamp
S10	*Equisetum fluviatile* swamp	swamp
S12	*Typha latifolia* swamp	swamp / 'reedbed'
S13	*Typha angustifolia* swamp	swamp / 'reedbed'
S24	*Phragmites australis–Peucedanum palustre* tall-herb fen	rich fen / fen / reedbed
S25	*Phragmites australis–Eupatorium cannabinum* tall-herb fen	rich fen / fen / reedbed
S26	*Phragmites australis–Urtica dioica* tall-herb fen	rich fen / fen / reedbed
S27	*Carex rostrata–Potentilla palustris* fen	poor fen / rich fen / fen
W1	*Salix cinerea–Galium palustre* woodland	fen carr / woodland
W2	*Salix cinerea–Betula pubescens–Phragmites australis* woodland	fen carr / woodland
W3	*Salix pentandra–Carex rostrata* woodland	fen carr / woodland
W4	*Betula pubescens–Molinia caerulea* woodland	fen carr / woodland
W5	*Alnus glutinosa–Carex paniculata* woodland	fen carr / woodland
W24	*Rubus fruticosus* agg.–*Holcus lanatus* underscrub	underscrub
W25	*Pteridium aquilinum–Rubus fruticosus* agg. underscrub	underscrub

---

[1] Some (perhaps most) of the basin mires in northern England and southern Scotland, which are currently valued (by conservationists) primarily for their fen vegetation, are former bog sites from which most, or all, of the ombrotrophic peat has been stripped away, presumably by domestic cutting (*e.g.* Cliburn Moss (Cumbria), Heart Moss (Kirkcudbrightshire). Examples from elsewhere include Woodwalton Fen (Cambridgeshire) and Wartle Moss (Aberdeenshire).

category (endangered) beetles present at Thorne & Hatfield Moors (viz. *Bembidion humerale* and *Curimopsis nigrita*) appear to be associated with either exposed peat or relatively dry *Calluna*-dominated vegetation. Conversely, as discussed above for *Sphagnum* species [2.3.5], in some sites, wet peat cuttings may provide an important refugium habitat for some invertebrates where the uncut surface has become too dry (*e.g.* König, 1992).

The extensive, bare surfaces left by milling may be less amenable to recolonisation by typical bog invertebrates than are small-scale hand peat cuttings, though as most milling fields have yet to be abandoned and rewetted, evidence for this proposition is mostly absent. Nonetheless, the large size of milled surfaces would suggest that comprehensive recolonisation is likely to be slower than in small, hand-cut sites.

The invertebrate fauna that may colonise peat cuttings in fen peat is potentially extremely rich, but it is beyond the scope of this report, not least because comprehensive data do not exist. [This is partly because many fen and raised-bog sites have not received detailed invertebrate surveys but particularly because it is not clear to what extent records refer to peat cuttings; this is a particular problem in many cut-over fen sites as their status as peat cuttings is often not visually evident.]

Birds

The response of bird communities to peat extraction and associated changes is complex because of the diverse nature of the changes that can be induced by such activities. Many species which occur on intact bogs also occur on modified sites, provided that sufficiently large areas of their preferred habitat remain. Small-scale hand cutting may result in an increase in available habitat, and an increase in bird species-richness. Conversely, at Thorne Waste for example, large reductions in populations of wildfowl, waders and birds of prey have been attributed to the effects of the expansion of intensive peat extraction (Limbert, Mitchell & Rhodes, 1986).

Disturbance, lack of food sources and nest sites is likely to severely limit the use of cut-over areas by birds. However, as bare areas revegetate, the bird species which recolonise will depend on such factors as the distribution and amount of open water and the type of vegetation which develops, and the site's geographical location. Thus, for example, an increase in open water habitat is likely to attract waders, wildfowl and gulls. However, as open water becomes occluded by vegetation, such species may be eventually displaced.

Some species of conservation importance may have 'unnatural' spatial distributions on damaged bogs, for example, species naturally occurring in scrub or fen around the margins of little-damaged bogs may extend into the central areas of damaged examples where there is an increase in these habitats [see also 2.2.2]. Restoration objectives need not be in conflict with the conservation of these species provided sufficient effort is put into ensuring the availability of sufficient suitable habitat in the appropriate sector of the bog. For example, Thorne Waste is estimated to hold almost 2% of the British breeding nightjar population (Roworth, 1992), but it has been suggested that those currently nesting towards the centre of the bog may be accommodated on the bog margins through proper management of over-dense scrub there.

Heathland bird species are likely to increase on a dry, cut-over site. Tree pipit, whinchat and stonechat are important additions to some cut-over bogs; the drier conditions in combination with the provision of song posts, in the form of birch scrub, undoubtedly favour the spread of these species on certain sites. An increase in open scrub habitat may benefit species such as nightjar [2.2.2].

A wide range of bird species are potential recolonists of peat cuttings in fen peat, and may include such species as sedge warbler, reed warbler, water rail, moorhen and coot. They are likely to be determined particularly by the character and area of the vegetation and depth of water. Extensive reedbeds occur in some fen peat cuttings and may support such species as bittern, bearded tit and marsh harrier as well as various wildfowl. The avifauna associated with other types of fen vegetation and habitats has not been systematically studied, but a range of wetland birds may be supported: Fuller (1982) provides some summary information. Fen carr mostly supports woodland birds, rather than wetland specialists, but may nonetheless provide a very rich bird resource. The perceived desirability of populations of, say, nightingales within a raised-bog site is likely to depend upon particular views of the aims and objectives (and practical possibilities) of conservation and restoration at particular sites [Chapter 3]. Some former raised-bog sites on the Somerset Levels have already developed into nationally-important wetlands for birds.

PART II

Principles of Restoration

Chapter 3

Aims and general principles for peatland restoration

3.1 Options for after-use of damaged peatlands

Peatland sites that have been damaged by peat extraction or other operations have various possible after-uses. In the past, these have often included afforestation, conversion to agriculture, use as refuse tips *etc.* and there has sometimes been a presumption that similar use might be made of some current workings, once they had been abandoned. However, changing attitudes and circumstances, coupled with a recognition of the conservational value of some peatlands and their potential for regeneration, have led to the view amongst conservationists and others that the after-use presumption for many, if not all, peat-cutting sites should be for nature conservation. It is this possibility which is the subject of this report.

Lowland peatlands are perceived to be important for various features additional to their potential for exploitation. These include their value as a 'peatland landscape', for their archaeological and palaeoecological archive and for wildlife. The requirements for the preservation or, where appropriate, restoration of these features are not identical. For example, it may be possible to preserve some of the features of a 'bog landscape' or the archival value of a raised-bog peat deposit without necessarily retaining, or redeveloping, all of the characteristic biota of such an ecosystem. Conversely, in an extensively cut-over raised bog it may be possible to regenerate a typical bog surface, with characteristic biota, but the peat archive cannot be replaced and the redevelopment of a 'bog landscape', whilst probably·possible, is likely to be long-term and outwith the foreseeable future. This report focuses on the requirements for reinstatement of wildlife interest in damaged peatland sites. No attempt is made to specify conservation policy by recommending particular objectives – rather, some possible objectives and options are identified and discussed.

3.2 Aims of restoration

3.2.1 The concept of restoration

The word 'restoration' has a broad compass (Wheeler, 1995), but is nonetheless often misused, sometimes because of a failure to recognise that it must refer to a specific object or objective. In all of its nuances of meaning, restoration implies an attempt to return an object to something like its 'former condition'. However, peatland ecosystems often undergo considerable changes as they develop and a damaged site may have had several distinct 'former conditions'. Semantically, it would be legitimate to try to restore a site to any of these, be it the last-known state or an earlier condition. However it is not possible, semantically, to restore a site to something it has never been. Thus, strictly-speaking it is not possible to 'restore' a damaged raised-bog site to grassland, but in many cases it could be 'restored' to fen. Of course, it is semantically acceptable to restore 'wildlife interest' to a damaged raised-bog site by converting it into grassland.

The specific connotations of 'restoration' have led some workers to search for other terms to refer a non-specific recreation of natural history interest. 'Rehabilitation' is sometimes used for this, but with no more legitimacy than 'restoration'. 'Renaturation' may be a better, neutral term, though it has little general currency in English.

3.2.2 Restoration objectives

Foci of conservation interest in lowland peatland sites can be recognised at various levels:

- plant and animal species;
- vegetation-types ('communities');
- habitat-types;
- mire system.

Conservation priorities and restoration preferences for damaged peatlands will be influenced by the perceived importance of these foci. For example, it is possible to maintain or recreate typical bog plant communities

Table 3.1 Occurrence of physiognomic categories of vegetation within cut-over peatlands. (For identity of physiognomic categories, see Table 1.5).

	Remnants	Peat workings
'Bog-*Sphagnum*' vegetation	√	√
'Para-bog-*Sphagnum*' vegetation	√	√
Wet heath	√	√
Dry heath	√	√
Molinia grassland	√	√
Bracken stands	√	√
Birch scrub	√	√
Reedbeds		√
Fen (including fen meadow and carr)		√
Open water	(√)*	√
Woodland	√	√

* Pool systems are widespread on some UK mire remnants; bog lakes do not appear to occur

without attempting to rebuild or re-establish an entire, regenerating mire (this is possible, for example, where recolonised peat workings are situated within a truncated, remnant mire massif).

Whereas *conservation* initiatives and priorities often relate to the maintenance or enhancement of existing 'interest' of peatlands, *restoration* initiatives can have a broader scope as, often, badly-damaged sites may have very limited existing interest and various restoration possibilities can be explored.

Restoration objectives (for nature conservation) are usually a combined product of the perceived desirability of a particular option, its cost and possibility. The first two of these considerations are essentially determined by choice and budget; only the latter provides an absolute constraint.

An assessment of the conservational 'desirability' of these objectives may need to take into account:

- the intrinsic interest and importance for nature conservation of the habitat-type and associated biota, locally, regionally and nationally;
- the scarcity of the habitat-type and biota, locally, regionally and nationally
- local objectives for nature conservation;
- national (and international) objectives for nature conservation.

Freedom of choice of restoration options is sometimes constrained by existing conservation interest. This may be the case, for example, where raised-bog sites have been badly damaged but have developed a replacement habitat with high conservation value centred on species and habitat conditions that are atypical of raised bogs. In this circumstance, restoration of ombrotrophic conditions may not be universally welcomed. In some former raised-bog sites 'restoration' consists of *preventing* spontaneous redevelopment of bog, in order

to retain prized fen habitats (Beltman, van der Broek & Bloemen, 1995).

Damaged raised bogs can support a variety of vegetation-types and habitats, depending upon specific conditions [Table 3.1]. An informal assessment of the intrinsic 'interest' and scarcity of these is given in Box 3.1. A number of these may be seen as an acceptable, or desirable, focus for conservation, restoration or renaturation.

3.2.3 Choice of options

In practice, cut-over raised bogs in Britain are valued for various reasons. Their actual or potential perceived importance for nature conservation can be broadly ascribed to three main foci. Some sites are perceived to be important for more than one of these.

(i) Maintenance or recreation of wildlife interest not pertaining to bogs

A number of former raised-bog sites in Britain are currently prized and conserved partly or completely for habitats and species that are *not* typical of raised bogs. This category of 'interest' is rather broad.

One category of replacement habitat that is conserved on a number of former raised-bog sites is fen (often with open water habitat). This has usually developed either because past peat extraction has exposed underlying fen peat or mineral soil, or because the ombrotrophic surface has been lowered sufficiently to allow ingress of groundwater (or both) (*e.g.* Brackagh Bog, Armagh [Plate 3.1]; Somerset Levels; Leighton Moss, Lancashire [Plate 3.2]; Woodwalton Fen, Cambridgeshire). In some examples baulks retain a reservoir of bog species. whilst cuttings contain fen species. Such sites may have very considerable interest, both for their vegetation and for other taxonomic

Box 3.1. *Informal physiognomic vegetation categories in relation to restoration objectives*
[For the identity and characteristics of physiognomic categories, see Table 1.5 and Box 2.1]

'Bog-Sphagnum' vegetation.

Bog-*Sphagnum* vegetation is particularly characteristic of little-damaged bogs; it is uncommon and is often cited as the preferred, or ultimate, vegetation goal of restoration initiatives in raised bogs, in terms of the species it supports and because of its (inferred) association with regenerating, self-sustaining mires.

'Para-bog-Sphagnum' vegetation.

This broad category represents vegetation that may contain a wide range of bog species. In richer examples it may be possible to find most of the characteristic species of bog-*Sphagnum* vegetation, though perhaps scattered over large areas and often with various additional species, particularly taxa associated with drier conditions. Such vegetation may be a natural component of some bog sites, but it tends to be regarded as not being 'true' bog vegetation and in many instances may represent a derivative of 'bog-*Sphagnum*' vegetation associated with some form of damage. Nonetheless, it may provide a substantial reservoir of bog species. It is often susceptible to invasion by birch though this cannot be taken as axiomatic (birch establishment upon some moribund surfaces can sometimes be very slow, especially where there is minimal disturbance).

Wet / dry heath

Typically rather species-poor vegetation, not confined to bogs. Wetter examples may support a smattering of bog species, including some Sphagna. Drier examples are referable to various types of dry heath. May support some uncommon bird and invertebrate species and is regarded as an important component of some damaged bog sites (*e.g.* Thorne and Hatfield Moors). Widespread in some parts of the UK but uncommon in many lowland agricultural districts. In some areas, dry raised bogs provide important heathland sites. Some examples are susceptible to invasion by birch and, in dry situations, bracken.

Molinia *grassland*

Examples on bog peat range considerably in character from richer examples that support a small range of typical bog species to those that are very species-poor and coarse. Robust *Molinia* is often effective in suppressing associates, even in quite wet conditions. Usually regarded as 'undesirable' by conservationists. May be susceptible to invasion by birch. Widespread outwith peatlands. Examples on fen peat may be much more species-rich.

Bracken

Typically species-poor vegetation, confined to dry sites in bogs. Widespread in other habitats. Potential associates are suppressed by the strongly-dominant fern. May invade and replace drier examples of heathland and *Molinia* grassland. Generally regarded as 'undesirable' by conservationists.

Birch scrub

Birch can colonise over a wide range of wetness conditions and is a potential invasive species of some bog, heath and *Molinia* stands. Its ground vegetation is strongly determined by the character of the vegetation colonised by the birch. Early stages of birch encroachment may have little impact upon the character of the biota, but the development of closed-canopy scrub is usually associated with a considerable change in the character of the ground vegetation and fauna. For this reason birch encroachment is usually regarded as 'undesirable', though sometimes various bog species can persist beneath even closed-canopy scrub. Note also that in some conditions some

Sphagnum species have been reported to survive better beneath young birch scrub than they can in more open vegetation, presumably on account of increased humidity and shade. Birch scrub may support a quite rich avifauna, comprised mainly of woodland species.

Open water

Large expanses of deep open water within bog peat generally have a sparse vegetation. Shallower examples can develop dense mats of aquatic Sphagna which may be a precursor to the redevelopment of regenerating bog vegetation. Open water in peat workings within fen peat can support a rich assemblage of aquatic macrophytes and some abandoned peat workings are prized by naturalists for this. In some cases (*e.g.* Norfolk Broads) once-rich macrophyte populations have largely disappeared, largely in consequence, it is thought, of complex food-chain interactions. When present, some aquatic plants are thought to form the basis of fen-raft development. Open water is also susceptible to hydroseral colonisation (by swamp species) from the margins.

Reedbeds

Beds of *Phragmites australis* and *Typha* spp. occur widely as recolonist species of shallow-water peat pits, often, but not exclusively, in sites irrigated with nutrient-rich water. They often have very low botanical diversity but may support notable bird species (especially in the more extensive examples). [Note that the term reedbeds is also sometimes applied to more diverse, mixed fen vegetation which is dominated by reed; these may have greater botanical value.] Widely distributed, but extensive (>20 ha) examples are infrequent. Drier examples are often susceptible to scrub encroachment.

Fen vegetation

A wide range of types of non-reed fen vegetation can develop in peat pits, including some types that are nationally scarce. Some former raised-bog sites are now prized for their extensive fen vegetation. Broadly, the botanical diversity and scarcity of fen vegetation is inversely proportional to the nutrient-richness of the irrigating water; examples developed under the influence of nutrient-poor but base-rich water are often particularly scarce and valued by conservationists. Base-richness and water level also influences vegetation composition. Many types of open fen vegetation require management to maintain species diversity and to retard scrub colonisation, which often leads to loss of some uncommon species typical of open fen. Invasion by Sphagna can also occur, in some cases as part of the process by which fen develops into bog.

Fen meadows

Various types of fen meadow vegetation can occur on fen peat surfaces, ranging from examples dominated by rushes (*Juncus* spp.) and sedges (*Carex* spp.) to fen grassland communities. Some of these communities may be species-rich and have considerable biological value.

Fen woodland

Much conservation management of fens attempts to prevent extensive development of scrub and carr. Nonetheless, fen woodland is often rich in plant species, though many taxa of open situations are absent from dense shade. It may also support a rich avifauna, most typically comprised of woodland species. Various types of fen woodland occur.

Plate 3.1 Recolonisation of fen peat by herbaceous fen vegetation; Brackagh Bog (Armagh).

Plate 3.2 Lake and reedbeds at Leighton Moss RSPB reserve (Lancashire).

Plate 3.3 Lake with islands and reedbeds, created using clay bunds. Burtle, Somerset Levels.

groups. Some are deliberately managed as fen (reed-beds) for their ornithological interest (*e.g.* Leighton Moss – Plate 3.2). Some examples are likely to develop spontaneously into bog, but this will be at the expense of much or all of the fen habitat and species and such an event may be regarded as undesirable by some conservationists.

Also included in this category are conservation sites which support replacement habitats of relatively low conservation interest assessed nationally, but which may be important locally as wildlife habitats or as landscape features. Examples of this include wetland sites within worked-out peat-extraction sites [Plate 3.3] and dry raised bogs that have developed into birch woods; some are managed as nature reserves, others have trees protected by Tree Preservation Orders.

(ii) Maintenance or re-establishment of viable populations of typical bog species

The object of conservation and restoration management of many raised-bog sites is to maintain or re-establish viable populations of typical bog species. In many instances, the objective is to re-establish *Sphagnum*-rich vegetation (comparable to the M18 community-type of the *National Vegetation Classification*) over some or all of the site. In other cases it is considered that it may only be feasible to retain or recreate

communities typical of damaged bog surfaces (which may nonetheless support a very wide range of typical bog species).

In a number of peat extraction sites, typical bog species are supplemented by some species of other (drier) habitats, usually in some form of habitat mosaic. Some of these species are themselves uncommon and form an important part of the perceived conservation importance of the mire. It is recognised that at some sites (*e.g.* Danes Moss, Cheshire) management that favours the development of bog may be detrimental to some non-bog bird species.

In some peat extraction complexes, the re-establishment of typical bog vegetation (especially M18) may represent a 'value-added' approach, in that the vegetation present prior to current peat extraction was not 'good-quality' bog vegetation.

(iii) Maintenance or re-establishment of a regenerating, self-sustaining bog ecosystem

The object of conservation and restoration management of a number of raised-bog sites is to restore them to a regenerating, self-sustaining ecosystem with the appearance and composition of a 'natural' (*i.e.* little disturbed) bog. This is particularly the case for those remaining bogs which have retained 'good quality' bog vegetation over substantial parts of their surface along with an appropriate topographical conformation (*e.g.* Cors Caron, Wedholme Flow) but it may also be seen as a desirable restoration objective for sites that have been much-damaged by peat extraction. Such an objective is obviously well suited to the maintenance, or increase, of populations of typical bog species, but it may be detrimental to non-bog species that form part of the existing wildlife resource of some sites.

Regeneration of a 'new' raised-bog system does not of necessity have to occupy the entire former area of the cut-over bog; moreover, in large cut-over sites it would be possible to initiate more than one regenerating mire.

In some peat-extraction complexes, the re-establishment of a 'regenerating bog' may represent a 'value-added' approach, in that the mire had been considerably damaged prior to current peat extraction.

3.2.4 *Species-centred* versus *mire-centred restoration*

There are at least two rather different approaches adopted for the conservation and restoration of natural history interest on damaged raised bogs. They are not, of necessity, mutually exclusive. One is essentially species-centred and aims to maintain or re-establish viable populations of typical bog (or other) species. The other approach is mire-centred, and aims to maintain or recreate a developing raised-bog ecosystem.

The species-centred approach does not demand a regenerating mire. It is possible to maintain or re-establish populations of many bog species on damaged bog surfaces or in peat pits. Is some, but not all, cases plant species may form a vegetation similar to that of little-damaged bogs. Such artificial situations may maintain numbers of typical bog species as effectively as on a little-damaged or regenerating bog. Biodiversity may even be increased relative to a little damaged bog by the growth of supplementary species on damaged sites, sometimes reflecting the habitat mosaics which have been produced by peat extraction. This is seen clearly in former block-cut sites where wet cuttings support regenerating bog vegetation (equivalent to M18) whilst the adjoining baulks have wet and dry heath. This juxtaposition of contrasting habitats accounts for the high biological interest of some cut-over raised-bog sites, especially when the interface between adjoining habitats supports specialised organisms.

Restoration initiatives which attempt to restore the whole site as a single, regenerating mire are less likely to result in a close juxtaposition of contrasting habitats and may produce sites with lower biodiversities than is the case with a species-centred approach, but the biota will be comprised mainly of typical bog species.

The choice between species-centred and mire-centred conservation and restoration initiatives is likely to be influenced by a variety of considerations, not least practicability and cost.

Attempts to regenerate the entire mire as a growing entity are arguably more 'natural' than is the maintenance of artificial habitat mosaics. Indeed, sometimes the latter strategy is effectively a form of 'bog gardening' with an ongoing requirement for periodic 'weeding' (*e.g.* birch clearance *etc.*) and sometimes even 'watering' (*e.g.* supplementary irrigation). A practical consequence of this is that the maintenance of artificial bog habitat mosaics will usually have a recurrent management cost whereas this will be less true of a naturally regenerating bog. However, the initial outlay of attempts to regenerate an entire mire may be considerably greater than that required just for the protection of existing interest, though this will depend strongly upon the starting point.

In some cases, it may be possible to provide suitable habitats for atypical bog species of great conservation value around the periphery of a regenerating mire, thus combining to some extent the species-centred and mire-centred approaches.

Ultimately, the choice between the species-centred and mire-centred approaches is likely to reflect personal preference, philosophy and practicality rather than to have a clear objective resolution. Both approaches have validity and there seems no objective necessity to impose a single, universal restoration solution upon all sites. Eggelsmann (1987) comments that the purpose and objective of all rewetting and regeneration measures taken in Germany is to produce such ecological conditions that in the long term natural processes will achieve an actively growing raised bog, without further human intervention. But he also recognises that this may not always be achievable. For individual sites, the choice may ultimately be resolved by practicability. For example, in some remnant massifs it may be impractical, either through constraints of topography or cost, to rewet the area sufficiently well for bog regeneration without further removal of peat. In this situation there may be little choice but to accept that it may be possible only to maintain, or create, artificial habitat mixtures. These will at least help ensure the survival of bog species on the site (though recurrent management costs and possible on-going hydrological instability may mean that this is not always in perpetuity). By contrast, where extensive, flat peat fields become available for restoration, it may be more appropriate to look towards habitat regeneration rather than just species survival.

3.2.5 Restoration opportunities in current peat workings

In general, where parts of cut-over raised-bog sites have considerable existing conservation interest, be it an 'original' bog surface on a remnant massif, or bog species that have recolonised abandoned peat pits, or areas of fen which have developed in minerotrophic workings, there is often an understandable desire amongst conservationists to maintain the *status quo*, or to enhance it. By contrast, there may be more scope for an open choice of restoration objectives in plans for current workings where the existing biological interest is minimal.

Even in current peat workings restoration opportunities may be constrained by practicalities and what is considered desirable may have to be subsumed to what is feasible. For example, in sites where operational peat extraction is now largely in fen peat (as in the Somerset Levels), or where a base-rich subsoil has been exposed, or where the workings are subject to ingress of groundwater, there is little option but to accept that wet restoration will, in the first instance, be to a minerotrophic habitat. In such situations, if revegetation processes are open to some possibility of environmental manipulation, the only real choice is in the *type* of minerotrophic wetland that is to be recreated (or, or course, some form of alternative 'dryland' habitat).

Where fen peat remains covered by bog peat, direct re-establishment of raised bog is more feasible, but even here it would, of course, also be possible to deliberately expose the minerotrophic deposits to recreate fen over all or part of the site. For whilst there is sometimes a tendency to regard the exposure of fen peat in cut-over raised bogs as a restoration problem, it can also be seen as a restoration opportunity. It would not be difficult to argue that as the bog initially developed from fen it would be a more 'natural', and possibly more stable, way of regenerating it by re-establishing the conditions from which it originated (*cf.* Chambers, Lageard & Elliott, 1992); or that as minerotrophic mires are less extensive (in aggregate) than are ombrotrophic mires, in the UK, there may be merit in their recreation, especially in those situations where the expected fen-type would itself be specified as a 'priority' habitat in the EC Habitats Directive.

Peatland restoration offers a wide range of opportunities for the creative restoration of mires. Whilst a *laissez faire* approach may be undesirable, equally with some 36,000 ha of damaged raised bog potentially available for restoration [1.6], there is scope for a variety of objectives to be realised. However, there is a real need to develop objective ground-rules to help decide restoration and renaturation options, priorities and areas in situations, such as denuded peatlands where there may be much scope for choice.

As one of the main objectives of bog restoration is to create a *Sphagnum*-based bog vegetation and a regenerating bog, and as this is likely to be considerably more difficult than the redevelopment of some other spontaneous vegetation-types (*e.g.* birch scrub), this will provide the main focus of much of this report. However, some attention is also given to the options for the creation of certain types of fen vegetation. The circumstances likely to lead to the development of some other types of habitat with natural history value are summarised in Chapter 6.

3.2.6 Constraints on restoration objectives

The realisation of particular restoration options is determined by considerations of feasibility and practicability. Some potential constraints include:

- unfavourable starting conditions (see below);
- lack of resources;
- legal constraints (for example, obligation to maintain drains in or around site);
- obligations to neighbouring land-owners (for example, need to avoid waterlogging of adjoining land);
- conflicting conservation aims:
    these may be induced, for example, by the presence of a rare species, which is not typical of the bog habitat. Opinions vary on the merits of conserving atypical, rare species *versus* regeneration of the mire. This partly reflects the 'species-centred approach' and 'mire-centred approach' to restoration. In some cases the rare species may have legal protection. It is sometimes possible to accommodate their needs, or those of other special interests, without abandoning an objective of bog restoration.

A summary of the main factors affecting restoration options is given in Table S2 [Summary].

3.3 Some principles of peatland restoration

3.3.1 Scope of restoration

The term 'restoration' can be used to apply to various objects. Some workers use it loosely to refer just to process of reinstatement of habitat conditions thought to be appropriate to the objectives. Thus rewetting of a peatland is sometimes referred to as 'restoration'. It is, of course, semantically legitimate to claim to have 'restored' former water levels to a drying-out site without taking into account the wider repercussions of this process. However, comprehensive site restoration implies not only reinstatement of former environments, but also redevelopment of a biota similar to a former condition and, where applicable, re-establishment of the 'natural ecosystem processes' which sustain the site. In this report, the unqualified term 'restoration' is used in this comprehensive sense.

Effective restoration *sensu lato* has two main features: (i) the establishment of appropriate environmental conditions and (ii) subsequent colonisation by target species. Kuntze & Eggelsmann (1981) subdivided restoration, conceptually, into three distinct but overlapping phases:

- *rewetting*
- *renaturation*
- *regeneration*

'Rewetting' may be too narrow a term for general use in peatland restoration as in some cases environmental manipulation other than, or additional to, rewetting may be required (*e.g.* nutrient stripping). Nonetheless, the establishment of appropriate water levels is usually the primary task in the restoration of peatlands damaged by commercial peat extraction.

'Renaturation' refers to recolonisation of the peatland by plant and animal species and the formation of characteristic communities. 'Regeneration' refers to be re-establishment of some ecosystem processes, such as peat accumulation. This phase is fundamental to restoration strategies which aim at whole mire regeneration, but is of less consequence when the objective is primarily to maintain species populations.

3.3.2 Approaches to restoration

As different species and restoration objectives may have markedly different environmental requirements, the creation of appropriate habitat conditions can only be considered in terms of the specified objectives. The purpose of rewetting damaged peatlands is not just to make them wet, but to provide conditions appropriate for the desired renaturation and regeneration objectives. The development of restoration strategies needs to consider the conditions required to realise the specified objectives, whilst recognising, for example, that the conditions needed to *re-establish* desired types of vegetation may differ from those required to *maintain* existing examples.

Two broad approaches to peatland restoration can be distinguished: *repair* and *rebuilding. Repair* usually entails relatively minor restorative operations (ditch blocking *etc.*) and aims at *direct reinstatement* of the desired objectives. It is particularly appropriate for sites with limited damage. *Rebuilding* involves the *redevelopment* of the peatland and implies that the desired endpoint cannot be produced directly but requires phased reconstruction, with a starting point often rather different from the final product. In some cases, further 'damage' may be required to produce a secure foundation for rebuilding. Depending on the

restoration objective, the restoration of bogs extensively damaged by commercial peat extraction will usually require rebuilding rather than repair.

3.4 Principles for restoration of raised bogs

3.4.1 Introduction

In principle at least, the restoration of damaged raised bogs may be easier than that of some other habitats. This is because, whilst peat extraction considerably damages raised bogs, it does not affect the most fundamental condition required for their formation and growth, namely a climatically-controlled precipitation excess. Moreover, raised bogs are thought to be climax ecosystems that have, in the past, developed spontaneously from a variety of starting-points, including fen and wet mineral soil. This suggests that renewed development of raised-bog ecosystems may be possible in a quite wide range of circumstances. Indeed, given appropriate conditions, it may be difficult to *prevent* 'ombrotrophication' from taking place.

There are two major requirements for raised-bog restoration: (i) availability of an adequate supply of precipitation of appropriate quality and its sufficient retention at the bog's surface to provide effective rewetting; (ii) availability of suitable recolonist species for renaturation. However, there are several reasons why these conditions cannot always be met, even in some former raised-bog sites [see also Box 3.2]:

(i) the peat surface may not readily retain rainwater (usually because of drainage systems, because the surface conformation tends to shed water and because the capacity of the natural bog surface for hydrological self-regulation has been lost (see below);

(ii) deep land drainage around the bog may substantially affect its water balance (this is not invariably the case);

(iii) drainage beneath the bog may substantially affect its water balance (this may occur when groundwater is abstracted from a permeable substratum beneath the bog; its importance in Britain is not known);

(iv) the peat surface may be minerotrophic in character (usually because of exposure of fen peats by excavation, ingress of groundwater or other contamination); bog vegetation may not be able to develop directly in such situations, though it may be able to develop indirectly by longer-term successional processes;

(v) atmospheric pollutants may be detrimental to the growth of some bog plants;

(vi) recolonist species may not be available close to the bog because of destruction of their refugia.

Box 3.2 *Hydrochemical constraints on bog restoration*

Individual cut-over raised-bog sites vary considerably in their conditions and characteristics. Although certain features (such as the presence of a layer of ombrotrophic peat) may *facilitate* some restoration options, and hence determine their feasibility, or priority, in a resource-limited context, this does not mean that sites lacking such attributes cannot be restored. As raised bogs are climax ecosystems, which have developed spontaneously, they are likely to be able to redevelop from a range of starting conditions on sites where they once occurred, though undoubtedly this process will take considerably longer from some starting points than others. Ultimately, there are two main constraints on the potential of sites to redevelop into raised bogs: (i) *availability* and *retention* of an *adequate supply* of meteoric water of *appropriate quality*; and (ii) *availability* of *recolonist species*. The first of these may be influenced by conditions external to the raised bog and, because of this, be particularly intractable.

The input of sufficient meteoric recharge water to bog surfaces is a prerequisite for bog development and climatic conditions provide a primary regulation of bog restoration options [Chapter 1], though the exact nature of climatic constraints upon ombrotrophic peat development and the range of climatic conditions under which this may occur is not known with precision: suggested threshold values of annual precipitation recharge required for bog development have been derived mainly by correlations based on the known distribution of bogs and the seasonal distribution of precipitation is almost certainly important in determining the growth of bogs [see Chapter 1], though its effect has not been well quantified. Workers in NW Europe (Kuntze & Eggelsmann, 1982; Streefkerk & Casparie, 1989) consider that the current precipitation : evaporation balance is suitable for raised-bog development in much of this region, though it is difficult to predict effects of future climatic patterns. In some sites, groundwater discharge may also have some importance to the overall water balance of the bog even though the surfaces are fed exclusively by precipitation [Chapter 1]. The interaction of this with other components of the water balance in relation to threshold precipitation values is not well known.

The *suitability* of meteoric water for raised-bog redevelopment, in parts of NW Europe at least, is open to question. It is possible that atmospheric contamination of rainwater ('acid rain') plus dry deposition of atmospheric N may constrain the possibilities for bog growth, especially with regard to the growth of certain *Sphagnum* species. As discussed elsewhere [4.5] the significance of this problem is not really known, but may be serious.

The *retention* of water within bog sites may be determined both by conditions within the mire and by those outside it. Retention problems internal to the mire can often be remedied (though it may not always be cost-effective to do so): drains that remove water from the bog can be blocked; lateral water loss across peat surfaces can be prevented by bunding; temporary water shortage can be alleviated by storing water in lagoons at times of surplus. External influences upon the water balance may be less tractable, such as those created by regional changes in hydrology. A lowering of groundwater levels is seen as a considerable constraint upon bog restoration in parts of NW Germany and The Netherlands where bogs have developed over permeable substrata in which a high groundwater level has effectively provided the base of the perched water mound. The extent to which this is an important component in the water balance of British bogs is

not known, but it is almost certainly a feature of some sites. It cannot be divorced from other conditions within the peatland. Thus, the 'problem' of ditches which cut through to the mineral substrata is only likely to affect substantially the hydrological integrity of the mire where the mineral ground acts as a water sink; otherwise such ditches can be readily dammed, as any other drain. Similarly, it may be of greater importance in peat cutting sites where only a thin layer of residual bog peat is available to constrain downwards seepage of water (Schouwenaars, 1993).

The *retention* of water within *specific parts* of bog sites is constrained by the same considerations mentioned above, but may be determined additionally by the surface topography created by peat extraction (Joosten, 1992). This may demand additional attention, if it is intended to rewet all, or most, of the site.

In many cut-over sites, water retention problems are strongly exacerbated by the lack of adequate water storage within the peat. Peat extraction usually removes the upper fibrous layers of moss and peat and exposes the lower, more humified peat layers. The latter, more highly decomposed peat, typically has a much lower water storage capacity than the former (the original acrotelm [1.8, 2.3]). Moreover, the plant species that often readily colonise such surfaces (*e.g. Molinia caerulea*) may induce high rates of evapotranspirative water loss and make summer surface conditions even less suitable for *Sphagnum* regeneration (Poschlod, 1988, 1992; Schouwenaars, 1992). In a little-damaged bog the *Sphagnum* layer is reported to be able to reduce evapotranspiration losses by forming a 'mulch' in its upper layers, whilst in the early stages of renaturation, the *Sphagnum* layer, if present at all, is not thick enough to regulate evapotranspiration losses effectively. Strategies aimed at regenerating bog vegetation may need to find surrogate methods for increasing surface storage as a precursor to re-establishing an acrotelm with an effective capacity for its own water regulation. In some climatic regions this may be achieved only by permanent inundation (Schouwenaars, 1992). This demands some substantial hydrological control of a disturbed or regenerating mire before attention focuses on revegetation.

The impact of minerotrophic surface conditions (created by exposure of underlying fen peat or mineral soil, or by ingress of telluric water) upon restoration prospects depends largely upon their character. Many bog plant species are able to grow in weakly minerotrophic (poor-fen) conditions, and some grow better in such conditions than in bog [1.9]. Weakly minerotrophic workings thus often support a mixture of species found both in bogs and fens. By contrast, few typical bog species normally grow in rich fens and where peat workings receive base-rich or nutrient-rich water, their vegetation is strikingly different to that of bog. It is possible that bog will eventually develop spontaneously from fen in such conditions, but it is likely to take longer than in poor fen. This is, however, partly dependent upon the water regime: given appropriate conditions ombrotrophic communities can develop from rich fen within c. 100–200 years, especially where peat cuttings are sufficiently inundated to permit the development of semi-floating rafts of vegetation.

It may be noted that some of these constraints are internal to the peatland, others are external; some may prevent restoration, other may just retard it; some can be readily remedied, others not so; some apply to intact bogs, others are confined to, or intensified in, cut-over sites. Very often 'external' constraints are less easily remedied than are 'internal' ones.

3.4.2 Conditions required for the establishment of bog species

The main focus of raised-bog restoration initiatives is to provide conditions suitable for colonisation and growth of species typical of little-damaged bogs, especially species of *Sphagnum*. The broad requirements for this are usually to:

- create, or maintain, permanently wet ombrotrophic conditions at the growing surface;
- minimise water fluctuation at the growing surface;
- prevent or reduce input of telluric water to the growing surface.

The establishment of *Sphagnum*-based vegetation is of great importance to raised-bog restoration, because (i) development of a 'bog-*Sphagnum*' vegetation is often a prime focus of restoration initiatives; (ii) it contributes to the regulation of surface wetness and to re-development of a characteristic bog acrotelm; and (iii) growth of *Sphagnum* may help regulate the chemical environment of the developing mire by acidification (especially important to the development of ombrotrophic nuclei within minerotrophic conditions).

The exact conditions required for effective establishment of *Sphagnum* species on damaged peat (or other) surfaces are not well known and are likely to vary somewhat between species and sites [1.9, 9.2]. Sphagna can colonise a quite wide variety of situations, though a common feature of these is generally a high and fairly stable water level. This may be provided:

- by high and frequent precipitation input (some climates permit *Sphagnum* growth in a range of situations, including sloping ground);
- by a mat of vegetation semi-floating within (shallow) water;
- by a *stable* water table, at or just below the surface of the substratum.

Bog plant species, including bog-*Sphagnum* species, have some flexibility in their growth requirements and may be able to grow in conditions that do not conform exactly to those characteristic of a little-damaged bog surface. For example, many can grow well in weakly minerotrophic conditions and some bog species can colonise open water, fen peats, mineral soils and artificial habitats (floors of quarries, railway ballast *etc.*) when conditions are appropriate. Establishment of a *Sphagnum* cover in such situations does not mean

that bog will *necessarily* develop in these sites, but it does suggest that ombrotrophic vegetation can be regenerated from a range of possible starting points.

Note that in some instances a stable, slightly subsurface *minerotrophic* water table in fen peat or mineral soils can provide a satisfactory basis for *Sphagnum* establishment. This is usually most suitable when base-rich water does not directly flood the surface; when the uppermost soil horizons are intrinsically acidic; and in regions of high precipitation input.

3.4.3 Pathways of bog restoration

Reflecting the range of circumstances from which raised bogs can naturally originate, restoration of damaged raised bogs can follow four main pathways.

1. direct colonisation of bog peat by plants associated with typical bog vegetation (M18);
2. colonisation of ombrotrophic water by plants and mosses associated with bog pools followed by successional invasion of other bog species;
3. colonisation of fen peat (or wet mineral soils) by fen plants followed by successional development to bog;
4. colonisation of minerotrophic water to form fen and thence bog.

The first of these pathways can be considered to be a form of *repair*. The other three are forms of *rebuilding*. Of these, pathways (3) and (4) may represent the mechanism by which the bog naturally developed, whilst pathway (2) is more artificial in these sense that bogs are not normally *initiated* in ombrotrophic water (though they may subsequently develop ombrotrophic flooding surfaces or bog lakes).

3.4.4 Starting conditions

In bog restoration initiatives, the pathway, speed and extent to which conditions suitable for the growth of typical bog species can be realised depends strongly on the starting conditions at each site (Table 3.2). Bog restorers need to assess the conditions and problems specific to each site and, from these, determine the most appropriate restoration possibilities and procedures. In some cases it may be desirable, if possible, to modify some starting conditions to facilitate the restoration process. The principles and methods by which this can be achieved form the main focus of the remainder of this report.

3.4.5 Suitability of sites for restoration

Various workers have pointed out that cut-over peatlands may vary considerably in their potential for restoration, depending both upon their situation (especially climatic constraints) and their condition (see *e.g.* Rowell, 1988; Eggelsmann (in Heathwaite &

Göttlich, 1993)). In some cases 'difficult' restoration circumstances (such as the effect of groundwater abstraction beneath a bog) may prevent effective rewetting, or make it very costly, and it may then be appropriate to consider more feasible restoration objectives, or to allocate resources to more tractable sites. Similarly, there may be some situations in which rewetting may not be feasible, for example on small or strongly sloping peat remnants.

As the character and configuration of a cut-over surface can have a critical influence upon successful recolonisation by bog plants, the best prospects for restoration may result from active collaboration between conservation bodies and the peat companies - which have the expertise and machinery for manipulating cut-over surfaces - in implementing an agreed restoration strategy. This would help to ensure that when the peat workings are eventually abandoned, they are in a conformation optimal for revegetation. Where some workings have been abandoned without such agreement, surface conditions may be such (*e.g.* very irregular topography) that renaturation will be almost impossible, or at least impractical, without a great deal of manipulation. There are numerous examples of such sites in which 'renaturation' has produced little more than thickets of birch and swathes of bracken.

Table 3.2 Summary of possible starting conditions on cut-over bogs.

Topography

Topography may be very variable across an abandoned peat extraction complex, depending on the method and extent of peat extraction. Two situations can be distinguished, at several scales [2.1]:

Massifs	blocks with an overall *convex* or *water shedding* profile.
Depressions	hollows with an overall *concave* or *water holding* profile.
	Note that *depressions* may occur within *massifs*.

Block cutting often produces a regular system of baulks, flats and trenches, but can sometimes result in a largely flat surface.

Milling often produces a series of long peat fields, usually as cambered beds.

Peat workings are often lower than adjoining refugium areas (which may be uncut remnants or revegetating cuttings).

Water conditions

Peat extraction and drainage modify or destroy typical bog vegetation and the characteristic bog acrotelm. They also typically induce dry conditions in cut-over areas and may also affect adjoining upstanding remnants either directly or indirectly [Chapter 2]. In consequence:

- water levels are generally too low for growth of peat-building *Sphagnum* species (except perhaps in some hollows);
- water levels tend to fluctuate to a greater extent than in 'intact' bog;
- water storage capacity of the peat is typically lower than in 'intact' bog;
- water loss may be exacerbated if the mineral subsoil is exposed.

Physical and chemical conditions

The peat surface of a little-damaged bog is typically acidic and nutrient poor. Peat extraction and drainage may lead to changes in the physical and chemical characteristics of the peat available for recolonisation [Chapter 2]. For example:

- rewetting dried peat may lead to release of nutrients;
- rewetting dried peat may lead to further acidification;
- peat extraction may expose fen peat or mineral ground;
- bare, dry peat provides an inhospitable physical environment for vegetation establishment.

Vegetation

The vegetation of remnant peat surfaces and of abandoned peat workings can be extremely variable, depending upon such constraints as degree of damage, depth of extraction, topography, base status, nutrient status, water level (and source) and length of time since last worked [Chapter 4]. Areas to be restored may thus include the following [see Box 3.1].

- bog-*Sphagnum* vegetation
- para-bog-Sphagnum vegetation;
- 'dry' bog vegetation;
- fen vegetation;

- non-wetland vegetation;
- completely bare surfaces
- open water

Chapter 4

Recolonisation of peat workings

4.1 Introduction

The most obvious feature of peat extraction is that it removes the living vegetation from a bog to leave a bare and often dry surface. Although natural, spontaneous colonisation by vegetation of some sort will undoubtedly occur on such surfaces without further intervention, the aim of most restoration schemes will be to try to optimise conditions to encourage colonisation and establishment by species appropriate to a specific restoration objective.

The revegetation of cut-over bogs is considered here giving attention to factors that may constrain or influence the renaturation processes. The techniques available to facilitate recolonisation of vegetation are considered in Chapter 9.

Studies on the natural revegetation of cut-over sites have indicated that the vegetation of such areas can be broadly categorised into four groups [2.3.5; 3.2]:

- bog-*Sphagnum* vegetation;
- para-bog-*Sphagnum* vegetation;
- vegetation typical of 'dry' bogs;
- vegetation typical of fens.

In some instances, natural colonisation of abandoned hand-cut, or commercial block-cut, areas has included many more bog species than spontaneous colonisation of a recently-abandoned, unmodified milled surface. This is due to factors such as topography, water levels, possible 'shoeing'[1] and availability of propagules and age (time since last cut). There is little evidence to suggest that vegetation typical of undamaged raised bog, with a cover of actively growing *Sphagnum,* will spontaneously return to extensive milled surface without some degree of intervention.

Water regime appears to be the primary factor affecting recolonisation by wetland plants, but both physical and chemical conditions of cut-over bog may differ significantly from the undisturbed bog environment [Chapter 2]. On milled peat fields there are usually fewer areas where water is 'naturally' retained than in block-cut areas, and abandoned areas are likely to be drier (unless constructs are made to impound water). Spontaneous recolonisation often results in vegetation

similar to that in the dry areas of block-cut sites, often with few, if any bog species (*e.g. E. vaginatum, Molinia*) accompanied by a range of dry-land or 'weed' species [see below].

Preliminary botanical data (*e.g.* Shaw & Wheeler, 1991) indicate that peat cuttings in fen peat support, overall, most of the characteristic fen plant species and many distinctive fen vegetation-types occur widely in revegetated workings. Moreover, abandoned peat cuttings provide the main reservoir for some species and vegetation-types, especially in England. This is because such peat cuttings help to provide a wet fen and hydroseral environment in circumstances which would otherwise be comparatively dry and solid. Several of the species and communities which are restricted, or almost restricted, to peat cuttings are rare and have high conservation importance, most notably those in Broadland, Norfolk (Giller & Wheeler, 1986, 1988).

The main factors affecting the revegetation of cut-over peatlands can be identified as:

- availability of recolonist species;
- physical and hydrochemical conditions, including type of peat;
- water regime.

These factors must be taken into account in considering the potential for revegetation of cut-over areas, and what, if any, measures should be taken in order to facilitate the recolonisation by typical bog (or fen) species.

4.2 Recolonisation of peat workings by plant propagules

4.2.1 Seed banks

Rather little examination has been made of the character of seed banks in undamaged ombrotrophic mires, but it is nonetheless clear that various bog plant species have a capacity to produce persistent seed banks, and that various assemblages of viable seeds have been recovered from the uppermost peat of some *Sphagnum*-dominated mires (*e.g.* McGraw, 1987;

---

[1] Return of vegetation to the cuttings

Poschlod, 1988, 1990, 1995). Permanent diaspore banks have also been found for many mosses and liverworts [Appendix 3].

However, the characteristics of seed banks are substantially irrelevant to many peat extraction sites, as the lower peat exposed by extraction does not retain viable seeds (Curran & MacNaeidhe, 1986; Salonen, 1987a). In some circumstances, the top spit of peat can retain a viable bank of various bog species (Poschlod, 1995), though this depends upon its exact nature, origin and the conditions in which it has been kept. Seed banks may also have some significance in other contexts. For example, the upper layers of uncut remnants may retain viable seed, which may respond to rewetting initiatives. 'New' diaspore banks may also develop in abandoned, revegetating peat cuttings, but very often they are comprised of the seeds of various 'weed' species, atypical of bogs, which have been derived either from sources external to the bog or by the spontaneous recolonisation of the abandoned cut-over surfaces. In many such cases the species concerned will be unable to regenerate in a rewetted area, but they may provide a reservoir for a few species, such as *Juncus effusus* and *Molinia caerulea*, which may be considered 'undesirable', at least in large quantities.

4.2.2 Diaspores and dispersal distances

The lack of a seed bank in the peat of newly-abandoned cut-over surfaces means that spontaneous revegetation is dependent upon the dispersal of viable diaspores from nearby sources. It has been suggested (Moore, 1982) that bog plant species are readily dispersed and can spontaneously recolonise some cut-over peatlands in appropriate conditions. This may well be largely correct, though it is not supported by some studies (*e.g.* Poschlod, 1995). There is rather little reliable information on actual rates of dispersion for most bog species – indeed, in some cases the dispersal agent is not conclusively known. It is likely that most rapid colonisation would be selective towards species with wind-dispersed diaspores. Diaspores of various bog species have been recorded in the diaspore rain upon commercially-cut peatlands, though seed input does not guarantee re-establishment (Salonen, 1987a, b). *Sphagnum* species may be well adapted to long-distance dispersal by their minute spores, but effective dispersal distances are not well known, nor indeed is the ability of *Sphagnum* to establish onto bare peat from germinating spores. However, wind dispersal of *Sphagnum* is not necessarily restricted to its spores. Vegetation fragments of various bryophytes can be wind-dispersed to peat surfaces upon which they can regenerate (Poschlod, 1995).

There is at least some evidence of the rapid colonisation of the wet floor of an abandoned sandstone quarry by bog species, including Sphagna, apparently colonised from a source some 14 km distant (Andreas & Host, 1983). However, the limits of dispersability are not really known and recolonisation of isolated mires may possibly be constrained by this. Recolonisation rates will probably depend upon the proximity of the worked-out areas to a source of propagules, though input of colonists from refugia may also depend on the character of the intervening habitat, for example, the presence of woodland or scrub around a remnant may reduce the influx of propagules of species usually dispersed by wind. The importance of 'corridors' for wildlife conservation has received recent attention, but the significance of these to bog plant species is unclear.

It is important that, where possible, reservoirs of populations of bog species are maintained close to peat extraction sites as the presence 'on site' of typical bog species is likely to considerably enhance the rate and 'quality' of natural recolonisation of bare surfaces or floating rafts and increase the speed of development of the more 'desirable' communities. Even where there is no uncut refugium for bog species, the survival of Sphagna in drainage ditches has been shown to be of value as a source for the spread of *Sphagnum* onto cut-over surfaces and the subsequent formation of floating rafts. In sites lacking refugia, it may be necessary to re-introduce species (see below).

The availability of appropriate propagules is, of course, no guarantee of revegetation by these species within abandoned peat workings as the conditions provided may be unsuitable for their establishment (*e.g.* Salonen, 1987a). Thus, for example, sites with dry, abandoned surfaces may become colonised almost entirely by 'weedy' species (Curran & MacNaeidhe, 1986), even if there is some remnant bog vegetation nearby, particularly where there is also adjoining farmland. Nonetheless, it is possible for a range of typical bog species ultimately to establish on abandoned surfaces after several years given suitable hydrochemical conditions.

Dispersability obviously regulates colonisation by 'weed' species as well as by desired ones. Anecdotal evidence from various workers has suggested that the rate and extent of birch colonisation of bogs is related to the proximity of mature trees[1], but that colonisation and establishment of 'undesirable' species is reduced where water levels are sufficiently high. However, the evidence suggests that it would be desirable to control populations of 'weed' species both within and around revegetating mires to reduce the potential invasion of such species [see Chapter 10].

---

[1] Note that this is a problem on some little-disturbed mires and mire remnants as well as in peat cuttings.

Plate 4.1 Risley Moss, Cheshire: vegetation recolonisation clearly reflects the topography of the block peat cuttings and relation to water level: baulks dominated by *Molinia caerulea*, the base of cuttings by *Eriophorum angustifolium*, and the trenches mainly open water. *Sphagnum* species (*S. squarrosum, S. fimbriatum, S. palustre, S. recurvum*) were recorded in the base of the cuttings and trenches. [See also Plates 2.14 and 2.15]

4.3 Effects of hydrological conditions on revegetation

4.3.1 *Significance of water level*

The importance of water level to the vegetation composition and structure of little-damaged raised bogs is outlined in Chapter 1, and discussed more fully in the working document on which this report is based [see Background]. The hydrological regime is one of the main factors affecting the recolonisation of cut-over bogs by different plant species. Individual wetland plant species may occupy rather distinct zones with respect to water level [1.9], although the actual water level 'preferences' of most bog and fen plant species, (including bryophytes) have yet to be established with precision. Thus, for example, some species are especially tolerant of (and may 'prefer') quite deep water conditions (*e.g. Typha* species); others seem tolerant of only shallow inundation (*e.g.* many forbs[1]); yet others may help form, or at least grow upon, floating rafts of vegetation. *Sphagnum* species show trends in microtopographical distribution with respect to water level [see Figure 1.10]. The depth of water (above or below the surface) in abandoned cut-over

surfaces may therefore be expected to have an important gross control upon the composition of recolonist vegetation [Plate 4.1], although any simple prediction of likely developments of vegetation in given water level conditions is hampered by effects of the mechanism of recolonisation [4.3.2], and may be influenced by the chemical conditions [4.4]. Optimal depths of inundation are discussed in Chapter 5.

The stability of the water table is also clearly important in influencing which species may recolonise peat workings. A strongly fluctuating water table may be inconducive to the colonisation of many typical bog species (and most importantly to Sphagna) and favour the growth of less desirable species as *Molinia* and birch. Rewetting requires not just a high water table; it also requires one that is relatively stable. This may be difficult to achieve in practice, as the limited water storage capacity in the peat remaining in many peat extraction complexes can exacerbate water level fluctuation. One solution is to try to stabilise the water level *relative to the vegetation surface* by creation of shallow lagoons, thereby helping to increase water storage, reduce water level fluctuations and to promote the establishment of wetland species, particularly floating *Sphagnum* rafts [see Chapters 5 & 9].

---

[1] *Forbs* are non-graminoid herbs

Table 4.1 Vegetation recolonisation of cut-over surfaces by *rooting* (plants establish by attachment to the "solid" substratum) or *rafting* (growth of plants and vegetation, floating in or on (sometimes shallow) water).

	Rooting	Rafting
Requirements:		
Water levels	Sub-surface / shallow flooding	Deep and persistent inundation (optimum depth is probably c. 50 cm, unless supplementary flotation mechanism available).
Surface configuration	No specific configuration required, other than for general retention of water; pools or pits should have gradually sloping sides.	Steep-sided pools / pits; may be necessary to create sub-divisions of large peat fields using baulks to reduce potential for damage to developing raft by wind or wave action.
Vegetation		Occurrence of plants with sufficient buoyancy to float (either on the surface, or at least within the photic zone).
Examples of possible colonising species in different conditions:		
Wet, base-poor	*Eriophorum angustifolium, E. vaginatum, Erica tetralix, Rhynchospora alba, Sphagnum* spp.	Aquatic Sphagna, *Eriophorum angustifolium, Drepanocladus fluitans, Cladiopodiella fluitans, Menyanthes trifoliata*
Wet, base-rich	*Typha* spp., *Scirpus lacustris, Phragmites australis, Eleocharis palustris, Equisetum fluviatile, Glyceria maxima.*	*Menyanthes trifoliata, Typha* spp, *Phragmites australis, Alisma plantago-aquatica, Carex pseudocyperus, Juncus effusus, Glyceria maxima, Eriophorum angustifolium, Carex rostrata, Potentilla palustris, Equisetum fluviatile*
Dry, base-poor	*Molinia caerulea*, birch, *Calluna vulgaris*	[not applicable]
Dry, base-rich	*Holcus lanatus, Dactylis glomerata, Rubus fruticosus, Ranunculus* spp., *Deschampsia cespitosa, Carex nigra, C. demissa, Cirsium* spp., *C. dissectum.*	[not applicable]
Facilitation of recolonisation	Inoculation with seed or rooted plant material and 'seeding' with *Sphagnum* fragments.	'Seeding' with *Sphagnum* fragments, with subsequent inoculation with rooted plant material. Use of 'nurse' species such as *Molinia caerulea* or *Eriophorum vaginatum* to protect floating *Sphagnum* mats from wind and wave action. Water levels must be raised once *Sphagnum* has become established. May be possible to use birch brashings, floating debris or an artificial material to accelerate recolonisation and reduce wind and wave action. Loose peat debris ± existing vegetation may detach from the bottom and float.
Advantages	Does not require inundation. Existing 'desirable' vegetation (if present) is not destroyed.	Inundation of the surface allows substantial water storage and may help to retard or even prevent establishment of species such as birch, *Molinia* and *Calluna*. Such species may also be killed by inundation. Vertical mobility of the raft allows the developing vegetation to accommodate some vertical flux in the mire water levels. This is particularly important in those situations where large seasonal fluctuations in the mire water table are known to occur. May help to "short-circuit" the terrestrialisation process by forming a 'skin' of vegetation before cuttings have filled with peat, thereby allowing precocious invasion of species that will not grow in deep water environments. Rafts may create conditions and support the vegetation that are known precursors of the natural development of raised bogs, e.g. lawn and hummock-forming *Sphagna*, even in base-rich conditions. Peat cuttings in fen peat have provided conditions for the development of conservationally-desirable plant communities.
Disadvantages	Vegetation change tends to be slow (e.g. birch may die gradually, but *Molinia* remains dominant and species such as *Eriophorum vaginatum* and *Sphagna* may establish and increase only slowly). Susceptible to water level fluctuations; may require management.	Requires adequate control of water levels to ensure permanent inundation and to prevent "grounding" of the raft before the area is self-sustaining; may require subdivision of large peat fields into smaller areas to avoid excessive damage to a fragile developing raft of vegetation by wind and wave action. Existing 'desirable' vegetation (if present) potentially destroyed (although in some circumstances may become detached from the bottom and float, thus accelerating revegetation).

One potential problem in the creation of large flooded lagoons is the possible attraction of certain birds (particularly gulls and wildfowl), which may lead to nutrient enrichment through inputs of faeces, possibly giving rise to the establishment of atypical vegetation, such as a dominance of the rush *Juncus effusus*. However, the extent of the problem and the precise conditions which may encourage such birds have yet to be established, and there is at least some evidence that bog vegetation can establish over *J. effusus* at the sites of former gull colonies (Baaijens, 1984, *cit.* Joosten & Bakker, 1987).

It is often suggested that an additional advantage of very wet conditions in recolonising peat workings is that they help to suppress undesirable species such as birch or *Molinia*. Whilst in gross terms this is probably correct, both of these species can often show surprising tenacity to survive, even in very wet conditions. However, consistently high water levels do seem to be able to restrain new colonisation by these species [see also Chapter 10].

4.3.2 Colonisation mechanisms

Introduction

In many situations, establishment of plant species upon peat surfaces is by direct *rooting*[1], but when the surface is inundated another mechanism may operate – *rafting,* in which the plants form a semi-floating raft, sometimes extending from, and anchored to, the sides of the cuttings. Not all wetland plants can form rafts, but many are able to grow upon rafts formed by other species.

In attempts to revegetate abandoned peat workings it may be possible, depending upon the local circumstances, to select a recolonisation mechanism. In practice this choice usually means either attempting to keep the water table close to the peat surface to permit rooting, or attempting to have deeper flooding, to promote rafting. In some sites the possibility for even crude control of the water levels may not exist, but in those situations where it does, it becomes important to assess the merits of the two colonisation pathways. Salient features of rooting and rafting are summarised in Table 4.1.

Rooting

The identity of species colonising peat surfaces depends upon the depth and behaviour of the water table (coupled with the chemical conditions) [4.3.1; 4.4]. If the water table is substantially below the surface of the peat for all or part of the year, this will select against species largely dependent upon permanently, consistently high water tables (such as some *Sphagnum* species) in favour of those that have more drought tolerance (such as *Eriophorum vaginatum)*. Conversely, if the water table remains high, either permanently or seasonally above the peat surface, this may select against species that are intolerant of much flooding, in favour of emergent species (*e.g. Eriophorum angustifolium*). When the water exceeds a certain depth the water will become too deep for most species to survive rooted to the peat, and colonisation will depend on species able to float and form rafts (see below). It is difficult to specify a mean critical water depth because:

a) it varies between species;

b) it differs for the new colonisation of plants compared to the *persistence* of established plants. In general, many wetland plants are able to survive, rooted, in considerably deeper water than that in which they would be able to establish (from seed).

Where pools of water are too deep to permit the invasion of any given particular species by rooting, unless rafting takes place its establishment is deferred until shallower conditions prevail. This may occur because of the gradual accumulation of organic muds and peats within the pool, as part of autogenic[2] terrestrialisation of the water (hydroseral infilling); by inputs of allochthonous[3] sediments (*e.g.* wind-blown peat); or through a sustained lowering of the water level.

Rafting

The term 'rafting' is used here to refer to the growth of plants and vegetation, floating in or on (sometimes shallow) water. By definition it requires some degree of at least seasonal inundation. The identity of species forming the rafts will largely depend upon the chemical conditions; raft-forming species include *Menyanthes trifoliata*, *Phragmites australis*, *Typha* spp., *Eriophorum angustifolium* and aquatic *Sphagnum* species). Individual plants may be free-floating or they may be attached to the margins of the pools, from whence they have expanded across the water. When well developed, rafting may short-circuit the usual terrestrialisation process by producing a skin of vegetation at the water surface in deep cuttings before they have filled with peat. It therefore permits the early invasion of plant species that will not grow in very wet conditions. The term 'rafting' also includes the growth of loose mats of *Sphagnum etc.* within the water [Plate 4.2]. These may or may not ultimately form a surface floating raft, depending on topographical and water

---

[1] Strictly speaking the term 'attachment' is more correct, as bryophyte species do not have roots.

[2] autogenic = 'self-made'

[3] allochthonous = externally derived

Plate 4.2 *Sphagnum cuspidatum* forming a raft in a flooded lagoon within worked-out peat cuttings; Amsterdamsche Veld (Bargerveen, The Netherlands).

conditions, and in shallowly-flooded sites they may be grounded for at least part of the year.

Where a raft of vegetation forms, it is usually initially fragile; decomposing portions may detach and fall to the floor of the pool and contribute to upward accumulation of organic material. But rafts usually increase in thickness, both by an increase in living plant material and by entrapment of muds and peat. In so doing the raft will gradually stabilise and ultimately will be able to support trees (see below).

The occurrence of a rafting colonisation process does not mean that colonisation of the water body is independent of its depth. For example, some of the more aquatic Sphagna (*e.g. S. cuspidatum*) grow well in fairly shallow open water but less well in deep conditions, possibly because of limited supply of dissolved carbon source (*e.g.* Baker & Boatman, 1990; Paffen & Roelofs, 1991; Joosten, 1992; Money, 1994). It seems likely that the 'optimum' inundation regime for the promotion of aquatic Sphagna will usually be a trade-off between a need to avoid deep inundation to maximise *Sphagnum* growth and a need to store as much excess water as is needed to avoid desiccation during dry periods. Depths greater than *c.*50 cm seem generally unsuitable for good growth of aquatic Sphagna in bog water (*e.g.* Money, 1994), though exceptions also occur, for example, *S. auriculatum* is

known to grow in a lake at depths up to 10 m at Jesioro Zielone, Poland (*pers. obs.*).

Although rafting recolonisation may result in an initial eradication of 'undesirable' species such as birch, rafts may not be free from subsequent colonisation by these. This is because as the raft matures, although it may sink beneath its own weight, even before it has 'grounded' the surface may remain slightly proud of the water and may be suitable for establishment of seedling birches *etc.* The degree to which this is a problem may vary between sites. It is not difficult to find floating rafts in which sapling birches have become held in 'check' and show little subsequent growth. Elsewhere trees may progressively sink through an unstable raft as they become heavier and ultimately become moribund or die. It cannot be concluded that floating rafts of *Sphagnum* will remain free from woody cover, but this may, of course, be part of a natural successional progression towards raised bog. The problem is exacerbated when the raft is only developed in shallow water, as 'grounding' of the peat raft may lead to surface-dry conditions.

Restoration strategies aimed at the production of rafts of vegetation seem to be particularly effective approaches to the rewetting and revegetation of peat workings in both bog and fen peat in that (i) they require inundation of the mire surface (*i.e.* they permit substantial water storage); (ii) they allow the developing vegetation to accommodate such vertical water flux as may occur (at least within limits) by their own vertical mobility and help to create permanently wet surface conditions. In principle they seem a more potent approach to mire restoration than strategies just aimed at keeping the water level close to the peat surface, particularly in those situations where large seasonal fluctuations in the mire water table are known to occur. Rafting is also a potentially important mechanism for re-establishing *Sphagnum* vegetation in (former) bogs where substantial base-enrichment has occurred, as the hydrological stability and mobility of the raft prevents its inundation. However, the potential importance of rafting should not just be seen in terms of the production of small-scale ombrotrophic floating rafts, important as they may be, but also as a fundamental strategy for regenerating an acrotelm-like structure over large areas of derelict raised bogs. In such situations the development of floating rafts may be the *only* effective way of re-establishing mire vegetation, although there are some limitations.

4.4 Physical and chemical influences on revegetation

4.4.1 Introduction

Different plant species are adapted to grow under different environmental conditions. The conditions prevailing at a given site largely determine which available species are able to colonise and establish. The major environmental influences upon the composition of mire vegetation are: water supply (rainfall amount and frequency, water depth and flow); base status; nutrient status and (in a few cases) salinity. There may also be physical constraints on revegetation, particularly of bare peat surfaces. The effects of some of these variables are identified below. In addition to environmental variables, vegetation management practices have a critical role in controlling and maintaining the character of many herbaceous vegetation-types, particularly in fens – these are considered further in Chapter 10.

4.4.2 Physical factors

Bare peat surfaces are likely to provide an inhospitable environment for establishment of plant propagules [Plate 4.3], although the 'difficult' environmental conditions found on an exposed peat surface may sometimes serve more to *retard* plant establishment than to *prevent* it (Salonen, 1987b). Summer drought may not only have a directly adverse affect upon the survival of seedlings of bog plants, but may also lead to crust formation and cracking of the peat.

Conversely, frost-heaving in winter is likely to affect seedling establishment on bare peat surfaces. Bare peat is also prone to erosion by wind or water, particularly where sloping (Tallis & Yalden, 1983) [Plate 4.4]. Such physical instability of the substratum is perhaps best reduced by the development of a vegetation cover, but it may sometimes be necessary to use artificial stabilants before this can be achieved.

Dark, bare peat is likely to absorb heat – increased temperature will exacerbate moisture loss and may affect plant establishment. A cover of vegetation can also help to buffer against fluctuations in water content and temperature of the surface peat, for example by reducing the drying effect of the wind, and providing a more favourable microclimate for the establishment of *Sphagnum* species (Grosvernier, Matthey & Buttler, 1995). It may be possible to achieve similar results by 'planting' the peat surface with plastic plants (Salonen, 1992), but in general the development of a natural cover is to be preferred.

Plate 4.3 Bare peat surface created by surface milling, sparsely colonised by *Narthecium ossifragum*.

Plate 4.4 Unstable and eroding, sloping peat surface remaining after surface milling, partly colonised by *Eriophorum vaginatum*. Wendlinger Filz (S. Germany).

If a peat surface is too unstable for vegetation to establish, it may be appropriate to use a surface mulch or artificial stabilants, over small areas at least. It is not possible to make firm recommendations of methods, as these have not been widely tested.

Plate 4.5 *Polygonum amphibium* and *Typha latifolia* colonising peat cuttings in fen peat; Somerset Levels.

Plate 4.6 *Polygonum amphibium* colonising reflooded, marl-based peat workings at Turraun Bog (Ireland). [See also Plate 2.13]

4.4.3 Chemical factors

In Britain, an important control on the pattern of spatial and temporal variation in plant species distribution in ombrotrophic mires is rainfall quantity and quality, itself controlled by factors such as proximity to the sea and degree of atmospheric pollution (Proctor, 1995). Two further major influences upon the species composition of mire vegetation are the base and nutrient status of the substratum.

Base status

Base status exerts a primary influence upon the composition of fen and bog vegetation. The base status of the water in peat workings is determined primarily by the characteristics of the peat (and underlying substrata) and the quality of any irrigating water inputs. These influences will substantially constrain the character of the invading vegetation, though other influences may modify some of their effects, for example, whilst fen plant species are the typical recolonists of peat cuttings with base-rich water [Plates 4.4 and 4.5], the development of a semi-floating raft of vegetation may facilitate the establishment of *Sphagnum*-dominated vegetation even over the most base-rich waters (Giller & Wheeler, 1988; Mallik, 1989).

Few chemical data exist for peat extraction sites in the UK. Those that are available for ombrotrophic peat workings suggest that the concentration of most ions is generally higher in the water and peat from peat workings than from less disturbed situations and sometimes provide chemical conditions more like those of poor fens than ombrotrophic bogs [2.3.3]. There is also evidence to suggest that in some circumstances, chemical changes resulting from drainage of the peat and seasonal fluctuations in water levels can lead to increases in acidity (pH<3.0) which may be inimical to the establishment and growth of some bog species, including some Sphagna (*e.g.* Austin & Wieder, 1987; Money, 1995).

The domes of ombrotrophic peat that form a raised bog have sometimes developed over fen peat, which usually has greater base-richness than the former, as can be readily shown in chemical profiles. Where peat extraction has exposed fen peat, the chemical environment is thus likely to be more conducive to the establishment of fen plants rather than bog vegetation (White, 1930; Poschlod, 1989, 1992). The outcome of rewetting strategies on fen peat will depend both upon the character of the irrigating water and the level at which it is maintained. As a general rule, assuming that some irrigating water is minerotrophic, when the peat is kept wet, there will be redevelopment of a fen vegetation, which may include some *Sphagnum* spp., and which may have a long-term potential for development into ombrotrophic bog. By contrast, if the peat is flooded, there is potential for development of a seral, floating fen vegetation which may provide a template for more rapid redevelopment of bog vegetation.

It is possible that where only a small thickness of peat remains at the base of peat workings there may be some chemical influence from the underlying mineral ground. The effect of this will depend upon its character – *Sphagnum* can recolonise base-poor sands and gravels quite readily and some excellent *Sphagnum*-based communities have developed hydroserally in small pits within glacial sands (*e.g.* Delamere Forest, Cheshire).

Nutrient status

The ombrotrophic bog environment is typically nutrient poor and infertile. However, disturbance of the peat through peat extraction operations or dehydration can lead to mineralisation of the drying peat and nutrient release [2.2.2; 2.3.3]. There is little evidence that this is inimical to revegetation prospects by *Sphagnum* species, but data are sparse. In many sites it is not obvious whether augmented N concentrations derive from disturbance of the peat or atmospheric contaminants (or both). More substantial nutrient (and base) enrichment may occur when eutrophic water from rivers or land drainage is allowed to enter peat workings. Exposure of underlying fen peat or clays can, in principle, also expose a substratum that is more nutrient-rich than was the overlying ombrotrophic peat. The quality of irrigating water inputs from sources other than precipitation should be carefully assessed, and if necessary, polluted water diverted away from the site.

A wide range of fen communities have been recorded from recolonised peat workings, developed either on solid peat or hydroserally. As a general rule, those which are particularly welcomed by conservationists for their intrinsic value are those which have developed in conditions of low fertility; such vegetation-types are often species-rich, frequently contain various uncommon plant species and are themselves rare. Nutrient-enrichment of abandoned fen peat workings, particularly by nitrogen or phosphorus, is typically associated with the development of a vigorous, coarse and species-poor vegetation that has limited botanical value, although it may still provide an important habitat for other groups such as birds or invertebrates.

4.4.4 Peat-type

The nature of the peat surface presented for recolonisation may depend on the type of peat exposed [1.8; 2.3]. Weakly-humified peat is thought to provide better conditions for revegetation than strongly-humified peat

(*e.g.* Eigner & Schmatzler, 1980; Nick, 1985), apparently reflecting its physical properties, such as looser structure, and, particularly, its greater water storage capacity (Schouwenaars & Vink, 1992; Roderfeld, 1992). It may be able to retain water better than strongly-humified peat, to the extent that it may swell upon rewetting and thus take on some of the functional attributes of the original bog acrotelm. However, it has also been suggested that some little-humified peat is too deficient in nutrients to sustain good regrowth of some bog species (J. Blankenburg, *pers. comm.*), and there is little clear evidence to suggest that the weakly-humified peat is *necessarily* more desirable for encouraging revegetation of cut-over surfaces than is strongly-humified peat as this is also related to the nature of the rewetting strategy [Chapter 5]. Evidence from The Netherlands (*e.g.* Joosten, 1992) suggests that weakly-humified peat thrown back into peat cuttings as a type of *bunkerde* [9.5] may facilitate the formation of a floating raft on which *Sphagnum* and other species could colonise.

Exposure of fen peat will undoubtedly influence the composition of the recolonist species, as the chemical environment is likely to be more conducive to the establishment of fen rather than bog vegetation (see above).

4.4.5 Depth of residual peat

In broad terms, the effect of residual peat depth upon the prospects for rewetting and subsequent revegetation is likely to be important in two main ways:

- the intrinsic characteristics of the peat-type that is exposed at a particular depth;
- the effect of the thickness of the residual peat layer as a buffer against underlying conditions and vertical water loss by seepage.

The intrinsic characteristics of the peat are related to, and partly determined by, its position in the peat profile [1.8]. The chemical composition may be of particular significance [4.4.3] but differences in physical properties such as water storage capacity (if any) [2.3.2; 4.4.4] may be overcome by inundation [Chapter 5].

In peat cutting complexes, the depth of residual peat that is needed to minimise, to an acceptable level, downward seepage losses into the underlying mineral substrata in appropriate sites is likely to depend strongly on the permeability of the peat. Studies are hampered by difficulties of making an accurate estimate of vertical seepage. Schouwenaars, Amerongen & Booltink (1992) provide evidence that rates of downward loss are inversely related to residual peat depth. A 'critical depth' against seepage has not been established, but Blankenburg & Kuntze (1987) suggest that at least 50 cm of a low permeability, strongly-humified peat is needed to keep downward seepage losses below what they considered to be an acceptable rate of 60 mm a^{-1}. Similarly, Schouwenaars (1993) suggests that at least 50 cm of strongly-humified peat (H $\geq$ 7) is mostly sufficient to guarantee limited water losses, whereas for less strongly-humified peat (H 5–7) a minimum thickness of 1 m may be required, unless the water pressure in the underlying aquifer lies above the base of the peat. Such possible losses by vertical seepage may be largely inconsequential to those many UK sites which are over impermeable substrata, but there is a need for a more careful evaluation of this water balance term in those sites where this is a possibility; experience elsewhere suggests that it may have profound repercussions for the success of restoration initiatives.

A minimum depth of *ombrotrophic* peat may be needed to help prevent enrichment from underlying base-rich substrata (fen peats or mineral ground), either directly or through plant roots being able to tap any underlying enriched conditions. Again a critical depth has not been established, but various considerations point to a depth of 50 cm as a desirable minimum, a view shared by various workers (*e.g.* Eggelsmann, 1980).

Note also that the depth of residual peat considered must take into account the depth beneath the floor of drainage channels and the disposition of the peat fields in relation to the underlying topography of the mineral sub-soil [see also Chapter 6].

4.5 External constraints on revegetation

4.5.1 Introduction

Earlier sections of this chapter have considered the relationship between some internal conditions of cut-over sites to their revegetation prospects, for example, lack of recolonist species and hydrological and chemical factors. However, there are also some external processes which may influence the characteristics of the site which it may not be possible to manipulate directly.

4.5.2 Effects of atmospheric pollution

Introduction

As raised bogs are irrigated directly and more-or-less exclusively by precipitation inputs, and as their component plant species may be well adapted to 'scavenge' solutes from dilute solutions (as seen perhaps most notably in species of *Sphagnum* (Malmer, 1988)), they may be particularly susceptible to

atmospheric contaminants [1.9.4]. These may influence the growing plant species either by some direct toxic effects or by a more indirect perturbation of the 'chemical balance' of the mire water, such as enrichment with nutrients that would normally be growth-limiting.

Possible implications for bog growth and restoration

The assessment of the effects of atmospheric pollutants and implications for growth of bog species is hampered by lack of data and the difficulty of relating plant response to specific concentrations of different pollutants. However, it seems likely that in present circumstances the deposition of nitrogen oxides and ammonia may have more significant effects on growth of bog species than sulphur dioxide. Atmospheric pollution has probably influenced the composition of the vegetation of some bogs in the past and it is possible that atmospheric nitrogen enrichment may affect raised-bog vegetation in certain regions at present, though this is not clearly established. Threshold values for the possible detrimental effects of nitrogenous contaminants upon lowland bogs are not known, but it is possible that these may differ for the *maintenance* of existing bog vegetation compared to the *recreation* of bog communities on cut-over sites, not least because the latter may be subject to additional sources of enrichment in consequence of disturbance, mineralisation *etc.* [2.3.3]. Further work is required to provide critically definitive evidence in order to establish whether current levels of atmospheric pollution are disadvantageous to the prospects for regeneration of raised bogs.

4.5.3 Lowering of regional groundwater levels

A decrease in regional groundwater tables may influence the water balance of some sites [2.3.2], although it may be possible to mitigate these effects by retaining a sufficient depth of low permeability peat [4.4.5].

4.5.4 Climatic constraints

The climate at a given site may influence the opportunities for revegetation by bog species, and hence the most appropriate restoration strategies. A precipitation input of 700 mm a^{-1} has been suggested as a threshold below which permanent moisture shortage will occur in North Germany and The Netherlands (Casparie & Streefkerk, 1992) but it is not clear how accurately this has been established. It is difficult to specify a universal threshold value as factors such as the amount and distribution of rainfall, temperature, humidity and evapotranspiration may all affect the water balance of the mires and the potential for regeneration of bog vegetation. In the UK, the most crucial period for wetland vegetation is during the summer months, when evaporation typically exceeds precipitation. In addition, constraints imposed by specific climatic regimes can sometimes be accommodated by the rewetting strategy that is chosen.

The conditions suitable for the maintenance of a peatland vegetation are likely to be different from those necessary for its establishment. For example, a closed carpet of Sphagna is able to preserve moisture by forming a 'mulch' over the surface, and 'bleaching' of the Sphagna on dehydration helps to reflect incident radiation, thereby helping to reduce the loss of water from the peat surface / acrotelm (Schouwenaars, 1990). However, until a closed carpet is achieved, the individual plants are more likely to be susceptible to desiccation during periods of low rainfall and humidity.

4.6 Recolonisation of peat workings by invertebrates

Very little is known of the colonising abilities of raised-bog invertebrates, but it is likely that dispersal will be limited in flightless species or those having reduced wings (as in the case of some beetles and bugs). However, the carabid beetle, *Agonum ericeti* is known to be flightless in the UK and indeed over much of its range (Thiele, 1977: 291; Lindroth, 1985) but it is nevertheless widely distributed in suitable oligotrophic mires. In some species mobility may be effected by methods other than flight, though it may also reflect in part, a greater contiguity of raised-bog areas in the past.

The importance to dispersal of the habitat-type between the refugium and areas to be colonised depends greatly on the mode of dispersal of particular species. For large, highly mobile and relatively strong-flying species such as dragonflies (Odonata) and some flies and Lepidoptera, intervening habitat-type may be relatively unimportant. Some species of dragonflies, for example, are markedly migratory in their behaviour (though some notable raised-bog species are more-or-less sedentary). At the other extreme, many flightless species such as some beetles and bugs, may be unlikely to enter areas of unsuitable habitat (*i.e.* areas that are too shady, dry, friable, alkaline, *etc.*); Thiele (1977: 214) intimated that substratum type was probably an important determinant of movement in carabid beetles. Nevertheless, studies have shown that a surprisingly large number of invertebrate species are capable of colonising even remote islands of suitable habitat given sufficient time.

Rates of recolonisation of cut-over areas are likely to be strongly influenced by the character of the vegetation developed within the workings, and also by the proximity of refugia for 'desirable' invertebrate species – nothing is known about the potential to inoculate regenerating areas with appropriate invertebrates in the absence of nearby refugia. Nevertheless, studies by Heaver & Eversham (1991) of extraction sites at Thorne Waste which had been worked up to the 1970's but which were since largely undisturbed and wet, show that colonisation of at least some species can occur fairly rapidly (including in this case some 27 scarce or rare taxa). Such successful recolonisation was probably dependent on the persistence of the recolonising species in nearby refugia, but provides at least some evidence that conservationally-worthwhile, more or less balanced invertebrate communities can reassemble within *c.* 50–70 years given the presence of adjacent refugia, perhaps even less, although the communities that exist at this time are undoubtedly still transitional. However, rates of recolonisation will clearly also depend on the availability and proximity of potential recolonist species

There have been very few studies of the behavioural or physiological selection processes that restrict peatland insect species to particular types of habitat, although it has been suggested that factors such as pH and climate may influence distribution in some species (*e.g.* Paje & Mossakowski, 1984; Peus, 1932). Availability of specific food sources (plants, animals or detritus), vegetation height and structure are also likely to be important determining factors, as are the amount and distribution of open water and hydrological regime (*e.g.* Key, 1991). For example, an increase in provision of open water habitat by management such as ditch blocking or creation of pits or scrapes, often leads to an increase in dragonflies (*e.g.* Fox, 1986b). In general, dragonflies do better where there is some protection from the wind and so are favoured by sites with peat walls, adjacent scrub or at the edges of raised bogs where woodland may act as a windbreak (R.G. Kemp, *pers. comm.*). It should be remembered that the habitat requirements of a species will be governed by both the requirements of the adult and also, the larva, pupa, *etc.*, and that these may be rather different, necessitating the presence of two or more different and perhaps even spatially separated features.

4.7 Recolonisation of peat workings by birds

Although most birds show strong site fidelity for nesting, roosting *etc*, ringing recoveries clearly show that many species do not remain in the same area (or even the same continent!) throughout the year. In view of such natural mobility it might be assumed that birds would readily abandon a site following adverse habitat change, or high levels of disturbance. Refugia may be located far from a disturbed site, and may be either temporarily or permanently adopted by the displaced populations. However, where species are displaced from sites located close to the limit of their geographical range, the chances of recolonisation of the site following restoration measures would be considerably reduced.

A distinction can be recognised between areas which have previously been hand cut for peat and those which have been worked using current technology. In the former, a mosaic of wet and dry habitats results over a relatively long timescale and colonisation from adjacent intact or recently colonised areas can be expected to be reasonably rapid if suitable habitats result. By contrast, extensive commercial extraction techniques remove all breeding birds from extensive working areas in the short term. No data are yet available on the colonisation characteristics of extensive cut surfaces in the longer term.

Disturbance, lack of food sources and nest sites is likely to severely limit the use of expansive areas of newly cut-over bog by birds. As these areas become revegetated birds may readily colonise, although re-establishment of a community which is characteristic of little-damaged raised bog is unlikely in the short term. The species which colonise will largely depend on the distribution and amount of open water and the type of vegetation which develops (as well as the site's geographical location), being influenced by such factors as suitability and availability of food sources, nesting sites, roosting sites, vegetation structure *etc.*. For example, increased provision of open water has been shown to attract breeding waders and duck (including teal) which may be attributed to increased food availability (*e.g.* aquatic invertebrates, including Odonata, Hemiptera, Coleoptera and Diptera) (Fox, 1986a). The development of birch scrub attracts species typical of woodland: willow warbler being the most characteristic species of pioneer birch woodland, with a number of other passerine species also being represented. Where fen vegetation develops in old peat workings, additional species such as sedge warbler, reed warbler, water rail, moorhen and coot can be attracted to breed. Conversely, loss of suitable habitat as a result of rewetting may reduce the numbers of such species as nightjar and skylark.

Chapter 5

Rewetting damaged and cut-over peatlands

5.1 Introduction

In any project aimed at restoring or recreating wetland ecosystems, long-term success depends upon the provision of a hydrological regime appropriate for the establishment and maintenance of the target wetland biota. It is not possible to give a simple, or universal, prescriptive solution to the problems of rewetting peat extraction complexes as this will depend critically upon such site-specific factors as topography, disposition and character of the peat fields, peat type and climate as well as the objective of restoration. However, it is possible to identify some general principles, problems and solutions, based upon attempts at restoration [see specific references and Appendix 6], and to discern some broad categories of context in which bog restoration is likely to occur. In this chapter, the principles, potential and limitations of various rewetting procedures are discussed. The adoption of these, in relation to specific restoration objectives, is discussed further and summarised in Chapter 6. The primary focus is upon producing conditions appropriate for the maintenance or re-establishment of a typical, *Sphagnum*-rich, bog vegetation, but some alternatives are considered briefly.

5.2 Establishment of suitable hydrological conditions for raised-bog restoration

5.2.1 Principles of rewetting damaged and cut-over bogs

The exact character of water management in bog restoration and conservation may depend on whether the aim is to *maintain* an existing bog surface or to *renature* a damaged surface (*i.e.* one that may be rather dry and which may have lost the original bog acrotelm layer and most or all of its former species). It will also depend upon the topography of the area (*e.g.* whether a *massif* or a *depression* [2.1]) but in all such situations the primary problem of rewetting is that of retaining sufficient meteoric water so that the peat surface remains consistently wet year-round. A characteristic feature of little-damaged bogs is that saturated

conditions are maintained close to the surface for much of the year, *i.e.* they have a consistently high water table. Although bog plants have some capacity to tolerate occasional dry periods (depending on their duration and magnitude), successful bog regeneration also requires permanently wet conditions. Low water levels are not only unsuitable for the growth of many bog plant species but may also promote further oxidative decomposition of the peat. On an ombrotrophic peat surface, precipitation is the sole source of recharge, and hydrological management must seek to retain as high a proportion of this as is possible[1] to initiate mire regeneration or to maintain existing surfaces.

Both the 'base-line' water level in raised bogs (*i.e.* the limit of permanent saturation) and the magnitude of fluctuations above this, are regulated by similar (though not identical) processes. The limit of permanent saturation is provided by the position of the 'groundwater' mound surface in relation to the mire surface and is a reflection of the variables that determine this [1.7]. In a damaged site it may be located well below the peat surface.

Water-level fluctuations are restricted to the peat horizons above the limit of permanent saturation. They are essentially a reflection of the consistency of precipitation recharge, the capacity for water storage in the upper layers (which is a function of the storage capacity of the peat, fraction of open water *etc.*), the vegetation, climate and the regulation of water losses through run-off and evapotranspiration. In disturbed mires, drainage and peat extraction may reduce water storage capacity at or near the peat surface (Joosten, 1992) relative to that of intact mires (Galvin, 1976; Eggelsmann, 1981, 1988a); removal of the acrotelm[2] also removes some natural capacity for hydrological self-regulation; and recolonisation by plant species such as *Molinia* or *Betula* may increase rates of

---

[1] while allowing for discharge of periodic water excess.

[2] The term 'acrotelm' refers to the surface layer of a peatland that is above the limit of permanent saturation. In this broad sense, cut-over bogs also have an acrotelm, but one which lacks some of the distinctive features of the acrotelm layers of a little-damaged bog surface, such as its apparent capacity for hydrological self-regulation. In this report, unless qualified, the term 'acrotelm' is restricted to refer to the 'fully-functional' surface layers such as characterise little-damaged bogs. [see Box 1.4]

evapotranspiration relative to a little-damaged *Sphagnum*-dominated surface; and, in some cases peat fissures develop which may create channels of preferential water flow and help to drain the surface. In combination, these processes often result in damaged bog surfaces having a much greater amplitude of water level flux than is found in a little-damaged site (*e.g.* Streefkerk & Casparie, 1989; Beets, 1992; Schouwenaars & Vink, 1992; Money, 1994).

5.2.2 Establishment of an acrotelm characteristic of little-damaged bog

In a little-damaged bog, the character, integrity and on-going growth of the system is in considerable measure maintained by the functional characteristics of the acrotelm [1.7]. This helps to maintain a 'stable state' at the bog surface, by various feed-back mechanisms, so that water level change is minimised and bog plants are able to grow, or at least survive, even during periods of drought. When the original acrotelm of a raised bog has been destroyed (as by peat extraction), its capacity for water storage and run-off regulation is reduced and an alternative 'stable state', may develop, but one which is essentially characterised by relative instability of various environmental variables, especially water level. This condition is supported by various feed-back mechanisms, including the growth on a summer-dry peat surface of various deep-rooted plant species with high rates of evapotranspirative water loss. The importance that loss of the original bog acrotelm has to renaturation of damaged sites is partly determined by the frequency and volume of recharge as well as by the water storage characteristics of the 'new' acrotelm (*i.e.* the unsaturated zone formed by the upper layers of the remaining peat). However, in many situations the net result is that whilst in wet (winter) conditions the surface may become saturated, or even flooded, in dry (summer) periods it dries considerably. In such situations, the water level fluctuations may be of sufficient magnitude to prevent recolonisation of the peat surface by bog (especially *Sphagnum*) species and hence to prevent redevelopment of an acrotelm which has the functional characteristics of a little-damaged bog acrotelm.

As Bragg (1989) observed, in damaged bogs, "the acrotelm should be reinstated as soon as possible", but the critical question is '*How ?*'. The central problem of restoration of bog vegetation on a damaged ombrotrophic surface is that of 'kicking' the system from the 'damaged surface' stable state to a 'bog-acrotelm-based' stable state. The difficulty of this is that the conditions required to redevelop an acrotelm with the properties typical of a little-damaged bog surface are in considerable measure provided by this sort of acrotelm

itself. A solution to this problem is to try to construct devices that mimic some of the properties of the original acrotelm and which permit its redevelopment by sustaining the growth of typical bog species. Many of the different approaches to bog restoration essentially represent different ways of attempting to solve this problem.

5.2.3 Approaches to rewetting

The main aims of water management for the restoration of raised bog can be summarised:

- identify causes of dry conditions;
- increase retention of nutrient-poor precipitation input;
- elevate level of permanent saturation as far as possible;
- reduce water-level fluctuations;
- prevent or reduce water inputs from other sources (*e.g.* mineral / nutrient-enriched or polluted water sources).

Various approaches to rewetting damaged raised bogs are discussed below. They are mostly different methods of attempting to elevate the level of permanent saturation within the peat or of reducing the amplitude of water level fluctuations near the surface, usually by increasing water storage (or both).

Rewetting procedures depend upon whether the aim is (i) to rewet a remnant of upstanding peat (or to retain its wetness); or (ii) to provide appropriately wet conditions in extensive cut-over surfaces. The separation of these two situations – *massifs* and *depressions* [2.1] – is sometimes rather arbitrary but they provide a simple conceptual basis on which to consider different approaches to peatland restoration and help in the formulation of generalised restoration strategies applicable to more than one site and for different scales within an individual site.

'Rewetting' of mires implies the creation of surface-wet conditions, but there is scope for variation in the degree of wetness which may be desired or that can be achieved. The following terms are used here with specific connotations:

Soaking: Water level is close to the surface of the peat (usually sub-surface) for much of the year.

Flooding or *inundation*:   Water level is above the surface of the peat for at least part of the year. The degree of flooding can vary typically between *shallow* (< *c.* 20 cm) and *deep* (< *c.* 50 cm).

5.3 Rewetting options for raised-bog massifs

5.3.1 Introduction

As used here, the term 'massif' may comprise entire bogs (damaged or not), uncut remnants or upstanding blocks within peat extraction complexes [2.1]. In all of these situations, the retention of water is ultimately dependent upon the maintenance of a water table perched above that in the surrounding depressions. 'Groundwater' mound concepts [Box 1.5] are thus appropriate for considering various conceptual options for the rewetting of bog massifs.

Various strategies for rewetting bog massifs are identified below, based upon approaches that have either been used or proposed. Some cannot be regarded as well tried and tested and, where appropriate, their limitations are identified. The choice, and effectiveness, of any of these options is likely to be influenced strongly by:

- the causes and extent of dehydration / damage;
- the nature of the peat;
- the nature of the climate;
- the exact topography of the site.

The choice of option will also be determined by whether the aim of rewetting is to *maintain* an existing bog vegetation or to *renature* a badly-damaged peat surface [Chapter 6].

The surfaces of residual bog massifs may be dry for several reasons [2.2.2], for example:

- basal area is too small to maintain a perched water mound near the surface over some or all of a site;
- site has been drained;
- excess vertical seepage occurs from the catotelm into the underlying aquifer.

Various feedback mechanisms may exacerbate these effects:

- development of vegetation with greater rates of evapotranspiration than typical for a little-damaged bog surface;
- development of fractures and fissures within the peat consequent upon drying;
- loss of some of the attributes of the original acrotelm.

The concept of the basal area of a peatland being too small to maintain the perched water mound close to the peat surface derives from the 'groundwater' mound theory, in which the height and shape of the water mound that defines the upper limit of the catotelm is related to the basal area and plan of the mire. This is illustrated in Figure 2.3. However, it is not axiomatic that a reduction of basal area will *necessarily* lead to a reduction of the height of the water mound over all or much of the bog. This is because in some bogs, especially large ones, the actual height of the peat surface is less than the hydrological maximum predicted by 'groundwater' mound theory (either because it has not had sufficient time to accumulate peat to the hydrological equilibrium position or

because on-going peat decomposition in the catotelm prevents the hydrological maximum being reached (Clymo, 1984)). Thus in large bogs it *may* be possible to make a considerable reduction of the total area without lowering the height of the water mound over much of the remnant. However, when the remnant is small, relative to its height, then it is likely that the water mound may drop to a position that is substantially subsurface.

The effect of drains upon a bog surface will depend upon their disposition, depth and frequency. They are likely to cause particularly marked water drawdown on the acrotelm, as it has a higher hydraulic conductivity than the catotelm. Indirect effects may also be important, for example through changes in water storage and species composition [2.2].

Loss of water by vertical seepage downwards from the peat into an underlying aquifer is only likely to occur in bogs that are located over permeable substrata (porous bedrocks, many glacial sands and tills) in which the groundwater head, which was once at, or above, the level of the bottom of the peat, has since been reduced consequent upon groundwater abstraction *etc.* This is considered to be an important source of water loss in many bog remnants in The Netherlands and N Germany (*e.g.* Schouwenaars *et al.*, 1992). Its importance in the UK is not known, though it may well affect both Thorne and Hatfield Moors. The possible significance of this for restoration in relation to residual depths of peat is discussed in section 4.4.5.

The potential water drawdown induced by marginal damage upon a mire massif is illustrated conceptually in Figure 2.3. Whatever the actual position of the reduced perched water mound, one main object of rewetting is to bring it back to an 'appropriate' position with respect to the peat surface over all or part of the mire. Deciding what is 'appropriate' may be an important subsidiary issue [3.2]. The second main object is to reduce water level fluctuations above the permanent perched water mound.

A number of approaches for rewetting bog massifs have been identified [see Box 5.1]. The salient features, limitations and appropriateness of these approaches for different situations are considered below. Note that these approaches are not mutually exclusive. It is often possible, and may be necessary, to combine different techniques to achieve optimum rewetting of massifs, due to the heterogeneous nature of many peat extraction complexes. All of the approaches assume that drainage ditches are blocked. For one, this is the only requirement. Three main types of bund have been identified – these are illustrated in Figure 5.1.

Box 5.1 *Potential approaches to rewetting bog massifs*
[see Figures 5.1 to 5.4].

Procedures based mainly on soaking:
(a)   *Elevation of the water level by ditch blocking*
(b)   *Non-intervention – natural subsidence of peat to the position of the perched water mound*
(c)   *Sculpting of the peat surface to the position of the perched water mound*
(d)   *Elevation of the water level by containment within wall bunds*
(e)   *Elevation of water level by increasing water levels in the surrounding area*

Procedures based mainly on inundation:
(f)   *Inundation using parapet bunds*
(g)   *Inundation by reduction of the level of the peat surface to form lagoons*

Other procedures
(h)   *Provision of supplementary water*

5.3.2 *Methods*

(a) Elevation of water level by ditch blocking

Fundamental to all rewetting options of peat massifs is blockage of any ditches that drain them [Figure 5.2 (i)], and this is the main focus of many restoration projects [Appendix 6]. Ditch blocking is essentially a *soaking* strategy. Its likely efficacy as the sole rewetting strategy for massifs (and cut-over bogs) will depend on the factors contributing to their dryness (including the hydraulic conductivity of the peat and underlying substrata) (see, for example, Schouwenaars, 1995). In some cases where superficial ditches provide more-or-less the only reason for dehydration, ditch-blocking alone may be sufficient to provide effective rewetting of the mire surface, or, particularly, to maintain the existing interest of a little-damaged mire surface. Indeed, in some little-damaged sites spontaneous

occlusion of (small) ditches has occurred.

Limitations

- The prime limitation is that in some sites periodic surface dryness may be a consequence of factors other than drains. Where dryness has been induced by an overall shift in the height of the water mound consequent upon a reduction of the basal area of the mire, it is unlikely that ditch blocking will effectively rewet the massif, though it may lead to wet conditions in and along the ditches.

- Where ditches have been particularly deep and extensive, slumping and wastage may have caused considerable change in the topography of parts of the massif. In this situation the topographical position of such ditches may mean that even when full of water they have little effect upon impeding drainage from some higher parts of the bog. In

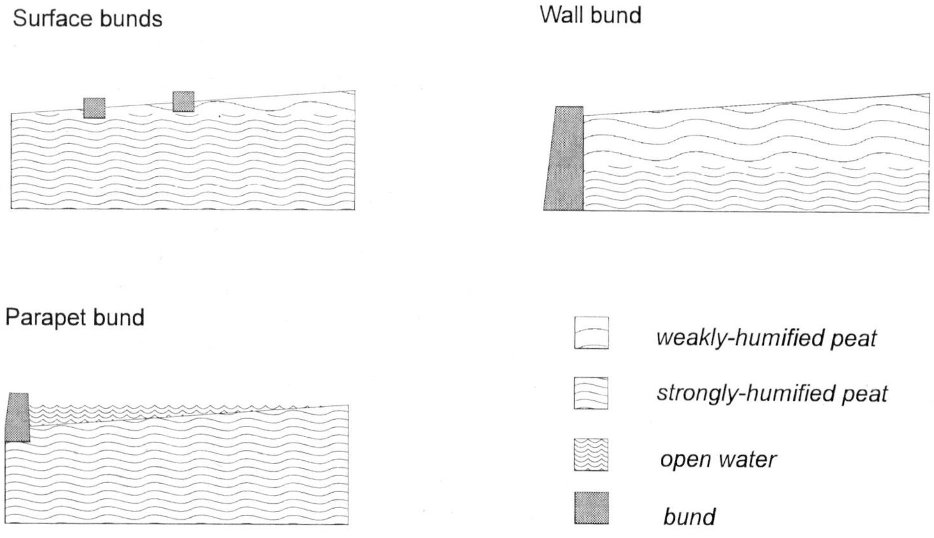

Surface bunds   Wall bund

Parapet bund

weakly-humified peat

strongly-humified peat

open water

bund

Figure 5.1 The three main types of bund which have been identified as being used in bog restoration projects. *Surface* bunds restrict lateral run-off through the upper horizons of weakly-humified peat; *parapet* bunds extend above the level of the adjoining peat massif, to form a long, low surface dam against which water may be impounded; *wall* bunds aim to elevate the water mound within the peat massif by reducing water losses due to marginal seepage and flow around some, or all, of its periphery.

some circumstances a stepped cascade of dams may be used to circumvent this difficulty.

- In damaged massifs without an acrotelm characteristic of a little-damaged bog, ditch-blocking may not be adequate to ensure a water table that is sufficiently stable close to the peat surface to permit the extensive establishment of *Sphagnum* species. This is mainly because evapotranspirative water loss, coupled with dry episodes lead to a reduction

of water level. The extent to which this limitation is important depends upon the topography of the massif and its climatic situation. It is especially important on surfaces with limited water storage and in regions that experience periodic and sustained droughts.

Possible application

- Blocking of active ditches is essential in any rewetting initiative.
- Ditch blocking is likely to be particularly effective in rewetting large bogs, with shallow slopes, where ditches are the principal cause of surface dryness.
- It is likely to be particularly effective in *maintaining* an existing bog vegetation but less well suited to *renaturation*, especially in drier parts of Britain.

Potential for vegetation restoration

In appropriate conditions, ditch blocking has been shown to help maintain existing bog vegetation, and to improve the condition of somewhat degraded vegetation (*e.g.* Roudsea Moss, Cumbria). We know of no examples where ditch-blocking alone has led to the widespread regeneration of an M18-type vegetation on a badly-damaged massif, though it seems likely that this process could occur on a small scale in badly-drained hollows within a massif. Ditch-blocking of a badly-damaged massif surface may sometimes create conditions suitable for some individual bog species. In the cooler and wetter parts of Britain, these may include some species of *Sphagnum*. In other situations, it is more likely to produce wet heath or, where particularly ineffective, a 'dry bog' community.

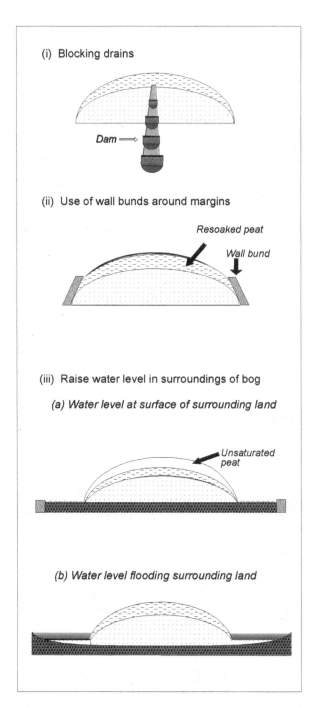

Figure 5.2 Approaches to rewetting badly-damaged remnant peat massifs based on resoaking.

(b) Non-intervention – 'natural' reconformation of peat to position of perched water mound

Perhaps the simplest approach suggested for the rewetting of bog massifs where the peat surface is elevated above the position of the water mound over all or part of the site is one of non-intervention, *i.e.* to permit natural processes of water drawdown, wastage and subsidence to occur. Its underlying presumption is that upstanding peat blocks will, by oxidation, slumping *etc.*, eventually reconform to the position of the 'new' groundwater mound within the massif. In such a process, increased humification of the superficial peats may help form a partial seal to the collapsing mire (Schneebeli, 1989; Joosten, 1992). It is essentially a *soaking* strategy.

Limitations

There is little, if any, evidence for the efficacy of this process in badly damaged massifs, but there is strong reason to believe that it has been important in a degree of 'accommodation' of the effects of marginal damage on otherwise little-damaged bogs (*e.g.* Wedholme Flow, Cumbria; Clara Bog, Ireland). Its potential value probably depends very strongly upon the starting conditions, in particular the prevailing climate. Two extreme starting conditions are considered below.

A: Site with badly-damaged surface with water mound well below surface

This situation is typical of a number of dry remnant massifs, where the surface is fairly dry over much of the expanse, supporting heath, *Molinia*, bracken, birch *etc.* and perhaps a few bog species that are relatively tolerant of drier conditions (*e.g.* *Eriophorum vaginatum*). In this situation the limitations to a passive restoration procedure based on wasting processes are:

- the wastage process may be protracted (measured in decades and possibly centuries, depending on the height difference between the peat surface and the position of the surface of the perched water mound);

- during this period part, or all, of the surface may be rather dry and incapable of sustaining a bog vegetation, and the value as even a temporary 'refugium' for bog species may be diminished;

- even when some bog species persist the site may need sustained management (birch removal *etc.*) to maintain the surface against invasive species; tree growth on damaged mires can lead to a loss of their characteristic fauna and flora, and sometimes induce considerable loss of hydrological integrity of the peat by fissuring;

- the presumption that the wasting peat surface will equilibrate at some stage at the zone of permanent saturation is questionable [see Figure 5.3]. In a diplotelmic mire an important role of the acrotelm is to supply water to the catotelm and hence maintain the zone of permanent saturation. By contrast, when a badly-damaged peat surface has wasted (let it be assumed) to the position of the perched water mound, other than in climatic regions where there is a near-constant input of meteoric water, the position of the water mound will continue to sink periodically below the peat surface in response to periods of dryness. Hence as the peat surface subsides, the zone of *permanent* saturation will also sink beneath it. Such periods of surface dryness may not only constrain the re-establishment of bog species; they may also permit ongoing wastage. It is then possible that the eventual consequence of a 'natural wastage' scenario will be the loss of the entire ombrotrophic peat deposit. This process is likely to be exacerbated if the subsiding surface is rather dry and supports a vegetation with high rates of evapo-transpiration (*e.g.* dominance of *Molinia* or birch);

- even when peat has wasted to a position proximate to the perched water mound, the water table may not be sufficiently stable close to the peat surface to permit the establishment of bog (especially peat-forming, *Sphagnum*-based) vegetation except, perhaps, in climatically-favoured localities.

B: Site with well-developed bog vegetation subject to minor marginal water drawdown

This situation is representative of a site which has suffered some marginal damage (for example, by peat extraction) and water drawdown, but where a well-developed bog vegetation exists over much of the surface and where the water-mound remains near the surface over much of the mire. In this situation the effect of marginal damage may have limited impact upon the rest of the mire, or processes of small-scale reconsolidation and slumping may permit rapid reconformation of the affected part of the surface to the surface of the new position of the perched water mound. The main limitations of non-intervention may then just be:

- drying of the margins of the massif will occur, the amount being determined by the degree of water drawdown;

- the edges may gradually conform to the edge of the water mound by slumping, oxidation *etc.*; they may, however, not rewet, and may continue to oxidise.

Possible application

There is little evidence to suggest that natural reconformation of the peat surface of a badly-damaged bog massif to the perched water mound will occur or will produce suitable rewetting of the peat surface, other than in a few specific cases.

- A non-intervention approach is unlikely to restore surface wet conditions in the foreseeable term to sites that have been badly damaged and where the water table is strongly sub-surface.

- A non-intervention approach is unlikely to preserve the character of 'good' quality bog vegetation when the mire is subject to an extensive reduction in the height of the perched water mound.

Situations where a non-interventionist approach to 'rewetting' may be acceptable are likely to be ones where the effects of drying will be small or where other rewetting strategies are not feasible, for example:

- in a mire site which supports 'good' quality bog vegetation over much of its area and where only the marginal areas are dry, if it is considered that drier margins are acceptable, and no lowering of the water table is anticipated;

- in sites where there has been a relatively small drop in the water level which has affected only a rather

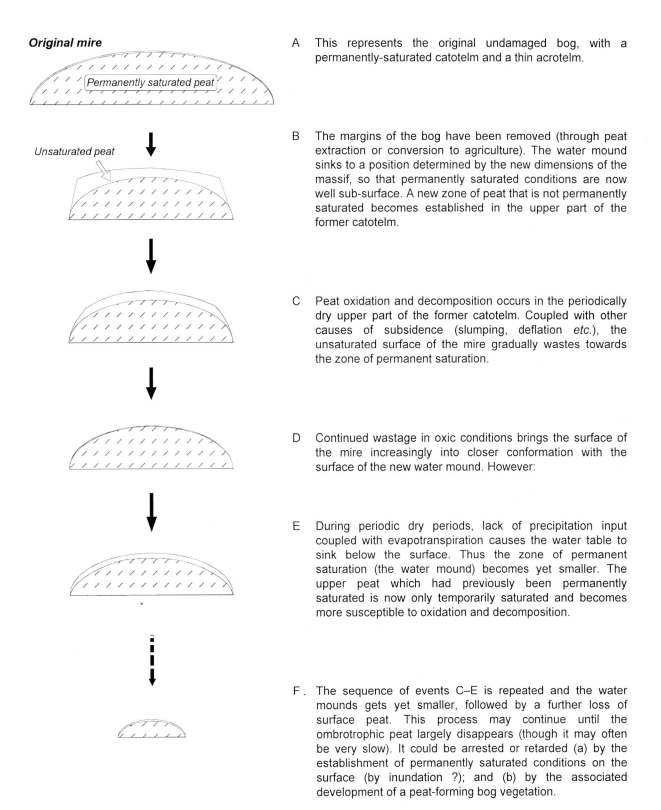

Original mire

Permanently saturated peat

Unsaturated peat

A   This represents the original undamaged bog, with a permanently-saturated catotelm and a thin acrotelm.

B   The margins of the bog have been removed (through peat extraction or conversion to agriculture). The water mound sinks to a position determined by the new dimensions of the massif, so that permanently saturated conditions are now well sub-surface. A new zone of peat that is not permanently saturated becomes established in the upper part of the former catotelm.

C   Peat oxidation and decomposition occurs in the periodically dry upper part of the former catotelm. Coupled with other causes of subsidence (slumping, deflation *etc.*), the unsaturated surface of the mire gradually wastes towards the zone of permanent saturation.

D   Continued wastage in oxic conditions brings the surface of the mire increasingly into closer conformation with the surface of the new water mound. However:

E   During periodic dry periods, lack of precipitation input coupled with evapotranspiration causes the water table to sink below the surface. Thus the zone of permanent saturation (the water mound) becomes yet smaller. The upper peat which had previously been permanently saturated is now only temporarily saturated and becomes more susceptible to oxidation and decomposition.

F . The sequence of events C–E is repeated and the water mounds gets yet smaller, followed by a further loss of surface peat. This process may continue until the ombrotrophic peat largely disappears (though it may often be very slow). It could be arrested or retarded (a) by the establishment of permanently saturated conditions on the surface (by inundation ?); and (b) by the associated development of a peat-forming bog vegetation.

Figure 5.3 Suggested scenario for the likely changes in badly-damaged peat remnants subject to natural processes of peat wastage. It is relevant to suggestions for rewetting of peat massifs by just allowing wastage to take place and to proposals to remove upper peat down to the predicted position of the water mound. The scenario assumes that seasonal dry periods regularly occur; the suggested changes are likely to take place more slowly in regions characterised by consistently high precipitation.

small area of the bog remnant; where the bog remnant is large and peripheral damage has been sustained gradually, or where the water drawdown at the edge of the massif affects only a narrow marginal zone (*e.g.* because the height difference between the surface of the massif and adjoining areas is small or because the peat is of low permeability);

- in situations where redevelopment of a *Sphagnum*-rich bog vegetation is not desired or is unlikely to be feasible for other reasons;

- where the surface configuration (*e.g.* hollows or block peat cuttings) of the massif permits the retention of locally wet conditions despite some degree of drying of more elevated parts;

- where 'good quality' bog vegetation towards the centre of the massif is already separated from the margins by a zone of damaged surface, which contains the drawdown and functions as a 'buffer zone'.

Non-intervention may be inevitable, for purely practical reasons, in peat-extraction complexes where there are numerous small block remnants at different levels.

Further considerations

As isolated peat massifs left to reconform by wastage may be rather dry, over some or all of their surface, and are perhaps colonised by large stands of birch and bracken, they may be vulnerable to incendiary events. Severe fires, which ignite the dry peat, may sometimes accelerate the restoration process by causing considerable loss of peat mass. At Thorne Waste, severe fires are thought to have caused a loss of some 30–40 cm of peat on some dry baulks (R. Meade, *pers. comm.*) and to have made them more conformable with the adjoining wet cuttings. Such 'combustion levelling' may, for several reasons, not be seen as a desirable management tool, but there can be no doubt of its efficacy in accelerating peat wastage. Nonetheless, wastage induced by this mechanism is likely to be subject to the same limitations as natural wastage if used as the sole restoration 'strategy'.

Potential for vegetation restoration

In some situations, some natural wastage may be compatible with the maintenance of existing *Sphagnum*-rich bog vegetation. However, where badly-damaged bog surfaces have been left to waste, the redeveloping vegetation is, in the short term at least, usually *Molinia,* bracken, birch scrub or heathland. Some of the more drought-tolerant bog species (*e.g. Eriophorum vaginatum*) may recolonise such situations. It is possible, particularly in the wetter regions of the UK, that a wider range of bog species

may ultimately establish on 'wasting bogs', but we have no evidence to support this.

(c) Sculpting of the peat surface to the position of the perched water mound

A more interventionist version of the 'natural wastage' approach is provided by the interesting suggestion of Bragg (1989) that peat could be removed to form a profile which, derived from 'groundwater' mound equations, would conform to the predicted position of the perched water mound in a peat remnant. Such an approach would reduce the potentially long time-span involved in natural wastage processes. Like natural wastage, it is essentially a *soaking* strategy.

Limitations

The fundamental limitations of this approach are the same as for the 'natural wastage' approach, especially that the zone of permanent saturation is likely to sink beneath the position of the sculpted surface during dry periods [Figure 5.3]; in addition:

- it may be difficult to predict the ultimate position of the perched water mound;

- it may be difficult (and costly) to sculpt the peat mound with the exactitude that is required;

- the surface thus produced may not be amenable to good renaturation due to water level fluctuations.

Possible application

- An innovative small trial restoration project undertaken by the Somerset Trust for Nature Conservation is currently in progress, in which a small area of peat (Getty's Mire) was contoured to the predicted shape of the 'groundwater' mound [Plate 5.1]. Water level measurements have shown that the water table was convex in the winter, following quite well the shape of the mound, but became concave during the summer. This corroborates some of the limitations identified above.

- Sculpturing of the peat surface in the way proposed may provide suitable conditions for the establishment of some bog species in some situations, but it is difficult to see what practical benefits this approach confers in comparison with some of the other, technically more simple, approaches discussed below.

Potential for vegetation restoration

As this approach has been little tried, few factual comments on its efficacy can be made. It seems *likely* that it would be possible for some of the more drought-tolerant bog species to establish on some surfaces and in appropriate climatic regimes, even that some *Sphagnum* species could colonise. However, we have no supporting evidence for this.

(d) Elevation of the water level by containment within wall bunds

An alternative, more elaborate approach to reducing the peat surface to the position of the perched water mound, is to elevate the water mound within the peat massif by reducing water losses due to marginal seepage and flow around some, or all, of its periphery [Figure 5.2 (ii)]. This can be achieved using a wall bund, made of low-permeability peat or, if this is unavailable, of inert materials such as plastic (or both) [8.2]. In effect, this raises the impermeable base of the bog and elevates the position of the perched water mound. In the simple form described here, this is essentially a *soaking* strategy, but can be modified to form a *flooding* strategy (see below).

Limitations

- It is relatively expensive to bund all or part of a bog, particularly if it is done well [7.3].

- As this approach involves elevation of the water mound above its natural position, it is potentially unstable. The bunds have to be substantial, well made and maintained to retain the water; weak bunds may be susceptible to collapse (for example, through a build-up of pressure behind the bund). It is possible that, in the long term, bunds may disintegrate through oxidative decomposition. As yet there is little direct evidence for this, but some allowance for on-going maintenance of at least the marginal bunds may need to be made. Provision must also be made for the control of water levels to allow discharge of excess water during periods of high rainfall.

- In steeply convex, or irregular, massifs it may be necessary to have two or even more concentric bunds if wet conditions are to be maintained at the summit; as well as being very costly these will inevitably cause local damage and interrupt the natural appearance of the massif.

- The water table may not be sufficiently stable close to the peat surface, particularly on badly-damaged surfaces. This may mean that the surface is not necessarily amenable to 'good' renaturation with *Sphagnum*-rich bog vegetation.

Note that most sites where substantial bunding has been used to retain water on a remnant massif are those with a considerable thickness of weakly-humified peat (*e.g.* Meerstalblok and Engbertsdijksvenen, The Netherlands). The relatively high permeability of this type of peat means that such massifs are particularly prone to water loss at the cut margins. In such situations wall bunds need not extend to the bottom of the peat deposit; it may be sufficient just to insert a plug of strongly-humified peat (or other low-permeability material) into a trench within the weakly-humified peat [see below and Figure 8.1].

Possible application

- This approach has been used, with some success, in rewetting raised-bog remnants in The Netherlands and Germany, for example at the Meerstalblok.

- This is an appropriate strategy for *maintaining* good quality bog surfaces on bogs where lateral water loss threatens survival. It may be less effective as a sole method for renaturation of badly-damaged massifs, particularly in drier climates, as it is essentially a *soaking* approach.

- This approach is appropriate for maintaining good quality bog vegetation upon massifs adjoining (or within) peat extraction sites. In principle, it is possible to maintain a wet surface across a considerable height differential between the top of the wall bund and the level of the adjoining ground, but very tall bunds are likely to be unstable and, where the height difference is great (>2 m) a series of stepped bunds would be desirable (or the surface from which peat is being removed should be graded up to the remnant).

- Even where long-term stability cannot be guaranteed, this approach may be important in sustaining bog refugia during peat extraction from its surroundings.

- Note that in principle it may also be possible to create a 'wet bund' by maintaining artificially high water levels near the edge of a peat remnant using pumped water. Nonetheless, a UK attempt at this approach by Heathwaite (1995) (the Ditch Recharge system at Thorne Waste) was unsuccessful.

Plate 5.1 Getty's Mire, Somerset Levels. Former peat workings mechanically contoured to the predicted shape of the 'groundwater' mound [see text].

Potential for vegetation restoration

This approach has been used with some success to maintain, and improve the quality of, existing bog vegetation (*e.g.* Meerstalblok, The Netherlands). Its efficacy as a starting point for renaturation of a badly-damaged massif surface is less clear; it seems likely that fluctuations of the water table may be inimical to the establishment of a *Sphagnum*-based vegetation, in drier regions at least.

(e) Elevation of the mire water level by increasing water levels in the surrounding area

A further possible method for elevating the surface of the water mound in a residual peat massif is by raising the water level in the surrounding land (peat-workings, farmland *etc.*) [Figure 5.2 (iii)]. In situations where a deeply sub-surface water mound in a peat massif has resulted from a reduction of the basal area of the mire, some hydrological control of the surrounding land, particularly that which once formed part of the original bog, may help to stabilise water in the mire remnant, for example by helping to reduce water loss to agricultural drains. However, it is far from certain that mere control of the drainage of the surrounding peat workings or claimed land will be sufficient to so elevate the water mound within the remnant massif as to rewet its surface adequately. The nature and magnitude of any such effects will depend primarily on the topography and relative heights (hydraulic head), as well as the amount of recharge to the catotelm and hydraulic conductivity of the peat. However, if it is possible to increase the water level on the land surrounding the remnant sufficiently (*i.e.* by flooding it) this could provide an effective method for resoaking the remnant massif.

Limitations

- The main problem with this approach is its practicality and likely cost.
- In some cases it would require the flooding of adjoining agricultural land.
- It may often be difficult to elevate the water table over the adjoining land sufficiently to re-soak the massif. This largely depends upon topography. Where the bog is in a closed basin it may sometimes be relatively easy to flood the surrounding land within the basin confines. However, many bog massifs are on floodplains or flat valley bottoms, and elevation of the surrounding water table would probably require a complex series of lagoons to impound the water.
- The water table may not be sufficiently stable close to the peat surface, particularly on badly-damaged surfaces. This may mean that the surface is not necessarily amenable to 'good' renaturation with *Sphagnum*-rich bog vegetation. It is likely that inundation around the periphery of the massif might damp water level fluctuations, though the significance of this would partly depend upon the configuration of adjoining inundated areas.

Possible application

- This approach could possibly be used to help rewet bog massifs in small basins.
- It could be used as part of a co-ordinated strategy for the restoration of a remnant massif and surrounding peat workings. [This is discussed further below.]
- This approach could also be used if it was thought desirable that agricultural land once claimed from the bog should be returned to a form of wetland.

Box 5.2 *Efficacy of re-soaking approaches to rewetting*

Re-soaking approaches (*i.e.* approaches aimed at elevating the surface of the perched water mound close to the peat surface) have achieved variable success in bog restoration, depending upon their situation and climatic context. We have noted the following, from field observations and reports:

(i) they can be very effective in *maintaining* or even enhancing a massif surface which is still in quite good condition (*i.e.* with a 'reasonable' development of bog vegetation and an acrotelm characteristic of little-damaged raised bog);

(ii) they are reported as being appropriate for sites which are damaged but which retain a thick horizon of fresh, weakly-humified peat, which can store water well and, in appropriate conditions, even swell in response to this, thus taking on some of the properties of the original acrotelm; this may be particularly the case in wetter, cooler climates but there seems to be little critical information;

(iii) they do not seem to provide an adequate basis for rewetting sites where the peat has high humification and low water storage characteristics.

Where re-soaking approaches do not lead to successful renaturation, the main limitations seem to be either that they do not address the root cause of dryness (as is the case with some ditch blocking procedures); or that they do not provide a stable water table that remains sufficiently close to the peat surface year round, in part because they do not necessarily increase water storage capacity at or near the bog surface. This is a particular problem in sites where the exposed peat has low water storage characteristics or in regions subject to long dry periods. In these cases the only realistic way of minimising the effects of fluctuating water levels may be by inundation strategies. These are not likely to be provided just by a 'groundwater' mound profile which, at best, is likely to be at the surface for only part of the year.

- As this is potentially an expensive restoration option, it is only likely to be appropriate for prestige projects where the aim is to protect a mire massif of much existing conservation value and to renature adjoining peat workings *etc.*

- There is little evidence to suggest that a return of the entire former area of a raised bog to a wetland condition is *necessarily* essential to maintain hydrologic stability in a remnant massif. This is because (a) in large sites the actual height of the peat surface may be considerably lower than the predicted hydrological maximum, *i.e.* the water mound can be sustained at this level with a bog basal area considerably less than that of the original mire; and (b) the construction of any lagoons that may be necessary to elevate the water level across the adjoining land may be a less stable approach than is the construction of wall or parapet bunds around massifs. Nonetheless, some control of drainage in the surrounding land (as in 'hydrological buffer zones' [8.3]) may well in some circumstances ameliorate some difficulties of rewetting the peatland.

- This approach may be useful as part of an overall restoration strategy in situations where loss of water through downward seepage is thought to be a problem.

Potential for vegetation restoration

Elevation of water tables over peat workings around a remnant massif has been used with considerable success at the Bargerveen reserve in The Netherlands and is discussed more fully below.

(f) Inundation using parapet bunds

The use of parapet bunds for rewetting [Figure 5.4 (i)] represents a development of the bunding approach discussed above [5.3.2(d)]. Both approaches, in effect, raise the impermeable base of the bog and elevate the position of the perched water mound. The difference is that with parapet bunds the bunds extend above the level of the adjoining peat massif, to form a long, low surface dam against which water may be impounded, and it is possible to accumulate water on the top of the peat massif. The extent to which this is possible will depend upon the topography of the massif. If it is domed then the effect will be to produce a moat of water; if flatter, it may be possible to inundate larger areas.

Limitations

- The limitations of this approach are similar to that discussed under 'wall bunding' [5.3.2(d)]. However, because this approach provides for some surface inundation, it effectively increases water storage in the vicinity of the peat surface. This may

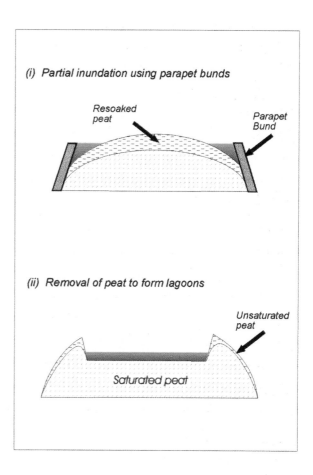

(i) Partial inundation using parapet bunds

(ii) Removal of peat to form lagoons

Figure 5.4 Approaches to rewetting badly-damaged remnant peat massifs based on reflooding.

reduce the amplitude of water-level flux and provide an environment more conducive to the establishment of typical bog species on degraded bog surfaces.

- One of the main problems with the use of this approach is that on sloping massifs it may not be possible to rewet more than a small proportion of the surface. In strongly domed bogs it may be necessary to have a series of concentric bunds if more widespread surface inundation is required.

Possible applications

- This approach has been used to rewet some bog massifs in The Netherlands. In some instances it has been adopted in consequence of the failure of other, more simple, procedures to produce the desired goals. For example, parapet bunding has been constructed in part of the Engbertsdijksveen [Plate 5.2], in recognition of the failure of ditch blocking to rewet the mire remnant. In other sites (*e.g.* Meerstalblok), previous wall bunding has been extended upwards to form a parapet to permit flooding of parts of the mire surface.

Plate 5.2 'Parapet' bund, causing flooding at the margin of an upstanding peat remnant; Engberts-dijksveen (The Netherlands).

- This is an expensive restoration procedure, but is one that may be more suited to the renaturation of badly-damaged surfaces than is wall-bunding. In some instances it may be the only practicable way to rewet massifs within peat extraction complexes. It would, for example, be appropriate for some of the elevated massifs at Thorne Waste which are currently difficult to keep wet. In view of its likely cost, it is particularly appropriate to apply this approach to areas which already have a known and important biological interest.

- Where the vegetation of the massif is already of 'good' quality, there may be little to be gained by using parapet bunds compared to wall bunds, unless there is a perceived need to increase the water level.

Potential for vegetation restoration

This approach has been used with some success to maintain, and improve the quality of, existing bog vegetation. It has also been used with some success to rewet degraded bog surfaces, though as these initiatives are mostly recent, it is difficult to judge their long-term potential for renaturation.

(g) Inundation by reduction of the level of the peat surface to form lagoons

An alternative restoration option attempts to resolve the rewetting problem not by elevating the water level but by decreasing the elevation of the peat surface, to form a lagoon [Figure 5.4 (ii)]. It differs from the approach of sculpting the peat surface to the water mound [5.3.2(c)] in that it aims to produce a series of hollows that can store water. The inundated areas may be configured to act as *growth lagoons* for direct plant colonisation or as *feeder tanks* to help soak adjoining baulks of peat. This approach has, inadvertently, been

widely used to maintain wet conditions within peat massifs, as in some mires old peat workings within upstanding blocks of peat provide wet conditions with regenerating bog vegetation. This approach may provide a more stable solution to rewetting than does elevation of the water level using wall bunds, in that it is less dependent upon bunding for its success, and also because it involves reducing the height of much of the peat surface to a position where the lagoons will hold water. It also often leads to larger flooded areas than does inundation using parapet bunds [Figure 5.4 (i)]; note that the construction illustrated in Figure 5.4 (ii) is purely conceptual; in practice it would often be desirable to subdivide the main lagoon into a series of smaller compartments.

Limitations

- Depending on its scale, this approach may involve substantial peat extraction, with attendant practical, conservational and palaeoecological problems.

- It is directly damaging to peat surfaces and would be detrimental to any existing wildlife interest.

- It is obviously artificial and is most likely to contribute to a species-centred conservation strategy (aimed at the preservation of bog species) than a mire-centred one (regeneration of an entire, growing mire), particularly if only small-scale hollows are excavated.

- It cannot be *assumed* that hollows excavated on a massif surface will necessarily retain water; this will be determined by the hydrodynamics of the massif. Moreover, ongoing wastage of the drier surroundings may mean that this is not sustainable in the very long term.

Possible applications

- This type of renaturation has occurred, inadvertently, at many raised-bog sites, where hollows and lagoons currently provide some of the main reservoirs for bog species and *Sphagnum*-rich vegetation (*e.g.* Thorne Moors, S. Yorks.). [See Chapter 2].

- It is particularly well suited to renaturation of badly-damaged bogs in drier regions as it can readily provide the flooded conditions appropriate for the development of semi-floating rafts of *Sphagnum.*

- It is likely to be an effective rewetting strategy for peat massifs comprised largely of strongly-humified peat.

- It is particularly appropriate for surfaces that have limited existing biological interest.

- If constructed as part of an agreed commercial peat extraction process it would be considerably cheaper than most other restoration strategies that are likely to be effective in comparable situations.

Potential for vegetation restoration

Numerous examples illustrate that peat cuttings can provide the main repository of typical bog species in some massifs and that they have potential to develop into examples of *Sphagnum*-rich vegetation comparable to M18 communities.

Further considerations

The value of excavation of pits to optimise water level conditions in mires has long been recognised by conservationists; shallow scrapes or deeper excavations have been dug for various purposes. The evident value of topographical depressions is seen in a number of mires that are otherwise rather dry, where peat cuttings, or other hollows provide the only reservoir of bog species. Even where extensive ditch blocking or bunding operations are being considered to raise water levels, small scale cuttings may help to provide a temporary habitat for Sphagna, to act as foci from where the *Sphagnum* can expand across the surface once an adequate water regime has been reinstated[1] Clearly the scale of any peat excavation operations will also depend on other management being considered and the desired end-point, and, of course, the condition of the existing vegetation (if any).

Removal of a layer of surface peat on some drained sites prior to rewetting may have other potential benefits. It may remove dry mineralised surface layers of peat, which may be enriched (Eigner & Schmatzler, 1980; Jortay & Schumacker, 1989), though it is far from clear if this is an important consideration. It can also remove short-term seedbanks of potentially undesirable species such as *Molinia* and, of course, physically removes any unwanted species as well.

This restoration approach, deliberate or spontaneous, can be very effective at creating a series of 'bog gardens' within damaged massifs. These may support a large reservoir of typical bog species, but this approach is more obviously 'artificial' than are some other rewetting strategies. The perceived suitability of this approach thus depends strongly upon the objectives formulated for restoration. One of its features is that parts of the massif surface are not rewetted and are particularly susceptible to ongoing oxidation and wastage, which may threaten the long-term stability of the 'bog garden'. Of course, this constraint applies to all rewetting approaches where part of the surface is aerobic for much of the year and does not support peat-producing plants.

---

[1] In some sites this role may in fact be played by the water in the dammed ditches, or borrow pits.

(h) Provision of supplementary water

An alternative approach to the problems of water retention is to directly irrigate peat massifs (or indeed peat workings) with water. This is generally only appropriate for small peat remnants because of the large volume of water and resources that are required. This approach has also been little tried (examples include Dosenmoor, Germany (Müller, 1980); Shapwick Heath, Somerset; Thorne Waste, S. Yorkshire). Clearly, the original causes of dehydration and current water losses also need to be carefully investigated (and remedied as far as possible) in order to assess the feasibility of providing supplementary water through a pumping scheme.

Possible applications

For most situations, the use of elaborate pumping schemes should be avoided as they are non-sustainable. However, pumping may be considered in certain circumstances, for example:

- to 'kick-start' the system – *i.e.* to provide an initial input of water to 'prime' the system;
- to preserve archaeological artefacts and palaeo-ecological values;
- to maintain water levels in boundary ditches to reduce outputs from the site;
- to keep specific areas wet as a temporary measure before full remedial action can be taken due to ongoing peat extraction;
- to maintain water levels as a temporary measure during periods of drought.

Clearly, if this approach is considered, then to maintain an ombrotrophic vegetation it is important that only ombrotrophic water should be introduced, as the consequence of introducing minerotrophic water is to promote the development of fen vegetation. Where only nutrient-enriched minerotrophic water is available, it may be possible to achieve some improvement in water quality by passing the water first through a 'buffer zone', for example, using a reed bed.

Limitations

- This approach is generally only appropriate for small peat remnants because of the large volume of water and resources that are required.
- Unless provision has been made to store large volumes of meteoric water, in many cases the only supplementary water available is likely to be minerotrophic.
- Oxygenation and movement of the water may stimulate decomposition of peat and archaeological artefacts by micro-organisms.

Box 5.3 *Approaches to rewetting based on surface inundation*

Many of the approaches to rewetting described here are based upon resoaking of the peat rather than inundation. Resoaking strategies may help to elevate the level of permanent saturation within a massif, but the water table may still show considerable fluctuation and may not provide the consistently wet peat surface that is required for renaturation. Restoration based upon surface inundation thus provides a rewetting approach, which, on the basis of field evidence, can provide a very satisfactory basis for the development of *Sphagnum*-dominated vegetation, particularly in drier regions (Schouwenaars & Vink, 1992). This has been observed in various restoration schemes on the near-Continent and by experimental studies on *Sphagnum* re-establishment (Money, 1994, 1995). It is corroborated by the occurrence, in many bogs, of well-developed *Sphagnum* vegetation (M18a) in abandoned, flooded peat cuttings coupled with an absence of such vegetation on adjoining uncut surfaces. Such cuttings initially develop loose rafts composed of the more 'aquatic'

Sphagnum species, but species such as *S. capillifolium*, *S. magellanicum* and *S. papillosum* can subsequently establish.

The value of some surface inundation is primarily (a) that it increases the water storage at the surface of the bog; (b) that any decrease in water levels will be less relative to the peat surface when the area starts inundated with water than would be the case for a similar drop where the maximum water level is at the peat surface; (c) it provides a good medium for colonisation by some *Sphagnum* species and (d) it is conducive to the development of floating rafts of vegetation, which can remain wet even with considerable water-level fluctuations. This approach does, however, have its own limitations, in particular that optimal inundation conditions for effective recolonisation are not known with certainty. They are determined *inter alia* by such considerations as: (i) optimal water conditions for growth of some *Sphagnum* species; (ii) mechanisms of rafting; (iii) problems of wave damage; (iv) problems of damage by wildfowl attracted to open water.

Potential for vegetation restoration

At Shapwick Heath, Somerset, an elaborate pumping scheme is operated to maintain wet conditions around an ancient wooden trackway (The Sweet Track, see Plate 1.7). As the only water supply available was minerotrophic, this has unfortunately lead to the development of fen woodland on the *Sphagnum* peat. At Thorne Waste, water has been pumped from drains in the area of active peat workings into some abandoned cuttings. As this has only been carried out recently, it is too early to comment on the success of this approach, although there is preliminary evidence that flooding has retarded the previously-vigorous growth of some birches.

5.4 Rewetting options for extensive peat workings in bog peat

5.4.1 Introduction

Peat workings most often represent topographical depressions with respect to any adjoining peat massif and rewetting may often be easier to achieve than on a massif. This is because problems of lateral water loss may be less acute; because the workings may serve as sumps which collect water from adjoining slopes and higher peat ground and because the hydraulic head is smaller than for an upstanding remnant. They also provide the opportunity of conforming the peat surface to maximise its potential for water storage. Ideally, agreement on final desired conformations would be reached by negotiation between conservationists and the peat industry.

The two main problems of rewetting peat extraction complexes are related: (i) providing adequate water

storage; and (ii) preventing lateral (and possibly vertical) water loss. The solutions to these problems will depend upon (a) the topography and disposition of the peat fields; (b) the nature of the remaining peat exposed; and (c) the climatic context.

Situation, topography and rewetting

Approaches suitable for rewetting abandoned peat workings depend very much upon their situation and character. Workings can occur as large complexes clearly distinct from remnant massifs, but also as depressions within massifs. In some cases, such as where there are small peat cuttings within a dome of raised peat, or where only a limited amount of peat has been removed, so as to leave a damaged but still upstanding dome, the problems of maintaining a positive water balance and the options for rewetting may be much the same as those for the mire massifs, as discussed above[1]. Indeed, in some cases former peat extraction has inadvertently produced a condition similar to that suggested as an option for rewetting of some raised-bog remnants [Figure 5.4].

In other cases extraction of peat has progressed so far as to remove most traces of the original peat dome and to leave a sometimes complex arrangement of peat fields, ditches and baulks largely unrelated to the former topography of the mire. In this situation the rewetting strategy need take little direct account of the former disposition of the peatland as the solution becomes essentially one of engineering. This may include artificial manipulation of the water table and construction of lagoons *etc.*

---

[1] Note, however, that this will in some considerable measure depend upon the character of the residual peat.

Even in sites that have been largely cut-over, the considerations advanced for the rewetting of upstanding blocks still sometimes apply. This is because in some cases the cut-over complex may still form a massif with respect to the surrounding landscape and thus shares the problems of rewetting of a massif.

The approach adopted to rewetting peat workings is likely to be determined primarily by the topography of the residual peat, or of the underlying mineral substrata. The surface topography of abandoned peat extraction complexes is sometimes not well suited for easy restoration. Cut-over surfaces may sometimes occur at various levels which can mean that it is difficult to achieve a wide-scale rewetting by simple procedures. The peat fields may also sometimes be quite steeply sloping, which not only causes problems of water retention, but may also induce some measure of surface gullying and erosion.

Water levels

The critical question of 'desirable' water levels in renaturation strategies may need to be addressed even more for peat extraction areas than with the upstanding remnant peat massifs. In particular, whereas with the latter the question of what is desirable may become subsumed by the practicalities of what is possible (depending on the rewetting strategy), in abandoned peat fields there may be a much greater opportunity to specify desired conditions, by engineering *etc.*

On flattish peat surfaces (such as are produced by peat milling) it is usually difficult to maintain a fairly stable water table at around the peat surface without some engineering. In such situations the lack of water provision within the peat needs to be compensated by some other supplementation mechanism, especially retention of surface water (*i.e.* inundation). In this circumstance, the rewetting of peat extraction complexes becomes a question of how water can be impounded (which is largely a function of topography) and to what appropriate depth.

Areas of open water can function (i) as *growth lagoons* (*i.e.* to provide an aqueous matrix for pioneer bog vegetation); or as (ii) *feeder tanks* (to rewet adjoining blocks of solid peat by water seepage). Experience has shown the importance of the former approach in the development of floating rafts of vegetation [4.3], and the use of open water as a *growth lagoon* is therefore considered as being of primary importance. This is not necessarily incompatible with their use as *feeder tanks*, depending on the water balance.

Where peat has been removed close to the base of the mire, the lowered surface may be increasingly susceptible to inputs of minerotrophic water from the surrounding landscape. Unless it is thought desirable to

recreate fen vegetation (or such water is base-poor), such supplementary water is undesirable and it is necessary to ensure that a sufficiently impermeable strip of peat remains around the mire as a buffer zone, to prevent ingress of groundwater [8.3]. For this same reason, deliberate pumping of groundwater into the workings to help maintain a high water level would be similarly undesirable [5.3.2(h)]. Removal of peat close to the base of the mire is also likely to increase rates of vertical seepage downwards, in situations where this process can occur (*e.g.* Schouwenaars, 1993).

5.4.2 *Block cuttings*

Introduction

Extraction of peat using the block-cutting method often produces a regular system of baulks, flats and trenches[1] [2.3.1]. The disposition of these is important to restoration options, as they can be used to increase water retention. Block cut sites are sometimes thought to be particularly amenable to restoration. This is usually because the peat cuttings may already be 'bunded', in whole or in part, by baulks which confer some hydraulic integrity upon the cutting. Block cuttings are also often quite small and this, with its associated high edge:area ratio, may provide both protection from wind and wave action in inundated sites and facilitate colonisation by plants and animals.

Many re-flooded block cuttings have been spontaneously colonised by *Sphagnum*-based bog vegetation (sometimes referable to M18) and in some sites sustain a rich biological resource. The close juxtaposition of wet cuttings with contrasting habitats (*e.g.* heathland on separating baulks), and the interface between them, may contribute to the high biodiversity and natural history interest of such sites. However, it not axiomatic that block-cutting sites are rich repositories of bog species, nor that they are always readily rewetted.

It is sometimes suggested that block cuttings are more amenable to recolonisation than, say, milling fields because of plants and animals that have survived upon (or have recolonised) the intervening baulks of peat (or within the trenches). This is very likely to be correct with comparatively small-scale peat operations, but it is not a universal feature of block-cutting procedures. In some block-cutting complexes, the environment and vegetation of the baulks has been so modified (*e.g.* by damage and dehydration) as to permit few bog species to survive, even where there is a long period between successive cuts. In other cases, the block-cutting cycle

---

[1] Note that this is not always the case: extensive block-cutting can eventually produce a largely flat surface comparable to a milling field.

of has been of such short duration as to 'sterilise' the surface of the baulks as effectively as any milling operations.

Ditch-blocking is likely to be a prerequisite for the rewetting of block-cut sites, and in some situations it may also be necessary to reduce rates of vertical water loss into the subsoil by completely filling the drainage ditches. The presence and functioning of tile or mole drains across the peat fields should also be assessed, and drains blocked as necessary. However, the effectiveness of ditch-blocking alone for rewetting will largely depend on the topography of the site. [See also 5.4.3]

Effects of topography

In an appropriate topographical context (*e.g.* where block cuttings form natural sumps), it may be sufficient to ensure that the cuttings are sealed for them to rewet (ditch blocking alone may be sufficient (Meade, 1992)). They partly then function as tanks that store (winter) rainfall. This may buffer them against excessive water-table drop during dry periods, and they can serve either as growth lagoons or as feeder tanks.

In some situations rewetting of block cuttings may be difficult. For example, when the cuttings are located upon a residual peat massif the water level in the cuttings may be dominated by the behaviour of the perched water mound in the massif as a whole, and rewetting of the cuttings will be dependent upon rewetting strategies for the massif (see above). Cuttings situated within weakly humified peat may be

particularly influenced by the behaviour of the water table in a surrounding peat massif and in circumstances where the perched water is low they may be particularly susceptible to dehydration, despite any greater storage properties of such peat. However, many abandoned commercial cuttings are within quite strongly-humified peat.

Some block-cutting sites possess a very uneven topography, with various states of revegetation [see Figure 5.5]. Where cuttings have been made at very different levels, it may be possible to rewet individual cuttings, but more difficult to integrate this into an overall rewetting strategy. Particularly intractable problems may be presented where there are residual massifs of strongly-humified peat within a cutting complex. In this situation it may be difficult to devise a rewetting strategy that provides optimal water level conditions for a large number of cuttings, at least without a large amount of earthworks. Here, it may be necessary to consider an integrated approach using ditch blocking and parapet bunding (possibly in addition to and extending existing baulks) together with some removal of peat to produce a more level field.

The problem of baulks

Although the network of baulks in a block-cutting site may be beneficial, for example, in helping to retain water in cuttings and for access, the baulks themselves may be difficult to rewet permanently. This frequently gives rise to a characteristic patterned landscape of wet, revegetated cuttings separated by strips of heath or,

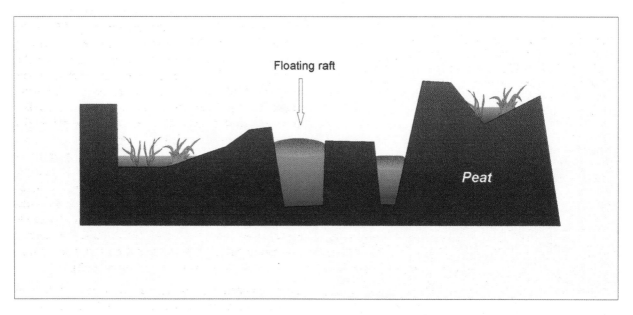

Figure 5.5 Revegetation of re-wetted block-cut peatland. In this configuration of cutting surface, the shallow pools periodically dry out and support only vegetation with purple moor-grass and cotton grass. The deeper pools show similar water level flux but have developed a floating raft of *Sphagnum* which accommodates this change. The uneven topography permits good revegetation of some individual cuttings, but is less well-suited to re-wetting of the entire complex.

where continued management is not possible, by scrub or woodland (*e.g.* Risley Moss, Cheshire; Crowle Moor, Lincs.). Where the cuttings are themselves narrow, development of scrub, or even vigorous *Eriophorum vaginatum,* on the baulks may eventually shade much of the cuttings as well as the baulks [Plate 5.3]. Moreover, as long as the baulks remain summer-

Plate 5.3 Revegetated block cuttings at Lichtenmoor (Germany). Dense growth of *Eriophorum vaginatum* on the floor of the cuttings shades growth of Sphagna in the ditches. Baulks are dominated by *Molinia caerulea.*

Plate 5.4 Block peat cuttings flooded to the level of the top of the baulks; Fenns Moss (Clywd).

dry they will effectively ensure that bog regeneration is confined to the cuttings.

One solution to this difficulty, in those situations where it is possible, is to try to elevate the water table in the cuttings to be level with the surface of the baulks [Plate 5.4], so that they can be more effective as feeder tanks. However, there is little current evidence that it is possible, just by maintaining high water levels in the cuttings, to rewet peat baulks sufficiently so that tree growth will be prevented (though it may be reduced) or so that a wide range of bog species will establish. This is not least because water tables tend to drop during the summer months, though the magnitude of this will partly depend upon the climate. One suggested solution may be to promote irrigation of the baulks by a network of grips extending from the cuttings, but we have not seen this employed in practice. This would also depend on maintaining water levels so that the grips did not act as drains in periods of low water supply.

An additional consideration with regard to raising the water level in the cuttings is the height difference between the base of the cutting and the surface of the adjoining baulk, when this is great (> 50 cm). The resultant deep water in the cuttings may not be optimal for growth of even aquatic *Sphagnum* species [5.4.1; 5.4.4].

Alternative approaches to the problem of too many baulks are to reduce their height, total area or frequency (especially where the cuttings comprise a large number of thin, parallel baulks), as carried out at Peatlands Park (Armagh) [Plate 5.5]. Such operations all require the removal of peat which may be expensive when peat extraction at a site has ceased, although it may be possible to use the peat to help fill in the ditches. It is also difficult to carry out once rewetting has started. Where manipulation is possible, careful consideration should be given to the most desirable ratio of baulk to cuttings in terms of achieving rewetting objectives and to the height of the baulks. Increases in the ratio of open water to baulk (by levelling selected baulks) may help to reduce water level fluctuations as open water has a higher water storage coefficient than peat (it would also be feasible to use the peat from the 'redundant' baulks to block trenches and drains). If the baulks around the open water area are too thin (< *c.* 5 m), a sufficiently stable water table may not be maintained owing to leakage and slumping of the baulk, and the water balance may show greater losses than gains (Beets, 1992).

If it is impractical to reduce the height or area of baulks, and where high water tables in the adjoining cuttings do not adequately rewet their surface, consideration may be given to inundation of the baulks by elevated water levels across part or all of the cutting complex. The feasibility of this will depend largely on

Plate 5.5 Recolonisation of former block peat cuttings; Peatlands Park (Armagh). Lowering baulk heights and raising water levels resulted in extensive colonisation by *Sphagnum cuspidatum*. The area is normally flooded in winter.

the topographical situation of specific sites. Where the cuttings form a large topographical bowl, it may be possible to achieve this just by blocking outfall ditches. However, where this is not the case (for example, where the cuttings are located upon a peat massif) then it will be necessary to create an artificial seal around the cutting complex, for example using a parapet bund [Figure 5.4; Plate 5.6].

Conclusion

It may be concluded that, in certain circumstances, block-cut surfaces may provide a good template for revegetation, but that this is not an invariable property. Also, even where successful revegetation has occurred within block-cuttings, the developing pockets of mire vegetation may not readily spread from the cuttings to coalesce across baulks. Approaches to the restoration of block-cutting complexes may therefore need to be phased to consider (i) the water management and revegetation of individual cuttings (*i.e.* the nucleation of bog regrowth and (ii) the wider issue of water management and revegetation of the entire peat-cutting complex. It should be noted that once substantial parts of the site are wet and regenerating, options for subsequent human intervention (engineering *etc.*) become progressively more limited.

5.4.3 Milled-peat workings

Introduction

Many current peat operations use some form of surface milling [2.3]. In this, a succession of thin layers of peat are shaved from the surface of cambered beds during each harvesting season. The fields are usually large, and are typically drained by a series of deep drains, sometimes fed by mole or tile drains beneath the peat surface. The surfaces remaining after peat extraction ceases are usually bare and dry, and when abandoned,

Plate 5.6 Extensive bunding around former peat cuttings; SE Bog, Cors Caron (Dyfed) [Photo: J. Davis] [See also Plate 8.2]

the fields may have only a shallow depth of typically strongly-humified, compressed peat. The surface may be flat or sloping. Sometimes the fields may be confined within un-worked peat banks, usually at very infrequent intervals.

Milled peat fields are sometimes thought to be some of the most difficult peat surfaces to restore, apparently on account of their extensive area and featureless, and sometimes sloping, topography. Where they have exposed strongly-humified peat they may be inconducive to adequate water storage and retention. Water retention is particularly problematic on sloping fields, which normally suffer rapid runoff and, sometimes, erosion. Nonetheless, there is little reason to suppose that milled fields are necessarily more difficult to rewet than would be block cuttings made on a similar scale. This is because milling fields can themselves be sculpted to provide a topography analogous to block cuttings, or can be bunded to retain water. Both of these activities require investment of resources into surface preparation for restoration. There are currently few examples of long-term restoration projects on milled surfaces, but it is likely that restoration will only be possible if successful attempts are made to retain precipitation, to prevent erosion and to accelerate vegetation colonisation by manipulating the surface relief (Pfadenhauer, 1989).

(a) Ditch blocking

Blocking of drainage ditches is essential to prevent water loss from milled peat fields. As for block-cuttings, in some situations it may also be necessary to reduce rates of vertical water loss into the subsoil by completely filling the drainage ditches and to take into account the effects of any mole or tile drains across the peat fields.

Limitations

- The effectiveness of ditch blocking in rewetting milled surfaces will depend largely upon the topography of the site. Where the milled fields are sloping, ditch blocking is unlikely to retain water at or near the surface of the peat, though it may maintain high water levels in and along the ditches (as at Breitenmoos, Germany). In flatter sites, ditch-blocking may retain water levels close to the peat surface for at least part of the year.

- Even on flat sites, ditch blocking alone is unlikely to produce a water regime conducive to the re-establishment of a full complement of bog species. This is because there is often considerable flux of the water table. In dry periods, the water table typically sinks some considerable distance below the surface. This may not be so great a problem in regions that are consistently wet, but generally milled peat extraction is impractical in such regions.

- Except in favoured topographical situations, ditch blocking alone is unlikely to provide much surface inundation. It thus offers little potential for increasing storage of surplus precipitation water, nor provides conditions for establishment of bog species other than those which are most tolerant of periodic dryness.

Possible applications

- Ditch-blocking is likely to be a prerequisite for the rewetting of all milled surfaces.

- In most cases ditch-blocking is unlikely to be sufficient for regeneration of a bog vegetation on milled peat fields. An exception to this is where milled fields are surrounded by high peat baulks which permit inundation just by blocking the main ditch outflow through the baulks. Even here, it is likely that some more complex constructs would be beneficial to revegetation (see below).

Potential for vegetation restoration

Except in situations which are in some way confined, ditch blocking by itself is unlikely to support regeneration of bog vegetation, except perhaps very locally in shallow depressions. Usual observed developments are species-poor *Molinia* grassland, birch scrub *etc.* Where the milling fields are topographically confined, so that surface inundation is possible, it should be possible to encourage the redevelopment of *Sphagnum*-rich bog vegetation.

(b) Impoundment of water in lagoons

One approach to rewetting milled peat surfaces is to create a series of lagoons which impound meteoric water [Plate 5.7]. These not only prevent, or reduce, lateral water run-off but also serve to store water. This helps to prevent the occurrence of low sub-surface water levels during prolonged dry periods and also provides an appropriate growing medium for pioneer, aquatic species of *Sphagnum*. Such lagoons provide the same sort of habitat as do the cuttings of block-cut peatlands. They can be created either by leaving baulks of peat *in situ* during extraction (unless these have become too dry to be effective) or by building walls of peat after operations have been completed. They are essential if water is to be retained on sloping surfaces and are probably also beneficial on flat surfaces, by subdividing what would otherwise be extensive stretches of water, subject to considerable wind and wave action *etc.*

On sloping surfaces problems of rapid runoff exacerbate lack of water storage. In this situation lagoons can be constructed as a paddy-field-like

Plate 5.7 Experimental restoration project in former milled peat workings, involving impoundment of water in constructed lagoons; Gardrum Moss (Falkirk). [Photo: C. Turner]

cascade [Figure 5.6] (see Nick, 1993). These reduce erosion on slopes to a minimum, hold precipitation water on to the area and regulate discharge of surplus water, ideally to retain sufficient water to be favourable for *Sphagnum* growth. Lagoon cascades can also be used, in principle at least, for *gradient feeding* (Joosten & Bakker, 1987). This is appropriate for sites that are particularly subject to summer drought and uses the upper lagoons as reservoirs to store winter water to help top-up lower lagoons during dry periods, an approach which may help to ensure hydrological stability in at least part of the site.

The dimensions and disposition of the lagoons will depend on the fall in height across the surface of the area to be rewetted, but areas of 1–10 ha have been suggested. The size may also depend on the disposition of the proposed lagoons in relation to the surrounding land, as in some situations, the creation of such lagoons may come under the provisions of the Reservoirs Act, if permanently flooded [Appendix 2]. The natural disposition and accumulation of water across the surface should be studied and the information utilised in any design solution. Each lagoon should have an outlet at the bottom to allow excess water to escape after heavy rain or snow to avoid damage to the peat walls. However, it is thought that these walls need not be completely water tight, as water will seep into the lagoons lower down in the series.

Limitations

- Construction of lagoons is more expensive than ditch blocking.

- Construction requires an adequate availability of a relatively impermeable construction material (ideally strongly-humified peat) if the walls are to be built rather than being created from peat left *in situ* (which may have become too dry to be effective). In some cases, dark peat at the bottom of a bog may be suitable. In this case it is important to ensure that a sufficient thickness of peat remains to supply material for wall building as well as to limit any downward seepage, without penetrating to underlying fen peat or mineral soil in those sites where this would disadvantage the desired renaturation.

- Lagoon walls may require some maintenance for long-term stability. In practice this may be of consequence only for the outer peripheral walls as, ideally, renaturation should be well advanced by the time that internal walls deteriorate. Nonetheless, it is always possible that heavy storms could cause premature damage to internal walls.

- On flat surfaces at least, the lagoons are likely to provide a rather uniform water depth which may restrict, at least initially, colonisation just to those species that are well adapted to those specific

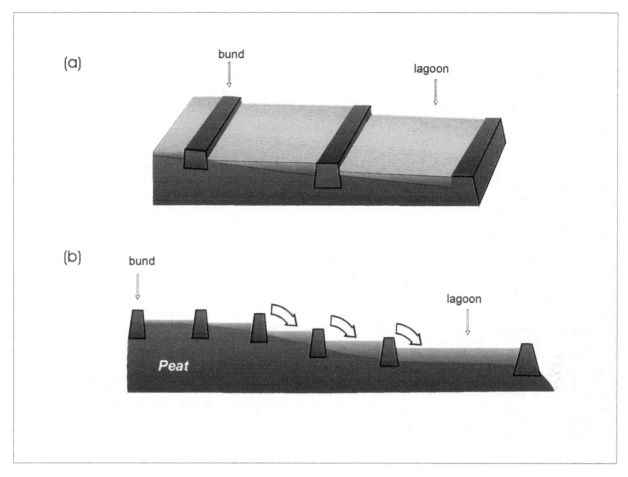

Figure 5.6 Terraced cascade re-wetting of sloping cut-over peat surfaces. Overflow water from the upper lagoons can be used to augment water in the lower ones.

conditions (*e.g.* aquatic Sphagna). However, in practice, even ostensibly 'flat' lagoons may show some topographical variation; moreover, this apparent limitation may actually be beneficial, because if the surfaces are not flat, any relatively dry areas with lagoons may be subject to invasion by birch *etc.*

- Small-scale topographical manipulation and heterogeneity may assist the establishment of a greater variety of species, but these may well include birches and *Molinia* on the drier places.

- Areas of open water may be attractive to wildfowl.

Possible applications

- This appears to be the single most useful technique for rewetting extensive milled surfaces, when the aim is to regenerate a *Sphagnum*-rich vegetation.

- A technique such as this is essential to rewet sloping surfaces

- This rewetting technique could also be used on milled fen peat surfaces and would provide considerable opportunity to influence the character

of the recolonist vegetation by manipulation of water levels.

Potential for vegetation restoration

This rewetting technique has been used effectively to rewet abandoned peat surfaces in The Netherlands and NW Germany (*e.g.* Lichtenmoor and Leegmoor, Germany; Amsterdamsche Veld, The Netherlands), and has led to the establishment of extensive carpets of *Sphagnum cuspidatum*, often with species such as *Molinia caerulea* and *Juncus effusus* [Appendix 6]. In some cases, these latter seem to encourage growth of *Sphagnum* species [9.2]. Peat stratigraphical studies have shown that in numerous raised bogs the development of a bog-building vegetation (with species such as *Sphagnum magellanicum, S. papillosum*) has arisen from a wet phase of *Sphagnum cuspidatum*. Thus, whilst most examples of this restoration strategy are still in their infancy and have not progressed much beyond the *S. cuspidatum* phase, it is to be expected that, providing a positive water balance is maintained, they will follow a comparable developmental pathway (as has occurred in some older, block-cut sites). Given the isolation of some sites it *may* be necessary to re-introduce some species that have been lost from the near vicinity. It is also possible that atmospheric contaminants (especially NH$_4$) may inhibit the re-establishment of some *Sphagnum* species, or otherwise influence the development of the vegetation.

(c) Impoundment of water in sculpted hollows

Another approach to the rewetting of extensive milled fields would be to scrape large, shallow hollows in the peat, to produce a scalloped surface which stores water in the depressions. In principle, this is similar to the construction of lagoons, but relies upon the excavation of peat rather than the construction of walls. It has been suggested that sculpted hollows may appear more 'natural' and be intrinsically more stable than a lagoon-based approach.

Limitations

- This approach may be better suited to flat surfaces rather than sloping ones.
- If the hollows are to be extensive and deep enough to store much water (to *c.* 50 cm depth) this approach would require substantial excavation and movement of peat.
- In sites which have retained only a thin layer of ombrotrophic peat, substantial excavation may be impractical, or is likely to expose underlying fen peat or mineral soil. The effect this would have upon revegetation will depend upon the exact character of these materials.
- The sloping sides of the scallops provide a substantial hydrological gradient from flooded to fairly dry. Whilst this may well increase the range of species that can quickly establish on the peat surface, it is also likely to provide considerable opportunity for the massive establishment of 'undesirable' species such as *Molinia* and birch in the drier areas.

Possible applications

- In principle this approach could be used in many of the same situations as lagoons. The choice between the two methods is likely to rest mainly upon depth of residual peat, engineering convenience, slope of the site and on whether it is desired to regenerate bog across most of the milling field surface or just within excavated hollows.
- We know of no site where this approach has been used on more than a very limited scale (*viz.* by excavation of surface scrapes) (*e.g.* Somerset Levels).

Conclusion

In some sites, milling has produced natural hollows and basins within the peat, which may provide a focus for water storage but these may be small. In others, an entire milling field may form a very large basin bounded by walls of uncut peat and in this situation it may be possible to keep the floor suitably wet with few additional constructions just by blocking the main drains (as at the Amsterdamsche Veld, The Nether-lands). In this situation some small-scale sculpting of the surface, as a series of depressions and hummocks (Eggelsmann, 1987, 1988b – see also Nick, 1993; Heathwaite & Göttlich, 1993), may help to increase storage [Plate 5.8]; and subdivision of the field by baulks may help to reduce damage to developing vegetation by wind turbulence and wave action (though the evidence that this is *necessarily* desirable is inconsistent). A further benefit of small-scale topo-graphical manipulation is that the heterogeneity may assist recolonisation and establishment of various species. Unfortunately, some of these latter may include birches and *Molinia* on the drier spots and in some instances such approaches to rewetting take on more the appearance of the cambered beds used by foresters to plant conifers in waterlogged soils than that of an exercise in mire restoration!

The optimal strategy for rewetting and restoring milled surfaces will partly depend upon particular site circumstances. In general, the approach adopted in North Germany (*e.g.* Leegmoor) has much to commend it, with the construction of paddy-field like lagoons (1–10 ha may be an appropriate size), though possibly with a slightly greater degree of inundation (see below). This appears to be the only effective strategy where the milling fields are sloping – design of the restoration of the mire will be strongly dependent

Plate 5.8 An attempt to increase microtopographical variation by small-scale sculpting of the peat surface as a series of depressions and hummocks; Leegmoor (N. Germany).

upon topography. This will be not just to use topographical features to help retain water, but also, in low rainfall circumstances, to devise configurations that can benefit, if necessary from 'gradient feeding' or some other form of water supplementation. Where the surface is flat and confined, few earthworks may be necessary, but even here some degree of compartment-alisation may be desirable. If there is next-to-no topographical variation within the lagoons thus created, some minor topographical manipulation of the peat surface could be countenanced but it is not evident that this offers much material advantage. As an alternative to formal lagoons, excavation of shallow depressions scraped within the milling fields could be tried.

It has been suggested that peat extraction could be planned so as to leave, at completion, a residual surface configured as a dome of peat approximating to the predicted position of the 'groundwater' mound (Bragg, 1989). However, there appear to be inherent practical problems with this approach, and it cannot be recommended until there is further evidence that it may prove to be an appropriate strategy [5.3.2(c)].

5.4.4 Depth of inundation

As within peat extraction complexes there is considerable opportunity to determine and manipulate the maximum height of the water table by engineering, it is necessary to identify an appropriate water level. Various considerations will influence this.

Approaches to rewetting based on just soaking the peat are likely to be unsuccessful due to excessive water loss during dry periods. This is a particular problem in sites on peat with limited storage capacity (*e.g.* Blankenburg, 1992) and in summer-dry climates. Thus such soaking may not provide an adequate basis for revegetation of such sites, except where some supplementary water (such as is provided by gradient feeding) is available to help maintain water levels in the cut-over peats. By contrast, some degree of surface inundation increases water storage, provides a suitable growth medium for pioneer species of *Sphagnum* and permits the development of floating mats of vegetation which can better accommodate water level flux than can plants growing on solid peat surfaces [Figure 5.7]. It may also help to control the growth of 'undesirable' plant species, such as *Molinia caerulea* [Plate 5.9] and birch [see Plates 10.2 and 10.3].

The depth of water impounded within lagoons *etc.* may not always be easily regulated – the depth will reflect water availability, topographical or constructional feasibility rather than ecological desirability. However, choice of an 'ideal' water depth is influenced by several considerations:

- In a block-cut peatland, deep filling of the (bunded) cuttings may be desired, to help rewet the adjoining uncut peat. The feasibility and suitability of this will depend upon the height difference between the top of the uncut peat and the bottom of the cutting.

- In any cut-over peatland, the depth of winter

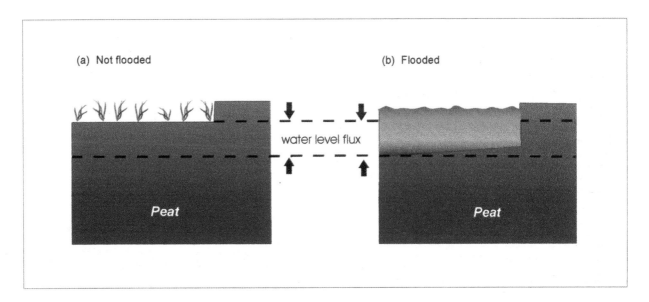

Figure 5.7 Restoration of peat excavations by inundation. In (a) the maximum water level only reaches to about the level of the cutting surface. Thus in dry periods the declining water level leaves the cutting surface relatively dry. Fluctuations in water level of this sort are mainly conducive to the growth of a small number of species such as cotton grass and purple moor grass. In (b) the cutting surface is relatively lower, so that for most of the year it is inundated. In dry periods the water level may sink slightly below the cutting surface, but it does not become dry. The relatively deep water may preclude growth of rooted species, but will permit rafting by species such as *Sphagnum*. The floating mats rise and fall with water level flux and thus experience relative hydrological stability.

flooding will be partly determined by water loss during the summer – *i.e.* it needs to provide sufficient storage to prevent water levels going too far below the surface for long periods during the summer. Depths of winter inundation of some 0.2–0.6 m have been calculated to be appropriate (*e.g.* Schouwenaars, 1995).

- Growth of pioneer *Sphagnum* species (especially *Sphagnum cuspidatum*) is promoted by water depths that are continuously supra-surface, but not too deep (50 cm summer depth seems to be an optimal maximum value, unless there is some additional aid to flotation).

- Some of the 'best' examples of revegetation seen was as floating rafts on deep (*c.* 1 m depth) water (*e.g.* Meerstalblok and Haaksbergeveen, The Netherlands; Wieninger Filz, S. Germany), but the mechanism of raft formation in such circumstances is not always well established.

The approach of shallow-water flooding used in some

Plate 5.9 Tussocks of *Molinia caerulea*, killed by flooding; Fochteloërveen (The Netherlands).

Plate 5.10 Extensive colonisation of former bare peat surfaces by *Sphagnum cuspidatum* and *Molinia caerulea,* within shallowly-flooded lagoon; Lichtenmoor (N. Germany).

north-German peatlands (*e.g.* Leegmoor – Plate 5.10) has been very successful in permitting the colonisation of extensive bare peat surfaces by *Sphagnum* species and may provide an appropriate way forward. It still remains subject to considerable water level fluctuation, though it may be expected that this effect will diminish as a thicker mat of *Sphagnum* accumulates.

In situations where it is readily possible to have deeper water flooding (as in cutting bays within a block-cut complex) one revegetation strategy would be to have a phased inundation: (a) to initially establish a base of ombrotrophic vegetation in shallow flooded conditions; and then (b) to impose deeper inundation upon this. There is some evidence that the established vegetation may lift to form a floating raft when flooded.

Attention should also be given to inoculation of rewetted areas with plant material (including *Sphagnum* species), the use of artificial aids to rafting and the possibility of enhancing recolonisation by such treatments as fertilisation [9.6]. These have already shown some potential value on a small scale (Money, 1994, 1995) but they will need to be scaled up before a firm conclusion on their potential benefits can be reached.

5.5 Rewetting extensive peat workings in fen peat

5.5.1 Introduction

In Britain, commercial extraction of fen peat (both within and without former raised-bog sites) is practised now only in the Somerset Levels. However, extraction of fen peat once occurred much more widely, and former excavation of bog peat has led to the exposure of underlying fen deposits in numerous mire sites.

The topography of fen peat workings shows internal variation (reflecting excavation techniques) and variation with respect to the surrounding landscape, reflecting events both in the mire and the wider landscape. Some deposits form massifs slightly elevated above the surrounding landscape, much as with bog peat massifs. This configuration may arise because of drainage and shrinkage of the surrounding land. In other sites, the exposed peat surface may be more-or-less level with the surrounding land, or peat removal may have produced depressions below the general ground level. When abandoned, these sometimes readily flood with telluric water.

In broad terms the rewetting of fen peat surfaces is subject to many of the same constraints as those of bog peat surfaces of comparable topography, and similar rewetting strategies may be appropriate. However, an additional consideration is possible inputs of telluric water. The fact that fen peat has formed indicates that at one time this horizon of the developing mire had been irrigated by telluric water. This may have originated from various sources (springs, river inundation *etc.*) which today are not always readily identifiable (and may no longer exist), on account of natural or man-made changes to the hydrology of the mire's catchment (*e.g.* embankment of rivers, construction of drains *etc.*). In consequence, possible telluric present-day water sources (and water quality) available to rewet fen peat workings may bear little relationship to those under which the fen peat was laid down.

Because there are various possible sources of telluric water input into cut-over fen peat (and sometimes the possibility of no obvious source at all) it is correspondingly difficult to make generalisations about water management options applicable to many fen peat workings.

The restoration significance of any telluric water inputs to the rewetting of cut-over fen surfaces depends upon the desired objective of restoration. On the one hand, such inputs may sometimes be instrumental in helping to rewet the site; on the other, they promote the redevelopment of fen vegetation. If this is not seen to be a desirable development (*i.e.* if the restoration objective is bog), it may sometimes be possible to build peripheral bunds or dams both to impound meteoric water and to exclude telluric inputs. In this situation, revegetation will still re-commence upon minerotrophic peat, but an absence of further telluric water inputs should help to shorten the fen phase. The success of this approach will depend considerably upon the topography of the deposit, the character of telluric inputs (if any), and the quality of precipitation recharge. Where the fen peat surface has only just been exposed, and where the peat deposit stands proud of the surrounding land, precipitation can be the major source of water input, and rewetting considerations are then much the same as with bog peat. However, where pits have been dug into the fen peat, so that the peat surface is below that of the surrounding landscape, it is correspondingly more difficult to exclude telluric inputs. And whatever the topographical situation it may be difficult to exclude telluric inputs when these are derived from upwelling groundwater springs.

The outcome of rewetting strategies on fen peat depends both upon the character of the irrigating water and the level at which it is maintained. As a general rule, assuming that some irrigating water is minerotrophic, a re-soaking strategy is likely to lead to the re-development of a fen vegetation which may have only a long-term potential to re-develop into bog. A flooding strategy (especially if with nutrient-poor water) is likely to produce a seral, floating fen vegetation which may have great intrinsic value as well

as a potential for quite rapid (100–250 years) re-development of bog vegetation (*e.g.* van Wirdum, 1995).

5.5.2 Rewetting of flat fen peat surfaces

The following broad strategies can be adopted, either individually or in combination:

(a) Ditch blocking

The potential value of ditch-blocking depends upon the topography of the site. Where the peat surface is elevated with respect to some or all of the surrounding water table, ditch blocking will help retain water on the site and will usually be a prerequisite of restoration initiatives. It may principally retain meteoric water inputs, though retention of minerotrophic water may also occur in some situations.

If adopted as the sole approach to rewetting, ditch blocking is liable to be subject to the same limitations identified above for bog peat. The main differences are (a) that it may be easier to maintain a permanently high water table, depending on the relationship of the peat workings with the surrounding landscape and water table and (b) that, even if periodically low water tables occur, the vegetation that re-develops (some form of fen or fen meadow (if grazed or mown) or fen carr (if unmanaged)) is more likely have higher conservation value than would the vegetation developed on bog peat in a similar situation. (This is because low-productivity vegetation on moist, base-rich peat is itself uncommon and often species rich.)

In some topographical situations, ditch-blocking may be needed, not to retain water on the site, but to prevent the ingress of minerotrophic water, should this be regarded as undesirable.

(b) Irrigation by telluric water *via* ditches or by surface flooding

Minerotrophic water from sources internal or external to the peat deposit can be distributed around the cut-over surface by ditches, either with or without more general surface flooding at times of water surplus. External water sources may include adjoining rivers and drains, but where the peat deposit is above the level of the adjoining land, external water may have to be pumped into the mire. The effects of these procedures depends upon the topography of the site; slight depressions may accumulate water whilst mounds may remain largely dry. Fen sites depending on river-flooding or ditch irrigation can show considerable seasonal water flux. Much of the peat may be waterlogged during the winter months, but during the summer there will be a tendency for the water table to fall. This occurs particularly in land parcels distant from the ditches. Care must also be taken to prevent the ditches acting to remove water, especially during dry periods.

Rewetting by periodic flooding or ditch irrigation can reinstate some form of fen vegetation upon the peat surface, but its character depends primarily upon the degree and permanence of soil saturation, the chemical composition of the peat and the irrigating water and type of vegetation management (if any). The most likely development is of a form of fen vegetation typical of summer-dry fens (such as fen woodland when unmanaged or fen meadow when mown or grazed). This is likely to be rather coarse and species-poor if the irrigating water is nutrient-rich. This approach to restoration is in current use at Woodwalton Fen, Cambridgeshire (a former cut-over raised-bog site).

It is likely to be inconducive to the re-development of bog, not least because of the incidence of low summer water tables. It is most appropriate for situations where maintenance, or recreation of fen vegetation is a restoration objective, or as a specific, short-term measure.

(c) Impoundment of water in lagoons or sculpted hollows

A fen peat surface can be engineered to produce lagoons or sculpted hollows that retain water (as described above for peat workings in bog peat [5.4]), as in the Somerset Levels, and Turraun Bog, Ireland [Appendix 6]. These can be used either primarily to impound precipitation inputs or to hold minerotrophic water (from various possible sources). Revegetation in the first situation may be subject to much the same constraints as described in section 5.4, with the additional constraint that it may be necessary to take steps to exclude minerotrophic water when appropriate. However, proximity to minerotrophic water sources can also mean that a more stable water table is more readily maintained. Where lagoons are designed to produce surfaces inundated with minerotrophic water, likely developments are as in 5.5.3.

Note that some types of fen peat may be a less suitable (less cohesive and more permeable) constructional material than some bog peats.

5.5.3 Rewetting of fen peat basins

Peat extraction in mires has sometimes created discrete pits and basins, either dug in bog peat and floored by fen peat, or excavated largely (or entirely) within fen peat. These may occur at various scales, sometimes just as trenches produced by block-cutting or as much larger depressions. Some former (now revegetated)

peat excavations in fen peat have been large (>16 ha). Such peat cuttings are very widespread in fens. Some current excavations in the Somerset Levels form comparable basins.

The water budget of cuttings in fen peat may be more complex than that of comparable examples in bog peat and water management options again will depend upon topography, available water sources and restoration objectives. In some sites drains which have been dug to evacuate water from the workings may need to be blocked to permit reflooding; in other situations such drains may provide an important supply of minerotrophic water. In some cases it may be necessary to install devices that can regulate the water level to a predetermined maximum.

Where such hollows are rewetted with minerotrophic water, fen vegetation can redevelop rapidly, its character being determined largely by water depth and fluctuation, base-richness, nutrient-richness and management regime (if any). Spontaneous rewetting of peat-cut basins within fen peat has occurred in a large number of mire sites in the UK (some of them former bog sites). When they are reflooded, hydroseral recolonisation can occur, often producing floating mats of fen vegetation. These rafts, when irrigated by water of suitable quality (nutrient poor but relatively base-rich) can provide a suitable basis for spontaneous succession to bog, as well as having much intrinsic value (some prime examples of fen vegetation in Britain occur in recolonised peat cuttings).

In some instances it may be possible to exclude minerotrophic water from fen peat basins by damming inflow ditches *etc.*, so that they are irrigated primarily by meteoric water. This may be particularly appropriate where the minerotrophic sources are rich in nutrients and where it is desired to recreate a nutrient-poor wetland.

5.6 Integrated restoration of remnant massifs and commercial peat fields

5.6.1 Introduction

In some commercial peat workings, peat extraction has occurred across almost all of the surface, leaving an expanse of peat fields with no remnant massifs. In other sites the peat fields are interspersed with upstanding remnant massifs, of various dimensions. Remnant massifs may vary considerably in their characteristics. Small remnants are often dry and may have rather little biological interest. Other examples, particularly larger ones, may retain a wealth of typical bog organisms, either as a surviving part of the original bog surface (*e.g.* Wedholme Flow, Cumbria), or as species that have recolonised older peat workings upon the massif (*e.g.* Thorne Waste, S. Yorkshire). The retention of the species complement of such sites is important both in its own right and because it provides a proximate source of recolonist species for the operational peat workings [Chapter 2]. The peat stratigraphy and archive of the massifs may also be considered important. Where 'good-quality' massifs occur it is desirable that they are maintained in a suitably wet condition for the duration of the adjoining peat extraction operations. However, remnant peat massifs can impose their own constraints upon the development of restoration strategies for the entire site, particularly if the objective is *whole bog* restoration. This is because the surface of the massif may be so elevated above the level of peat fields that it requires independent water management to that of the latter. It should be recognised that in some peat workings, the surface topography of massifs (*e.g.* sloping surfaces, large variations in height) may make their restoration to surface-wet conditions practically impossible. Co-operation between restorers and the peat industry is desirable in order to produce, on cessation of peat-extraction, topographies amenable to restoration.

The approaches appropriate for the restoration of composites of massifs and peat fields are dependent upon (a) the height difference between the massif and the final cut-over surface and (b) the surviving biological value of the *massif*. The height difference is important in several respects. For example, where the height difference is great then the rewetting of the massif will usually have to be independent of that of the peat fields. The massif is also likely to remain proud of the peat fields for a considerable period and may require water management for this time. The biological value is also an important consideration, as it will influence the desirability of maintaining surface wet conditions within the massif.

In some sites it may be appropriate to focus water management activities upon the restoration of just one of the two components: for example, where the massif is large relative to adjoining peat fields it could form the main focus of restoration initiatives; where it is small, it may perhaps be regarded as a dispensable feature, (though in some cases one which provides a refuge of bog species until conditions in the adjoining, rewetting peat fields are appropriate for recolon-isation). The biological and archaeological resource sustained by the massif are likely to influence this choice: where massifs have limited current importance as reservoirs of bog species it may be inappropriate to engage in costly water management initiatives additional to those of the peat fields. However, in other situations it may be desirable both that the remnant has

long-term protection whilst the peat fields are also restored.

The options for the water management of composite sites, where the aim is to restore bog conditions in both the peat fields and the massif, are essentially:

(i) to treat the massifs and peat fields largely as separate objects; this approach involves the artificial maintenance of high water levels in the massif and does not attempt to restore the bog as a single entity. The possibility of future integration, as accumulating peat over the peat fields coalesces with that on the massif, is not precluded but is unlikely to occur rapidly;

(ii) to unify the massif and the extraction fields by encouraging or engineering a common water mound appropriate to maintain, or recreate, wet conditions in the massif. The possibilities for this depend upon the salient characteristics of the water mound associated with the remnant massif. Two approaches which have been suggested are (a) to reduce the height of the massif to the level of a sustainable water mound (by creation of lagoons); and (b) to elevate the water levels (over the peat fields) around the remnant massif [5.3.2(e)].

5.6.2 Independent water management of massifs and peat fields

(a) Preservation of the peat massif by bunding

As discussed above [5.3] remnant massifs can be maintained in a wet condition, or rewetted, by appropriate bunding of their margins, in large measure independent of surrounding conditions. Bunded massifs can be maintained within composite peat extraction complexes, but they will often be effectively independent of the water management of the peat fields and they may have to be managed as independent entities (for the foreseeable future) rather than as a single, regenerating mire. An exception to this is where the height difference between the massif surface and the peat fields is small, when early coalescence between the growing surfaces of both components may be expected.

5.6.3 Reduction of height of all or part of remnant massif

(a) Natural reconformation of the surface of the massif

One beguiling suggestion, in terms of simplicity and cost, is a non-interventionist approach in which remnant massifs are allowed to waste and slump until they eventually naturally reconform to a position in equilibrium with the water regime maintained in the surrounding peat fields.

Limitations

- The limitations identified above [5.3.2(b)] with respect to the possible rewetting of individual massifs by 'natural wastage', of course, apply also in composite peatland sites, *viz.* that there is little reason to suppose that the surface of damaged massifs will necessarily rewet satisfactorily just in response to wastage. It is possible that the massif would completely, if gradually, waste away to the position of the water level maintained in the peat fields.

- The feasibility of this approach for rewetting of the massif depends upon the topography of the site and the possibility of impounding water over the peat fields to a depth sufficient to saturate a significant proportion of the massif (see below).

Possible applications

This approach to integrated restoration may sometimes be determined by lack of resources for more elaborate approaches. It may be particularly appropriate:

- where the height difference between the massif surface and the peat field surface is small;

- where elevation of the water level within the surrounding peat fields (usually inundation) elevates the position of the perched water mound within the massif to a position close to the surface;

- where the massif retains a 'good quality' bog vegetation and where it is acceptable to permit some drying of the margins (and probably loss of vegetation 'quality' at the periphery) *either* because the total area of the 'good quality' vegetation is large *or* because the amount of peripheral damage is predicted to be small;

- where the climatic regime is suitable (*i.e.* cool and consistently wet) for the direct establishment of *Sphagnum* on damaged or wasting bog surfaces;

- Where the massif is already badly-damaged so that there is likely to be little loss of biological interest upon wastage, whatever the outcome.

(b) Reduction of the height of the massif by peat removal

An alternative approach to permitting wasting processes *etc.* to run their natural course is to substitute for them by peat extraction, to reduce the height of the massif to a level at which it can be adequately rewetted integral with water management of the adjoining peat fields.

Limitations

- Peat removal would remove the peat archive. [This may also eventually occur by processes of natural wastage].

- Peat removal would remove any biological value associated with the remnant. The extent to which this represents a constraint depends upon (a) the nature of the biological resource of the remnant massif; and (b) the likely long-term stability of this resource in the absence of other water management measures.

- Peat removal may destroy the reservoir of species for recolonisation of adjoining peat fields. [It is possible that this could to some extent be mitigated by transfer of the massif surface directly to the peat fields, provided that the latter had been rewetted into an appropriate condition to receive it.]

Possible applications

An exception to the above situations may be provided when the vegetation *etc.* is *demonstrably* not stable and where 'interest' is likely to be lost anyway. In this situation a 'rescue' operation (*i.e.* transfer of some or all of the remnant surface to adjoining peat fields in a suitable receptor condition) could be contemplated.

Peat removal from remnant massifs could be considered when:

- the massif has limited value as a reservoir for bog species or archaeology;

- the massif is unlikely to become effectively rewetted by other procedures, because of problems of 'difficult' topography or lack of resources;

- when the height difference between the surface of the massif and peat fields is great and when the massif area is small.

Planned peat removal from remnant massifs may not seem an attractive option to some conservationists. However, it should be recognised that in some cases its effects may be similar to those that will be produced more slowly by natural processes of wastage *etc.* Ideally the potential for the rewetting of massifs should be considered with respect to the cessation of peat extraction: there may be little to be gained if premature curtailment of peat extraction results in a bog topography that is particularly difficult to rewet.

5.6.4 Elevation of the water table around a remnant massif

(a) Elevation of the water table in basins

An alternative approach to an integrated restoration of remnant massifs and surrounding peat fields is to elevate the water table over the peat fields sufficiently to effectively rewet the remnant massif. In suitable topographical situations (such as a closed basin) it may be possible to do this just by allowing the peat fields to fill with water, confined by the basin topography [Figure 5.8(a)]. However, this approach is inappropriate for many commercial peat workings, which are often on rather flat, unconfined sites. In this situation the alternative approach, if possible, is to elevate the

water mound around the residual massif by appropriate bunding. Note that in either case consideration must be given to the depth to which the peat fields will flood, both in terms of their potential for revegetation and considerations of safety.

(b) Reconstruction of the water mound around a remnant massif on flat sites

On flat surfaces, elevation of the water table on the peat fields relative to the massif surface is more difficult than in a basin and will inevitably entail the construction of bunds to impound water. In situations where the height difference between the surfaces of the massif and the peat fields is small, the construction of simple lagoons across the peat fields may be sufficient to maintain high water levels in the massif. However, when the difference is greater, this approach may be inadequate to maintain the surface of the massif in a suitably wet condition [Figure 5.8 (b,i)].

A more elaborate approach, appropriate for this situation, is to reconstruct the water mound around the remnant massif. The principle of this approach is illustrated in Figure 5.8 (b,ii). It differs from simple inundation of the peat fields in that lagoons of increasing elevation are used to build the water mound in a series of steps. On level surfaces this may be achieved by a series of bunds of varying height; on peat surfaces which rise up to the massif, there will be less need for tall bunds and associated deep lagoons.

Limitations

- This approach involves considerable bunding and may be expensive, though the magnitude of the operation will depend upon the height difference between the surface of the massif and the peat fields.
- Where the surface of the peat fields is more-or-less level, bunds near the massif will be tall and the associated lagoons will be deep. Consideration must be given both to the stability of the bunds and to the prospects for revegetation of deep lagoons.
- Where the surface of the peat fields rises up to the massif, shorter bunds will be needed, but the slope may require bunds at frequent intervals.

Possible application

- This approach could be used for the integrated restoration of many composite peat workings. Where the height difference between the remnant massif and the peat fields is not great, it may be little more expensive than the normal cost of creating lagoons on abandoned peat fields.
- Where substantial peat engineering is required, this approach is perhaps best seen as a prestige approach, that may be used in sites where the

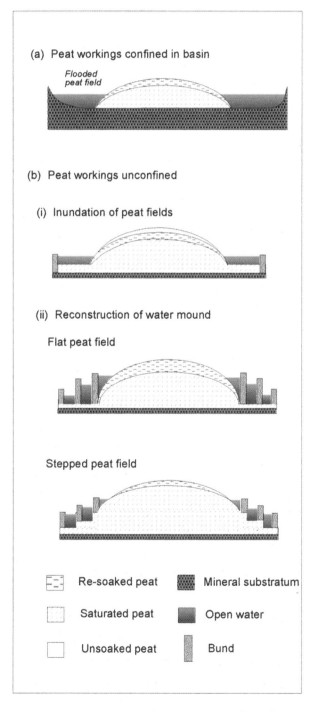

Figure 5.8 Rewetting of remnant massifs and peat fields

residual massif has particularly great conservation importance.

Potential for vegetation restoration

This approach has been used with considerable success in the restoration of the Meerstalblok in the Bargerveen reserve (The Netherlands). Here, lagoons peripheral to the remnant massif, over worked peat surfaces, have helped to rewet the massif, and have themselves revegetated well [Plate 5.11]. At this site, some adjoining agricultural land is also to be flooded to help maintain the water balance of the area. [This stems partly from a desire to prevent the possible development of oxidising conditions *beneath* the peat mass as a result of lowering groundwater tables.]

5.7 Maintenance of remnant massifs during peat-extraction operations

5.7.1 Introduction

In sites where peat extraction is taking place adjacent to peat massifs that sustain important populations of bog species, it may be desirable to protect these from excessive water loss, occurring in consequence of the extraction operations. Factors associated with peat extraction which may contribute to water loss include: (a) direct drainage of the adjoining massif (either as a deliberate policy to drain the massif, or as a consequence of ditches dug across the massif to evacuate water from the operational peat workings); (b) reduction of basal area of the massif; and (c) increase in hydraulic gradient between the surfaces of the massif and the peat fields. The requirement to minimise any water drawdown and loss in the massif induced by ongoing peat removal will depend largely on the importance of the massif for bog species. Where the bog massif already supports few bog species, but is, for example, heathland, there may be little need to protect it against water loss (although this does not necessarily mean that rewetting should not be attempted.) Where the massif supports 'high quality' bog vegetation, some form of protection is likely to be necessary.

Whilst peat operations are in progress, the priority requirement is likely to be to protect any existing interest rather than to attempt restoration of areas which are already badly-damaged [see Chapter 6], unless these can be incorporated into an integrated strategy at an early stage. Thus, water management strategies will most often be those which aim to *maintain* wet conditions rather than to *restore* wet conditions. For such purposes, strategies which aim at *re-soaking* are likely to be appropriate.

Plate 5.11 Floating rafts of vegetation (including *Sphagnum cuspidatum, S. recurvum, Eriophorum angustifolium, Erica tetralix*) developed in reflooded, bunded block-peat cuttings; Meerstalblok (The Netherlands).

5.7.2 Bunding

Peat massifs can be protected from water loss by the construction of an impermeable bund around all or part of their periphery. Bunds can be constructed from low permeability peat or from an artificial, inert low-permeability material. Various arrangements of bunds can be used, as discussed in previous sections. The required character of the bunds will depend upon the height difference between the massif surface and the peat field surface and also upon the character of the peat. When the deeper peat is of sufficiently low permeability, relatively shallow bunds may be used to contain water in the upper, more transmissive peats rather than needing complete wall bunds down the entire depth of the massif edge [Figure 5.9].

Limitations

- Bunding is comparatively expensive.
- Where the height difference between the surface of the massif and the cut-over peat is large, bunds will need to be particular well constructed and maintained. Alternatively a series of stepped bunds may be required [as in Figure 5.8].

Possible applications

- Bunding can be used in a large number of situations to protect a remnant peat massif from excessive water loss [5.3].

- In many situations it may be desirable to configure the peat excavation so that there is a series of steps up to the base of the remnant [Figure 5.8]. This will help to reduce the hydraulic gradient, be more stable and will permit shorter, less robust bunds to be used.

5.7.3 Non intervention (except ditch blocking)

The main alternative to some form of bunding is a policy of non-intervention, other than the blocking of any ditches that drain the remnant massif. This approach has the advantage of being cheap and simple, but it is unlikely to be universally acceptable as, in general, it is an approach based upon the *accommodation* rather than *prevention* of damage associated with water loss [5.3.2(b)].

Limitations

- In many situations non-intervention may lead to sustained and increasing damage of the bog habitat supported on the remnant massif.
- The extent to which damage will occur will depend upon the character of the massif biota and the extent to which water loss is induced by adjacent peat extraction. This latter will be determined *inter alia* by the hydraulic gradient, the transmissivity of

(a)

(c)

(b)

(d)

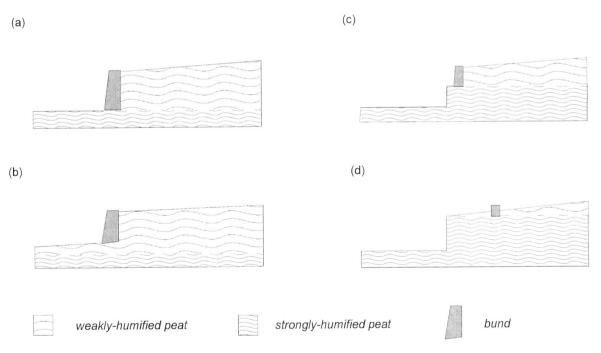

weakly-humified peat   strongly-humified peat   bund

Figure 5.9 Protection of massifs alongside peat extraction by bunding. When the exposed massif is composed of permeable peat, a wall bund the height of the edge of the massif may be needed to retain water (a), although its height can be reduced to some extent by removing less peat immediately alongside the massif (b). When the permeable peat is underlain by a low permeability peat, the wall bund need only protect the edge of the permeable peat (c). In some cases, it may be possible to maintain the surface-wet conditions over much of the massif just by the use of surface bunds to prevent excessive water loss through the acrotelm (d).

the peat and the configuration of the massif surface.

Possible applications

Non-intervention in the protection of bog massifs may be acceptable in some circumstances [5.3.2(b)], for example:

- where the character of the biota on the massif is not critically dependent upon high water tables;
- where the water-drawdown at the edge of the massif affects only a narrow marginal zone (*e.g.* because the height difference between the surface of the massif and the peat fields is small or because the peat is of low permeability);
- where the surface configuration (*e.g.* hollows or block peat cuttings) of the massif permits the retention of locally wet conditions despite some degree of drying of more elevated parts;

- where 'good quality' bog vegetation towards the centre of the massif is already separated from the margins proximate to the peat operations by a zone of damaged surface, which contains the water drawdown and functions as a 'buffer zone'.

5.7.4 Conclusion

There is no doubt that, in appropriate situations, it is possible to maintain wet conditions in close proximity to peat-extraction operations, depending on such features as surface topography and peat permeabilities. However, as the latter, in particular, are difficult to characterise accurately, it is correspondingly difficult to make generalisations and accurate predictions of the potential impacts of peat extraction upon adjoining massifs.

Chapter 6

Restoration options and peat-working practices

6.1 Introduction

Practical experience of wetland restoration and creation suggests that chances of success are likely to be improved by defining clear objectives and identifying appropriate management strategies for their achievement (Treweek, 1993). In most situations, the adopted options and associated outcomes of raised-bog restoration are likely to be a combination of desirability modified by practicability. The practicability of specific objectives will be determined primarily by the starting conditions available for restoration, *viz.* the environmental context of the site and the particular conditions created by peat extraction or other forms of damage.

The following objectives are currently adopted in the conservation management of some UK raised-bog sites:

- *the maintenance or re-establishment of wildlife interest (not necessarily pertaining to bogs)*
  This may include the flora and fauna of, for example, heath (wet and dry); rough grass; birch scrub and woodland; open water; reedbeds; herbaceous fen; fen meadow; fen woodland.

- *the maintenance or re-establishment of bog species*
  This may include bog species–populations maintained on badly-damaged bog surfaces or re-developed within peat workings *etc.* Examples of the latter may be akin to vegetation of the *NVC* M18 bog community (*Erica tetralix–Sphagnum papillosum* raised and blanket mire [1.9]). Such sites may support, and be valued for, a range of non-bog species, (some uncommon).

- *the maintenance or re-establishment of a 'natural' regenerating, self-sustaining mire system*
  This includes the maintenance of the on-going development of a little-damaged bog; the regeneration of a damaged peat massif; and initiation of 'new' raised bogs in peat workings. In vegetation terms, such sites have, or, it is hoped will redevelop, vegetation referable to the M18 bog community over all or part of their surface.

6.2 Restoration options for ombrotrophic peat surfaces

Development of an ombrotrophic mire is thought to be a 'natural', spontaneous successional process which can be induced from several starting points [Box 1.3], and acidification and establishment of a *Sphagnum*-dominated vegetation is known to occur in a quite wide range of conditions. Thus, in principle the regeneration of a *Sphagnum* bog may be able to occur, sometimes spontaneously, in a variety of situations. In consequence, provided that there is sufficient precipitation input of appropriate quality, and that conditions of impeded drainage can be maintained (by blocking of drainage ditches *etc.*) it may be thought that redevelopment of a raised-bog ecosystem within the ramparts of an old one will almost inevitably recur. In some cases, such a view may ultimately be correct, but it is also clear that some starting conditions are more immediately suitable for raised-bog redevelopment than are others. Where the object of restoration initiatives is to regenerate an ombrotrophic ecosystem within the foreseeable future, it is likely to be necessary to consider procedures that will optimise and facilitate such a process, rather than to adopt a *laissez faire* approach in which the natural processes of mire development are just left to 'sort themselves out'.

6.2.1 Climatic regimes and restoration options

The re-instatement of a *Sphagnum*-based vegetation on a damaged ombrotrophic surface is widely regarded as a most desirable aim of restoration of damaged raised bog. It requires the establishment and maintenance of consistently wet surface conditions. The extent to which this is possible will be regulated by the main water-balance terms of each bog, *viz.* rate of precipitation input, rate of water loss (lateral and vertical discharge and evapotranspiration) and water storage at the peat surface.

Recharge of the bog is dependent upon climate, in terms of precipitation input. Rates of water loss from the bog are regulated *inter alia* by the topography of the surface (whether sloping or flat; its relationship to the position of the perched water mound); permeability of the peat (including fissures and other channels of preferential flow); and vegetation composition and climate (both of which influence rates of water loss by evapotranspiration). Water storage capacity at, or on, the peat surface is influenced by the intrinsic storage capacity of the peat and the topography of the surface (depressions tend to store water). Thus, the problems of rewetting of a peat massif will be most acute:

- in climates with a prolonged dry period;
- where water inputs are readily lost by surface flow;
- where the topography (*e.g.* small area in relation to height) leads to the limit of the zone of permanent saturation being some distance below the peat surface;
- where vertical water loss occurs into the underlying mineral soil;
- where the vegetation and climate are conducive to high rates of evapotranspiration;
- and where the surface peat has little capacity to store water.

Conversely, in climates that are cool and consistently wet, where a bog has been little damaged other than by drainage and where the surface peats retain a high storage coefficient, rewetting and renaturation may be achievable with minimal effort. In climates which are sufficiently wet and cool (as in those which sustain blanket peat formation) even sloping damaged bog surfaces may renature, though such regions have generally not been the focus of commercial peat exploitation.

Whilst some relationship between climatic conditions and restoration procedures for damaged bogs is evident, its exact character is not known and it is not yet possible to specify climatic thresholds for particular restoration options. This is partly because climate is just one of the variables which may affect the rewetting of damaged bogs. It is also because the importance of different aspects of the climate to revegetation is not well known. For example, total amount of precipitation may not be as significant as its frequency or seasonal distribution for the maintenance of ombrotrophic surfaces in a consistently wet state. Moreover, yearly variation in rainfall patterns and totals makes generalisation difficult: a series of wet summers may engender success in rewetting options that would normally be untenable.

6.2.2 *Assessment of restoration options*

Tables 6.1a and b present an assessment of different restoration options for ombrotrophic surfaces and their likely outcomes. They are based upon:

(a) the current condition of a wide range of raised-bog sites and the spontaneous (*i.e.* unplanned, but not necessarily unmanaged) revegetation of abandoned peat workings found within them; these data are derived from personal observations and published and unpublished reports for sites in England, Wales, Scotland, Northern Ireland, Eire, The Netherlands, Germany, Switzerland, Scandinavia and North America; and

(b) upon the results of attempts to restore raised bogs damaged by peat extraction [see Appendix 6].

Existing restoration initiatives vary considerably in their character and situation. Some have only been started recently; others have not always been well documented or monitored. Some of the most innovative and elaborate attempts to restore both remnant massifs and extensive commercial peat fields have been undertaken in The Netherlands and various parts of Germany and the problems and results of these initiatives are of particular importance. Many of these endeavours have been in regions which, whilst climatically comparable with many raised-bog areas in England, are generally both drier and warmer than some raised-bog regions of Scotland. Moreover, they have sometimes also had to address the difficulties imposed by vertical loss of water from the catotelm into the underlying aquifer – a problem that may affect some raised-bog sites in the UK, but which probably does not influence the majority of them. Thus, some of the Dutch and German experience relates to circumstances that are intrinsically less conducive to rewetting than is the case for some, perhaps many, UK sites. However, this does not mean that their experience is inapplicable elsewhere: observations on various cut-over sites in England, Scotland, N. Ireland, Eire and N. America, suggest that many of the problems of rewetting damaged raised bogs, particularly commercial peat fields, that have been experienced in The Netherlands and Germany, are common to many other cut-over sites; and, although a wetter, cooler climate may be expected to mitigate some of the problems of rewetting, there is little factual evidence currently available to show that it will necessarily overcome them. Ultimately, the only way to establish the true potential of different restoration options for badly-damaged raised bogs in cool, wet climates will be to try different approaches.

TABLE 6.1 Summary of the likely outcomes of different options of raised bog restoration, from a contrasting range of starting conditions.

The starting conditions (represented in the table by headings in bold type and with a single number identifier (*e.g.* **1**)) have been chosen as representative starting conditions that have been observed in a number of damaged sites. It should be recognised that variants of these may occur and that some sites will present a range of starting conditions – *i.e.* the options are not mutually exclusive.

For each type of starting condition, various management options have been presented (designated by a double number identifier (*e.g.* 1.1)). These are not comprehensive but represent the main options that seem likely to be applicable. Various permutations of them can be made, for example to cover various different starting conditions present on one site. Because of this, to avoid excessive repetition not every option has been entered for every starting condition.

It is assumed that in all options simple attempts will be made to retain water on the mire, *i.e.* that as a base-line minimum outfalls and ditches will be adequately blocked. Thus the 'no bunding' option assumes that ditch blocking, but nothing else, will take place.

Assessment of the probable effects on water tables, vegetation, revegetation and implications for conservation and management are based on practical experiences of restoration together with current knowledge of bog and fen ecology outlined in this report. The suggested outcome is therefore not 'guaranteed', but presented as the most likely outcome in the given circumstances.

The implications of the different options for working practices and subsequent possibilities for restoration need to be carefully considered, as do the potential impacts of peat extraction on the uncut or abandoned areas and the viability of such areas in the absence of positive management. In some cases, restoration of such areas may represent a 'value-added' approach in that the biological value may be enhanced by appropriate management techniques (for example, replacing a dry, birch–*Molinia* mix with a wet, *Sphagnum*-dominated system).

Table 6.1a Restoration options for uncut peat remnants (bog peat) (see text)

Starting conditions / Management	Probable effects on water tables	Other hydrological considerations	Probable effects on vegetation and revegetation	Conservational assessment	Conservation / management implications
1 Peat remnant large with respect to marginal damage; surface little-damaged (*Sphagnum* cover etc. retained);					
1.1 No bunding	Drying near margins; central area remains wet; subsidence may occur to reconform the shape of the mire		Original surface maintained in centre. Development of heathland, *Molinia* grassland or birch scrub near margins unless surface reconformation occurs rapidly.	Original character and conservation interest retained, at least in centre. Edges may become heathy and susceptible to birch encroachment. They may provide a habitat for some organisms otherwise absent from the bog.	Birch control may be necessary, particularly around margins.
1.2 Surface bunding of weakly-humified peat on remnant.	Drying near margins; wetter central area more extensive than 1.1; subsidence may occur to reconform the shape of the mire	Water mound similar to 1.1 but marginal damage has less effect upon *acrotelm* conditions because of shallow bunding.	Original surface maintained in centre to greater extent than 1.1. Development of heathland, *Molinia* grassland or birch scrub near margins unless surface reconformation occurs rapidly.	Original character and conservation interest retained, at least in centre and to a greater degree than 1.1. Edges of remnant (outside bunds) may become heathy and susceptible to birch encroachment.	Birch control may be necessary, particularly around margins.
2 Peat remnant small with respect to marginal damage; surface little-damaged (*Sphagnum* cover etc. retained)					
2.1 No bunding	Drying across most or all of site, especially near margins		Ultimate loss of many components of original surface, except, perhaps, some more drought tolerant bog species (*e.g. Eriophorum vaginatum*). Replacement by wet heath, dry heath, *Molinia* grassland, bracken *etc.*	Much original conservation interest likely to be lost. Replacement habitat may have new conservation value as dry/wet heath. Birch encroachment a problem across entire site.	Vegetation management depends on objectives for non-bog habitats. Peat may be subject to ongoing oxidative decomposition.
2.2 Surface bunding of acrotelm / 'white' peat on remnant.	Drying across most or all of site, especially near margins. Possibly localised wet areas.	Surface bunding has little effect on the overall position of the water table.	Ultimate loss of many components of original surface except, perhaps, a few drought tolerant bog species (*e.g. Eriophorum vaginatum*). Replacement by wet heath, dry heath, *Molinia* grassland, bracken *etc.*	Most original conservation interest lost. Replacement habitat may have new conservation value as dry/wet heath. Birch encroachment a problem across entire site.	Vegetation management depends on objectives for non-bog habitats. Peat may be subject to ongoing oxidative decomposition.
2.3 Wall bunding around remnant margins	Retention of high water table over much of site.	Marginal bunds have elevated base-level of water mound. Will affect most of remnant unless it is strongly domed.	Retention of original surface and species.	Original character and conservation interest is retained. Important *per se* and as a reservoir from which recolonisation of surrounding cuttings can occur.	Remnant left isolated above general level of mire. Bunds need to be well made if height difference is great and may require long-term maintenance. Series of concentric bunds may be required if strongly domed.

3 Peat remnant with dehydrated and damaged surface (little or no *Sphagnum* cover remaining)

3.1	No bunding	Drying across most or all of site, especially near margins. Possibly localised wet areas (*e.g.* in blocked drains)	Bog species reduced or lost (depending on climate and severity of damage). Prospects for unaided recovery depend on climate and nature and severity of damage. In many situations redevelopment of M18-type vegetation is unlikely, but *may* be possible to retain a number of species in wetter regions. Elsewhere, replacement by wet heath, dry heath, *Molinia* grassland, bracken, birch *etc*.	Original character of mire surface lost and unlikely to redevelop readily. In some regions, a number of bog species may persist in reduced abundance. Elsewhere replacement habitat may have new conservation value as dry/wet heath. Birch encroachment a likely problem across entire site.	Vegetation management depends on condition of surface and objectives for a 'damaged bog' or 'non-bog' habitat. Peat likely to be subject to ongoing oxidative decomposition.
3.2	Surface bunding of weakly-humified peat on remnant.	As 3.1	As 3.1	As 3.1	As 3.1
3.3	Wall bunding around remnant margins	Retention of high water table over some or much of site.	Success of rewetting may depend on original degree of dehydration / damage to peat and on dimensions of remnant	Possible redevelopment of M18-type bog vegetation on rewetted surface of remnant, but unlikely in any areas with protracted dry periods. Replacement habitats may persist.	Remaining bog species likely to survive and some potential for increase bog conservation interest over all or part of remnant. May require inoculation of vegetation. Birch encroachment a potential problem.	Remnant left as isolated remnant above general level of mire. Bunds need to be well made if height difference is great and may require long-term maintenance. Series of concentric bunds may be required if strongly domed. Removal of existing vegetation (*e.g.* birch) likely to be a problem.
3.4	Parapet bunding around remnant margins	Retention of high water table over some or much of site, with local inundation.	Success of rewetting may depend on original degree of dehydration / damage to peat and on dimensions of remnant.	Possible redevelopment of M18-type bog vegetation on rewetted surface and, particularly, in shallow-flooded areas, even in drier climates. Replacement habitats may persist on higher areas..	Remaining bog species likely to survive and some likelihood of redevelopment of 'good quality' (M18) vegetation over at least part of remnant. May require inoculation of vegetation. Birch encroachment a potential problem in drier places.	Remnant left as isolated remnant above general level of mire. Bunds need to be well made if height difference is great and may require long-term maintenance. Series of concentric bunds may be required if strongly domed. Removal of existing vegetation (*e.g.* birch) likely to be a problem.

contd

Table 6.1b Restoration options for cut-over surfaces (bog peat) (see text)

	Starting conditions / Management	Probable effects on water tables	Other hydrological considerations	Probable effects on vegetation and revegetation	Conservational assessment	Conservation / management implications
4	**Cut-over peat massif with original surface lost, exposure of deeper, more humified peats etc. Surface relatively flat.**					
4.1	No bunding	Surface shows strong fluctuations in wetness. May be very wet during winter rains but dries out during summer dry periods	Fluctuations in 'wetness' created by lack of sufficient water storage in residual peat	Little recolonisation by bog species except, perhaps, a few drought tolerant taxa (e.g. *Eriophorum vaginatum*). Replacement by wet heath, dry heath, *Molinia* grassland, bracken *etc*.	Little redevelopment of original conservation interest of bog. Replacement habitat may or may not have conservation value as dry/wet heath. Birch encroachment a problem across entire site	Massif left as dry remnant above general level of mire. Vegetation management depends on objectives for non-bog habitats. Peat likely to be subject to ongoing oxidative decomposition
4.2	Wall bunding around massif margins	Unless bund is extended upwards into a parapet (4.3) surface may still show strong fluctuations in wetness.	May have little impact in reducing lateral wall loss as residual peat is likely to be of inherently low permeability.	Little recolonisation by bog species except, perhaps, a few drought tolerant taxa (e.g. *Eriophorum vaginatum*). Replacement by wet heath, dry heath, *Molinia* grassland, bracken *etc*.	Little redevelopment of original conservation interest of bog. Replacement habitat may or may not have conservation value as dry/wet heath. Birch encroachment a problem across entire site	Massif left as dry remnant above general level of mire. Vegetation management depends on objectives for non-bog habitats. Peat likely to be subject to ongoing oxidative decomposition
4.3	Parapet bunding	Creates surface flooding over all or some of massif. Still strong fluctuations in water level but surface water storage reduces effects of summer droughts.	Bunding around exposed edge of massif not required if *in situ* dark peat has low permeability.	Potential for recreation of typical bog vegetation on rewetted surface of massif. May require inoculation of vegetation.	Potential for regeneration of bog conservation interest over all or part of massif.	Massif left as isolated remnant above general level of cut-over mire. Periodic maintenance of parapet may be needed, but as most of impermeability is a product of low permeability peat left *in situ*, system is likely to be inherently more stable than 2.3.
4.4	Peat removal	Creates conditions of 4.3 by excavation of peat from all or part of massif.	Bunding around exposed edge of massif not required if *in situ* dark peat has low permeability.	Potential for recreation of typical bog vegetation on rewetted surface of massif. May require inoculation of vegetation.	Potential for regeneration of bog conservation interest over all or part of massif.	Massif (or parts of it) no longer substantially elevated above general level of cut-over mire.
5	**Block-cut surfaces in massif with only strongly-humified ('black') peat**					
5.1	No bunding	Peat cuttings / hollows tend to remain wet; intervening baulks show strong fluctuations in water level and tend to dry during summer.	If peat is low permeability, wet conditions can be maintained even in hollows close to margins of massif.	Potential for regeneration of bog vegetation within peat cuttings. Baulks develop a drier vegetation (wet heath, dry heath, *Molinia*, bracken, birch *etc*.).	Mosaic of wet and dry habitats and their interface gives range of conservation interest, including elements of bog.	Not uniform bog. Usually considerable birch development on ridges (≡ cambered beds of foresters). Potential for bog expansion out of cuttings onto baulks uncertain. Massif may be left as isolated remnant above general level of cut-over mire. Dry peat likely to be subject to ongoing oxidative decomposition.

No.	Treatment					
5.2	Wall bunding around massif margins	If dark peat has low permeability, Wall bunding is unlikely to have many advantages upon 5.1.		As 5.1	As 5.1	As 5.1
5.3	Parapet bunding	Creates surface flooding upon the baulks over all or some of the massif as well as in the peat cuttings.	Wall bunding around exposed edge of massif not required if in situ dark peat has low permeability.	Regeneration of bog vegetation within peat cuttings. Also bog regeneration on flooded or wet conditions of baulks. May require inoculation of vegetation.	Potential for regeneration of bog conservation interest over all or part of massif.	Massif left as isolated remnant above general level of cut-over mire. Periodic maintenance of parapet may be needed, but as most of impermeability is a product of low permeability peat left in situ, system may be quite stable.
5.4	Peat removal – as 4.4					

6 Block-cut surfaces in massif. with weakly-humified peat

No.	Treatment					
6.1	No bunding	Peat cuttings and hollows wet; intervening baulks show strong fluctuations in water level and tend to dry during summer.	Wet conditions unlikely to be maintained in hollows close to margins of massif.	Potential for regeneration of bog vegetation within peat cuttings. Baulks develop a drier vegetation (wet heath, dry heath, *Molinia*, bracken, birch *etc.*).	Mosaic of wet and dry habitats and their interface gives range of conservation interest, including elements of bog.	Not uniform bog. Usually considerable birch development on ridges (≡ cambered beds of foresters). Potential for bog expansion out of cuttings onto baulks uncertain. Massif may be left as isolated remnant above general level of cut-over mire. Dry peat likely to be subject to ongoing oxidative decomposition.
6.2	Wall bunding around massif margins	Unless bund is extended upwards into a parapet (6.3) surface of baulks may still show strong fluctuations in wetness.	Marginal bunding may not be needed to prevent water loss through lower peats of small permeability.	Potential for regeneration of bog vegetation within peat cuttings. Baulks develop a drier vegetation (wet heath, dry heath, *Molinia*, bracken *etc.*).	Mosaic of wet and dry habitats and their interface gives range of conservation interest, including elements of bog.	Not uniform bog. Birch encroachment on baulks likely to be a problem. Potential for bog expansion out of cuttings onto baulks uncertain. Massif may be left as isolated remnant above general level of cut-over mire. Dry peat likely to be subject to ongoing oxidative decomposition.
6.3	Parapet bunding	Creates surface flooding upon the baulks over all or some of the massif as well as in the peat cuttings.	Wall bunding around exposed edge of massif not required where in situ dark peat has low permeability.	Regeneration of bog vegetation within peat cuttings. Also bog regeneration on flooded or wet conditions of baulks. May require inoculation of vegetation.	Potential for regeneration of bog conservation interest over all or part of massif.	Massif left as isolated remnant above general level of cut-over mire. Periodic maintenance of parapet may be needed, but as most of impermeability is a product of low permeability peat left in situ, system may be quite stable.
6.4	Peat removal – as 4.4					

contd

Table 6.1b (continued) [Options for cut-over surfaces (bog peat)]

Starting conditions Management	Probable effects on water tables	Other hydrological considerations	Probable effects on vegetation and revegetation	Conservational assessment	Conservation / management implications
7	**Milled surface of ombrotrophic peat: surface sloping**				
7.1 No bunding	Surface does not retain water.	Surface run-off + lack of storage means that surface is dry except during wet parts of year.	Development of vegetation with few, if any bog species – heath, *Molinia*, bracken, birch scrub.	Little redevelopment of original conservation interest of bog. Replacement habitat may or may not have conservation value. Birch encroachment a problem across entire site.	Vegetation management depends on conservational objectives for non-bog habitats. Likely to be ongoing oxidative decomposition of residual peat.
7.2 Terraced, bunded lagoons	Water retained in lagoons.	Creates surface flooding. Reduces run-off. Still wide fluctuations in water level but surface water storage (and, in some situations, 'cascade feeding') reduces effects of summer droughts.	Potential for development of bog vegetation within wet areas in lagoons. Possibly wet heath/*Molinia* in less wet higher areas. May require inoculation of vegetation.	Potential for redevelopment of bog vegetation. Encroachment by birch and some other species a problem on drier areas.	May also need to have marginal bund (or residual baulk) to reduce water loss from site margins and to prevent ingress of enriched water. Birch encroachment of drier areas may need to be checked. Likely to be ongoing oxidative decomposition of areas that are not rewetted. Marginal bunds may require periodic maintenance.
8	**Milled surface of ombrotrophic peat: surface ± flat**				
8.1 No bunding	Surface shows strong fluctuations in wetness. May be very wet during winter rains but dries out during summer dry periods.	Fluctuations in 'wetness' created by lack of sufficient water storage in residual peat.	Little redevelopment of bog vegetation except, perhaps, for a few more drought tolerant bog species (e.g. *Eriophorum vaginatum*) and in sites in wet regions. Heath, *Molinia*, bracken, birch scrub are likely developments.	Little redevelopment of original conservation interest of bog. Replacement habitat may or may not have conservation value. Birch encroachment a problem across entire site.	Vegetation management depends on conservation objective for non-bog habitats. Likely to be ongoing oxidative decomposition of residual peat.
8.2 Bunded lagoons	Water retained in lagoons.	Creates surface flooding. Reduces run-off. Still wide fluctuations in water level but surface water storage reduces effects of summer droughts.	Development of bog vegetation within wet areas in lagoons. Wet heath/*Molinia* in less wet higher areas. May require inoculation of vegetation.	Potential for redevelopment of bog vegetation. Encroachment by birch and some other species a problem on drier areas.	May also need to have marginal bund (or residual baulk) to reduce water loss from site margins and to prevent ingress of enriched water. Birch encroachment within lagoons unless well inundated. Likely to be ongoing oxidative decomposition of areas that are not rewetted. Marginal bunds may require periodic maintenance.

9   Milled surface of ombrotrophic peat: surface scalloped or forming depressions

9.1	No bunding	Water retained in hollows	Creates surface flooding. Reduces run-off. Still strong fluctuations in water level but surface water storage reduces effects of summer droughts.	Development of bog vegetation within wet areas in hollows. Wet heath/*Molinia* in less wet upper areas. May require inoculation of vegetation.	Potential for redevelopment of bog vegetation. Encroachment by birch and some other species a problem on drier areas. May be extensive, depending on surface configuration.	May need a marginal bund (or residual baulk) to prevent ingress of enriched water. Birch encroachment within lagoons unless well inundated. Likely to be ongoing oxidative decomposition of areas that are not rewetted.

10   Shallow peat deposits upon permeable substrata with lowered groundwater tables

10.1	No bunding	Effect of lowered groundwater tables upon surface condition is partly dependent upon depth of residual peat. 50 cm of strongly-humified ('*black*') *bog* peat seems the minimum needed to reduce vertical seepage to an acceptable level.	If residual peat is too thin rewetting of surface is likely to be impossible. No form of remedial action is known. [Even with sufficient peat depth, any ditches close to or penetrating the subsoil must be filled with low permeability peat.]	Development of heath, grassland and scrub. No redevelopment of bog.	Little redevelopment of original bog conservation interest. Replacement habitat may or may not have conservation value. Birch encroachment a problem across entire site.	Vegetation management depends on conservation objective for non-bog habitats. Likely to be ongoing oxidative decomposition of residual peat.
10.2	Intervention ?	It is likely that the only way this problem may be mitigated in sites with insufficient residual peat will be the management of landscape hydrology to re-elevate water levels generally.			

contd

Table 6.1c Restoration options for fen peat surfaces (in peat cuttings) (see text)

11 Flat surface of fen peat

Starting conditions		Probable effects on water tables	Other hydrological considerations	Probable effects on vegetation and revegetation	Conservational assessment	Conservation / management implications
	Management					
11.1	No action	Wetness of surface will depend upon site topography and the intrinsic properties of the local hydrological environment. May be subject to large fluctuations in wetness, very wet (perhaps inundated) in winter but quite dry in summer	Fluctuations in 'wetness' created by lack of sufficient water storage in residual peat coupled with absence of water-retaining structures. In large sites ditch network may be used to regulate water levels	Development of wet grassland vegetation, or some form of rough fen or fen carr, depending upon water levels and management	Developing vegetation can include species-rich pastures or hay meadows when managed, and these may have considerable conservation value (e.g. *Molinia–Cirsium* fen meadow). Elsewhere, rough or dry fen (e.g. *Phragmites–Urtica* fen, *Phragmites–Eupatorium* fen), fen woodland etc. is likely to develop. This may have limited conservation value as fen vegetation (unless in exceptional hydrological situation) but habitat may have 'general wildlife' value.	Without management only a rank species-poor herbaceous or wet woodland vegetation will develop. Likely to be ongoing oxidative decomposition of residual peat. This may contribute to nutrient status of substratum.
11.2	Ditch blocking	Effect depends on topography and water source. Can be used to retain meteoric water; to exclude telluric water; or to retain a mix of both water supplies	When used to retain meteoric water effects are likely to be similar to 11.1, unless underlain by high & stable groundwater table. When used to retain telluric water, high water levels can sometimes be maintained	As 11.1, except (a) where underlain by stable groundwater table (which may then provide a suitable basis for various types of fen and possibly *Sphagnum* in climatically-suitable areas); and (b) where used to retain minerotrophic water, in which case wider development of fen vegetation may be expected.	As 11.1, but potential for more development of wetter fen communities, at least locally	As 11.1

11.3	Ditch irrigation or periodic flooding	Effect depends upon topography and availability of water source. If sufficient supply of telluric water, parts of fen can be kept permanently wet	In dry episodes there will be a tendency for the fen to dry out away from irrigation ditches. Flooding will be episodic and may lead to periodic dryness across much of the site	Ditch-irrigated sites can maintain fen vegetation (but not usually wet-fen types). If there is no other water source, sites irrigated by episodic flooding usually support dry, coarse fen vegetation or fen grassland. Quality of water is also important, especially in flooding episodes: input of high nutrient loadings typically lead to impoverished vegetation. Flooding not suitable for bog regeneration but if ditch irrigation can maintain permanently high subsurface groundwater table it *may* provide a basis for local *Sphagnum* invasion, especially in wetter, cooler regions.	Ditch irrigated systems can develop fen vegetation of considerable conservation interest (*Phragmites–Peucedanum*, *Phragmites–Eupatorium* fen, *Molinia–Cirsium dissectum* fen meadow). Sites just irrigated by episodic flooding may support low-quality vegetation (e.g. *Phragmites–Urtica* or *Phragmites–Eupatorium* fen if unmanaged; wet grassland if mown or grazed); however, these may have much ornithological value, especially during winter flooding episodes.	Some form of management is likely to be required (summer mowing or grazing) to help maintain a species-rich vegetation and to prevent successional development of scrub and woodland. May be some ongoing oxidative decomposition of peat, depending upon maintained water levels.
11.4	Lagoons or sculpted hollows	Rainwater retained in lagoons. Creates surface flooding. Reduces run-off. Still strong fluctuations in water level but surface water storage reduces effects of summer droughts.	Note also that in some sites lagoons may also help impound telluric water. The capacity of fen peat to create walls for lagoons is not well known.	Development of various types of fen vegetation, probably mostly characteristic of low-fertility environments, though this may not be the case if telluric water inputs exist.. Vegetation character dependent on depth, base-richness and nutrient richness of water (see 12, below).	Some fen communities could have high conservation value. Will require some management and (perhaps) recreation of hydrosere to maintain interest in perpetuity. Possibility of *Sphagnum* invasion into terrestrialising lagoons	May also need a marginal bund (or residual baulk) to prevent ingress of enriched water. Scrub (birch, willows, alder) encroachment within lagoons unless well inundated. Dry areas may be subject to ongoing oxidative decomposition of peat.

12   Cuttings within fen peat

12.1	No intervention (except block outfalls)	Wetness of cuttings will depend their topography and the intrinsic properties of the local hydrological environment.	Intrinsically more stable water table than 11.1 because cuttings help to retain water surplus.	Fen community that develops will depend upon water sources and levels.	May generate conservation interest. Difficult to speculate on the large number of possible communities that could develop in this condition.	Without management, vegetation will develop into a form of fen woodland. Herbaceous fen communities may have great conservation value.
12.2	Soaking with nutrient-poor water (precipitation + groundwater)	Water near or just above water level	Water level manipulated by inflow ditches, sluices, pumps etc.	Potential for development of species-rich fen vegetation.	Fen communities may include: *Carex rostrata–Potentilla*, *Phragmites–Peucedanum* fen, *Juncus–Cirsium*, *Molinia–Cirsium* fen meadow and various forms of fen woodland.	Without management, vegetation will develop into a form of fen woodland. Herbaceous fen communities may have great conservation value.
12.3	Soaking with nutrient-rich water (precipitation + enriched river / land-drainage water)	Water near or just above water level	Water level manipulated by inflow ditches, sluices, pumps etc.	Potential for development of a coarse fen vegetation.	Fen communities may include: *Phragmites–Eupatorium* fen, *Phragmites–Urtica* fen, various types of tall herb fen and fen woodland.	Without management, vegetation will develop into a form of fen woodland. Heavy management may help enhance floristic 'interest' of herbaceous vegetation, but never likely to be of great interest. Such situations may be best managed for birds.

contd

Table 6.1c (continued) [Restoration options for fen peat surfaces (in peat cuttings)]

Starting conditions / Management	Probable effects on water tables	Other hydrological considerations	Probable effects on vegetation and revegetation	Conservational assessment	Conservation / management implications
12.4 Shallow flooding with nutrient poor water (precipitation + groundwater)	Water level >0 <50 cm	Water level manipulated by inflow ditches, sluices, pumps *etc.*	Potential development of rich aquatic and wet fen vegetation, including raft-forming communities. These latter may form a basis for *Sphagnum* re-invasion.	Potential communities include: *Carex rostrata–Calliergon* mire; *Carex rostrata–Potentilla palustris* fen; *Carex elata, C. rostrata, Equisetum fluviatile, Typha angustifolia* swamps *etc.*	Scrub invasion unlikely initially but will occur as peat accumulates unless some form of management is introduced. [In some cases carr formed in such conditions can have considerable interest.] Herbaceous fen communities may have great conservation value.
12.5 Shallow flooding with nutrient-rich water (precipitation + enriched river / land-drainage water)	Water level >0 <50 cm	Water level manipulated by inflow ditches, sluices, pumps *etc.*	Potential development of rather coarse fen communities.	Potential communities include: *Carex rostrata–Potentilla palustris* fen; *Juncus effusus, Phragmites australis, Phalaris arundinacea, Glyceria maxima, Typha latifolia* swamps *etc.*	Scrub invasion unlikely initially but will occur as peat accumulates unless some form of management is introduced. Management is unlikely to improve quality of fen vegetation.
12.6 Deep flooding with nutrient-poor water (precipitation + groundwater)	Water level >50cm	Water level manipulated by inflow ditches, sluices, pumps *etc.*	Formation of deep-water emergent swamp communities (regulated by precise water depth) Possible formation of floating rafts (which may the provide a basis for *Sphagnum* establishment) but mechanism and occurrence of rafting in very deep water (> 1.5m) is uncertain.	Potential communities include: *Scirpus lacustris* swamp, *Typha angustifolia* swamp, *Phragmites* swamp (reedbeds). If floating rafts can develop then *Potentillo-Cariceta* and *Acrocladio-Cariceta* and *Sphagnum*-dominated communities can also form	Management not required until substantial terrestrialisation has occurred, though reeds can be harvested in such situations. Herbaceous fen communities may have great conservation value.
12.7 Deep flooding with nutrient-rich water (precipitation + enriched river / land-drainage water)	Water level >50cm	Water level manipulated by inflow ditches, sluices, pumps *etc.*	Formation of deep-water emergent swamp communities	Potential communities include *Typha latifolia* swamp and *Phragmites* swamp (reedbeds). *Glyceria maxima* swamp may occupy some peripheral locations.	Management not required until substantial terrestrialisation has occurred, though reeds can be harvested in such situations. Unlikely ever to be of prime botanical importance and perhaps best managed for other taxonomic groups.

In general, rewetting problems are often greater on massifs (which are typically water-shedding areas) than they are in depressions (which are typically water-holding areas) [2.1]. Various approaches can be used to rewet massifs [Table 6.1a; 5.3], but particular difficulties can be experienced with badly-damaged remnants. Likewise a series of upstanding blocks, at different levels, which are found in some (usually abandoned) peat extraction complexes can present particularly intractable problems for restoration. In some situations it may have to be accepted that effective rewetting of the whole complex is not feasible, in which case the remnants may be left to support some replacement habitat, which may include some bog species, though they are ultimately likely to be wasting assets.

Because of their situation, peat fields may ultimately provide a more satisfactory basis for bog restoration (especially 'whole-mire' regeneration) than some uncut massifs. This is because they may provide a less topographically-varied surface; because, when close to the mineral ground, they may be intrinsically more stable, both in terms of water regime and peat wastage; and because their effective rewetting [Table 6.1b] may be technically less difficult than rewetting of massifs. Nonetheless, in many cases some technical intervention will be required to produce structures that impound water against lateral flow and increase storage, although this will depend upon the topography and disposition of the abandoned surfaces. The flat or gently sloping surfaces of modern commercial peat fields may be quite well suited to rewetting over extensive areas.

Nonetheless, rewetting of peat fields cannot be divorced from that of peat massifs. This is partly because cut-over surfaces are themselves sometimes located on a massif well-elevated above the surrounding land, in which case considerations pertinent to the rewetting of massifs become equally applicable to the peat fields (this is a lesser consideration when peat has been removed nearer to the base of the deposit). It is also because an obvious effect of peat removal is to accentuate the height difference between the peat field surface and the surface of adjoining peat massifs. In this situation it may still be possible to maintain an independently high water table in the massif, but is likely to be more expensive and difficult to do so (depending upon the characteristics of the massif). An additional consideration is that of linking the regeneration of the peat field surfaces to the maintenance of the massif, particularly when the aim is to regenerate a bog across the whole site, integrating both peat fields and the massifs. This difficulty can be ameliorated in various ways. One option, in those situations where it is possible, is to have the peat surface grading up to the

massif, by removing less peat close to the massif. [This does, of course, produce an inclined surface which, depending on its slope, may be much more difficult to rewet than a flat one.] Where the massifs are badly damaged, of limited biological or palaeoecological interest and difficult to rewet, an alternative approach would be to remove peat from them so that they are more conformable with the peat fields. In other situations, where the massifs have considerable conservation value there may be little choice but to engineer independent water management strategies for the massifs and the peat workings.

6.3 Restoration options for minerotrophic peat surfaces

Considerably less attention has been directed towards the deliberate restoration of raised-bog sites where peat extraction has exposed underlying fen peat. Indeed, the full occurrence of this circumstance is not even well known. This is because, whilst in some sites it is obvious that peat cutting of ombrotrophic peat has uncovered fen peat (*e.g.* Brackagh Bog, Armagh), in others bog peat has been removed so comprehensively that there is little evidence for the former existence of bog (*e.g.* Woodwalton Fen, Cambridgeshire). However, increasing evidence suggests that a number of sites that are now regarded as good examples of fen have originated by the removal of overlying bog peat and this phenomenon may be much more widespread than is currently recognised. Although at present the peat workings in the Somerset Levels form the only area for commercial extraction of fen peat, restoration options for minerotrophic surfaces are applicable to a number of other wetland sites. It should not, however, be assumed that all raised-bog sites are underlain by substantial thicknesses of fen peat. In some sites, especially those which have developed by paludi-fication, the fen phase may have been only short-lived; and in others, the fen peat may show few chemical differences to the bog peat.

Peat workings within fen peat in apparent former raised-bog sites can provide a wide variety of habitats. They are valued for conservation for various reasons and in some cases are managed to maintain or redevelop these interests:

- *Open water* (interest mainly ornithological and entomo-logical);
- *Reedbeds* (interest mainly ornithological and entomological);
- *Herbaceous fen* (various types);
- *Fen woodland*;
- *Fen meadow*;
- Sphagnum *bog*.

The type of vegetation that develops in abandoned peat

workings in fen peat is primarily a function of water depth (and stability), water quality (particularly base-richness and nutrient-richness) and management regime (if any). Many herbaceous fen vegetation types require regular management to maintain their character and to prevent their colonisation by trees. Such management is often most feasible when it is associated with some economic return. Grazing or summer mowing is possible in some circumstances and can produce conservationally-desirable communities, as with some of the fen meadows of the Somerset Levels. Such objectives, when coupled with summer-dry conditions, are usually incompatible with the redevelopment of bog, although in certain circumstances, mowing may enhance the initial development towards bog.

The formulation of desirable restoration options for fen peat sites is often more difficult than for sites based on bog peat, because there is usually more scope for habitat manipulation and renaturation. In some instances circumstances will dictate the most feasible restoration option, but in others it may be possible to choose from several possibilities. A primary decision is whether to focus on the recreation of bog or fen, though these options are not mutually exclusive, especially as some forms of fen can give rise to bog vegetation. If the fen option is selected, the choice then becomes the type of fen desired. This can sometimes be determined by choice of water sources and levels. For example, fen cuttings can be flooded with nutrient-rich water from adjoining rivers, in which case the resulting vegetation (*e.g.* reedbeds) is likely to have little botanical interest but, possibly, much orni-thological value; if, however, such sources are excluded and precipitation inputs are adequate to reflood the cuttings, then a vegetation of more botanical interest may develop, together with a greater likelihood of the successional development of bog. The choice of objectives is thus likely to be determined by topography, availability (and quality) of minerotrophic water sources and implications for on-going management and maintenance as well as by conservational desirability.

In general, regeneration of bog within fens occurs most readily as a hydroseral development from fen vegetation in peat workings flooded with nutrient-poor (but not necessarily base-poor) water[1]. In appropriate circumstances *Sphagnum* can grow rapidly and thick-nesses of *c.* 1 m depth of *Sphagnum* peat accumulating within *c.* 100 years have been reported (van Wirdum,

pers. comm.). However, as the organisms associated with the fen phase of the succession are themselves often of great interest to conservationists, this spontaneous process of 'ombrotrophication' may not be universally welcomed.

It is obvious that if cut-over surfaces in fen peat are to redevelop fen vegetation (and perhaps ultimately bog) they require water input, but because of the likely (and usually unknown) complexities of the hydrology of individual minerotrophic systems and, with the contribution and quality of possible water sources also varying amongst sites, it is difficult to specify the effects of specific minerotrophic water sources upon the revegetation process. It is, however, possible to identify broadly the likely effects of the irrigating water in terms of its quality (nutrient poor *versus* nutrient rich) on restoration [Table 6.1c]. In this table, the assumption has been made that the residual fen peat is intrinsically not very fertile. This assumption may be inapplicable to some sites. Restoration options for sites with fertile residual peats will probably be similar to those at sites where peat extraction has exposed fertile freshwater clays [6.4].

Rewetting strategies for fen peat will depend strongly on the surrounding topography of the peat workings. In general, rewetting can be achieved most readily where the workings form a closed depression (within bog peat, fen peat or mineral soil) or where they have been deliberately bunded. In this situation it may be possible to inundate the depressions. In other situations cut-over fen surfaces are flat and located at about the same level as, or even higher than, surrounding farmland. In this case attempts to maintain a permanently high water table on the peat surface with minerotrophic water may be difficult without causing (at least temporary) water-logging of adjoining land. Bunding may be used to help hold water on the site, both to prevent flooding of adjoining land and to maintain a high water level in the fen peats.

6.4 Restoration options for mineral substrata

In some sites peat has been extracted to expose large areas of the underlying mineral substrata. Specification of restoration options for this may be subject to the same problems as for fen peat with respect to variation in the character of water sources. It is further complic-ated by the great variability of physico-chemical characteristics of the substrata. For example, the pH range of the substrata beneath ombrotrophic bogs is known to vary between about 3.0 (acid sands and gravels) to 7.5 (calcareous marls). Where it has been exposed, these characteristics of the substrata considerably determine restoration options and have

---

[1] It may also occur on solid fen peat where there is a *stable*, slightly subsurface water table, especially in wetter regions. The potential for raised bog development from this starting point is not well known - it may be suspected that it will be slower initially than from a semi-floating origin and in some situations may not occur at all.

obvious ramifications with respect to desirable water sources *etc.* Growth of Sphagna and other bog species may be just as good (if not better) on acid gravels as it is on ombrotrophic peats. Clays are perhaps the most widespread underlying substratum type and are often (but not always) relatively base rich. Where they represent some form of estuarine deposit they may also be brackish.

Rather little is known about the recolonisation of rewetted mineral substrata in the peatland context, but the outcomes of restoration initiatives upon base-rich, nutrient-poor substrata are probably similar to those on fen peat irrigated with nutrient-poor water; whereas those upon base-rich, nutrient-rich substrata are probably similar to those on fen peat irrigated with nutrient-rich water. There is even less information about revegetation pathways on rewetted brackish clays. In wet (inundated) sites characteristic colonist species are *Phragmites australis, Scirpus tabernae-montanae, Typha angustifolia* and *T. latifolia.*

6.5 Optimisation of peat-working practices and starting conditions for restoration

6.5.1 Introduction

It is not possible to set out universal guidelines on desirable working practices to optimise starting conditions for restoration following extraction, as these will partly depend upon site-specific features:

- conservation objectives;
- character of the existing biological resource;
- character and configuration of the remaining peat deposit (especially topography and peat properties);
- environmental context of the sites (especially climate, but also characteristics and use of the adjoining landscape).

Here, some of the underlying principles are identified and working practices suggested which facilitate the restoration process.

6.5.2 General requirements

The following requirements are likely to be applicable in many restoration initiatives:

- a scientific assessment of the character of the site, possibly by independent environmental scientists (Akkermann, 1983), with particular regard to features important in determining desirable and feasible restoration options, based on factors identified in *Chapter 7*; [1]

- a restoration strategy should be devised and agreed for the site, based on the scientific assessment and conservation objectives [*Chapter 3*];
- where feasible, peat extractors should optimise and phase working operations to facilitate the agreed restoration strategy;
- working practices should aim to minimise further damage to abandoned areas and refugia, and, where feasible, enable restoration work to commence on some working areas as soon as possible;
- at cessation of operations (in parts or all of the site), peat fields should be configured into an (agreed) condition that will optimise restoration (*i.e.* to maximise use of *in situ* machinery, operators and infrastructure) [*Chapters 5 & 8*].

6.5.3 Working practices for restoration during peat extraction operations

Once restoration options have been defined for a particular site ongoing peat operations should aim to minimise damage to remnants and refugia that have been agreed as having an important and sustainable conservation value or which are in some other way critical to restoration objectives. They should also aim to optimise the conditions upon abandonment to facilitate the realisation of the objectives. The following principles should be taken into consideration, and implemented where possible:

- Important refugia (which may include little-damaged areas of bog, as well as revegetated cuttings or damaged areas with an important biological resource) should be identified and steps taken to preserve or enhance their existing conservation interest. Such areas should not be subject to further peat extraction, unless as part of an agreed rolling programme of peat extraction and restoration.

- If feasible and necessary, a buffer zone should be designated around the core part of any refugium areas, which should also remain uncut. [This requirement will partly depend upon the topographical circumstance and the method used to protect the remnant massif; optimum widths will be site-specific. See Chapter 8.]

- Work should start on the restoration of abandoned areas and maintenance of refugia as soon as possible, so that dehydration is minimised.

- Peat should be extracted in such a way as to leave upstanding baulks to a specified eventual height at agreed intervals. This height will be site-specific; 0.5–1 m is likely to be appropriate for many sites. It is recognised that in many existing workings, it would not be possible to achieve the final configuration of baulks in this way as the scale desired would be too small. In this case, residual

---

[1] These may include some assessment of: existing biological resource; characteristics of the residual peat deposit (peat topography, type, depth, permeability, storage coefficient and position of water table); downward water loss into mineral ground; character of minerotrophic water sources (if any).

baulks may be supplemented by constructed baulks after operations have ceased.

- If feasible, operations should be phased such that:
  (i)   Contiguous areas are completed in sequence.
  (ii) Areas closest to refugia should be abandoned first, leaving agreed depths of peat. [This would help to reduce the hydraulic gradient from the remnant across the cuttings, and may help to reduce drying-out. It will also make the design of a 'cascade paddy-field' system of lagoons more feasible. Note, however, that this feature will depend upon the existing topography and agreed restoration strategy for the site.]

- If the aim is to recreate ombrotrophic bog directly, it is recommended that *as a general rule* a minimum of 50 cm of *ombrotrophic* peat be left *in situ*. Sufficient peat should also be left to allow for constructs to impound water (bunds or a scalloped surface). [This suggested residual depth may vary according to the nature of the peat and the underlying substratum and its topography and restoration objectives. In sites subject to downwards seepage of water into the mineral substratum, a greater depth (> 1m) may be needed to seal to base of the bog, in others, a depth of 50 cm (or less) may be adequate [4.4.5]. The difference between a *minimum* depth of 50 cm and an *average* depth of 50 cm should be noted.]

- Drains should not be dug into mineral subsoil (unless this is impermeable and unlikely to lead to downward water loss). [This may be impossible to achieve where the agreed depth of peat to be left *in situ* is an <u>average</u> of 50 cm.]

- Where possible, 'nursery' pools for the 'farming' of *Sphagnum* should be initiated, to provide an inoculum for abandoned areas [9.2].

- Drainage operations should be assessed, and where possible redesigned to minimise impacts on remnants and areas undergoing restoration. In low rainfall areas it may be desirable to pump drainage water into abandoned peat workings *etc.*, although this will partly depend on the quality of the pumped water [*Chapter 5*].

6.5.4 *Operations following abandonment*

Once an area has been brought out of production, further operations should start as soon as practicable to facilitate rewetting and revegetation. This should be planned to ensure that rewetting initiatives do not preclude subsequent access or actions elsewhere on the site. In sites where peat extraction is ongoing in adjoining areas, it will usually be most cost-effective to make use of the machinery available on site for restoration work. More specific background and details are given elsewhere in this volume [in particular Chapters 5, 8, 9 & 10], but the main factors to be considered are outlined below.

Water management

All ditches and outfalls should be blocked where possible to increase retention of rainfall and reduce water loss *etc*. It may be necessary to further seal / fill ditches cut into mineral soil where these are thought to contribute significantly to vertical water losses [Chapters 2 & 4] or to provide undesirable mineral enrichment.

Topographical manipulation

Attention should be given to the creation of optimum conditions for rewetting and revegetation, including the building of constructs, such as bunds. Where possible, use should be made of the existing network of embankments *etc.*, raising levels where necessary, although the permeability of the baulks should first be determined to assess their efficacy. [The movement of peat and alteration of the configuration of abandoned peat cuttings should be carried out as part of an agreed restoration plan, usually in consultation with the statutory conservation and archaeological bodies.]

Milled surfaces

It may be necessary to subdivide large peat fields to create lagoons to facilitate rewetting and renaturation.

Block-cut surfaces

Depending on the configuration remaining, it may be desirable to flatten some of the baulks to achieve a more level area for rewetting, while utilising some baulks to retain water. It should be possible to use some of the material from the 'redundant' baulks to fill the ditches.

Control of vegetation invasion

Vegetation management should start as soon as production ceases in order to reduce the establishment of 'undesirable' species, especially if it is not possible to raise water levels within a short time [Chapter 10]. Where 'abandoned' fields lie within the zone of ongoing peat extraction, it may be possible to achieve this by running rotovating machinery over the surface each year to retard seedling establishment. Where this has not been done, it may be necessary to remove vegetation (*e.g.* birch and *Molinia*) from abandoned areas prior to rewetting.

6.5.5 *Maintenance*

Full renaturation and regeneration of rewetted peat fields is likely to be slow, partly on account of the impoverished nature of the ombrotrophic environment and the intrinsically low relative growth rates of bog plants. In consistently wet conditions, initial colonisation by pioneer *Sphagnum* species (*e.g. S. cuspid-atum*) may occur rapidly, but subsequent development to a more diverse bog surface is likely to take longer, possibly several decades [6.6]. There is scope for exploring possible means of artificial acceleration of colonisation by other bog species [Chapter 9]. As the cut-over areas regenerate into bog they may be expected to become increasingly self-sustaining. However, some degree of maintenance may be needed in the early stages of rewetting and renaturation, such as removal of scrub from dry sites within the peat fields (though the extent of this problem will depend partly on the success of the rewetting procedures). The condition of the peat bunds, especially the outer ones, will also require periodic inspection and, if needed, some maintenance. The expected intrinsically-slow renaturation of the peat fields is likely to mean that some (intermittent) maintenance may be required for much longer than an after-care period of 5 years. The restoration scheme should be designed to minimise on-going management requirements[1] but also to make it practicable for them to take place, if needed.

6.6 Prospects for restoration

An assessment of the prospects of restoration of lowland bogs damaged by peat extraction must be subject to the usual caveats of the precise objectives of restoration and the specific conditions of individual sites. Assessment of the desirability and the perceived success of restoration options also needs to take into account the condition of the sites prior to current peat extraction: some, but not all, sites were considerably damaged before current peat extraction operations (as a consequence of drainage, repeated burning, partial agricultural conversion or an earlier phase of peat extraction). In such cases successful restoration may serve to enhance the conservation value of the site.

6.6.1 Remnant peat massifs

Many of the 'best' remaining raised bogs in Britain have been subject to some degree of marginal damage and reduction in area, either through peat extraction or conversion for agriculture. The fact that they still provide a 'good quality' bog habitat points to the capacity of the systems to accommodate, naturally, some degree of marginal damage. The 'cost' of this capacity is usually some drying around the margins of the sites and the degree to which this is regarded as

acceptable will largely depend upon the proportion of marginal damage relative to the area of little-damaged bog and upon the consequential effects of the damage. In large sites, with just a small amount of marginal water draw-down, some loss of area may be acceptable (although long-term effects may be unknown). Greater problems arise where only a small peat remnant is left undamaged or where, perhaps because of a large height difference between the peat fields (*etc.*) and the remnant surface, marginal water drawdown affects most of the bog. Here the damage is likely to result in a loss or reduction of typical bog species over much or all of the massif, unless constructive measures are taken to prevent this. These may include the construction of bunds around some or all of the periphery of the remnant, an approach which has had some success in The Netherlands.

It is undoubtedly possible to retain existing interest upon a bog massif with a little damaged surface, though this may require some engineering. It is similarly possible to retain bog species upon a partly damaged surface, though not necessarily in the same proportions as when in a little-damaged state, and perhaps requiring some periodic management to remove 'undesirable' colonists such as birch. In this situation attempts to enhance the quality of the vegetation and habitat by further elevation of the water level (where possible) may also meet with some success, depending upon specific circumstances (though such procedures may not integrate well with attempts at restoration of adjoining cut-over surfaces). However, where a massif surface is badly damaged (so that it has lost many or most of its original species) effective rewetting may be much more difficult[2] and, whilst perhaps technically possible, may be impractical or cost-ineffective, except perhaps in the case of large massifs or sites located in particularly cool and wet regions. Elsewhere it may be more practical to permit the massif to develop into a replacement habitat of some more general wildlife interest.

6.6.2 Cut-over ombrotrophic surfaces

It is evident from examination of old peat cuttings that, where they have been kept (often fortuitously) in a suitably wet condition, recolonisation by typical bog species has occurred, to the extent that in some instances the appearance and composition of the vegetation is little different to that found on some little-damaged bogs, including some development of a hummock-hollow patterning. Such examples are typically some 50–150 years old. Although some such examples are quite large (several hectares) they are

---

[1] For example, by ensuring that the floors of lagoons can be kept inundated, to minimise opportunities for establishment of undesirable species; a strongly undulating, or sloping, surface may create periodically dry areas that are susceptible to birch encroachment *etc.*

[2] This will partly depend upon the reason why the massif is damaged and dry.

usually on a much smaller scale than current commercial operations; moreover, the conditions of their restoration may have been rather different to that of some present operations (*e.g.* close juxtaposition to sources of recolonist species), though in many instances critical information is lacking.

Restoration initiatives on large commercial cut-over sites are still in their infancy; moreover some of them have been in sites where problems of water management have been exacerbated by several unusually dry summers and by vertical loss of water down into a permeable mineral substratum. Nonetheless, it is evident (a) that a wide range of bog plant species can invade such surfaces (where there is a proximate inoculum source); and (b) that it is possible to rewet the peat fields to the extent that (c) carpets of aquatic Sphagna can rapidly colonise extensive areas. This latter event permits considerable optimism for regeneration prospects as it is evident (from studies on the natural development of bogs and of recolonised peat workings) that a wet *Sphagnum cuspidatum* phase has provided a basis for spontaneous successional development of a more diverse vegetation composed of more important bog-building species such as *Sphagnum papillosum* and *S. magellanicum* (*e.g.* Joosten, 1995). It is difficult to see why this process should not be repeated on commercially-cut over sites, provided that three conditions are satisfied:

(i) that the site is accessible to potential recolonist species (if it is not, then re-introduction of species will need to be considered) [Chapter 9];

(ii) that the chemical composition of precipitation inputs will support the growth of recolonist bog species and

(iii) that sufficient precipitation water can be retained on site.

If such conditions are not limiting, it seems likely that commercially-cut peat fields will redevelop a characteristic bog vegetation and that peat accumulation will recommence in time. Indeed, the long-term stability of bog development on flat peat-cutting surfaces may well be greater than that on upstanding bog remnants.

6.6.3 Cut-over minerotrophic surfaces

Prospects for restoration of minerotrophic surfaces will depend critically upon the topography of the site, the water level that can be maintained and the quality of the water used to achieve this. Fen vegetation of conservation value has spontaneously redeveloped on extensive cut-over fen peat surfaces, including examples that are flat and not flooded (*e.g.* Woodwalton Fen, Cambridgeshire (Poore, 1956)) and examples in large, flooded cuttings (*e.g.* Catfield &

Irstead Fens, Norfolk (Giller & Wheeler, 1986)). In both cases revegetation has occurred over large areas (tens of hectares), but the nature of the vegetation that has redeveloped in each is rather different. Some examples of revegetation within flooded peat workings has produced some of the prime areas of lowland fen within the UK. Such hydroseral situations are also susceptible to *Sphagnum* establishment and in some locations considerable thicknesses of *Sphagnum* peat have accumulated (up to 1m depth in *c.* 100–150 years). By contrast, *Sphagnum* re-establishment on solid fen surfaces is generally more limited, probably on account of periodic dryness and irrigation with base-rich water.

For the most part, the particular conditions that were operative at the start of the spontaneous revegetation of cut-over fen peats are not known. This makes generalisation from historical observations to present-day workings difficult, other than to recognise the importance of wet, shallowly-inundated, conditions to the prospects of re-establishment of specific types of fen and the development of bog. In principle, given appropriate water management, there seems little reason why ombrotrophication processes should not recur in fens sites which have formerly supported raised bog, subject again to (i) the possible limitations of availability of suitable recolonist species; (ii) deposition of atmospheric contaminants; and (iii) the stability of telluric water supply to the fen peat.

6.7 Holistic approaches to raised-bog restoration

In some situations the restoration of damaged peatlands *can* be approached piecemeal. This approach is likely to be most satisfactory when it is possible to provide independent hydrological control of particular land parcels. For example, in the fen peat basins of individual holdings in the Somerset Levels it may often be possible to rewet and renature each peat working independently of the others. Similarly, some sealed depressions within ombrotrophic peat may be rewetted independently of their surroundings; indeed, as noted above [6.2] such an approach may be the only practical possibility in some sites where cut-over surfaces have been left at widely differing levels. Such an approach may be very effective in maintaining populations of bog species within the landscape (*i.e.* production of a series of 'bog gardens') but it is less suited to the co-ordinated regeneration of a single mire [5.6].

These observations notwithstanding, habitat continuity is often particularly important in the restoration of mires because of their dependence upon a suitable water source (and sink). Whilst lack of such continuity may not prevent effective rewetting it may materially increase the complexity (and cost) of water management. This problem is sometimes most evident in attempts to restore fen ecosystems, where some separate peat cuttings may have become isolated from appropriate sources of minerotrophic water (inputs of river or seepage water). In principle, this problem is much less acute in ombrotrophic systems as the main water source (precipitation) is accessible across the entire site. However, even here, some surface configuration (e.g. a very varied block-cut topography) may require a mosaic of several individual rewetting schemes. In addition, rewetting of bogs in low rainfall regions may only be possible by some redistribution of water across the entire site (e.g. by a form of 'gradient feeding' [5.4]). Unless continued pumping is countenanced, this approach requires inputs from parts of the surrounding mire and hence an integrated water management plan.

An integrated approach to site restoration may also provide a rational basis for decisions upon conservation priorities in specific areas. For example, where workings in fen peat can only be rewetted by nutrient-rich river water, they may be appropriately managed for birds (as reedbeds); where they can be kept wet by nutrient-poor seepage water, then management for a species-rich fen vegetation can be considered. On ombrotrophic peat, restoration to *Sphagnum*-rich vegetation can be focused on those areas that are least difficult to maintain in a wet condition. This approach thereby avoids the problem that can accompany piecemeal restoration, namely attempts to recreate a specific habitat-type in circumstances that are not best suited to it.

In most instances, restoration of a raised bog need not demand the rewetting of adjoining land, even in those cases where it once formed part of the original peatland area. However, in some instances localised rewetting may be useful, for example, to enhance the coherence of the mire (e.g. at Wreaks and White Mosses (Duddon, Cumbria) where two massifs of peat are now separated by a narrow strip of agricultural land) or as part of a co-ordinated strategy for the restoration of a remnant massif and surrounding peat workings or drained land [5.6].

In some cases, effective rewetting of a bog may only be possible by some manipulation of the drainage in the surrounding land. This is likely to be the case where land-drainage systems directly (a) drain the mire (e.g. Fenns and Whixall Moss) or (b) indirectly drain it, in situations where the water table in fen peat or an underlying aquifer would otherwise form the 'impermeable' base to the perched water mound. Rewetting of peat workings in fen peat may have greater repercussions upon the adjoining land as often the ability to rewet the workings may depend upon water supply and retention that is determined, directly or indirectly, by adjoining land drainage systems.

Such considerations suggest that the restoration or recreation of wetlands as substantial landscape features would benefit from the development of a co-ordinated policy of land management. This would require integration of the activities and interests of the peat industry and the conservation bodies and also, in specific situations, of the Internal Drainage Boards, the Water Authorities, the National River Authorities and agriculturalists. Integration of restoration activities into an overall plan (and the available options) will also depend upon the timing of peat extraction in specific areas, particularly in those localities where there are several operators (e.g. Somerset Levels). In such situations the development of a holistic scheme for mire restoration would be enhanced if it was possible for the co-ordinating body to develop a proactive strategy for peat extraction rather than to just be responsive to individual applications.

It may also be noted that decisions concerning the desirability of the various wetland habitat-types that could form the most appropriate focus for wetland restoration schemes in different parts of the UK could benefit from the formulation of a 'national wetland strategy'. Amongst other things, this could help identify *objective* ground-rules for assessing priorities in wetland habitat recreation, based on such considerations as the perceived 'value' of particular habitat-types, their national and regional scarcity and the feasibility and appropriateness of their recreation in specific locations. Such an approach would help to provide a rationale for wetland restoration options based on assessed ecological and conservational merit and would thus reduce the chance of options being chosen on a purely *ad hoc* basis or in response to the overweening influence of a particular interest group.

PART III

Practical Aspects of Restoration

Chapter 7

Planning a restoration strategy

7.1 Introduction

The occurrence of spontaneous and 'desirable' reveget-ation of some abandoned peat workings shows that in some instances a measure of bog 'restoration' can be achieved without intervention or planning. However, the existence of large areas of rather dry cut-over surfaces dominated by birch, bracken or heather shows that this is by no means always the case. In most damaged peatland sites, particularly those subject to extensive commercial peat extraction, it will be important to develop a strategy in order to optimise restoration procedures to achieve specific objectives. This is required to ensure that:

- areas of existing natural history interest that will not be subject to further peat extraction are safeguarded;
- peat workings are left in a condition optimal for restoration;
- restoration practices and objectives for specific areas are well phased and integrated with one another;
- techniques appropriate to achieve specific restoration objectives are identified.

Formulation of a restoration plan for a cut-over bog site requires the acquisition of some information about the site in question (*e.g.* Turchenek, Tedder & Kranowski, 1993; Famous, *et al.* 1995; Ward, Hirons & Self, 1995). Information (environmental and biological) is required particularly: (i) to help select appropriate restoration options; (ii) to identify the constraints upon the chosen options and to enable informed decisions to be made on the most appropriate ways to achieve specific objectives; and (iii) to provide base-line data for monitoring purposes.

Consultation with various statutory and non-statutory bodies will form an important part of the planning phase of restoration. These include the local mineral planning authority, heritage, conservation and water resources bodies. It may also be necessary to engage specialists in order, for example, to carry out survey work; interpret the results; assist in the preparation of an appropriate restoration scheme with detailed specifications; and to provide legal advice.

The variability of starting conditions amongst damaged lowland peatlands means that a universal statement of 'data required' for formulating a restoration plan cannot be made. However, it is possible to identify some of the main types of information that may be needed, the objectives of restoration and the way in which restoration may be planned, although specific requirements are likely to vary between sites, depending upon their exact conditions.

7.2 Planning for restoration

7.2.1 Approaches to restoration planning

There are at least three broad approaches to peatland restoration in relation to the nature of information required.

Unplanned approach

The 'unplanned approach' is one in which, for example, spontaneous changes are allowed to take place in a way which it is hoped will produce a satis-factory result. Although several important conservation sites are a product of unplanned restoration, this cannot be commended as a reliable approach to realise a specific restoration goal. Nonetheless, in many restoration schemes, some events and responses are likely to be both unplanned and unexpected.

Empirical approach

The 'empirical approach' is one in which restoration is substantially based upon an intuitive appraisal of the requirements for habitat manipulation, rather than upon data acquisition and prediction. This approach has both merits and limitations:

- some successful restoration initiatives have proceeded in this way;
- ignorance of actual site conditions may mean that this approach involves a good deal of 'trial-and-error' in which certain options are tried and then, if necessary, modified; some errors may be acceptable if they are not too costly or irreversible;
- it is strongly dependent upon the personnel involved; some individuals have a clear intuitive appraisal of controls on particular conditions within peatlands with which they are familiar; others do not;
- this approach is often not readily communicable, nor are reasons for failure or success always easily identified;

- it is particularly suitable for *repair* of relatively minor damage to bog sites, where the options are fairly well circumscribed, where the operations are comparatively small-scale and can be reversed or replaced if unsuccessful;

- it is less suitable for the *rebuilding* of extensively damaged sites, where larger-scale and innovative habitat manipulation may be needed;

- even in extensively damaged sites this approach may have some contribution to make; for example, peat workers often have a good insight into the drains that have most control of the water balance of the bog, or of areas where water naturally accumulates; the identification of wet conditions to nucleate restoration may be more easily and accurately assessed by examining the natural accumulation of water than by attempting to predict it using topographical and hydrological measurements.

Measured approach

The 'measured approach' is one in which numerous data concerning site conditions are collected and analysed predictively to devise a well-researched, well thought-out restoration plan. This is often considered to be the 'best' approach. Nonetheless, it may have a number of limitations both in principle and, particularly, in practice:

- there is sometimes a tendency for data acquisition not to be focused upon specific questions, but to be part of a 'wish-list' of 'useful' information, or to be seen as a way of identifying the specific questions that need to be answered; sometimes the acquisition of such data, although of interest, may have little direct relevance to the development of a restoration plan and may even be counter-productive because:

- data acquisition is frequently expensive and in most cases this constrains the amount of information that can be collected; this usually results either in inadequate sample replication or inadequate site coverage. The latter may be of particular importance in large raised-bog sites and can lead to lack of information about quite large parts of the mire; it is quite common experience that even elaborate investigations do not generate the level of detail required for some restoration purposes;

- data interpretation may sometimes be difficult. This reflects both lack of knowledge and understanding specific to some areas of peatland ecology together with the more general problems of data interpretation. For example, it is simple to measure high concentrations of ammonium in the peat of some peat extraction surfaces but it is much more difficult to predict the threshold concentrations that may constrain re-invasion by typical bog plant species;

- measurements and analyses may not provide the level of predictive accuracy required for the exact formulation of restoration objectives. For example, there are various procedures available for modelling the behaviour of water table in peatlands, but they may have limited capacity to predict *accurately* the position of the water table with respect to the peat surface, especially in peat-cutting sites. This is because of intrinsic limitations of

some models; because the more sophisticated models are 'data-hungry'; and because of the difficulty of obtaining meaningful estimates of certain parameters for the models. Restoration initiatives may, of course, provide a valuable opportunity to develop and refine various ecological techniques, but there are obvious limitations in using methods with unknown propensities to study peatland sites with unknown properties.

In practice, many restoration schemes will rely on a sensitive interaction between the empirical and measured approaches. In most cases, empirical procedures require some 'hard' data to help ensure (and monitor) their success, but equally, the empirical approach may provide the only realist option when data acquisition is inadequate or of limited predictive reliability. To yield maximum benefits for restoration, data acquisition should be: (a) focused upon answering specific, defined questions that are critical to particular aspects of restoration; (b) sufficiently well resourced to ensure that reliable and usable data are collected; and (c) performed by experienced practitioners who are aware of the inherent problems and likely limitations of their studies. These comments are not intended to discourage acquisition of site data, but to emphasise the need for relevant and reliable data and for a considered appraisal, at the outset of planning a restoration strategy, of the salient questions and data that are likely to be required to answer them. The acquisition of information of limited relevance or reliability (*e.g.* because of inadequate replication) may ultimately provide little more than a loss of money!

7.2.2 Feasibility study

In view of the various sources of information potentially available and varying conditions at different sites, it is recommended that the formulation of restoration schemes should be preceded by a feasibility study which will provide the basis for choice of specific objectives for a site and the nature of any restoration work required. For sites currently under extraction, a restoration scheme should be formulated as soon as possible, before extraction ceases, even though this will involve an element of prediction (*e.g.* final topography, peat depths *etc.*).

The primary functions of the feasibility study are:

(i) to determine the practical and financial feasibility of restoration;

(ii) to determine the most suitable techniques for retaining and enhancing any existing wildlife or archaeological interest within or on a site (in particular raised-bog elements);

(iii) to determine the most suitable techniques for recreating an appropriate habitat (in particular, the raised-bog habitat) on a cut-over or otherwise damaged site, paying due regard to (i).

In some sites it may also be appropriate to consider the potential of the site for education and research and its potential for interpretation and public access.

Assessments will be based on information derived from (a) a preliminary 'desk study' by collation of existing information and (b) from on-site investigations. The latter, together with interpretation of the information, may require the expertise of specialists from several disciplines, although an indication of the importance and usefulness of the information is given in the appropriate sections below. Collection of superfluous information should be minimised by careful scoping of the site assessment programme; a reasonable balance must be achieved between collection of adequate data to facilitate informed decisions and the cost of collecting such data. The latter is likely to be a major limiting factor in peatland restoration. An example of the potential scope of a feasibility study is given in Table 7.1.

It is essential that accurate maps are prepared for use in consultations and survey work if not already available.

7.2.3 Consultation

Consultations should begin as early as possible in the planning stages of a restoration scheme. They relate both to the process of choosing the most appropriate restoration objectives for each site and the realisation of the specified objective. It will particularly help to identify at an early stage any known potential constraints on development. The main interested parties are given in Table 7.2. Key consultees include the statutory bodies, peat extraction companies and land or mineral owners involved with the site or adjacent land. There are also numerous non-statutory organisations who may be able to provide advice or information on various aspects of the site and proposed restoration schemes, some of whom may wish to be directly involved. Some of these are listed in Table 7.3.

Table 7.1 Potential scope of a feasibility study concerning the restoration of a cut-over or damaged peatland site.

1. Site description
  1.1 Site location, landscape setting, and boundary information
  1.2 Soils and geology (including peat types and depths)
  1.3 General topography (within site, and in relation to surroundings)
  1.4 Flora and fauna (past, present and potential) (including features of special interest or conservation value)
  1.5 Hydrology (including climate, regional and local water resources, 'undesirable' water inputs)
  1.6 Current and past management
  1.7 Archaeology / historic landscape / industrial landscape

2. Peat workings
  2.1 Extent, type, age, planning permissions (current and future)
  2.2 Topography and relationship to uncut areas
  2.3 Integration into restoration strategy

3. Ownership / Tenancies
  3.1 Details of land and minerals ownership of site and adjoining land which may be affected by any restoration scheme

4. Restoration options
  4.1 Objectives
  4.2 Constraints and opportunities
    4.2.1 Potential legal and land-use constraints on development (*e.g.* physical, legal, financial, wildlife, manpower, timescales, archaeology, adjoining land-use)
    4.2.2 Options available, and potential for financial and practical assistance
  4.3 Specification of restoration work including:
    4.3.1 Conservation of existing features of importance
    4.3.2 Optimisation of working practices to achieve optimal starting conditions for restoration
    4.3.3 Work needed to improve hydrological water balance (and water quality, if appropriate)
    4.3.4 Reconfiguration of topography
    4.3.5 Proposed schedule of restoration work (including phasing of the work, taking climatic, management and practical constraints into consideration)
    4.3.6 Proposals for on-going maintenance and management
    4.3.7 Proposals for monitoring progress

6. Costed options

The focus of the consultations may depend upon the initiator of the restoration scheme, for example a nature conservation body attempting to restore former peat workings or a peat company putting forward a plan when applying to a Mineral Planning Authority (MPA) for an updated or new planning permission. The guidance is also of relevance to MPA's in assessing the information provided in any applications submitted.

7.3 Financial considerations

7.3.1 Introduction

The feasibility of the various restoration options may depend on financial limitations, as well as practical and legal constraints. Unless funding for restoration work has been agreed in advance, an important part of the initial feasibility study will be to determine the potential for financial or practical assistance that may be available from different sources, including both statutory and non-statutory conservation bodies. The latter may be able to provide help with past records for the site, reconnaissance and recording. The costs of restoration are inevitably site specific, depending on such factors as the size of the site, the degree of damage, the extent of the remedial action necessary to achieve the stated management objectives (including archaeological mitigation), availability of materials, and the technical difficulties in carrying out the work. Some typical ranges of costs for different techniques are given in Table 7.4.

Table 7.2 Primary interested parties* in the formulation of a restoration scheme.

Organisation	Topic
Peat extraction companies	Involvement and co-operation in restoration schemes, advice on methods, use of machinery *etc.* Details of peat extraction history. Future plans for land when extraction completed. Possible financial support for restoration work.
Land and mineral owners involved with the site or adjacent land (if different from above)	Involvement and co-operation in restoration schemes. Legal aspects of site leases. Future plans for land following cessation of extraction.
Mineral Planning Authority	Guidance on planning and conservation issues (*e.g.* in development plans) Planning constraints relating to the site (*e.g.* existing conditions, rights of way); Site history (planning). Statutory designations, *e.g.* Local Nature Reserves (LNR), common land, Scheduled Ancient Monuments (SAM). Non-Statutory designations *e.g.* Local Nature Reserves. Possible financial support for restoration work.
English Nature, Countryside Council for Wales, Scottish Natural Heritage, DoE(NI), Countryside Commission.	Statutory designations *e.g.* National Nature Reserves, Sites of Special Scientific Interest (SSSI's), Areas of Special Scientific Interest (ASSI's), Areas of Outstanding Natural Beauty (AONB), National Parks, Special Protection Areas (SPA's) and Ramsar sites. Occurrence or likely occurrence of scheduled species *e.g.* adder, badger, great crested newt. Wildlife value of the site and existing records. Advice on species introductions and peatland restoration methods. Possible practical and / or financial support for restoration work.
National Rivers Authority (NRA) and Internal Drainage Boards (IDB); River Purification Boards (Scotland) ; DoE(NI).	Consent requirements for water abstraction, water impoundment, water discharge, works affecting drainage or flood defences. Location of any nearby water abstraction points. Pollution potential of discharges Possible collaboration with, practical or financial support for and advice on restoration work. Water quality information / data relating to catchment water supply / adjacent water courses / regional water resources *etc.*
The Ministry of Agriculture Fisheries and Food (MAFF), Department of Agriculture Northern Ireland (DANI), Scottish Office Agriculture and Fisheries Department (SOAFD), Forestry Authority	Catchment management. Current usage and possible effects on adjacent land. Designations of Environmentally Sensitive Areas (ESA's) Agricultural land quality (of site and/or surrounding areas)
English Heritage, Cadw, Historic Scotland, DoE (NI), County Archaeological Officers	Advice on archaeological interest and survey. Location and details of Scheduled Ancient Monuments (SAM). Possible practical and / or financial support for restoration work.

*   The relevant participants will depend on the party initiating or assessing the restoration scheme.

As with much conservation work, there is unlikely to be much tangible economic return on the investment, unless (a) the raised-bog objective is subsumed by more remunerative objectives such as provision of a fishing lake; (b) compensation payments are made; or (c) public access and financial contribution is encouraged. The major investments are likely to occur at the start of a project, but ongoing maintenance management may be essential for a long time. It is clear that the most cost-effective means of carrying out the work will be carried out by or in co-operation with the Peat Industry, where the machinery and expertise are already on site. Some of the most reliable guides to

costing come from NW Germany, where a number of bogs have now been prepared for restoration. These suggest that preparation costs of cut-over surfaces are in the region of £ 200–400 ha^{-1} when appropriate equipment exists on site and £ 800–1250 ha^{-1} when it has to be brought in.

The costs associated with restoration can be broken down under the following headings:

- Land - *e.g.* purchase of site or adjacent land.
- Restoration procedures and management:
    (a) personnel;
    (b) specialist advice;
    (c) management operations;

Table 7.3 Useful consultees in the formulation of a restoration scheme (in addition to those given in Table 7.2).

Source	Nature of information
Local Authority Record Office.	County Series Ordnance Survey maps. Estate plans. Early documents relating to peat extraction.
Local Authority archaeologists or Archaeological Trust; Council for British Archaeology; local archaeological organisations; wetland archaeological specialists	Site history. Statutory designations e.g. Scheduled Ancient Monuments. Information and advice on archaeological interest and value of the site. Possible practical support for survey and restoration work.
Royal Commission on Historical Monuments of England; Royal Commission on Historical Monuments of Wales; Royal Commission on Historical Monuments of Scotland; Historic Scotland	Hold the National Archaeological Record, which contains information on archaeological sites, and the National Building Record, which includes the National Record of Industrial Monuments.
Joint Nature Conservation Committee	Existing records for specific sites (including Invertebrate Site Register). Advice on conservation and management for specific species
The Wildlife Trust Partnership RSNC; Scottish Wildlife Trust; Ulster Wildlife Trust	Existing records for specific sites. Amenity and wildlife value of sites. Advice on restoration methods used in existing restoration schemes on Trust reserves.
Council for the Protection of Rural England; Council for the Protection of Rural Wales.	Landscape, wildlife, and historical details relating to local sites.
Royal Society for the Protection of Birds (RSPB), British Trust for Ornithology (BTO) and other national and local specialist bird groups	Ornithological records for specific local sites. Advice on conservation and management for specific species.
National and local specialist invertebrate groups (*e.g.* Royal Entomological Society; British Entomology and Natural History Society; Balfour-Browne Club; British Arachnological Society; British Dragonfly Society; British Butterfly Society; Bees, Wasps and Ants Recording Scheme.)	Invertebrate records for specific local sites. Advice on invertebrate conservation and management.
Various other national and local conservation / specialist species groups	Records for specific sites.
Biological Records Centre	Wildlife information covering a wide range of groups. Species evaluation.
Health and Safety Executive	Health and safety issues of the site.
Utilities	Location of gas, telephone, electricity, water supply and surface and foul drainage.
Meteorological Office	Climatic records and information.
Institute of Hydrology	Information and advice on hydrological aspects.
Scientific literature, local journals *etc.*	General and specific information on various aspects of peatlands, restoration, conservation, site / county records *etc.* In some cases, such information may be held by conservation / historical / archaeological groups *etc.*
Local schools and colleges *etc.*	If a site has been used as an educational resource, unpublished records may be held.

(d) monitoring and maintenance;

(e) archaeological survey and mitigation

These are considered further below. In some instances, financial assistance with the costs may be available through various schemes and organisations [see Table 7.5].

7.3.2 Land costs

The costs of purchasing or leasing land has been a major consideration in the conservation of several of the raised-bog sites in England and Wales, although obviously this will not be a consideration where the work is to be carried out by existing owners or occupiers, unless the scheme requires control of additional land. For example, the National Nature Reserve at Fenns and Whixall was bought in 1990 at a cost of £ 1.7m (for 137 ha) and £ 20,000 is spent annually[1] on rent for the leased land (302.3 ha). Costs of land purchase in the Somerset Levels were estimated to vary from c. £ 2,800 to £ 10,700 ha^{-1} depending on the amount of peat remaining (Hancock, 1991).

7.3.3 Restoration procedures and management

(a) Personnel

Most of the major restoration projects in the UK currently undertaken by the statutory conservation agencies involve a full time warden (site manager), with assistance from varying numbers of estate workers. Some sites are managed as nature reserves by the local Wildlife Trusts. Volunteer labour is often used but it is generally considered to be most cost-effective to leave tasks such as ditch blocking to contractors or permanent staff using mechanical methods, particularly where large scale operations are involved. However, even with experienced contractors, considerable time investment by site managers is usually needed to supervise the work to ensure that it is carried out to the required specifications and in the right place.

(b) Specialist advice

It is likely to be necessary to involve specialists in order, for example, to carry out survey work (topographical, biological, hydrological, archaeological); perform chemical analyses of water, peat or mineral substrata; interpret the results; assist in the preparation of an appropriate restoration scheme with detailed specifications, and perhaps occasionally to provide legal advice. This is likely to be relatively

expensive; typical consultancy fees may range from < £ 100 to £ 1000 per day, depending on the type of work, and experience necessary to carry it out. The information required should therefore be carefully identified before any such work is commissioned.

(c) Management operations

Approximate ranges of costs have been summarised for different management operations [Table 7.4], based on information provided by site managers, the peat industry and published information (e.g. Beets, 1993; Edgar, 1993). From these, the approximate potential costs of some restoration measures have been estimated for a hypothetical situation of a cut-over bog with an adjacent remnant, which could amount to around £ 140,000–200,000, excluding supervision, survey, monitoring etc. However, it should be recognised that costs will inevitably depend heavily on the extent of the remedial action required.

Machinery, equipment and materials

A variety of specialist machinery, adapted for work on boggy terrain (i.e. with low ground pressure) is likely to be required to carry out the various operations required for restoration (e.g. scrub clearance, ditch blocking, bunding, surface configuration). The choice of machine depends on the task and the operating conditions. Advice can be appropriately sought from the peat industry and the statutory conservation agencies with experience in restoration. It will be most cost-effective if the work can be carried out as a rolling programme of restoration alongside ongoing peat extraction, while the machinery is on site. In the absence of appropriate equipment on site, it will usually be necessary to hire the machines (and perhaps operators) from contractors; this is generally more expensive than standard agricultural contracting rates. Use of inexperienced contractors, although sometimes cheaper, is not recommended as practical experience suggests that these lack appropriate expertise and require more supervision.

For construction of peat dams and bunds, the most cost-effective option is to use the peat in situ, where this is available and judged to be sufficiently well decomposed. Excavation and transport of peat from one area to another substantially increases costs. It may also be necessary to reinforce the dams with an impermeable core, either of polythene, plastic-coated metal or wood.

Irrigation using pumps and piping requires purchase of hardware, plus installation and running costs.

It may be appropriate to provide boardwalks at some sites, for example, to facilitate management and monitoring or to provide public access.

---

[1] To be reviewed every three years.

Vegetation management

Scrub control is often a major problem of vegetation management, either on bog remnants that have dried out, or on abandoned surfaces [10.2]. Depending on staff and machine availability, this can either be carried out 'in house' or by using contractors. Costs quoted varied from *c.* £ 400 to £ 2,500 ha^{-1}, depending on the amount of scrub.

Grazing is only practised rarely in bog restoration projects in the UK, and is not generally considered to be economical (*i.e.* it costs more to maintain and supervise the flock than is recouped from sale of the wool or meat) although it could be considered to be a cost-effective management tool in certain circumstances, for example, in helping to control scrub invasion until water levels are sufficiently raised.

The active revegetation of cut-over areas, by transplantation of vegetation *etc.* [see Chapter 9] should be included in any costed options. This would mainly involve transport and labour costs, but may be as much as £ 2,000 per ha. Obviously, such procedures require careful planning and targetting.

(d) Monitoring and maintenance

The costs of monitoring and maintenance will mainly consist of personnel time, in terms of establishing and executing the work and taking appropriate remedial action (which may involve some machinery). The costs will depend on the options taken and methods used,

and whether the work can be carried out 'in house' or necessitates the engagement of suitably qualified specialists. Assessment of monitoring costs should include provision for regular data analysis and interpretation. [see also Chapter 11].

7.3.4 Financial assistance

Financial assistance with the costs of restoration of cut-over bogs may be available from a variety of sources. These should be investigated as part of the feasibility study, as they may have considerable bearing on what is financially practicable. Eligibility for assistance depends on such factors as ownership; details of planning conditions; conservation status (whether SSSI *etc.*); proximity to water or impact on water resources; presence of specially-protected species or habitats; whether located within designated areas *etc.* The applicability of each scheme will depend on the precise circumstances, and will usually be considered on merit. Specific details and qualifying conditions are available from the organisations concerned [see Table 7.5].

In certain cases it has been, or may prove, necessary to compensate owners for loss of revenue from a site, for example as a consequence of terminating peat extraction before a previously agreed limit; or prevention of land improvements, either on the site itself, or on adjacent land (as on certain SSSI's). This translates into income for the owners concerned.

Table 7.4 Approximate ranges of costs for selected restoration techniques used on lowland peatlands. These are mainly based on examples from a survey carried out in 1991–1992, using information provided by site managers and the peat industry.

Operation	Methods	Range of costs	Example potential costs for 50 ha site with 45 ha cut-over (milled) + 5 ha remnant*
Bunding of remnant	Peat embankments (*in situ* peat) Peat embankments (imported peat) Peat + plastic membrane	£ 1.8–6 m^{-1} £ 2–40 m^{-1} £ 15–45 m^{-1}	£ 2,160 – 7,200 £ 2,400 – 48,000 £ 18,000–54,000
Ditch blocking (includes operator / installation costs *etc.*)	Wide, palisade timber dams steel sheet dams peat dams ditch infilling	< £ 380 each c. £ 2.50 each £ 9–12 each £ 0.67– *c.* £ 30 m^{-1}	as appropriate as appropriate £ 9,000–12,000 (for 1000 dams) as appropriate
Surface configurations	Surface levelling, forming shallow bunds of peat and compacting, (may include transport of peat)	£ 200–1,250 ha^{-1}	£ 9,000–56,250
Scrub control	By hand or machine (may include chemical treatments)	£ 400–2,500 ha^{-1}	as appropriate
Transplantation of vegetation		< £ 2,000 ha^{-1}	< £ 100,000

* Assuming division of the cut-over into 9 polders of 5 ha, and 1200 m perimeter of remnant; with some damming of drainage ditches.

Table 7.5 Possible sources of financial or practical assistance for restoration schemes.

Organisation	Type of assistance possibly available
Statutory nature conservation agencies	Management agreements (on SSSI's / ASSI's)
	Grant aid (under the Wildlife and Countryside Act / Town and Country Planning Act) for restoration work through schemes such as Wildlife Enhancement Scheme or Species Recovery Programme. Potential for co-operative ventures
Water resources bodies (NRA *etc.*)	Practical assistance with machinery *etc.*
English Heritage / Historic Scotland / Cadw/ local authority archaeologist	Practical assistance with *e.g.* archaeological survey and mitigation.
Non-governmental conservation bodies (*e.g.* RSNC / RSPB / BTO)	May provide help with specific projects, for example survey and monitoring.
Local community groups / BTCV	May provide help with specific projects (including volunteer labour)
Peat Industry / land owners	Potential for co-operative ventures, help with machinery *etc.*
	Possibility of contributions from developers to longer-term management through Section 106 obligations under the Town and Country Planning Act, 1990.
Countryside Commission	Countryside Stewardship Scheme–offers incentives for positive conservation management in selected landscapes, including waterside landscapes. May be applicable to enhancement of existing vegetated areas (on and off site), but would not be applicable to restoration under planning conditions. Individual cases considered on merit.
MAFF / DANI / DAFS	Environmentally Sensitive Areas scheme (ESA). The designation is designed to ensure that traditional farming practices are continued within the area concerned, with financial incentives offered to farmers not to intensify their agricultural practice. Although not directly applicable to restoration of recently cut-over bog, the scheme could include the raising of water levels on adjacent agricultural land.
European Union	Funding may be available for selected restoration projects; relevant schemes may vary annually.

7.4 Preliminary collation of information (desk studies)

7.4.1 *Cartographic details*

Examination of maps will help to put a peatland site into its overall topographical, historical, industrial, geological and land-drainage setting. Features which may be determined by examination of various maps include the following:

- geology and soils;

- topography;

- main land drainage patterns and water courses (detailed site drainage will not normally be shown);

- infrastructure, buildings, access roads *etc.*;

- information on the historic and industrial landscape and structures;

- natural features of the site boundary.

Sources include Ordnance Survey, Soil Survey and Geological Survey maps.

Examination of a series of maps of different ages can be valuable in helping to establish the history of the site, particularly with respect to land-use changes. These include Tithe Maps, 1st edition Ordnance Survey, Enclosure Maps, Manorial Maps. It should,

however, be noted that cartographers have not always surveyed peatland areas in detail and some maps of peatlands may have limited accuracy. Moreover, successive Ordnance Survey revisions do not always include changes to the character of some peatland sites.

Soil and geology maps may help to put the site in a regional and local context, for example, in establishing the original extent of the peat body, of which the site may form only a small part. This may influence decisions on the best restoration strategy, for example whether it would be desirable or feasible to try to manage the entire peat area as a whole. At some sites, information shown on these maps may prove insufficiently detailed, and, if required, plotting a precise boundary of the peat body is likely to require further investigation in the field.

The amount of information that can be obtained from maps with direct value to peatland restoration is often strictly limited. For example, geological and soil maps may provide some useful background information on possible factors that may influence restoration management (*e.g.* type of bedrock surrounding and underlying the site), but in general do not provide information concerning, for example, the nature of the substratum beneath the bog. In these situations it is important to substantiate the information derived from maps with chemical analyses of the soils (see below) and, in most cases, any important influences will need to be substantiated by appropriate field investigations.

7.4.2 Use of aerial photographs

Aerial photographs are important aids to site characterisation and, when time-series photographs are available, may permit determination of the effects of recent activities on site. They are also useful in updating cartographic information and for locating features not readily evident on the ground, such as old peat cuttings and former drainage ditches, which although occluded, may still retain some drainage function. Aerial photographs are also useful in identifying vegetational features and boundaries. For example they may help to locate open areas otherwise hidden within dense scrub. They thereby provide an important aid to ground survey work and if possible recent photographs should be made available to field workers.

7.4.3 Ownerships and tenancies

Local occupants of the site and adjoining land should be consulted and involved at an early stage in the planning of any restoration project, particularly where their land may be affected by the restoration scheme. They may also provide a valuable source of local information. In addition, in some sites, it may be necessary to obtain permission to cross land, for example for vehicular access to the site during restoration procedures. It is therefore important that the relevant details (*e.g.* name, address, land affected) are collated.

7.4.4 Current management regimes and general site history

When possible, information should be gathered from site occupants on the current land-use and management practices on different areas of the site so that these can be incorporated into the restoration strategy, where appropriate, or possible constraints on development identified.

Information on the land use history of a site, including previous management regimes, can sometimes be gleaned by examination of maps, aerial photographs, literature and local sources *etc.* Although not critical for assessing restoration options, the information can provide valuable insights into the site. For example it can be used to chart the changing layouts of peat extraction operations, and help to date different cut-over areas. Such data are crucial to the archaeological, historical or industrial background of a site.

7.4.5 Hydrological information

Available existing information relating to climate, regional and local water resources, 'undesirable' water inputs *etc.* should be collated and assessed.

Climatic data can be obtained from the Meteorological Office and from published sources and maps (*e.g.* Smith, 1976). The most important factors are rainfall and potential evapotranspiration, particularly during the summer. The presumed relevance of meteorological data to individual bog sites is related to the proximity of the recording station, but in many cases it will be adequate to provide a broad outline of the likely climatic conditions, although it is not possible to specify critical threshold amounts [see Chapter 1].

It is important to set each site in its local and regional hydrological context, in terms of potential effects on both water inputs and outputs, for example, considering availability of water for supplementary supply, possible constraints imposed by flood defence or water abstraction. This is particularly important in areas such as the Somerset Levels where peat workings may be below regional groundwater levels, and areas where it is thought that there may be some connectivity between the perched water mound in the bog and regional groundwater levels. Information and advice concerning local and regional water resources will be available from the water resources bodies (*e.g.* NRA).

7.4.6 Wildlife conservation and archaeological interest

Existing records concerning the wildlife conservation, archaeological and palaeoecological interest of peatland sites can be collated from the sources identified in Tables 7.2 and 7.3. Available data are likely to vary considerably in quantity and quality, but may provide some useful background information and insights, for example concerning former conditions or species on the site.

7.4.7 Potential legal and land-use constraints on development

The relevant legislation (international, national and local) which may affect development should be investigated and its implications for restoration options set down. The most important areas to be considered concern legislation relating to planning, conservation and water resources. Further details are provided in Appendix 2.

Planning legislation

Peat is classed as a mineral under planning law and is subject to the same planning requirements as any other extracted mineral. Peat extraction requires planning permission, which may place conditions on working practices and specify after-use and after-care. It is important therefore that the details of any planning permissions are known, including the precise boundaries of the area affected and the implications of any specified conditions.

Wildlife and conservation legislation

Although one of the main aims of the restoration schemes considered in this document will usually be to maintain and enhance the conservation 'value' of a site, it should be recognised that all operations must be carried out with due regard to current conservation legislation. For example, there may be certain restrictions on the work that can be carried out without consent from the statutory conservation agencies and there may be circumstances where a conflict of conservational interest needs to be resolved (for example, where a statutorily-protected species of bird occurs in an area which would be disturbed through restoration operations). It is important that the relevant agencies are consulted about these aspects before carrying out any work.

Particular care should be taken where operations being carried out may directly or indirectly affect any of the following:

- Species specially protected under the Wildlife and Countryside Act 1981 (as updated and amended);
- National Nature Reserves;
- Sites or Areas of Special Scientific Interest (SSSI / ASSI);
- Special Areas of Conservation (SAC sites)
- Ramsar sites;
- Special Protection Areas (SPA's);
- Environmentally Sensitive Areas (ESA's);
- National Parks;
- Areas of Outstanding Natural Beauty;
- Heritage Coasts;
- Public Rights Of Way;
- Scheduled Ancient Monuments;
- Listed Buildings;
- Local Nature Reserves;
- Any further sites of environmental, archaeological or geological interest, such as those identified by Local Authorities and those owned/managed by the National Trust or voluntary conservation bodies.

Legislation relating to water resources

For any proposed restoration schemes which may impact upon water resources (*e.g.* blocking or diverting water courses; impounding, discharging or pumping water), the bodies with responsibility for those resources (*e.g.* National Rivers Authority, Internal Drainage Boards, River Purification Boards, DoE-NI) must be consulted at an early stage in the planning process, as there are several areas in which they must be specifically involved:

(a) Impoundment of water; blocking or diverting water courses

A *water impoundment licence* is required to impound water, for example if 'on-stream' water is impounded or an existing water course is blocked or diverted to provide water for an impoundment.

Regulations also impose safety provisions on reservoirs or artificial lakes not used for water supply purposes that retain more than 25,000 m^3 of water above the 'natural level' of any part of the adjoining land or have a dam higher than 4.5 m. The intention of this is to ensure that there is no potential danger to life or property through the sudden release of water due to the catastrophic failure of the retaining structures. The volume of water specified is equivalent to *c.* 4.5 ha flooded to 50 cm depth. It is therefore possible that parts of some restoration schemes may fall under the provisions of the legislation, where the intention is to create large lagoons, in which case it is recommended that advice is sought from a qualified engineer.

(b) Abstraction of water

Consent is needed to abstract water either from water courses or groundwater.

(c) Discharge of water

In some circumstances it will be necessary to make provision for the discharge of water from a bog. This will usually require a certificate giving the *Consent to Discharge*, unless drainage rights already exist. Situations where this may apply include the provision of specific outfalls from a bog and pumping of enriched water from a lagoon. It is necessary to provide details of the quality of the water to be discharged.

(d) Works affecting land drainage

Any works which interfere with existing drainage require *Land Drainage Consent.* This includes the building of any constructs on or adjacent to water courses, the diversion of any streams around a bog and the potential for causing flooding of land not within the site. Details of the proposed work must be notified to the water resource bodies, who, before issuing consents, must be satisfied that either the works will not adversely affect drainage on land owned by third parties or that those third parties agree to accepting the consequences of the proposals.

Miscellaneous legislation

Adherence to health and safety legislation should form part of the requirements for any work carried out in connection with restoration works.

Searches should also be made for possible constraints such as common land, turbary rights, rights of way, riparian rights, mineral rights, shooting rights, grazing rights, location of public utilities such as gas pipes, electricity pylons *etc*. The implications of any such constraints for the project should be assessed.

7.4.8 Summary

A preliminary examination and summary assessment should be made of the information gathered by the desk study in order to identify its nature and usefulness and where further details are needed, in order to facilitate the planning of further work.

7.5 Field investigations

7.5.1 Introduction

The aim of field investigations is to build on data gathered in the preliminary desk-study, enabling all the relevant options to be considered in the formulation of an appropriate restoration strategy. Suggestions of the type of information which may be gathered is outlined in Table 7.1 and considered in further detail below. This is intended as a guide to possible field investigations that may be needed at some sites, rather than a prescriptive list. It is recommended that 'hard' data acquisition is focused upon information that is specifically needed, rather than upon a general 'wish-list' of information that may be of interest, and that it is sufficiently well resourced and performed by experienced practitioners who, when appropriate, are aware of the likely limitations of their studies [see 7.2].

Appropriate field investigations are an essential requirement of site assessment and may require the services of various specialists. On-site investigation will allow the various specialists to familiarise themselves with the site and, when appropriate, to map data which they collect. All field workers should work with the same base maps if possible and preferably record data on topographical survey plans of the site. Locations of all transects, sample points *etc*. should be recorded on the base maps. Assessments of any health and safety measures which need to be taken should be made and action implemented to protect field workers prior to field work commencing.

Surveys of the site must necessarily gather information on a wide range of topics, but these inter-relate to a large extent. For example, information on the topography of the site would be required to assess the current and future hydrological regimes; in the planning of any earth-works and as an archaeological record. It is thus desirable to co-ordinate the efforts of different interested parties into an integrated approach to the site investigation. The advantages of this include the following:

- avoids unnecessary duplication and overlap (and therefore reduces costs);
- optimises the information gathered by each survey team, to provide input for other specialisms;
- minimises disturbance or damage to sensitive areas of the site;
- promotes on-site discussions between various specialists of the various restoration options and means of achievement;
- allows the early identification of any potential problems or areas of conflict of interests.

7.5.2 Site physical characteristics

A broad survey of the topography and physical characteristics of the site should be carried out to obtain information on the following factors, when considered necessary and if not already available in sufficient detail from existing documentation:

- general size and shape; extent of site in relation to whole peat body;
- surface and subsurface topography; peat depths;
- geology and soils underlying and surrounding the site;
- access for machinery and equipment;
- location of existing tracks, pathways, boundaries, buildings and other structures; location of potential hazards (*e.g.* rubbish tips).

These aspects are discussed below. A general plan of the site should be made, and relevant features mapped.

General size and shape; extent of site in relation to whole peat body.

In most cases the exact boundaries of the site under consideration will have already been established, but occasionally there may be a need for some verification and accurate mapping. The establishment of at least the approximate boundaries of the peat body will allow the site to be put into context [7.4.1]. In most cases it will be necessary to supplement information from existing maps with at least some field investigation to enable the plotting and provision of reasonably accurate maps of the site boundaries for further reconnaissance work. The potential for buffer zones can also be assessed at this stage.

Surface and sub-surface topography; peat depths

(a) Disposition of peat fields in relation to each other and any upstanding areas

Ideally, the detailed topography of the peat fields and any uncut areas should be carefully mapped and levelled to Ordnance Datum to facilitate the planning of a detailed restoration scheme. For example, it will help to identify any 'massif' areas [2.1]; identify the need and potential for any buffer zones [8.3]; allow predictions to be made of the movement or collection of water; facilitate the optimal siting of water control measures such as dams and bunds and provide a record of the historical and industrial land surface. The potential value of existing baulks *etc.* as water-holding structures should be assessed[1] .

It may also be important to determine subsurface contours, as this can have implications for the rewetting strategy, for example, when there is more than one basin, or when the subsoil slopes in a particular direction. In most cases the surface contours can be measured using standard professional surveying techniques. Subsurface contours can be measured in relation to the surface with peat coring equipment, augers or ground-penetrating radar. Sampling should be carried out using a combination of line transects and grids, plus examination of profiles where, for example drains have already been cut into the sub-soil. This will also provide the necessary information on peat depths.

(b) Relationship to surroundings

The general disposition of the site in relation to the surrounding land is important in assessing possible impacts both from and on the adjoining land. For example, the potential for inputs of minerotrophic or polluted water is greater if any of the exposed peat surfaces lie below the level of the surrounding land, but it may be easier to retain water on the site. Conversely, if the site forms an upstanding block in relation to its surroundings, it will increase the problems of water retention, and potential for flooding of adjoining land, but ensure that the only water inputs are atmospheric.

(c) Peat depths

The data available from the survey of the surface and subsurface contours will allow identification and assessment of:

* depth of peat remaining;
* areas with the most complete peat stratigraphical and palaeoenvironmental record;

---

[1] The efficacy of the baulks as bunds will depend on their size, intactness, degree of dehydration and humification of the peat, and its bulk density.

* areas where drains or peat extraction has exposed mineral soil;
* potential availability of peat for bunding, ditch blocking *etc.*

Where possible the recording of peat depths should be accompanied by some assessment of the peat types [7.5.5].

Geology and soils underlying and surrounding the site

Published geology (solid and drift) and soil maps provide some information to put a site into its regional and local context [7.4.1] but often the amount of information of direct value to restoration is strictly limited and, in those situations where it is considered important, it may be necessary to supplement the information derived from maps by on-site survey. Consideration of the geology may be particularly important when it is suspected that otherwise unexplained water losses may be caused by vertical seepage through the peat into a permeable substratum. If this is suspected, expert hydrogeological advice should be sought to assess the likely impact on restoration measures.

More detailed survey may also help to indicate the potential for mineral enrichment of water supplies (although this should also be substantiated by chemical analyses of the soils) and provide locational inform-ation of palaeochannels for palaeoenvironmental analysis.

Access for machinery and equipment

For most restoration schemes it will be necessary to maximise the use of machinery and equipment in carrying out management operations such as ditch blocking, bund building and scrub clearance. The field reconnaissance should therefore:

* identify access routes for machinery of different types (at least those potentially available) including light railways;
* identify areas where passage of machinery would be damaging to biological interest.

The strategy adopted should take into account the accessibility of different areas of a site to different equipment, both before and after rewetting. The planning of operations will also need to take into account the possible climatic constraints on the use of machinery at different times of the year

Location of existing features

Features such as tracks, pathways, boundaries, buildings and other structures, location of potential hazards (*e.g.* rubbish tips) should be carefully recorded on the base maps, where not already documented.

7.5.3 Land use

Where information has not been available from the preliminary 'desk study', or proves insufficient, the site and adjacent land should be surveyed to assess:

- current management activities (*e.g.* grazing) which may affect the options for restoration;

- risk of nutrient enrichment from agricultural activities (either through water or air) and assessment of possible remedial action that may be necessary (*e.g.* catch-water drains, shelter belts, diversion of polluted streams);

- potential damage to adjoining land caused by raising water levels in the bog;

- possible constraints on restoration options and potential for change of land-use in adjacent areas to one sympathetic to wetland conservation and restoration, or the provision of buffer zones (through purchase, management agreements, ESA schemes *etc.*).

7.5.4 Hydrology

Introduction

The maintenance of an ombrotrophic environment requires that the input of water from precipitation must equal or exceed the water losses (at least on an annual basis). The major problem for the restoration of most damaged raised bogs is the lack of an adequate and consistent ombrotrophic water supply at or near the peat surface to sustain the growth of peat-building Sphagna.

In some situations a mainly empirical approach to restoration of suitable hydrological conditions may be sufficient for effective restoration [7.2]. However, in order to formulate the most appropriate and cost-effective remedial strategy it is important to determine the main causes of dry conditions [see Chapter 2], to identify the main factors which affect the water inputs and outputs in different areas of the mire and to put the site into its local and regional hydrological context.

Available information collated as part of the desk study (see above) can be supplemented as required by further investigations and measurements, as outlined below.

It is recommended that expert hydrological advice is sought on the level of detail required for an adequate hydrological assessment of a site. Information which may be required could include the following (at least those items marked * are likely to be needed for most projects):

- climatic information*;
- details of water courses* (type, distribution, slope, degree of functioning);
- water outputs*;
- topographical disposition of peat fields* and remnants*; peat depths* and sub-surface contours;
- peat hydraulic conductivity;

- vegetation characteristics;
- distribution and stability of open water*;
- potential for water supply;
- local and regional context of the site.

(i) Climatic information

Construction of detailed water budgets for a site or hydrological modelling may require more localised information than that available from published meteorological records, as conditions on site may vary from those recorded some distance away, particularly in situations of varying topography. The most relevant data include seasonal variations in rainfall, temperature and evapotranspiration.

(ii) Reconnaissance of drains and water courses

A reconnaissance survey should be carried out of all drains and water courses impacting upon the site (including those outwith the site), and a map produced showing direction of flow; slope; degree of functioning; main outfalls and inputs; whether cut through to mineral subsoil and whether thought to be introducing minerotrophic or polluted water on to the site. This should include drains which are apparently already occluded by vegetation and also a general assessment of any 'buried' cross drains (usually slit drains or mole drains) across peat fields or cuttings. Aerial photographs can be an invaluable source of detail, particularly when trying to trace old drains and water courses. Potential impacts of external drains and water courses on the site should be noted, in terms of both water outputs and as potential sources of inputs (where appropriate).

This information can be used to prioritise ditch blocking operations and, at least in the initial stages, may be useful for achieving the optimum dispersion of water around the site. Note, however, that operatives of the peat industry often have a good working knowledge of the characteristics of the drainage system and consultation may be advantageous.

Measurement of the mean altitude of the water levels in the main drains and around the margins of the site can help to predict possible water draw-down effects.

(iii) Water outputs

Reconnaissance of water courses (see above) should provide information concerning the most obvious water losses from the sites. However, where appropriate, and possible, more indirect causes of dehydration should also be identified and assessed. This includes possible connectivity between the perched water mound and regional water tables; leakage through the base of the mire; losses through cut edges *etc.*

For sites currently being pump-drained, valuable information can be obtained from the pumping records. It may be useful to carry out some simple pump tests under different conditions.

(iv) Disposition of peat fields and remnants, peat depths and subsurface contours

These features should be identified by the topographic survey (see above) and will be useful in determining likely patterns of water distribution across the mire and potential for increasing water retention. For example, in any damaged peatland, particularly where the surface topography is uneven, it is probable that there will be areas where water naturally collects. These areas should be identified and the information incorporated into the design of any 'engineering' works (construction of bunds *etc*.). Although such areas may be identified from the topographical survey, if carried out in sufficient detail, an empirical approach will confirm whether the areas do in fact hold water. The areas are likely to be most evident after a period of heavy rainfall.

(v) Peat hydraulic conductivity

Measurements of peat hydraulic conductivity can be useful in several different contexts associated with hydrological modelling [Box 7.1]:

- prediction of (potential) perched water mounds within relatively 'intact' peat remnants [Chapter 1];
- prediction of the rates at which water is lost through peat in different areas (*e.g.* edges of remnants, through baulks or the basal layer of peat);
- prediction of the draw-down in potential buffer zones, and hence calculation of an appropriate buffer zone width [8.3];
- prediction of the effects of different peat extraction or management operations.

For such measurements and predictive hydrological modelling [Box 7.1], it will usually be necessary to employ the services of a competent hydrologist. It should, however, be recognised that good-quality hydrological data (such as meaningful estimates of actual values of hydraulic conductivity) may be both difficult and expensive to obtain.

(vi) Vegetation characteristics and distribution of open water

A field survey of the vegetation [7.5.6] will provide information on the distribution of different vegetation types across the site, together with open water and bare ground. This may facilitate some assessment of likely evapotranspirative losses and water storage characteristics in different areas should the information be required for hydrological studies. It is known, for example, that summer evapotranspirative losses are

---

Box 7.1 *Hydrological modelling*

Various hydrological models are available which can be used to explore the hydrodynamics of peatlands, including: an assessment of the hydrological relationships between bog remnants and their surroundings; hydrological relationships between different areas on a site; inter-relationships between the hydrodynamics of the bog and local and regional water tables; calculation of the appropriate width of buffer zones and prediction of the outcome of various operations (including peat extraction and management techniques) both on site and on adjacent land.

Some of the available hydrological models are most appropriate to relatively simple, uniform bog sites such as those which retain much of their original dome. In such situations 'simple' 'groundwater mound' models can, subject to various constraints, help to predict, for example (a) the effects that reduction of the area of a raised bog will have upon the water level in the remnant; or, conversely, (b) to estimate the basal area required to sustain a given 'groundwater' mound height. However, many damaged raised-bog sites are very heterogeneous in character, with cuttings, baulks, remnants and ditches *etc*., often at various altitudes and perhaps with varying (and usually unknown) hydraulic conductivities). Here application of 'simple' models is particularly difficult, not least because the assumptions of some models are inapplicable or because 'calibration' of some of their parameters may not be feasible. In such circumstances, finite element groundwater models may potentially be more useful than the simpler 'groundwater mound' models, as they are more flexible, can take into account more easily variability in parameters and may be able to predict changes as a result of different disturbance or management activities. In addition, some can

consider variables such as the acrotelm properties and, in particular, run-off and overland-flow elements that represent large losses to raised-bog systems in winter. Such models are, however, very 'data hungry' and have not been widely tested in peatlands.

It is beyond the scope of this report to provide guidelines on the most appropriate models and methods, not least because these are still being refined. The choice of model largely depends on the purpose of the modelling, the level of detail required, the resources available and the amount (and quality) of data available (Schouwenaars, 1995; Bromley & Robinson, 1995). In general, it may be suggested that at present the application of hydrological models is limited more by the difficulties of obtaining sufficient and accurate field estimates of some of their parameters than by deficiencies of the models themselves.

There can be little doubt that, in principle, hydrological models may be able to provide exact solutions to some critical aspects of the hydrodynamics and rewetting of peatlands, but, depending on the questions asked, at present there is little reason to suppose that they necessarily have sufficient predictive accuracy to provide more than a broad basis for practical peatland restoration and that empirical solutions will continue to be important. Nonetheless, further development of hydrological models, and of techniques for better estimating some of their terms, may be expected to make an important future contribution to peatland restoration.

Specific advice on the use of hydrological models should be sought from hydrological specialists.

higher from *Molinia*-dominated vegetation than from *Sphagnum*-dominated vegetation (Schouwenaars, 1990), but in general there is only a limited amount of comparative information currently available.

Identification of areas which are permanently inundated will also be useful in assessing approaches to revegetation, for example where there is existing potential for establishment of floating rafts.

(vii) Potential for water supply

The potential for supplementary water supply to specific areas may be an important consideration in some sites. The quality of such supplies is of critical importance [4.4.3] and needs to be established at an early stage if this approach is considered desirable.

7.5.5 Substratum characteristics and water quality

The chemical properties of water and peat will have a profound influence on the plants that will colonise a given area of peatland, and on the likely course of subsequent succession [1.9; 4.4]. They may also affect the long-term preservation of some archaeological structures. Thus some basic chemical data may be needed to make decisions on the most appropriate strategies and outcomes.

Simple measurements of pH and the conductivity (corrected for pH) of water inputs, including rainfall, made in a representative selection of peat fields can provide valuable information. Comparison between results (and with published values) will allow identification of anomalous values [see also Table 2.1]. Where some pollution or inappropriate minerotrophic input is suspected, it may be necessary to carry out further analyses to identify the nature and source of the problem. Analysis of the water (including the common 'heavy' metals), followed by comparison of the proportions of various ions with those in local rainwater inputs will give an indication of which ions might be coming in from sources other than rainfall.

It will also be important to establish the water quality of any potential supplementary water supplies [4.4.3].

Knowledge of the type of peat that is, or will be, present when restoration management commences is very important in assessing the potential and options for restoration. One of the most important considerations is whether the exposed peat is ombrotrophic (bog) peat or minerotrophic (fen) peat. Usually, this can be easily determined by simple measurement of pH, or by examination of the plant remains preserved in the peat (macrofossils) [see Chapter 1]. The degree of decomposition of the peat is also of importance as this will help to determine the water storage

capabilities and permeability of the peat, and its suitability for use in the construction of dams and bunds *etc*. Table 1.3 gives the basic details of the von Post scale of humification.

7.5.6 Survey and assessment of biological interest – flora and fauna

Introduction

A survey and assessment of the existing biological interest of any site is an important component in the formulation of a restoration strategy. Where possible, field survey should build on the information collated during the initial desk study [7.4].

The aims of the survey should ideally include the following:

- identification and assessment of any areas with existing biological interest;
- identification of any species or communities with special conservation status (*e.g.* statutory protection) either present on, or using the site; for the less common species, some assessment of the population size should be made;
- identification of any potential conflicts between existing conservation interest and aims of restoration strategy;
- assessment of the potential for 'natural' and 'assisted' recolonisation of damaged or rewetted areas (*i.e.* the availability of inoculum *etc.*);
- identification of areas with 'undesirable' species or communities (*e.g.* scrub *etc.*);
- identification of potential 'threats' to the existing flora and fauna;
- provision of base-line data for monitoring.

Flora

A broad survey of the vegetation and main habitat-types present should be carried out. Various survey methodologies are available, but it is recommended that the survey should at least conform to the Phase 1 habitat mapping used by the statutory nature conservation bodies (Nature Conservancy Council, 1990)). The survey should also identify the specific features outlined above. It is particularly important to identify species and areas of existing conservation interest, and those areas which may provide a reservoir of bog species for recolonisation of the cut-over areas. These species and specific areas should form the focus of the restoration scheme for the whole site.

An extensive cover of Sphagna, with a variety of *Sphagnum* species (including semi-aquatic species, lawn and hummock species) may help to identify a refugium as providing a good reservoir of bog species. However, good refugium areas need not necessarily take the form of a residual, uncut block of peat; old, revegetated peat cuttings can fulfil a similar role. The presence of a cover of birch should not be considered detrimental to the assessment of interest, providing the ground layer is still relatively *Sphagnum*-rich.

In some sites, existing wildlife interest of certain areas may not be as a refugium for bog species but for species of replacement habitats (dry heath, fen, birch woodland *etc.*). The rôle and future of such areas must be closely considered in relation to the strategy for the whole site; advice should be sought from the statutory nature conservation bodies.

As part of the field investigations, it would be desirable to initiate some fixed point photography, to illustrate key features, both as an aid to off-site discussions and as the basis of a monitoring programme [Chapter 11].

Fauna

Invertebrates

Assessment of the invertebrate interest of a site will ideally comprise reference to existing records, species lists, *etc.*, supplemented as necessary by field survey, together with expert appraisal of the likely habitat requirements of any rare or notable taxa.

Given the diversity of invertebrates and the difficulty and expense that would be associated with identifying all specimens in any reasonably-sized sample, field survey work will necessitate restriction to a limited number of groups and the participation of experts capable of accurately identifying material and of recognising notable and rare groups. Survey work of

this sort is very prone to adverse effects of weather conditions and sampling technique. To overcome such bias, surveys should employ several sampling procedures and be carried out on several occasions.

Methodological problems include the difficulties of accurately censusing the populations of different types of invertebrates (Beukeboom, 1986). The larger, actively flying, diurnal species such as dragonflies and butterflies are usually counted along line transects, and errant ground dwellers are usually sampled using pitfall traps. Undoubtedly a major problem with interpreting the abundance and distribution of invertebrates in raised bogs, and in particular in intact *Sphagnum* carpets, are practical difficulties of sampling from these low vegetation types. Nearly all studies have relied heavily on pitfall trapping and/or water pan traps and net sampling of water beetles [see Table 7.6]. These will undoubtedly tend to be biased in favour of errant species such as carnivorous beetles (*e.g.* Carabidae, Staphylinidae) and spiders, and will tend to underestimate more sedentary, phytophagous and sap-sucking groups (Coulson & Butterfield, 1985). Thus Kirby (1992a) notes that several species of delphacid bugs occurring in bogs seem to be difficult to find (and hence record), and though they may be caught in pitfall traps, these will undoubtedly miss many of these species unless very intensive sampling is carried out and quantifying more sedentary species such as many bugs has yet to be applied accurately to bog situations (Nelson, 1983/4; Kirby, 1992a). Even relatively common bog species such as the lygaeid bug *Pachybrachius fracticollis* may be overlooked unless

Table 7.6 Standard survey methods applicable to survey of invertebrates on cut-over peatlands.

Survey method	Comments
Aquatic netting	Water beetles and water bugs
Transect walks with visual counting	Butterflies, diurnal moths (Lepidoptera) and dragonflies (Odonata)
Waterpan trapping	Mainly for low-flying insects, may be useful for water beetles and bugs on *Sphagnum* carpet; floating waterpans can be used on water surfaces
Pitfall trapping	Errant ground invertebrates, notably beetles (especially Carabidae, Staphylinidae), various bugs (Heteroptera) and spiders; perhaps the best method for sampling from low vegetation sites though they may show certain biases (Southwood, 1978; Coulson & Butterfield, 1985)
U.V. light trapping	Moths (Lepidoptera) and several other orders (*e.g.* Neuroptera, Trichoptera)
	Insects may be attracted from a distance and therefore derive from habitats other than where the trap is located
Sweep-netting	Appropriate for a wide range of errant and more sedentary insects and spiders of the herb and scrub layer; can be difficult under wet or windy conditions (Coulson & Butterfield, 1985)
Hand searching	Particularly important for locating some bugs (Heteroptera) that frequent the ground layer (Kirby, 1992a)
Extraction of soil samples	Perhaps the most accurate way of surveying soil fauna though it may underestimate more errant taxa
Vacuum sampling	Difficult to apply to wet vegetation (Coulson & Butterfield, 1985)

its population level is very high and the weather conditions are particularly suitable (Kirby, 1992a).

Given the above, however, most standard survey methods for invertebrates are applicable to raised-bog site invertebrate communities, though to date, a limited subset have been most widely employed. These are summarised in Table 7.6. No one sampling method is likely to be adequate to make a thorough and useful assessment of the invertebrate interest of a site. The methods selected will no doubt normally reflect the availability of taxonomic expertise. However, pitfall trapping and UV light trapping should be used if possible as they have been the two most widely used techniques in past studies and therefore data obtained from these are likely to be more readily interpretable.

Given that most lowland raised-bog sites in the UK include a mosaic of habitats, it is important that invertebrate records for any site can be attributed to their particular habitats. In the past, many studies have failed to do so with the result that it is often unclear what aspects of the bog system may need to be protected in order to favour particular species. This is particularly important with lowland raised bogs, which in their undamaged state have few rare species that are specific to this habitat type, but at various stages of recovery from certain forms of peat extraction, notably from traditional hand-cutting, do provide important sites for a number of species of high conservation priority. Taxa which fall into this category include the two rare beetles *Bembidion humerale* and *Curimopsis nigrita*. Given this, it may be preferable to sample each particular habitat type intensively rather than attempting long transects that cover more than one distinct type of habitat.

Birds

Assessment of the ornithological status of a site may require field survey to supplement the information derived from the collation of existing records, together with expert appraisal of the likely habitat requirements of any rare or notable species.

A survey of breeding birds could be carried out using the method used in the British Trust for Ornithology's new Breeding Bird Survey (BBS). There is, as yet, no standard method for undertaking an assessment of populations of wintering birds, but methods involving transects, point counts or grid surveys may be appropriate. Basic details are provided by Bibby, Burgess and Hill (1992). However, bird census techniques are currently receiving much attention, and it is recommended that the British Trust for Ornithology (BTO) are contacted for up to date information on preferred methods.

Assessment of breeding and wintering birds will need to be carried out over a minimum of one year and should aim to provide an assessment of bird habitats not only within but also surrounding the site in order to put the site into its local context.

Non-avian vertebrates

Non-avian vertebrates (mammals, amphibians, reptiles) usually form a relatively minor part of the conservation interest of raised-bog sites, but efforts should be made to collate and review existing records so that the potential impact of restoration measures can be assessed. Records from raised-bog sites have included such species as otter, mountain hare, deer and adder. Bogs may also constitute important feeding areas for bats, especially around marginal habitats.

Assessment of wildlife 'value'

Following the reconnaissance surveys, an overall evaluation of the wildlife of the site should be carried out, in consultation with the statutory conservation agencies, in particular to identify key areas or species which require special protection. This should be coupled with an assessment of how such areas can best be maintained and, where possible, the ecological requirements of the relevant species.

Sites may be conservationally valuable either through the presence of notable or rare organisms or because they represent communities that are themselves interesting and/or vulnerable even if the species they comprise are not particularly rare (or specific to bogs). Conservationists and site managers may at times need to consider which sort of interest they consider to be more important [see Chapter 3].

7.5.7 Survey of archaeological and palaeoecological interest

The palaeoecological record contained within peat (pollen, plant macrofossils, fossil beetles *etc.*) can be used to reconstruct vegetation history, landscape development, climatic change, human activity *etc.* Organic and inorganic artefacts may also be found, giving further useful information on human activities. The historical and industrial landscape and buildings on a cut-over site may also be of interest, and may warrant recording before remedial action is undertaken. There may be existing documentation for individual sites in the literature or held by the bodies listed in Tables 7.2 and 7.3. Recent activities may have hidden or destroyed artefacts or may have exposed features not previously recorded. Contact should be made at least with the local authority or county archaeologists and the statutory archaeological bodies to seek advice on the potential archaeological interest of the site.

Where further evaluation is considered desirable, assessments of archival value can be made by wetland archaeologists or palaeoecologists. Archaeological investigations can include topographical and structural survey, palaeo-environmental analyses and site inspection, coupled with evaluation and mitigation. Some exploratory excavations may be required.

Specific points which should be considered during an archaeological investigation include:

- the 'value' of the site both in terms of the individual structures and artefacts and the site as a whole;
- the importance of the site in the context of others in the area;
- the historical and industrial landscape;
- the palaeoenvironmental record contained in the peat (pollen and macrofossil stratigraphy);
- the conservation needs of any finds and sites, and the potential for conflict with wildlife conservation aims (and restoration methods).

In some sites it may also be appropriate to consider the potential of the site for education and research and its the potential for interpretation and public access.

Following the archival work, survey and site inspection, further investigation may be needed, particularly where there is evidence of extensive archaeological interest or conflicts are identified between the archaeological and biological conservation needs. Any areas which would be affected by restoration proposals may need to be properly recorded prior to the works being carried out – advice should be sought from the Local Authority and other archaeologists (e.g. English Heritage).

7.5.8 Potential for control of fire

Fire is a potential hazard on any bog, and can cause extensive damage if uncontrolled. Provision should be made for the prevention and control of fires in the formulation of any site plan, concentrating particularly on areas that dry out in the summer. Access routes for vehicles carrying fire-fighting equipment, potential water sources and firebreaks should be identified. Where these are considered to be inadequate, it may be necessary to increase such provisions [see 10.5]. Advice may be sought from the statutory conservation agencies and the local Fire Authorities.

7.5.9 Engineering assessment

Where it is intended to carry out restoration work through the building of bunds, movement of considerable amounts of peat etc., it may be advisable to carry out an engineering assessment of the site, as part of the feasibility study for any particular restoration strategy. This would centre on the nature

and properties of the materials available on site, the existing topography, the condition of structures, the potential for building water-retaining constructs and the movement of water through the site.

Particular attention should be paid to the following points:

- access for machinery – existing availability vs requirements;
- hydrology;
- impoundment of water may bring the constructs under the provisions of the Reservoirs Act 1975 and thus be subject to inspections and remedial works [Appendix 2];
- design of 'new' landforms must take into account stability considerations.

7.5.10 Safety assessment

Safety assessments should consider:

(a)   physical hazards;

(b)   chemical hazards.

Physical hazards will be principally related to old or current peat workings and structures, and should be recorded during the field reconnaissance surveys. They may include:

- old peat cuttings with unstable, floating rafts of vegetation;
- unstable or unsafe buildings;
- drainage ditches – both extant and occluded;
- peat works machinery, light railway etc;
- debris from tipping.

Chemical hazards may be encountered where the site has been used for tipping (either officially or for fly-tipping). Where a potential problem is identified, the Local Authority should be contacted for guidance on disposal.

Consideration will need to be given to the safety of workers on site and the general public (if applicable, e.g. if rights of way exist). Adherence to other health and safety legislation should form part of the requirements of any contracts to be let in connection with restoration works.

7.5.11 Landscape assessment

Most cut-over raised bogs are found in a rural setting, but some occur in close proximity to housing or industry. Some have been used for waste disposal. One objective of a restoration scheme is therefore likely to be to produce a site in harmony with its landscape setting, reducing its prominence as a disturbed area with large expanses of bare ground, and to blend with its surroundings.

Where a site is close to housing, potential detrimental effects of rewetting to householders should be considered. For example, in at least one instance in The Netherlands, increased populations of biting insects, as a consequence of peatland rewetting, have led to an adverse reaction amongst the nearby inhabitants to restoration initiatives.

Chapter 8

Water management

8.1 Introduction

As discussed in Chapter 5, the three main problems of rewetting peat extraction complexes in the UK are related: (i) maintaining a consistently high water level in the peat; (ii) providing adequate water storage; and (iii) preventing lateral water loss. The solutions to these problems will depend upon the topography and disposition of the peat fields, the nature of the exposed peat; and the climatic context.

The retention of water in peat extraction complexes is partly a function of their topography and capacity for water storage. The latter is a property of the peat type [2.3.2]. Where the exposed peat has limited storage capacity, increase of storage may be possible only by storing water above-ground, by creating some form of reservoir on part or all of the cut-over fields [Chapter 5]. Such reservoirs can be used directly as the basis for recolonisation by rafting, or, in some situations, to in-filtrate water into adjoining peat. Lateral water loss can be reduced by damming drains and, where necessary, by creating bunds across extensive peat surfaces.

The nature of water management operations is partly determined by climatic considerations – in areas of high rainfall the desired water level control may be reached and maintained more easily than in drier areas – the main principle being to ensure a positive water balance. There will also be climatic constraints on the phasing of operations, for example there may be periods when access by machinery is not possible.

All water management operations should be carried out with due regard to the legislation relating to water resources (*e.g.* impoundment, abstraction or discharges of water), and to conservation interests (including archaeological or palaeoecological interest in the residual peat deposit). Possible constraints should be identified and resolved at an early stage in the planning of any restoration scheme [Chapter 7].

Some reconfiguration of the peat surfaces prior to rewetting may be needed to optimise the conditions provided for water retention and recolonisation, for example removal of existing vegetation; manipulation of the macro- or micro-topography through reduction or increase in the number or height of baulks, creation of lagoons for retention of water *etc.* [see Chapter 5].

8.2 Constructs for water retention

8.2.1 Introduction

Because the rewetting necessary to regenerate raised bogs can only be achieved by retaining the incoming precipitation, all drains, trenches and outfalls must be dammed (although it is recognised that there may be circumstances in which this is not possible due to external constraints). However, any measures used for reduction in outflow from the bog must have the capacity to deliver peak discharges from the bog other-wise erosion of the regenerating peat surface, damage to the dam network and bunds or to the recolonist vegetation may occur. Even in undisturbed raised bogs, high run-off occurs in autumn through to spring when precipitation exceeds evaporation. In designing the water level control system for a regenerating mire, high water flows must therefore be catered for and this may involve the installation of weirs or sluices.

Rowell (1988) deals with the general principles and practical aspects of control of water in peatlands. Brooks (1981) also gives practical advice, particularly on the building of dams and sluices or weirs. The techniques available to reduce hydrological change within refugia and rewetting cut-over sites include:

- ditch blocking;
- bunding;
- provision of supplementary water;
- buffer zones.

In most situations, it may be necessary to utilise more than one technique to optimise rewetting.

8.2.2 Ditch blocking

The following principles should be applied:

- all possible ditches should be blocked, including old, occluded ones as these may retain some function, even if apparently choked with vegetation;
- existing vegetation should be cleared out where dams are to be built, to ensure a good seal;
- a phased approach may be necessary, to integrate with other management operations, such as scrub removal;
- if required, particular care should be taken to seal ditches

cut into mineral soil, particularly where the latter is of high permeability;

- slit drains or mole drains in abandoned cut-over areas must be identified, and blocked if thought to be functioning (in some cases they will be effectively blocked by retention of water in the main drains);

- for large scale operations it is necessary to use machinery (rather than hand methods) to build the dams, but consideration must be given to potential damage to existing vegetation;

- in most cases, peat dams will be adequate if built correctly, but they may need to have an impermeable core of plastic, metal sheeting, wood *etc.*

- careful attention should be paid to the re-routing of drains carrying enriched or polluted water across a site;

- careful attention must be paid to legal constraints and potential effects on adjacent land;

- the number and spacing of dams will largely depend on the size, fall and orientation of the drain;

- on-going maintenance of dams is essential to correct as soon as possible any damage through factors such as shrinkage, slumping and erosion;

- adequate provision must be made for overflow.

Once blocked by dams, open ditches should be encouraged to infill as rapidly as possible, particularly with *Sphagnum* species. However, in some situations, it may be desirable to prevent too much vegetation colonisation and preserve the linear pools created by blocking ditches at intervals, which can provide an attractive habitat for wetland fauna (*e.g.* Fox, 1986a, b) and may help to temporarily provide increased water storage.

Damming and ditch-blocking techniques used in rewetting damaged bogs are illustrated in Plate 8.1.

8.2.3 Bunding

Bunds may be used to seal the edges of upstanding bog remnants, to reduce run-off from remnants, to impound water within existing peat cuttings or to create new lagoons. Depending on location and availability of source material, these may be constructed from materials such as clay, peat and plastic membranes, and usually involve the use of machinery. Note that clay bunds may help to enrich the mire water, although the significance of this to bog restoration is not well known. The construction material may be won *in situ*, or brought in from outside. The latter may only be appropriate in sites with existing infra-structure from peat cutting operations, for example tramways or roadways that permit the transport of materials in sufficient quantities, and would substantially increase costs. In many cases, existing tramways and roadways may act as bunds, and can be utilised or extended, although they may not necessarily be watertight. The efficacy of the baulks as bunds will depend on their size, intactness and degree of dehydration of the peat.

Use of bunding techniques is illustrated in Plates 8.2 and 8.3.

Peat

The construction of bunds raises several problems from the engineering point of view, as, although many embankments have been constructed from, and on, peat, there is still no accepted procedure for determining the engineering properties of these types of structure or standard engineering criteria on which to base a design. However, unless a major project with particularly large bunds is planned, an empirical approach would seem to be satisfactory, taking into account experience from other restoration projects. It should, however, be noted that the Reservoirs Act 1975 imposes safety provisions on reservoirs or artificial lakes not used for water supply purposes that retain more than 25,000 cubic metres of water above the 'natural level' of any part of the adjoining land or have a dam higher than 4.5 m; requiring that the construction be undertaken in accordance with the design and under the supervision of a qualified civil engineer [see Appendix 2].

For an effective bund, the peat recommended by most practitioners is wet, strongly-humified peat, although it should retain some fibrous structure (for example, peat of humification value H6–H8[1]). Where sufficient quantities of this are not available, it may be necessary to use less strongly-humified peat, in which case it will usually be necessary to insert a plastic membrane (see below). The main principle is to ensure a good seal of wet black peat to wet black peat. Thus any remaining weakly-humified or dry peat should be removed before the main bund construction (the former may be replaced on top of the strongly-humified peat once this is in place [Figure 8.1a]). It is not normally necessary to excavate down into the mineral subsoil if there is an adequate layer of strongly-humified, wet peat. Such bunds may be used to seal the edges of uncut remnants or constructed 'within' the remnant using this technique, although clearly potential damage to the vegetation needs to be taken into account.

An alternative approach for bunding within remnants used on some German sites (*e.g.* Hahnenmoor) is to excavate a trench down into the strongly-humified peat, then replace the weakly-humified peat first, followed by the strongly-humified peat on top [Figure 8.1b]. This has the effect of creating an impermeable seal within the weakly-humified peat, thus reducing seepage losses through the more permeable peats.

Where the bunding is based on existing baulks or tramways of peat, the drier surface peat and vegetation

---

[1]   von Post humification scale [see Table 1.3].

(a) Peat dams blocking narrow drainage ditch; Astley Moss (Lancashire)

(b) Peat dams across wide drainage ditch; Wedholme Flow (Cumbria).

(c) Sheet-metal dam across narrow drainage ditch, Glasson Moss (Cumbria).

(d) Sheet metal dam across wide fire-break; Risley Moss (Cheshire).

(e) Simple plywood-sheet dam across narrow ditch; Danes Moss (Cheshire).

(f) Palisade timber dam across broad erosion gully; Blawhorn Moss (Lothian).

Plate 8.1 Rewetting using damming and ditch-blocking techniques.

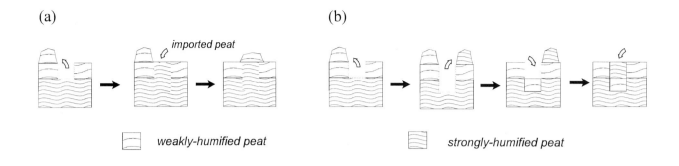

Figure 8.1 Construction of shallow, internal bunds: (a) by replacement of upper, weakly-humified peat with imported strongly-humified peat[1] ; (b) by interchange of strongly- and weakly-humified peat horizons in trenches.

will usually need to be removed, unless sufficient quantities are available to create a good seal through the weight of peat itself (as suggested at Cors Caron, Dyfed). Where new lagoons are to be created on cut-over surfaces, the peat may be bulldozed into position, if sufficient depth remains. Some compaction of the peat in the construction of dams and bunds is usually achieved by driving machinery across the surface. This may help to consolidate the peat so that subsequent slumping and erosion are minimised.

For builds around lagoons, it may be necessary initially to provide some protection from erosion through wind and waves using wooden baffles. Provision of a 'shelf' area would also help to dissipate the wave energy, thus protecting the main bund, and may help to provide a platform for the initiation of rafting vegetation.

Plastic membranes

These have been used in situations where there is some doubt about the permeability of the peat available for bunding. The plastic used is a heavy duty polythene (such as is available from builders merchants) which is inserted vertically into a narrow slit cut into the peat wall. This approach has been used in extensive bunding around massifs at sites such as Wicken Fen (Cambridgeshire), Corlea (Ireland; Plate 8.3) and Fochteloër-veen (The Netherlands). Such bunds are probably most appropriately used for 'external' bunding of massifs, as expense may prohibit their extensive use within peat cutting complexes. However, the material can also be used to improve the water retention of existing structures (dams or bunds) which are thought to be leaking.

Plastic membranes are non-biodegradable and have an indefinite (although unknown) life-span. The main potential problems suggested include damage by

burrowing animals, in particular rats and moles, and the potential formation of a vertical 'slip plane' down the outer face of the plastic membrane, particularly if the peat on the 'outside' becomes dry. Neither problem seems to have happened so far, although the possibility cannot be excluded. The plastic does not necessarily need to go down to the base of the peat, although should penetrate into the most highly humified peat if possible. Some seepage across the bund at a low-level may help to reduce the build-up of pressure behind the membrane, although this should be monitored. It may be possible to reduce the potential for a zone of enhanced water movement at the base of the membrane, which could lead to leakage and weakening of the bund structure, by inserting lengths of the plastic to different depths.

Mineral substrata

Embankments on peat or estuarine clay for river flood-control are usually constructed from peat or sandy materials around a clay core. Some of these have been reported to have problems due to weak foundations, piping, instability and leakage (Harris, 1979; A. Bullivant, *pers. comm.*). Such problems may be related to construction design and methods, and size. Where mineral materials are used, attention must also be given to the potential problem of leaching of bases and nutrients from the bund into an ombrotrophic system.

General comments

Bunds should be kept as wet as possible. To protect a bog remnant, Rowell (1988) suggests the construction of a trench on the remnant side of the bund to ensure there is a supply of water to keep the bund wet. In some sites this function may be carried out by the trench from which the peat used in the bund has been excavated (borrow-trench). At Corlea (Eire), in order to help counteract drying, part of the length of the bund has been constructed with a water trap half-way down the outside-slope, intended to contain water and release

---

[1] The source of the strongly-humified peat may be from elsewhere on the site, or from a trench dug along the inside of the position of the proposed bund.

Construction of a bund around old peat cuttings on the SE bog at Cors Caron (Dyfed). The lines of dams across ditches on the remaining 'dome' of the bog can also be seen. [Photo: J.E. Davis]. [see also Plate 5.6]

Shallow peat bunds forming lagoons within former peat workings at (*left*) Esterwege Dose (Germany) and (*right*) Kendlmühlfilze (Germany).

Plate 8.2 Rewetting using bunding techniques. [see also Plate 8.3]

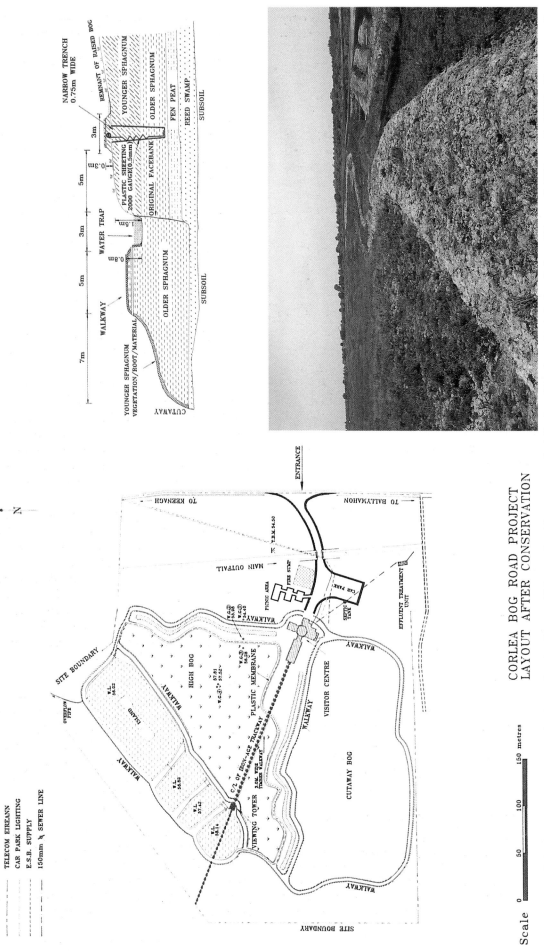

Plate 8.3 Scheme to protect an ancient wooden trackway within a raised-bog remnant at Corlea (Co. Longford, Ireland) (see Wynne & O'Donnell, 1993). Diagrammatic sketches of project layout and embankment (bund) construction and photograph of the bund (the remnant peat block is on the left of the photograph). [Sketches reproduced by permission of Bord na Mona]

it slowly in times of water deficit (Wynne & O'Donnell, 1993) [Plate 8.3]. As this project is new, there has been no opportunity to assess the effectiveness of this approach. Vegetation growth should be encouraged, to help bind the surface peat together and reduce erosion, but tree growth should be prevented, as this may increase drying and cracking.

There must be some provision for water-level control to prevent damage by excess water flowing over the top surface of the bunds. An adjustable collar-overflow pipe system laid through the bund, or a sluice can be used for this. An overflow system also has the advantage of providing specific discharge points for the water, whether into another lagoon or external drainage system as appropriate. The latter will help to avoid any potentially undesirable impacts on adjoining land. Careful consideration must be given to the materials and methods used for over-flow provision, so that lines of weakness are not created, and regular checks made for correct functioning.

On-going management of the bunds is necessary to ensure that any problems are dealt with promptly, for example rectifying slumping and removal of shrub seedlings. The height of the bunds around bog remnants may need to be increased periodically as the peat within swells. Maintenance of 'internal' bunds which subdivide peat fields in less important, once the cuttings have started to renature.

8.2.4 Provision of supplementary water

Supplementary water provision should only be considered in certain circumstances, for example to 'prime' the system, as in general it is time-consuming and costly to run [see 5.3(h)]. Sites where this approach has been used include Shapwick Heath (Somerset) and Thorne Waste (S. Yorkshire).

8.3 Buffer zones

On the European mainland an attempt has been made, in some cases, to surround uncut remnants, and regenerating cut-over areas with 'buffer zones', designed to help protect the sites against adverse influences of surrounding land use. Buffer zones may have varying functions:

A. Buffer zones on or adjoining the peat body:

- A buffer zone on adjoining land within which water levels can be raised. This may (a) help to reduce lateral water losses by reducing the hydraulic gradient between the bog and its surroundings; (b) help to prevent downward leakage of water from the bottom of the bog; or (c) reduce oxidation of underlying impermeable layers

or of the basal peats that might occur should an unsaturated zone develop beneath the bog. Note that (b) and (c) are likely to be important only in bogs subject to vertical water seepage [4.4.5] (See also Schouwenaars, 1995).

- An 'agricultural' buffer zone in which agricultural activities are controlled in order to reduce drainage and water abstraction and to prevent enriched water from entering the bog. Spray from agro-chemicals may also be a problem; to help ameliorate this, a shelter belt of trees (a non-invasive species) may be incorporated into the buffer zone.

- A buffer zone to provide an impermeable barrier around the margins of a peat-extraction complex to prevent ingress of enriched or polluted water into the cut-over areas, if these are situated at a lower topographical level than the surrounding land.

- A 'conservation' buffer zone – zone of semi-natural vegetation adjoining the bog.

B. Buffer zone on the peat body:

- A buffer zone which corresponds to the maximum width of the water drawdown zone at the margin of an upstanding peat block.

The principle of the establishment of buffer zones around both uncut remnants and cut-over mires is clearly an important one. The width of the buffer zone depends on such factors as climate, hydraulic conductivity of the peat, height differences and the distance to (and depth of) active drains. However, although the width of buffer zone required in different situations can be calculated using standard hydrological data and equations (see e.g. Eggelsmann, 1982; van der Molen, 1981; Robinson et al, 1992; van Walsum, 1992), the accuracy and value of such determinations have been little tested in practice, and may be limited by difficulties of obtaining meaningful estimates of some key hydrological variables. More research is needed to refine the modelling approach to calculate the appropriate buffer zone widths for different situations before it is possible to provide precise guidelines by such methods.

Widths of between 30 m and 100 m have been suggested to provide a sufficient hydrological buffer. However, work by Robinson et al (1992) suggested that in some circumstances, a buffer zone of 500 m might be needed to minimise the effect of peat extraction on an adjacent upstanding peat block, unless hydrological management measures were taken (e.g. ditch blocking or installation of an impermeable barrier).

Raising of water levels in a buffer zone within the adjoining land, while probably not sufficient in itself to effect much rewetting of an upstanding bog remnant (unless there is a very low hydraulic gradient) may provide the opportunity for the establishment of sympathetic management, for example in the creation of wet meadows. This would have the additional benefit of reducing the potential for agricultural pollution impinging on the site, either from water courses or aerial sources.

8.4 Practical implications of rewetting for adjoining land

As the major aim of most restoration strategies is to *reduce* water losses from the bog remnants, it may be thought that the measures taken to achieve this need not have an undue adverse effect on adjoining ground. However, this will depend on such factors as the hydraulic conductivity of the peat, the difference in height between site and surroundings, distance to drains, permeability of the underlying substratum *etc.*

Use of bunds should allow relatively independent control of water levels 'inside' the bog. In many circumstances, however, it may be necessary to maintain a marginal ditch to ensure the surplus water is carried away, as in a natural lagg. It would be preferable to keep the water level in the marginal ditch as high as possible to reduce the hydraulic gradient from the bog, but this could make it difficult to drain adjacent land. Where this is likely to cause a problem (for example on agricultural land) it may be possible to create a buffer zone extending away from the edge of the bog and bounded by a second ditch within which water levels can be lowered. The width of buffer zone necessary would depend largely on the permeability of the substratum and the required drainage capacity of the outer ditch. However, clearly this could have implications in terms of loss of the land for agriculture, and requires further investigation.

There is some evidence to suggest that in certain mires, particularly those underlain by a mineral subsoil which has a high permeability:

a) there may be some connectivity with the regional and local water tables, such that raising water levels in the bog may affect water levels in the surrounding land, or, conversely, drainage in the surrounding land will influence the hydrology of the bog (*e.g.* Poelman & Joosten, 1992);

b) the role of ground water recharge cannot be ignored, especially where the mire has been extensively cut-over and a relatively thin veneer of peat remains above the mineral subsoil.

The rewetting options that will have the most impact on adjoining land are those which require the water levels in this land to be raised [see Chapter 5] and either elevated above or returned to former groundwater levels. Such strategies may involve further substantial infrastructural works, which, besides direct costs of construction and maintenance, may also have obvious financial implications in terms of land purchase or compensation *etc.* Considerable problems in achieving such rewetting are likely to be encountered where the adjoining land is under multiple ownership or where land-uses other than agriculture and structures such as roads, railways and buildings are involved in former wetland areas where water levels are currently controlled by drainage schemes.

When surrounding farmland has been rewetted, it is important that base- or nutrient-rich or polluted water is prevented from reaching the site. In sites where drains entering or crossing the cut-over areas carry enriched drainage water from adjoining agricultural land, the water should be diverted away from the site as soon as possible.

The potential of the restoration measures for increasing the buffering capacity of the mire in terms of flood control of adjoining land should be considered as this may be perceived as beneficial by the water resources agencies and would enhance the 'value' of the restoration scheme. However, there is conflicting evidence in the literature concerning the role of undamaged, drained and rewetted peatlands in the 'damping' of peak flows following storms.

Chapter 9

Facilitation of revegetation

9.1 Introduction

Natural recolonisation of cut-over bogs by plants may take place quite readily where there are local refugia of typical bog species. However, where these do not exist, or have a sparse range of species, or where sites are particularly large, it may be necessary to consider 'inoculation' of damaged areas with suitable plant species, either by transplantation or by seeding.

Before areas are inoculated, it is important that other stages of the restoration scheme have been successfully carried out, and that any remedial work can be undertaken without damage to the vegetation. For example, if appropriate vegetation is to re-establish, it is important that the hydrological conditions, in terms of quality, quantity and stability of water supply, are appropriate [see Chapters 4 and 5]. Conversely, the restoration scheme developed should take into account the availability of plant inoculum.

9.2 Inoculation with *Sphagnum* species

9.2.1 Introduction

The main feature of the vegetation of an undamaged raised bog is the extent of the *Sphagnum* cover, which, besides being characteristic, may play various important rôles in the functioning of the mire [1.7]. The restoration of a mire to a self-sustaining system requires the reinstatement of an acrotelm which is comparable to that of a little-damaged bog surface. Thus, one of the most important considerations in the restoration of a damaged bog is the question of how to regain the *Sphagnum* cover. A characteristic of many damaged bogs is the lack of or limited areas of *Sphagnum*-rich refugia, which may hinder recolonisation.

In some sites, it is possible to inoculate damaged areas with plant material, such as *Sphagnum*, either as whole plants or fragments. For relatively small operations *Sphagnum* plants could be collected from areas in donor sites considered least 'sensitive', ensuring that damage is minimised. Donor sites should preferably be in the same geographic area to avoid undesirable translocation of non-local species or gene pools [see

also 9.4], particularly if the donor site is likely, or known to support scarce bog species. In sites where Sphagna do survive, for example in a mire remnant, old peat cuttings or in ditches, it may be possible to inoculate rewetted areas with Sphagna by hand. Many site managers have successfully spread *S. cuspidatum* in this way and it has been suggested that *Sphagnum fuscum, S. capillifolium, S. magellanicum, S. cuspidatum* and *S. recurvum* can all be transplanted in sods (Nilsson *et al.*, 1990). However, trials by Money (1994) suggest that hummock and lawn species of *Sphagnum* will regenerate more readily if a template of aquatic Sphagna is first created, than from direct 'broadcasting' of plants into open water pools.

For larger scale restoration, removal of large quantities of *Sphagnum* from donor sites is likely to be inappropriate. In these situations the availability of propagules may be increased by *Sphagnum* 'farming'.

9.2.2 Sphagnum *'farming'*

All *Sphagnum* species can reproduce vegetatively and techniques have been investigated to increase the amount of *Sphagnum* plants available using 'nursery' pools (Money, 1994, 1995). Aquatic Sphagna (such as *S. cuspidatum*) can be farmed readily and are likely to be more suitable for this treatment than hummock forming species (such as *S. papillosum*), which may require a 'template' of aquatic Sphagna on which to regenerate [9.2.3]. Further work is needed to formulate adequate guidelines for optimal conditions for sustainable farming of Sphagna to allow for harvesting on a regular, rotational basis. It may be recommended that 'nursery' pools are established as soon as possible in a restoration programme (if possible alongside ongoing extraction), so that inoculum is available as required.

9.2.3 Propagation of Sphagnum *from small vegetative fragments*

Effective inoculation of the extensive areas presented by commercial peat workings with whole *Sphagnum* plants would require large amounts of source material. Techniques have therefore been investigated for optimising the use of available plant material. It is known from numerous observations that *S. cuspidatum* regenerates remarkably well from fragments and also that the growth of lateral buds of *Sphagnum* can be stimulated by damage to the plant apex, for example, by decapitation. Small-scale trials have shown good regeneration of *S. cuspidatum* plants in pools into which fragments of plants in a suspension of water were 'broadcast' (Money, 1994, 1995). Regeneration from fragments will depend on provision of a suitable water regime as periodic desiccation on a dry peat surface inhibits regeneration, while regeneration also seems to be inhibited if fragments are introduced into deep water (>50 cm), unless some provision is made to assist flotation [9.2.5]. Colonisation of deep water by *S. cuspidatum* tends to occur by lateral spread from plants anchored to the edges of pools, thus regeneration is likely to be most successful initially at the peat–water interface and in shallow water (Money, 1994, 1995).

The regenerative capacities of other Sphagna are less clear (Money, 1994). Hummock and lawn forming Sphagna have been grown successfully from fragments in carefully controlled laboratory conditions (Sabotka, 1976; Baker & Macklon, 1987; Poschlod & Pfadenhauer, 1989; Rochefort, Gauthier & Lequéré, 1995) and viable vegetative fragments may sometimes persist in upper peat layers or be dispersed by water and air. However, growth from fragments of these Sphagna is generally less prolific than for *S. cuspidatum* and may require more precise conditions (such as permanently moist, rather than saturated conditions) for successful establishment. It may be necessary to consider inoculation as whole plants in clumps, to the edges of pools, or on to artificial rafts.

9.2.4 Regeneration of Sphagnum from spores

Regeneration of *Sphagnum* from spores is potentially an important process for recolonisation of damaged peatland as it would enable long-distance inoculation of areas devoid of a local source of propagules for certain species. However, the contribution to dispersal made by sexual reproduction of *Sphagnum* is poorly understood. Spores have regenerated successfully under laboratory conditions (*e.g.* Boatman & Lark, 1971; Sabotka, 1976; Baker & Boatman, 1985; Clymo & Duckett, 1986), but under nutrient poor conditions in the field it would appear that regeneration from spores may be less important than vegetative reproduction.

9.2.5 Facilitation of Sphagnum establishment and rafting

There is evidence that the establishment and spread of *Sphagnum* within embryonic bogs may be facilitated in some situations by the presence of 'nurse species' such

as *Molinia caerulea*, *Eriophorum vaginatum* and *Juncus effusus* (Joosten, 1992; Meade, 1992; Grosvernier *et al.* 1995). These may (i) afford protection against wind and wave action in flooded sites; (ii) provide a 'climbing frame' for *Sphagnum*; and (iii) provide a more suitable microclimate for *Sphagnum*. Joosten (1992) refers to this as 'tussock buffering'. However, a possible limitation of this approach is that a critical balance may exist between conditions that favour extreme dominance of species such as *E. vaginatum* and *M. caerulea* and those which permit these species to act as nurse species to *Sphagnum*.

The provision of 'artificial' constructs within the water such as birch brashings may also perform functions (i) and (ii). Rafting may also be encouraged by loose peat fragments (*e.g. bunkerde* - see 9.6) or particles floating in the pools, either washed in from the sides, or detached and lifted from the base of the cuttings (probably due to the formation of gas bubbles).

9.3 Inoculation with vascular plants

Commercial supply of seed of bog species is unlikely to be available, although seed mixtures are available from specialist seed merchants which could be used for the creation of 'wet meadows' at the margins of sites. Similarly, few bog plant species are likely to be commercially available in sufficient quantities for inoculation. Species not occurring naturally in the area should not be introduced. Where possible, transplantation from 'natural' sources is preferable, as the inoculum may contain propagules of a range of plant species, as well as invertebrates, which would be absent from specially raised sources.

There is little information available on the likely success of transplanting vascular bog species, but it is unlikely to be too problematic under a suitable hydrological regime and could be considered where there is no nearby source of propagules. However, it is likely to be practicable only over small areas, usually being restricted by the availability of suitable plant material and intensity of labour input required, although once established, plants will be able to spread.

Turves, whole plants or individual tillers may be used as transplants, either collected from another site, or grown and established from seed in the greenhouse. On blanket bog 'live mulching' (*i.e.* spreading material collected by machinery from an 'intact' surface) has been used to provide fragments of vascular plants and mosses, and a seed source (Bayfield *et al.*, 1991), although this technique is likely to be of use at only a few sites, as it presumably severely damages the surfaces from which the mulch is taken. These authors also suggest that turf transplanting at a density of 2–4 turves m^{-2} can be used to provide a good source of inoculum (at least on blanket bog).

Some of the techniques for revegetation suggested by Brooks (1981) and Hammer (1992) may also be applicable to raised-bog restoration, although mainly aimed at minerotrophic wetland restoration. For example, suggestions to overcome some of the problems of transplanting into open water such as using log or board baffles to help break the force of any waves and using bio-degradable cotton mesh or netting to hold the plants in position until established.

Planting should ideally be carried out in the autumn or early spring so that vegetation can establish before any onset of dry periods in summer. Plant material should be transplanted as soon as possible after collection – drying out in transit must be avoided. Maintenance of high and stable water levels are crucial for the successful establishment of bog species. It should be apparent after only one growing season whether transplantation has been successful. Any failures should be noted, the reasons for failure assessed and remedial action taken, before any replacements are made.

9.4 Legal aspects of transplantation

Concern is sometimes expressed about the use of inter-site transplants, as disturbance of regional gene pools is considered undesirable, as is the possible introduction of non-local plants and invertebrates. However, whilst intra-site transplants would be preferable, there may be insufficient material locally to make this possible and a choice has to be made as to whether or not such species are a desired component of restoration (this is partly determined by the restoration objectives for the site). While there is no specific legislation which covers transplantation, under the Wildlife and Countryside Act (1981) it is illegal to uproot any plant without the owners' consent and consent is required from the statutory conservation agencies for the removal of organisms from, or introduction to a Site (or Area) of Special Scientific Interest as this may be considered a potentially damaging operation. It is recommended that guidance on intra-site translocations of both flora and fauna is sought from these agencies, as the general guidelines are currently under review.

9.5 Mitigation of adverse chemical effects

9.5.1 Phosphorus fertilisation

In some circumstances, the chemical conditions prevailing in peat cuttings or on bare, milled surfaces, may

not be conducive to the rapid establishment of 'typical' bog species, due to particularly high acidity or low nutrient availability. The use of phosphorus has been shown experimentally to assist in the short-term establishment of certain *Sphagnum* species in peat cuttings (applied at a rate of 30 g NaH_2PO_4 in *c.* 4m^3 of water) (Money, 1995). However, to date, this has only been carried out on a very small scale; large scale trials are undoubtedly needed before firm guidance and recommendations can be made as to the use of fertiliser in facilitating revegetation. Any application of fertiliser should be regarded as experimental, and the results carefully documented. There is likely to be a fine dividing line between the stimulation of the growth of 'desirable' vegetation and the encouragement of 'undesirable' species, including algae. The potential for the stimulation of the microbiota and hence acceleration of peat decomposition must also be taken into account. The latter is an important consideration in terms of the preservation of the pollen record and archaeological artefacts. Note that similar comments apply to the use of some water sources for rewetting a site. Where water is pumped onto a site, it is also likely to be aerated to some extent, which may also help to accelerate decomposition.

9.5.2 Base- or nutrient-enrichment

Excess inputs of bases or nutrients (from telluric water, bird droppings *etc.*) may have an adverse impact upon redevelopment of bog vegetation, depending on the loadings in question. In most situations, the only method of mitigating any adverse effects will be to identify the source(s) and attempt to stop or reduce inputs, for example by diversion of polluted streams, providing flood-protection banks, scaring off birds *etc.* Once the inputs have been reduced, it may be possible to further reduce the nutrients cycling within the system by harvesting and removing the vegetation regularly, although this may involve reducing water levels to unacceptable levels to allow access by machinery.

Where it is possible to maintain water levels permanently above the peat surface, the promotion of vegetation rafting can help to initiate the hydrosere, and provide a buffer against the influence of poor-quality water [4.3].

9.6 Importance of '*bunkerde*' to revegetation

'*Bunkerde*' is a German term for the surface layer of vegetation and peat which is removed prior to peat cutting, and is probably roughly equivalent to the Irish 'scragh' and the English 'riddings'. The word is sometimes translated into English as 'top-spit'. It has no standard 'recipe', and its character and composition can be variously based upon the uppermost layer of 'natural' vegetation, or upon such recolonist vegetation that has redeveloped between cutting episodes, together with variable amounts of different types of peat. In Germany *bunkerde* is considered to be of great importance in the restoration of abandoned peat workings and there is a legal requirement for this material to be stored [Plate 9.1] so that a 30 cm thick layer can be replaced after extraction has ceased, to assist in the restoration. As storage necessitates the formation of quite thick layers which may remain undisturbed for a considerable period, the material is essentially composted, although it may be mixed with remnants of living vegetation before being spread back on to the bare peat surface.

The evidence for the general importance of *bunkerde* is inconclusive, perhaps due to the extremely variable nature of the material in question. There is little evidence that *bunkerde* necessarily improves restoration prospects, and in some cases may even be detrimental. Some *bunkerde* (that derived from a natural bog surface) can retain viable diaspores of a wide range of typical bog species (Poschlod, 1995). Other types contain few diaspores (or sometimes seed of 'undesirable' species such as *Molinia caerulea* and in this case any value of *bunkerde* may be more

through amelioration of growing conditions by physical properties than as a source of propagules. *Bunkerde* may provide a mulch, greater water storage, better rooting conditions and provide an important source of nutrients, particularly compared with strongly-humified peat (see, for example, Roderfeld, 1992). It may also float when flooded, thus providing a 'platform' for vegetation colonisation. Its rôle may be to accelerate revegetation, but this is likely to depend upon the water regime. It may be of greater value in sites where the water is not kept at a high level.

The use of *bunkerde* may be derived from the practice of 'shoeing' of peat cuttings with the living turf of vegetation which is removed from the bog surface prior to cutting. This occurs widely in small-scale peat operations in the UK, and was probably once more widespread. It encourages rapid regeneration and retains the vegetation resource (although this may have been an unforeseen beneficial consequence of the practice at the time). The use of *bunkerde* or living turf is unlikely to be relevant to the current context in the UK, as there has been no requirement for this type of material to be stored. However, should such material be available, its use should be carefully considered, particularly with respect to its quality and the hydrological conditions that will pertain in the rewetted areas.

Plate 9.1. Storage of *bunkerde*, alongside current peat extraction, for future use in bog restoration. Steinhuder Moor (Lower Saxony, Germany)

Chapter 10

Vegetation management and after-care

10.1 Introduction

One of the main objectives of raised-bog management and restoration schemes is to maintain or restore a sufficient area of actively-growing raised bog to enable the site to become a self-sustaining system, needing only minimal management inputs. However, some form of on-going management is often necessary for this to be achieved (which could amount to scores of years, depending on the rewetting strategy), in order to maintain or enhance the species composition and to reverse the adverse effects of damage. Vegetation management should form part of the restoration strategy for the bog, and should be planned to coincide with the phasing of peat extraction operations, and opportunities for rewetting.

One of the main problems associated with the abandonment of large, relatively dry, bare surfaces, is the colonisation by 'weedy' species [4.2]. In situations where cut-over areas are abandoned before adequate provision can be made to elevate water levels sufficiently to provide 'natural' weed control, other types of control may be necessary, for example, to prevent the establishment of species which may not be easily controlled by subsequent elevation of water levels. Mowing, grazing and burning or even the use of surface rotavation or chemical herbicides may need to be considered, both within and around revegetating mires. Consideration will also have to be given to the vegetation management of refugia. Clearly, the applicability of such management will be site specific, and depend on the overall restoration strategy adopted.

The most commonly used methods for the control of water levels are discussed in Chapter 8; here comment is made on the practices used widely in the management of vegetation on damaged bogs. Certain common principles can be identified:

- vegetation management is necessary to reduce the invasion and spread of 'undesirable' species, which are normally checked by high water levels;
- scrub invasion and its control is a major problem;
- there are few circumstances in which mowing or grazing are likely to be appropriate techniques if attempts are being made to restore raised bog, except as an interim measure;

- it may be necessary to consider the use of herbicides to control 'undesirable' species;
- adequate provision for control of fire is essential;
- ongoing maintenance of bunds and dams may be required.

Clearly, appropriate management techniques will depend on the restoration objectives for any particular site [see Chapter 3]. Rowell (1988) deals with the general principles and practical aspects of management of peatlands. Brooks (1981) also gives practical advice, particularly on aspects such as scrub control and building of dams and sluices. The frequency of management operations necessary will depend on factors such as water levels and nutrient status. Site-specific practical advice should be sought from the statutory conservation agencies.

10.2 Scrub control

Drying-out of a bog remnant, cuttings or baulks typically results in an invasion of woody species, most commonly birch, but also species such as pine and *Rhododendron* [Chapter 2]. This is generally thought to be detrimental to the bog vegetation due to shading, both from living leaves and smothering as litter; increasing water loss through evapotranspiration; reduction of water input through interception of rainfall; nutrient enrichment through leaf fall; provision of roosting posts for birds and a positive feedback through the production of seeds. In some circumstances, it is possible that a small amount of scrub may help to provide a more humid micro-climate which could help to promote *Sphagnum* growth in the early stages of regeneration, although this positive influence may cease once the canopy closes (Tüxen, 1976).

Where the peat is fairly thin, it is possible that trees may root through the peat into the mineral subsoil, thereby increasing the nutrient status of the peat by taking up nutrients, with subsequent release and re-cycling through the litter. Roots may also penetrate dams and bunds, thus causing leaks. In dry sites, tree roots may exacerbate the effects of dehydration by creating cracks and fissures in the peat.

Even with adequate control of water levels on a site, the control of scrub is likely to remain a major management feature in restoration work [Plate 10.1] until the bog can be returned to a self-sustaining system in which birch colonisation is naturally kept in check. Scrub removal should precede rewetting operations. After the initial clearance (by hand or machinery), and rewetting, sufficiently increased water levels should

Plate 10.1 Scrub cutting at Roudsea Moss (Cumbria).

Plate 10.2 Birch trees killed by deep flooding; Neustadter Moor (Germany).

Plate 10.3 Die-back of birch trees attributed to flooding; Thorne Waste (S. Yorkshire). [Photo: P. Roworth]

help to keep the birch in check. Deep flooding will prevent initial establishment, and in some cases, may stunt or even kill quite large birches rooted in the base of cuttings [Plate 10.2]. It has been suggested that the *in situ* dying or dead trees may help to reduce damage through wave action and facilitate the colonisation by *Sphagnum* [9.2]. However, birch can establish on floating rafts, and deep flooding is unlikely to kill these trees. It is also not clear whether raising the water table to below the level of the peat surface is sufficient to kill established birch trees, although it may help to reduce new colonisation and retard growth [Plate 10.3].

Disposal of the cut woody material is commonly a problem, particularly in areas inaccessible to vehicles. Brashings may be left or burnt *in situ* (usually on metal sheeting raised above the bog surface to avoid damage to the peat), or removed. Bulk may be reduced by chipping. In some circumstances, it may be possible to push the brashings into cuttings or drains to help reduce any flow of water, and to act as a 'climbing frame' for the *Sphagnum* (Chapter 9). It may also be possible to use the brashings in inundated areas, to reduce wave action and facilitate raft formation. Fears have been expressed over the possible nutrient-enrichment effect from decomposing plant material, and undoubtedly this occurs, although it seems that the phenomenon may only be short-lived, and the pulse of nutrients may sometimes be beneficial.

Regrowth can be treated with chemicals, such as 'Krenite', although this sometimes has limited success (*e.g.* Ruckley & Doar, 1991). Use of chemicals should be carefully controlled, following the appropriate Health and Safety regulations.

In some sites it may be considered important to retain a band of trees as part of a buffer zone around a site, in order to provide a shelter-belt to reduce transport and pollution from an aerosol of sprayed agro-chemicals. This may also help to create a more humid micro-climate on small sites by reducing wind effects. Rowell (1988) recommends that any shelter belt should be sited off the main peat body. Planned establishment of scrub at the margins of a site could be phased with the removal of scrub from the centre in order to maintain some continuity of habitat for birds and invertebrates, but it should be recognised that marginal scrub can act as a seed source for invasion of 'undesirable' species such as birch onto the bog – removal of trees (both on and off the site) has the advantage of removing the seed sources.

It should be noted that concern has been expressed by archaeologists over the potential damage caused to the archaeological and palaeoecological record by various scrub control methods. Advice should be sought from English Heritage on the most appropriate methods which will cause least damage.

10.3 Mowing

Bog vegetation is sometimes mown to control growth of *Calluna* and birch. The benefits of mowing are also thought to include retarding growth of *Molinia*; rejuvenation of *Calluna* and breaking-up and spread of *Sphagnum* hummocks over the bog surface (Eigner & Schmatzler, 1980). *Molinia* tussocks may be removed by brush-cutters in sites unsuitable for mowing (Rowell, 1988). It has also been suggested that it may be possible to accelerate the process of development of raised-bog vegetation through mowing and removal of vegetation in sites where nutrient levels are too high (see Joosten & Bakker, 1987). However, it should be noted that although mowing may be valuable in managing vegetation of a fairly dry or 'enriched' site, or as a 'holding-operation' on sites where rewetting cannot be achieved soon after abandonment of cut-over surfaces, it would not be appropriate in an adequately wet site, as the passage of the machinery is likely to cause more damage than benefits gained. Mowing of firebreaks and to control vegetation on bunds may also be appropriate in certain circumstances.

10.4 Grazing

Few raised bogs are grazed, other than on the claimed bog margins or cut-over areas, although it is not clear to what extent this occurred in the past [see Chapter 1]. In Germany, a special breed of sheep ('Moorschnucke') are used at some sites to control the heather and scrub and maintain conditions suitable for the golden plover. However, as with mowing, this is probably only really appropriate on sites which are drier than required for good growth or regeneration of Sphagna.

The main fears concerning grazing of bogs are the problems of damage by poaching and nutrient enrichment from dung. Sheep may do more harm than good, particularly on fairly wet sites, but could be useful to control scrub invasion or domination by heather where these are a problem. If used, the breed of sheep should be carefully selected, as modern breeds tend to be too heavy and not suited to the poor diet. The animals should be carefully shepherded, for example, driven across the bog during the day to spread the dung, and taken off the site at night to reduce dung inputs. Controlled shepherding also means that the more sensitive areas (*e.g.* breeding birds, rare plants), could be avoided. However, shepherding is costly, with little return from the poor-quality sheep products. Grazing is sometimes used in conservation management for certain moorland birds, such as Golden Plover, that need short, treeless vegetation. However, although it keeps the vegetation open, grrazing may still not provide some other habitat features favoured by birds, such as adequate variation in surface relief (Bölscher, 1995), and is not necessarily compatible with good regeneration of bog vegetation in the long term.

10.5 Fire

Effects of fire on bogs include damage to sensitive mire communities (flora and fauna) and micro-topography, encouragement of *Molinia* invasion, loss of peat and nutrient enrichment. Damage by fire can be severe (as at Glasson Moss, Cumbria and Cors Fochno, Dyfed), but communities can usually recover with time, providing the site is sufficiently wet and no new fires occur. Mosses and lichens are usually most severely affected, with a concomitant increase in *Calluna*, *Molinia*, *Eriophorum vaginatum* and birches. A succession of lichen communities can take seven or eight decades until a new climax is reached, even if no new fires take place (Masing, 1976).

Provision for prevention and control of fires is particularly important at most sites, particularly those with areas that dry out in the summer. Three main measures can be taken:

(i)   mowing of fire breaks around the main areas;

(ii) digging of trenches as fire breaks and

(iii) provision of 'lagoons' for a local water supply in the event of fire.

However, particular care should be taken if trenches are dug as these may function as drainage ditches if positioned incorrectly (as happened at Glasson Moss, Cumbria). One benefit of an elevation of water levels on damaged bogs is the reduction in cover of *Molinia*, which can present a significant fire hazard, particularly in winter. *Rhynchospora alba* is also said to be a fire risk when abundant (Slater, 1976).

Carefully controlled burning (preferably in winter) may be useful as a surface preparation measure, particularly to remove *Molinia*, as long as the area is subsequently flooded or grazed (Eigner & Schmatzler, 1980; Eigner, 1982). This may also be effective as a once-off measure for controlling woody species (Rowell, 1988).

10.6 Management and succession of herbaceous fen vegetation

Most of the herbaceous fen vegetation-types of particular value to conservationists (Wheeler, 1988) are not stable. They are either part of a hydrosere that will eventually succeed to some form of fen woodland, or they occur on solid peat but are maintained in their particular condition by some form of management (usually grazing and mowing). Such management regimes are 'traditional' and have shaped the character of the vegetation. Abandonment of such management usually means a loss of floristic diversity and 'quality' as the vegetation becomes overgrown, first by coarse herbaceous species and then by invading trees and shrubs. Attempts to recreate such seral vegetation-types in abandoned peat workings must therefore make provision for ongoing management to maintain them.

In flooded peat workings, continued growth of plants, and accumulation of peat, makes these pits increasingly comparable with areas of solid peat and is generally associated with a waning floristic interest. In this context, the Broads Authority and English Nature have recognised the need for cyclical excavation of peat in some East Anglian mires, aimed at periodically rejuvenating the hydrosere. Various studies, including experimental pits, have been established with this in mind. One of the major problems encountered is the excavation and, particularly, disposal of the unwanted peat.

Floristic and ecological parallels with the Broadland peat pits occur in some of the extensive peat workings in The Netherlands, particularly those in North-west Overijsel. In these mires, similar ongoing successional processes have been identified (*e.g.* Segal, 1966) including the acidification and replacement of rich-fen communities with a *Sphagnum*-dominated vegetation, which may provide the basis for the re-development of ombrotrophic vegetation. However, as this leads to the loss of prized plant species and communities, it is not universally welcomed, and some attempts are being made to manipulate the peat workings to maintain base-rich conditions (*e.g.* Beltman *et al.*, 1995). In Broadland, similar acidification and expansion of *Sphagnum* has occurred over (and mostly *only* over) the old turf ponds (Giller & Wheeler, 1988), but as yet its scale is sufficiently small, and its association with rare plants such as *Dryopteris cristata* (and, in this context, *Sphagnum* species) is sufficiently great for it not yet to be perceived as a 'problem'.

10.7 After-care of water control structures

Provision must be made in the restoration strategy for regularly monitoring the condition and maintaining all water control structures, although this will probably be at diminishing time intervals as the project progresses.

10.7.1 Ditches

In most situations, it will not be necessary to maintain ditches, as occlusion by vegetation is to be encouraged. However, situations in which this may need to be considered include:

- maintenance of outfall ditches adjacent to peat workings or agricultural land;
- maintenance of ditches carrying mineral- or nutrient-enriched water through the site;
- maintenance of open water habitat for invertebrates (*e.g.* dragonflies) (where this does not conflict with the main aims of restoration).

10.7.2 Dams

Maintenance of dams is essential to correct as soon as possible any damage through factors such as shrinkage, slumping and erosion. Checks should also be made for erosion channels around the dams and for scouring of the base of ditches caused by strong overflows. Conversely, during dry weather, checks should be made for evidence of shrinking and cracking of dams and ditch channels, and remedial action taken where possible to prevent subsequent loss of water due to preferential flow though these cracks. As rewetting progresses, it may prove necessary to increase the height of the dams, for example, if the adjacent peat swells.

10.7.3 Bunds

In general, bunds should be kept as wet as possible, and, as for dams, regular checks must be made to identify and remedy any problems caused by shrinkage, settlement, slumping, erosion, cracking *etc.* The height of the bunds may need to be increased periodically as the peat within swells. Maintenance of 'internal' bunds which sub-divide peat fields is less important than for 'external' bunds, particularly once the cuttings have started to revegetate.

Vegetation growth on the bunds may help to bind the surface peat together, but tree growth should be prevented, as this may increase problems of drying and cracking. Control of vegetation growth will also be beneficial as bunds are likely to be useful for access purposes for personnel and machinery. In certain circumstances this may be achievable using grazing animals, but in general, mowing is likely to be the most appropriate method.

Chapter 11

Recording and monitoring

11.1 Introduction

There are several reasons why it is important to record and monitor procedures and progress in bog restoration:

- all schemes must be regarded as essentially experimental, and therefore recording is important in increasing the knowledge of techniques *etc.*

- provision of 'base-line' data so that progress can be assessed and changes to the programme made where necessary;

- provision of 'hard' data so that current and future managers (and other interested parties) know the starting conditions, exactly what has been done and can continue to assess the degree of success, in order to formulate appropriate further management strategies;

- provision of information that can be used to assess the applicability and potential of similar schemes at other sites.

Without adequate monitoring it may be difficult to learn both from past mistakes or successes.

Monitoring procedures need to be set up with clearly-defined objectives and with identified yardsticks by which the direction and extent of change can be measured. In setting up a monitoring strategy, the questions which need to be addressed include the following (Usher, 1991):

- Purpose: what is the aim of the monitoring?

- Method: how can this be achieved?

- Analysis: how are the data, which will be collected periodically, to be handled?

- Interpretation: what might the data mean?

- Fulfilment: when will the aim have been achieved?

The questions are, of course, inter-related, each largely depending on the one above. To this list, perhaps a sixth question should be added – what resources are available for monitoring?

Monitoring can be approached at two levels:

1. provision of hard and detailed evidence of change in resource or conditions (or lack of it);

2. provision of casual data to give a broad indication of change.

Any preliminary surveys of the topography, hydrology and biological interest of the site made prior to the start of restoration measures [Chapter 7] can act as a base line for monitoring, and should be set up with this in mind. The information gathered will help to determine an appropriate monitoring strategy, for example by identifying areas, species, communities *etc.* to be specifically targeted.

Whereas detailed monitoring is considered to be desirable, in practice it is usually time-consuming and expensive. It may be difficult to carry out and to interpret it in a meaningful way. When detailed monitoring schemes are impractical, it should be possible to determine simple key factors such as whether water levels are responding to management, whether *Sphagnum* is expanding or *Molinia* and birch declining [see Table S4].

Where possible, it is recommended that a monitoring programme should be set up taking the following aspects into account:

- careful recording of management operations undertaken (including time taken and costs);

- base-line data on flora, fauna and water levels (based on field investigations, but with additional detail if possible);

- selected species or priority areas (*e.g.* those identified as refugia), plus species of special conservation status should be identified for regular monitoring checks to assess response to management operations;

- the hydrological and biological response within a representative selection of cut-over areas to be regularly monitored;

- dipwells or staff gauges inserted at key points for monitoring water levels;

- photographic record, for example:

    (i) 'fixed point' photographic records of selected representative areas, including 'before' and 'after' pictures and regularly thereafter;

    (ii) selected management operations (such as bund and dam construction).

- regular checks to be made on any water control structures (dams *etc.*) and remedial action taken as necessary;

- records should be made of events beyond the control of site managers (*e.g.* heavy storms, fires, vandalism *etc.*) which may influence the future interpretation of 'success' of the project;

- annual review of results to allow assessment of any changes needed to management programme.

11.2 Methods

Various methods are available for monitoring change. Selection of an appropriate technique and the monitoring intensity will depend on the objectives, the features being monitored and the level of detail required. It is likely that the monitoring protocol will have to be adapted as rewetting and renaturation progress. Similarly, the frequency of monitoring will need to be adjusted according to the response, and also the perceived success. Annual appraisal should allow results to be assessed, and the necessary changes to either the restoration programme itself, or the monitoring procedures to be implemented. Suggestions are made here of what and how to monitor – more specific discussion, details and advice should be sought in the literature (*e.g.* Goldsmith, 1991) and from specialists and practitioners, such as the nature conservation agencies (statutory and non-statutory) and the Institute of Hydrology.

11.2.1 Hydrology

Hydrological monitoring can be divided into (i) monitoring of hydrological change and (ii) inspection of the integrity of water-control structures.

Monitoring hydrological change

Equipment used for monitoring hydrological change can vary from simple, 'home-made' devices to sophisticated automated installations using computerised equipment. The former can provide sufficient information for basic monitoring of the success and effects of management [11.3.1], although the latter may be more appropriate for some specific applications. Advice on hydrological monitoring 'hardware' and techniques is available from the statutory conservation agencies or hydrological specialists such as the Institute of Hydrology.

A series of dipwells[1] installed across a site (preferably along a transect), or targetted on specific areas, would allow assessment of water table fluctuations. Where possible, the tubes should be anchored to prevent movement, either by direct installation into the underlying mineral ground, or by attachment to anchor posts. The tops of the tubes should be levelled to a fixed datum (preferably Ordnance Datum) to enable an absolute comparison of water levels between dipwells, as well as assessment of trends in water levels relative to the peat surface. In flooded areas, water levels can be assessed using graduated staff gauges, again preferably fixed into the mineral subsoil to minimise movement, and levelled to OD. Water discharges can

be measured using weirs. Fortnightly monitoring of water levels in selected areas allows assessment of general response and fluctuations. A new, low-cost field instrument, known as a WALRAG (WAter Level RAnge Gauge), is currently being developed (Bragg *et al.*, 1994). This records the highest and lowest water levels attained between site visits and thus provides more information on water table movements than the simple dipwells for the same recording interval.

It will be important to make at least some visits to the site during (or immediately following) heavy rain, as this may help to identify previously unrecognised water outlets.

Peat anchors[2] fixed in to the mineral subsoil will help to determine the degree of swelling of the peat surface in response to water level measurements, and ultimately the accrual of peat (note, however, that a clear distinction must be made between increase in peat *volume* and peat *mass*).

If there is no suitable local weather station from which records can be obtained, it may be desirable to set up a simple weather station to give basic climatic records for precipitation, potential evaporation, wind and temperature if such information is required for detailed hydrological monitoring.

Integrity of water-control structures

The functioning of drains, dams and bunds should be regularly checked, particularly following heavy rain events, so that any remedial action can be taken to repair damage *etc.* [10.7].

11.2.2 Vegetation

Discussion of various methods for monitoring vegetation changes are given by Goldsmith (1991) and advice may be obtained from the statutory conservation bodies. Appropriate methods include permanent quadrats, random quadrats and photographic records (fixed point photography) following selection of appropriate areas. Records should be made of plant species and their relative abundance. Recording the amount of bare ground (or open water) within the selected areas will allow assessment of the general rates of recolonisation.

It may be possible to devise a scheme whereby the response of selected indicator species only are monitored. Species selected for this will depend on the objectives of the restoration, and the stage of colonisation at which recording begins. Tables 11.1 and 11.2 give suggestions for some species which it

---

[1] Usually made from perforated plastic piping.

[2] The movement of a metal plate buried just below the surface is measured relative to a datum post fixed in to the mineral substratum.

would be appropriate to monitor when the objective is restoration of raised-bog vegetation.

After the initial base-line recording, it is suggested that a monitoring programme is set up to record the vegetation at intervals of 3–5 years.

Inoculated plant material: Careful records should be made of any transplants or inoculations, including sources, species concerned (and amounts), methods and locations. Monitoring protocol should aim to assess 'success' through recording vegetative expansion of individuals, flowering / seed setting and seedling establishment. Photographic records are also recommended.

11.2.3 Invertebrates

Few UK lowland raised-bog habitats offer large, uninterrupted areas of *Sphagnum* carpet or even just hand-cut areas in various stages of regeneration.

Damaged peatlands often contain a complex mosaic of habitats which have their own distinct invertebrate faunas. Detailed invertebrate surveys are time-consuming and expertise-intensive, and consequently can be costly. It is therefore desirable to consider whether the overall invertebrate conservation value of a site could be estimated by more selective screening, employing indicator species for habitat conditions or indices of species diversity and rarity (see *e.g.* Ball, 1992; Holmes *et al.*, 1993b).

Species of special conservation status

Lowland raised bogs in the UK support a number of Red Data Book (RDB) species (see Chapter 1), though all of these are associated with habitats other than bog-*Sphagnum* carpets (Shirt, 1987; Bratton, 1990; Falk, 1991a, b; Wallace, 1991; Kirby, 1992a, b), and only a few appear to be confined to the set of habitats that are associated with little-damaged lowland raised bogs in

Table 11.1 Suggested plant indicator species for monitoring progress towards a raised-bog objective.

Species	Notes
Sphagnum cuspidatum, S. recurvum	Often colonise areas with open / standing water
S. papillosum, S. magellanicum, S. capillifolium	Indicate satisfactory development of bog species
Eriophorum angustifolium	May invade precursor floating *Sphagnum* carpets, or root directly into peat (± inundated).
Erica tetralix / Scirpus cespitosus / Calluna vulgaris	These are only indicators of 'success' if associated with peat-forming Sphagna (*e.g. S. papillosum*) as they are also constant species of wet heath communities.
Other 'desirable' species include: *Vaccinium oxycoccos, Narthecium ossifragum, Drosera spp., Rhynchospora alba, Andromeda polifolia, Sphagnum subnitens, S. pulchrum, (S. fuscum, S. imbricatum)*	
'Weed' species, including birch / pine / *Molinia*	Reduction in vigour and spread of these species (through rise in water levels ± vegetation management) would be generally regarded as indicative of 'success'.

Table 11.2 Vegetational indicators of potential problems with respect to revegetation with bog species. Note that In many cases it should be possible to mitigate the effects of adverse conditions through management and it should not be assumed that these are necessarily irreversible [see Chapters 9 and 10].

Species	Potential problem
Juncus effusus	May indicate a eutrophication problem (*e.g.* from bird excrement or polluted drain) and / or disturbance.
Birch / pine / *Calluna* / *Molinia* / *Rhododendron*	Extensive invasion probably indicates conditions are too dry.
Sphagnum recurvum, S. fimbriatum, S. squarrosum	May indicate some base or nutrient enrichment (possibly atmospheric pollution)
'Heathy' Sphagna (*e.g. S. tenellum, S. compactum, S. molle*); plus other bryophytes (*e.g. Pleurozium schreberi, Dicranum scoparium, Hypnum cupressiforme*).	Although these species may be present in small quantities in M18a vegetation, their establishment and spread in the absence of the aquatic or main peat-building Sphagna would suggest that conditions are not generally sufficiently wet.
Fen species (*e.g. Typha, Phragmites, Salix, Alnus.*)	Indicates minerotrophic water source ± nutrient enriched.
'Weed' species, *e.g.* bracken, *Rumex acetosella, Chamerion angustifolium*, Graminae (*e.g. Calamagrostis canescens*).	Suggests that conditions are too dry and possibly disturbed.

this country. However, monitoring the response of such species to management may be desirable.

Monitoring response of different invertebrates species or groups to various management options

Changes in management regimes (*e.g.* water table level, scrub removal, peat extraction, creating or enlarging areas of open water) are liable to have significant effects on the population levels and even survival of many invertebrate species. It is therefore desirable to monitor effects such that they may be adjusted if necessary. In the case of dragonflies and butterflies, counting along transect walks has proved a useful monitoring procedure at some sites. For other groups it will be necessary to use one or more of the survey methods outlined in Table 7.6. However, it must be recognised that management that is appropriate for one species or group may not be so for another. Particular care should therefore be taken if a management action is likely to adversely affect populations of any RDB or notable species – any potential conflict between existing interest and management objectives should be identified at an early stage [Chapters 3 and 7].

11.2.4 Birds

A periodic survey of breeding and wintering birds could be carried out appropriately using methods described in Chapter 7 [7.5.6]. It will be particularly important to evaluate the relative density of those species characteristic of the various stages of habitat transition from relatively undamaged and extensive bogs to those which are more characteristic of damaged bogs [1.11; 2.2; 2.3.6]. Based upon data from the initial site assessment, changes of numbers of breeding territories and wintering populations can be assessed and related to changes in habitats.

Based on information derived from initial base-line surveys, it should be possible to monitor populations of selected target species only, for example, species of special conservation status, together with other species which are likely to be particularly responsive to change in habitat, for example a decrease in scrub / woodland or increase in open water. Appropriate species will clearly be site-specific, but suggestions include teal, snipe, raptors (hobby, hen harrier, merlin), lapwing, skylark, whinchat, stonechat, tree pipit, nightjar, willow warbler, general numbers of waders and ducks.

11.2.5 Water chemistry

In circumstances where 'undesirable' inputs of base or nutrient enrichment have been identified, it may be

necessary to carry out some ongoing monitoring of water chemistry [7.5.5], to assess the success of efforts that have been made to change the conditions.

11.3 Assessment of 'success'

The ultimate test of success is, of course, whether the desired objectives have been achieved. However, in view of the long time-scales over which restoration is likely to occur, it is important that a series of targets be identified so that progress towards the goal can be assessed, and adjustments to management operations *etc.* be made where necessary. In general, for the management operations considered in this report, the most immediate response is likely to be hydrological, followed by biological changes and ultimately regeneration of peat growth. Specific factors which can be assessed are outlined below.

11.3.1 Hydrology

Monitoring of water levels and regular checks on the condition of water control structures should allow the assessment of the success of water management operations, by assessing the answers to the following questions:

- Are water levels maintained at the levels required by the objectives?
- Have water levels stabilised and fluctuations been reduced sufficiently?
- Are water levels consistently higher in the ditches than previously?
- Are the dams or bunds damaged or leaking?

Note that assessment must be made with due regard to the actual and prevailing weather conditions.

Interpretation of the data collected can be carried out most easily using graphical techniques, for example by plotting the water levels recorded over time, and in relation to the peat surface (*e.g.* Mawby, 1995). One simple method for assessing water level fluctuations is to use 'duration lines', *i.e.* the number of days the measured water level is between certain limits, over a given time period.

11.3.2 Swelling and growth of peat

Increasing water retention within a formerly partly-dehydrated peat mass can be expected to cause 'swelling' of the peat mass, which will result in an increase in the relative height of the peat surface. This can be measured using peat 'anchors' [11.2.1]. There may be a relatively rapid response (for example, at the Meerstalblok, The Netherlands, the surface of parts of the remnant is thought to have risen some 50 cm in 5 years), and can be distinguished from the potential for longer term renewal of peat growth and subsequent accumulation, which is likely to be less than a millimetre per year. Swelling of the peat mass may result in the necessity for dams or bunds to be raised.

11.3.3 Vegetation

Whether the management measures have been truly successful in returning the site to a self-sustaining, growing raised bog will only be apparent after a long period of time (probably centuries), but it is possible in the short-term to assess the response by the vegetation, which will indicate whether the hydrological and vegetation management operations have been appropriate for the given objectives – for example, whether the vegetation is progressing towards bog or wet / dry heath. It is difficult to recommend precise indicator species through which to measure 'success', as most species found in M18a are also commonly found in other bog or even fen communities (e.g. blanket bog, wet heath or poor fen)[3] . It is the particular combination and relative abundance of different species which makes up each different community, rather than the presence of certain species. However, the establishment of *Sphagnum* species is one of the major objectives, particularly the aquatic and hummock-forming species, if a site is to be returned to a self-sustaining raised-bog system. Joosten & Bakker (1987) suggest that 'raised-bog regeneration' can be considered successful in the short term when 'durable' communities (*i.e.* stable over a period of about 10 years) have formed, which are able to form the basis for raised-bog development in the current climatic conditions; these include communities dominated by *S. papillosum*, *S. magellanicum* and *S. capillifolium*.

Table 11.2 suggests certain plant species which may help to indicate the presence of specific problems on the site. However, in many cases it should be possible to mitigate the effects of adverse conditions through management [see Chapters 9 and 10] and it should not be assumed that these are necessarily irreversible. For example, although *Juncus effusus* may be considered an 'undesirable' species, and perhaps indicate some nutrient enrichment, its presence does not necessarily preclude the invasion of Sphagna and eventual progression through to raised bog (providing steps are taken to reduce the nutrient source, and to prevent flooding of the *Sphagnum* with poor-quality water). It

may even have a beneficial rôle in acting as a 'nurse' species [9.2.5].

Inoculated plant material

In most cases, it will be evident fairly quickly whether transplants have initially 'taken' as under particularly unfavourable conditions the plants will just die! Successful establishment can be measured through vegetative expansion of individuals, or flowering / seed setting, followed by establishment of seedlings. For Sphagna inoculated by 'hydro-seeding' methods, the growth and establishment of new capitula should be measured in relation to the amount and distribution of the initial inoculum.

Rates of change

Vegetation of some sort can be expected to start to colonise a bare, abandoned surface within a few months (depending on the seed supply and season). Colonisation and establishment will progress until little or no bare ground remains, the rates (and species) depending on the prevailing hydrochemical conditions [Chapter 4]. Colonisation of open water is likely to be slower than bare peat, unless inoculated with plant material. For transplanted material, it should be evident within the first two growing seasons whether the plants are putting on new growth, and in the case of Sphagna, producing new capitula. In minerotrophic or nutrient-enriched conditions, revegetation can be expected to progress at a faster rate than under purely ombrotrophic conditions (particularly by non-bog species).

A floating raft of vegetation is likely to take many years to develop, unless positive steps are taken to speed up the process through provision of artificial constructs, inoculation with plant material *etc.* [see Chapter 9]. Evidence from the recolonisation of old hand peat cuttings suggests that the redevelopment of M18 -type vegetation may occur within 50–100 years given appropriate hydrochemical conditions (Smart, *et al.,* 1989; Money, 1994). van Wirdum, den Held & Schmitz (1992) showed colonisation of typical bog species (including *Andromeda polifolia*) within 100 years, from a rich-fen starting point.

11.3.4 Invertebrates

As for other factors outlined above, assessment of 'success' in terms of invertebrate species or populations will clearly depend on the objectives set for the restoration programme. However, it is possible to identify some species characteristic of little-damaged raised bogs [Table 11.3] or those of high conservation importance associated with sites which have suffered small-scale damage (*e.g.* by hand cutting) whilst

---

[3] Constant species of the *E. tetralix - S. papillosum* raised and blanket mire (M18a) are: *Calluna vulgaris, E. tetralix, E. angusti-folium, S. papillosum, E. vaginatum, S. capillifolium, S. tenellum, Odontoschisma sphagni. Calluna, E. vaginatum* and *Scirpus cespitosus* are usually associated with the drier areas (Rodwell, 1991).

maintaining (or regaining) a generally high water table [Table 11.4].

Coulson and Butterfield (1985) further note that lowland raised-bog invertebrate faunas are characterised by the absence of a number of species of which the following are probably most relevant from the point of view of assessing their status: *Dyschirius globosus*, *Bradycellus ruficollis*, *Olisthopus rotundatus*, *Trichocellus cognatus*, *Ormosia pseudosimilis*, *Cicadula quadrinotata*, *Agonum fuliginosum*, *Tipula subnodicornis*, *Moliphilus ater*. However, it should be emphasised that all these are generally common (at least locally) and therefore are all liable to turn up occasionally even on little-damaged lowland raised bogs.

An alternative view that might be taken with specific sites is to base the assessment of success on a defined species or group, for example sites might be managed so as to favour numbers and diversity of dragonflies (Odonata). Within a particular group, any change in the proportion of species typically associated with 'wet' or 'dry' habitats could be monitored at specific points on the bog, chosen in relation to the management. Assessment of success with such arbitrary objectives is

relatively straightforward.

Maintenance of a high water table (with associated *Sphagnum* carpet development) seems vital to ensure survival of most if not all notable bog associated invertebrates even though many of these [see Table 1.6] require an interface situation between *Sphagnum* and/or bare peat and drier zones. For example, drying out has been strongly intimated in the decline of the rare fly *Phaonia jaroschewskii* (= *crinipes*) on Humberhead Levels sites. Loss of open water pools due to plant (including *Sphagnum*) growth, will be detrimental to dragonflies (Odonata). Regular monitoring should enable such adverse trends to be recognised in time for remedy (if this does not conflict with the main restoration aims).

Rate of recolonisation is likely to be strongly influenced not only by the development of a *Sphagnum* carpet and associated flora, but also by the proximity of refugia for 'desirable' invertebrate species. Nothing is known about the potential to seed (inoculate) regenerating areas with appropriate invertebrates in the absence of nearby refugia. Available data for areas of lowland raised bog that were subjected to traditional

Table 11.3 Invertebrate species associated with little-damaged raised bogs, which may be useful in the assessment of 'success' of restoration initiatives.

Species	Order	Notes
Pterostichus diligens, P. nigrita and *Agonum ericeti*	Coleoptera	Individuals sampled in proportion 2:4:3 (Mossakowski, 1970);
Dolichopus atratus	Diptera	Abundant
Molophilus occulatus	Diptera	Abundant
Jassargus sursumflexus	Hemiptera	Should be absent or rare on little-damaged bogs because its foodplant is *Molinia*

Table 11.4 Invertebrate species associated with partly-damaged raised bogs, which may be useful in the assessment of 'success' of restoration initiatives.

Species	Order	Notes
Leucorrhinia dubia	Odonata	Present and abundant
Limnephilus elegans	Trichoptera	Present
Agonum ericeti	Coleoptera	Present and abundant relative to *Pterostichus diligens* and *P. nigrita* (Mossakowski, 1970)
Bembidion humerale	Coleoptera	At present only on Humberside levels; occurrence elsewhere would be a significant sign of success
Curimopsis nigrita	Coleoptera	At present only on Humberhead levels; occurrence elsewhere would be a significant sign of success
Acilius canaliculatus	Coleoptera	Present (an RDB 3 species)
Sorhoanus xanthoneurus	Hemiptera	Present; associated with *Molinia*; tends to avoid uplands (Kirby 1992a).
Dolichopus atratus	Diptera	Present (Coulson, 1992)
Molophilus occultus	Diptera	Present (Coulson, 1992; Coulson & Butterfield, 1985)
Hercostomus aerosus	Diptera	Abundant (Coulson & Butterfield, 1985); generally associated with wet, acid places
Ochthera mantis	Diptera	Present; also occurs in rich fens.
Coenonympha tullia	Lepidoptera	Present; associated with *Molinia* and / or *Eriophorum*; tends to avoid uplands

hand peat cutting but subsequently allowed to recolonise from adjacent uncut and other areas suggest that invertebrate faunas of considerable conservation interest can reassemble within a period of 20 years (Heaver & Eversham, 1991) though the communities that exist at this time are undoubtedly still transitional.

11.3.5 Birds

Re-establishment of a bird community typical of little-damaged and extensive raised-bog habitats may be an ultimate objective of the restoration programme, but this is unlikely to be achievable in the short-term. Mire restoration is likely to produce substantially changed conditions for birds, and is likely to dramatically change the existing bird community. For example, during rewetting, if large areas of open water are created initially, the site may become attractive to large numbers of wetland birds. If the ultimate aim is to restore a bird community which is characteristic of little-damaged raised bog, it is likely that such species would subsequently be displaced in the long term as the renaturation progresses. Progress towards such a goal could be assessed by comparison with bird assemblages characteristic of relatively undamaged raised-bog habitats and monitoring populations of species likely to be particularly responsive to changes in habitat such as woodland / scrub or open water [see 11.2.3].

11.4 General comments

It has been suggested that areas should be monitored for at least 18 months before deciding on the optimum surface configurations (*e.g.* where to put the bunds for lagoons), particularly where the water table fluct-uations are known to be erratic, although this may not be practicable in all cases. Similarly, once the lagoons are constructed, a further period of at least a year should elapse for water levels to stabilise before making decisions on any planting operations so that appropriate areas can be targeted, and any adjustments can be made without fear of damage to the vegetation.

It is recognised that monitoring of mire sites does present considerable problems, particularly in view of the sensitivity of some of the plant and bird species to disturbance. Once a site has started to rewet, there are also likely to be considerable practical difficulties (*e.g.* access) in effectively monitoring the redevelopment of the flora and fauna. In some situations it may be possible to overcome some of these problems, for example, providing chest waders, aluminium ladders or even an inflatable raft or boat! Clearly, however, adequate attention must be given to Health and Safety considerations at all times.

Even where monitoring data are collected, there may be problems in their analyses. Careful consideration must be given to developing an appropriate monitoring strategy with specific objectives, that will provide meaningful data, and provision made in the restoration programme for adequate analysis, interpretation and evaluation.

An important part of the monitoring of restoration operations is the provision of information that can be used to assess the applicability and potential for similar schemes at other sites. Thus it is important that the details and outcome (whether positive or negative) should be disseminated to others, either through publication in conservation and technical journals or through the production of regular reports, which can be made available on request to others with an interest in restoration.

References

Aaby, B. (1976). Cyclical climatic variation over the last 5000 years reflected in raised bogs. *Nature*, **263**, 281–284.

Aerts, R. & Berendse, F. (1988). The effects of increased nutrient availability on vegetation dynamics in wet heathlands. *Vegetatio*, **76**, 63–69.

Aerts, R., Wallén, B. & Malmer N. (1992). Growth limiting nutrients in *Sphagnum*-dominated bogs subject to low and high atmospheric nitrogen supply. *Journal of Ecology*, **80**, 131–140.

Akkermann, R. (1983). Abbau bestehender Konflikte zwischen Moorschutz und Moornutzung. *Telma*, **13**, 211–222.

Aletsee, L. (1967). Begriffliche und floristiche Grundlagen zu einer pflanzengeographischen Analyse der europäischen Regenwassermoorstandorte. *Beitrag Biol. Pflanzen.*, **43**, 117–160.

Andreas, B.K. & Host, C. E. (1983). Development of a *Sphagnum* bog on the floor of a sandstone quarry in NE Ohio. *Ohio Journal of Science*, **83 (5)**, 246–253.

Andreessen, B. (1993). Spinnen (Araneida) in Mosaikbiotopen eines degenerierten Hochmoorrestes in Niedersachsen. *Telma*, **23**, 181–197.

Andrus, R.E. (1986). Some aspects of *Sphagnum* ecology. *Canadian Journal of Botany*, **64**, 416–426

Andrus, R.E., Wagner, D.J. & Titus, J.E. (1983). Vertical distribution of *Sphagnum* mosses along hummock-hollow gradients. *Canadian Journal of Botany*, **61**, 3128–3189.

Austin, K.A. & Wieder, R.K. (1987). Effects of elevated H^+, SO_4^{2-}, NO_3^-, NH_4^+ in simulated acid rain precipitation on the growth and chlorophyll content of 3 North American *Sphagnum* species. *Bryologist*, **90**, 221–229.

Baker, R.G.E. & Boatman D.J. (1985) The effect of carbon dioxide on the growth and vegetative reproduction of *Sphagnum cuspidatum* in aqueous solution. *Journal of Bryology*, **13**, 399–406.

Baker, R.G.E & Boatman, D.J. (1990). Some effects of nitrogen, phosphorus, potassium and carbon dioxide concentration on the morphology and vegetative reproduction of *Sphagnum cuspidatum* Ehrh. *New Phytologist*, **116**(4), 605–612.

Baker R.G.E. & Boatman, D.J. (1992). The effect of nitrogen, phosphorus and carbon dioxide on cell development in branch leaves of *Sphagnum*. *Journal of Bryology*, **17**, 35–46.

Baker, R.G.E. & Macklon, A.E.S. (1987). A study of factors affecting the growth and morphology of *Sphagnum*. Unpublished report for Highlands & Islands Development Board.

Ball, S.G. (1992). The importance of the invertebrate fauna of Thorne and Hatfield Moors: an exercise in site evaluation. *Thorne and Hatfield Moors Papers*, **3**, 34–65.

Barber, K.E. (1981). *Peat Stratigraphy and Climatic Change*. Balkema, Rotterdam.

Barber, K.E., Dumayne, L. & Stoneman, R. (1993). Climatic change and human impact during the late Holocene in northern Britain. *Climate Change and Human Impact on the Landscape*, (ed. F.M. Chambers), pp. 225–236.

Chapman & Hall, London.

Barkman, J.J. (1992). Plant communities and synecology of bogs and heath pools in The Netherlands. *Fens and Bogs in The Netherlands* (ed. J.T.A. Verhoeven), pp. 173–235. Kluwer Academic Publishers, Dordrecht.

Bather, D.M. & Miller, F.A. (1991). *Peatland Utilisation in the British Isles*. Centre for Agricultural Strategy, Paper 21, University of Reading, Reading.

Batten, L.A., Bibby, C.J., Clement, P., Elliott, G.D. & Porter, R.F. (1990). *Red Data Birds in Britain*. Published for the Nature Conservancy Council and the Royal Society for the Protection of Birds, Poyser, London.

Bayfield, N.G., Picozzi, N., Staines, B.W., Crisp, T.C., Tipping, E., Carling, P., Robinson, M., Gustard, A. & Shipman, P. (1991). *Ecological Impacts of Blanket Peat Extraction in Northern Ireland*. Report to the Countryside and Wildlife Branch (DoE NI).

Bayley, S.E., Vitt, D.H., Newbury, R.W., Beaty, K.G., Behr, R. & Miller, C. (1987). Experimental acidification of a *Sphagnum*-dominated peatland: first year results. *Canadian Journal of Fisheries and Aquatic Science*, **44** (Suppl), 194–205.

Beckelmann, U. & Burghardt, W. (1990). Regeneration of bogs – obtainment of oligotrophy at the example of Burlo-Vardingholter Venn, NorthRhine–Westfalia, FRG. *Peat Use and Peatland Conservation* (eds A. Tóth & Szobó, P.) pp. 106–116. International Peat Society, Hungarian National Committee, Keszthely.

Beets, C.P. (1992). The relation between the area of open water in bog remnants and storage capacity with resulting guidelines for bog restoration. *Peatland Ecosystems and Man: An Impact Assessment*. (eds O.M. Bragg, P.D. Hulme, H.A.P. Ingram, R.A. Robertson), pp. 133–140. International Peat Society / Department of Biological Sciences, University of Dundee, Dundee.

Beets, C.P. (1993). Hochmoorregeneration nach Wiedervernässung industriell abgetorfter Hochmoore in den Niederlanden (Einrichtung, Kosten und Entwicklungen). *Telma*, **23**, 271–286.

Bellamy, D.J. (1967). *Ecological Studies on some European Mires*. PhD thesis, University of London.

Bellamy, D.J. & Bellamy, S R. (1966). An ecological approach to the classification of the lowland mires of Ireland. *Proceedings of the Royal Irish Academy*, B, **65**, 237–251.

Bellamy, D.J. & Rieley, J. (1967). Some ecological statistics of a "miniature bog". *Oikos*, **18**, 33–40.

Beltman, B., Van den Broek, T. & Bloemen, S. (1995). Restoration of acidified rich-fen ecosystems in the Vechtplassen area: successes and failures. *Restoration of Temperate Wetlands* (eds B.D. Wheeler, S.C. Shaw, W.J. Fojt & R.A. Robertson), Wiley, Chichester, *in press*.

Beukeboom, L.W. (1986). The dragonfly fauna of the peat moor Fochteloërveen, The Netherlands. *Proceedings of the 3rd European Congress of Entomology, Amsterdam, 1986, Part 3*, 405–408.

Bibby, C.J., Burgess, N.D. & Hill, D.A. (1992). *Bird Census Techniques*. Academic Press, London.

Blankenburg, J. (1992). Abtorfungsverfahren und Wiedervernäßbarkeit. *Telma*, **22**, 85–93.

Blankenburg, J. & Kuntze, H. (1986). Aspects of future utilization of cut-over bogs in Western Germany. *Socio-economic Impacts of the Utilisation of Peatlands in Industry and Forestry*, Proceedings IPS Symposium, International Peat Society, Finnish National Committee, 219–226.

Blankenburg, J. & Kuntze, H. (1987) Moorkundlich – hydrologische Voraussetzungen der Wiedervernassung von Hochmooren. *Telma*, **17**, 51–58.

Boatman, D.J. (1983). The Silver Flowe National Nature Reserve, Galloway, Scotland. *Journal of Biogeography*, **10**, 163–174.

Boatman, D.J. & Lark, P.M. (1971). Inorganic nutrition of the protonemata of *Sphagnum papillosum* Lindb., *S. magellanicum* Brid. and *S. cuspidatum* Ehrh. *New Phytologist*, **70**, 1053–1059.

Boatman, D.J., Hulme, P.D. & Tomlinson, R.W. (1975). Monthly determinations of the concentrations of sodium, potassium, magnesium and calcium in the rain and in pools on the Silver Flowe National Nature Reserve. *Journal of Ecology*, **63**, 903–912.

Bolte, D, Flügger, J. & Cordes, H. (1985). Untersuchungen zur Vegetationsentwicklung in einem gestörten Hochmoor. *Verhandlung der Gesellschaft für Ökologie*, **8**, 251–256.

Bölscher, B. (1995). Niche requirements of raised bog birds matching habitat attributes resulting from bog restoration. *Restoration of Temperate Wetlands* (eds B.D. Wheeler, S.C. Shaw, W.J. Fojt & R.A. Robertson), Wiley, Chichester, *in press.*

Boström, U. & Nilsson, S. (1983). Latitudinal gradients and local variations in species richness and structure of bird communities on raised peat bogs in Sweden. *Ornis Scandinavica*, **14**, 213–226.

Braekke, F.H. (1981). Hydrochemistry of low-pH soils of South Norway. 2. Seasonal variation in some peatland sites. *Meddelelser Norsk Institutt for Skogforskning*, **36**, 1–22.

Bragg, O. (1989). The importance of water in mire ecosystems. *Cut-over Lowland Raised Mires* (eds W. Fojt & R. Meade), pp. 61–82. Research and Survey in Nature Conservation No 24, Nature Conservancy Council, Peterborough.

Bragg, O.M., Hulme, P.D., Ingram, H.A.P., Johnston, J.P. & Wilson, A.I.A. (1994). A maximum-minimum recorder for shallow water tables, developed for ecohydrological studies on mires. *Journal of Applied Ecology*, **31**, 589–592.

Bratton, J.H. (1990). *A Review of the scarcer Ephemoptera and Plecoptera of Great Britain.* Research and Survey in Nature Conservation, No. 29. Nature Conservancy Council, Peterborough.

Bromley, J. & Robinson, M. (1995). Groundwater in raised mire systems: models, mounds and myths. *Hydrology and Hydrochemistry of British Wetlands* (eds J.M.R. Hughes & A.L. Heathwaite). Wiley, Chichester, *in press.*

Brooks, A. (1981). *Waterways and Wetlands.* British Trust for Conservation Volunteers (BTCV), London.

Burton, R.G.O. & Hodgson, J.M. (1987). *Lowland Peat in England and Wales.* Soil Survey Special Survey, No. 15. Soil Survey of England and Wales. Harpenden.

Butterfield, J. & Coulson, J.C. (1983). The carabid communities on peat and upland grasslands in northern England. *Holarctic Ecology*, **6**, 163–174.

Cadell, H.M. (1913). *The Story of the Forth.* James Maclehose & Sons, Glasgow.

Cajander, A.K. (1913). Studien über die Moore Finnlands. *Acta Forestalia Fennici*, **2(3)**, 1–208.

Casparie, W.A. (1972). Bog development in South-eastern Drenthe (The Netherlands). *Vegetatio*, **25** (1–4), 271pp.

Casparie, W.A. & Streefkerk, J.G. (1992). Climatological, stratigraphic and palaeo-ecological aspects of mire development. *Fens and Bogs in The Netherlands* (ed. J.T. A. Verhoeven), pp. 81–128. Kluwer Academic Publishers, Dordrecht.

Chambers, F.M., Lageard, J.G.A. & Elliott, L. (1992). Mire development on Mynydd y Drum, South Wales: restoration of an open cast site. *Peatland Ecosystems and Man: An Impact Assessment.* (eds O.M. Bragg, P.D. Hulme, H.A.P. Ingram, R.A. Robertson). pp. 388–391. International Peat Society / Department of Biological Sciences, University of Dundee, Dundee.

Clausen, J.C. & Brooks, K.N. (1980). *The Water Resources of Peatlands, A Literature Review.* Department of Forest Resources, College of Forestry, University of Minnesota.

Clausen, J.C. & Brooks, K.N. (1983a). Quality of runoff from Minnesota peatlands: I. A characterisation. *Water Resources Bulletin*, **19**, 763–767.

Clausen, J.C. & Brooks, K.N. (1983b). Quality of runoff from Minnesota peatlands: II. A method for assessing mining impacts. *Water Resources Bulletin*, **19**, 769–772.

Clymo, R.S. (1963). Ion exchange in *Sphagnum* and its relation to bog ecology. *Annals of Botany*, New Series, **27**, 309–324

Clymo, R.S. (1970). The growth of *Sphagnum*: methods of measurement. *Journal of Ecology*, **58**, 13–49.

Clymo, R.S. (1973). The growth of *Sphagnum*: some effects of environment. *Journal of Ecology*, **61**, 849–869.

Clymo, R.S. (1984). The limits to peat bog growth. *Philosophical Transactions of the Royal Society of London*, B **303**, 605–654.

Clymo, R.S. (1987). Interactions of *Sphagnum* with water and air. In: *Effects of Acidic Deposition and Air Pollutants on Forests, Wetlands and Agricultural Ecosystems* (eds T.C. Hutchinson & K.M. Meema). pp. 513–529. Springer-Verlag, Berlin.

Clymo, R.S. (1991). Peat Growth. *Quaternary Landscapes* (ed. L.C.K. Shane & E.J. Cushing), pp. 76–112. Belhaven Press, London.

Clymo, R.S. & Duckett, J.G. (1986). Regeneration of *Sphagnum. New Phytologist*, **102**, 589–614.

Clymo, R.S. & Hayward, P.M. (1982) The ecology of *Sphagnum. Bryophyte Ecology* (ed. A.J.E. Smith), pp. 229–291. Chapman & Hall, London.

Clymo, R.S. & Reddaway, E.J.F. (1971). Productivity of *Sphagnum* (bog moss) and peat accumulation. *Hidrobiologia*, **12**, 181–192.

Clymo, R.S. & Reddaway, E.J.F. (1974). Growth rate of *Sphagnum rubellum* Wils. on Pennine blanket bog. *Journal of Ecology*, **62**, 191–196.

Coles, B. (1990). Wetland archaeology – a wealth of evidence. *Wetlands: a Threatened Landscape*, (ed. M. Williams), pp. 145–180. Blackwell, Oxford.

Coles, B. & Coles, J. (1986). *Sweet Track to Glastonbury.*

Thames & Hudson, London.

Coulson, J.C. (1992). Animal communities of peatlands and the impact of man. *Peatland Ecosystems and Man: An Impact Assessment.* (eds O.M. Bragg, P.D. Hulme, H.A. P. Ingram, R.A. Robertson), pp. 297–308. International Peat Society / Department of Biological Sciences, University of Dundee, Dundee.

Coulson, J.C. & Butterfield, J.E.L. (1985). The invertebrate communities of peat and upland grasslands in the north of England and some conservation implications. *Biological Conservation,* **34**, 197–225.

Curran, P.L. & Macnaeidhe, F.S. (1986). Weed invasion of milled-over bog. *Weed Research,* **26**, 45–50.

Darby, H.C. (1983). *The Changing Fenland.* Cambridge University Press, Cambridge.

Department of Agriculture and Fisheries for Scotland (1962). *Scottish Peat: 2nd report of Scottish Peat Committee.* HMSO, Edinburgh.

Department of Agriculture and Fisheries for Scotland (1964–1968). *Scottish Peat Surveys.* Volumes 1–4. HMSO, Edinburgh.

Department of the Environment (1994). Report of the Working Group on Peat Extraction and Related Matters. Department of the Environment, London.

Doyle, G.J. (1973). Primary production estimates of native blanket bog and meadow vegetation growing on reclaimed peat at Glenamoy, Ireland. *Proceedings of IBP Tundra Biome Symposium, Production & Decomposition Processes, Dublin,* (eds L.C. Bliss & F.E. Wielgolaski), pp. 141–151.

Edgar, P. (1993). Contracting out heathland management. *Enact,* **1** (2), 11–14.

Eggelsmann, R. (1980). Okohydrologische Aspekte zur Erhaltung von Moorgewässern. *Telma,* **10**, 173–196.

Eggelsmann, R. (1981). *Okohydrologische Aspekte von anthropogen beeinflussten un unbeeinflussten Mooren Norddeutschlands.* Thesis, Oldenburg.

Eggelsmann, R. (1982). Anmerkungen zur Berechnungsmethode der Breite hydrologischer Schutzzonen im Moor (van der Molen, Telma 11, 1981). *Telma,* **12**, 183–187.

Eggelsmann, R. (1987). Ökotechnische Aspekte der Hochmoor-Regeneration. *Telma,* **17**, 59–94.

Eggelsmann, R. (1988a). Rewetting for protection and renaturation / regeneration of peatland after or without peat winning. *Proceedings of the 8th International Peat Congress, Leningrad,* **vol 3**, 251–260.

Eggelsmann, R. (1988b). Wiedervernässung von Hochmooren. *Die Geowissenschaften,* **11**, 317–322.

Eigner, J. (1982). Pflegemaßnahmen für Hochmoore im Regenerationsstadium. *Informationem zu Naturschutz und Landschaftspflege in Nordwestdeutschland,* **3**, 227–237.

Eigner, J. & Schmatzler, E. (1980). *Bedeutung, Schutz und Regeneration von Hochmooren.* Naturschutz Aktuell. Booklet 4.

Falk, S. (1991a). *A Review of the Scarce and Threatened Flies of Great Britain (Part 1).* Research and Survey in Nature Conservation, No. 39. Nature Conservancy Council. Peterborough.

Falk, S. (1991b). *A Review of the Scarce and Threatened Bees, Wasps and Ants of Great Britain.* Research and Survey in Nature Conservation, No. 35. Nature Conservancy Council. Peterborough.

Famous, N.C., Spencer-Famous, M., Daigle, J-Y. & Thibault, J.J. (1995). Coastal raised mire restoration: mosaic of peatland, salt marsh, and minerotrophic wetlands for avian habitat enhancement *Restoration of Temperate Wetlands* (eds B.D. Wheeler, S.C. Shaw, W.J. Fojt & R.A. Robertson). Wiley, Chichester, *in press.*

Ferguson, P. & Lee, J.A. (1980). Some effects of bisulphite and sulphate on the growth of *Sphagnum* in the field. *Environmental Pollution,* **21**, 59–71.

Ferguson, P. & Lee, J.A. (1982–3). The growth of *Sphagnum* species in the southern Pennines. *Journal of Bryology,* **12**, 579–589.

Ferguson, P., Lee, J.A. & Bell, J.N.B. (1978). Effects of sulphur pollutants on the growth of *Sphagnum* species. *Environmental Pollution,* **16**, 151–162.

Forrest, G.I. & Smith, R.A.H. (1975). The productivity of a range of blanket bog vegetation types in the northern Pennines. *Journal of Ecology,* **63**, 173–202.

Foss, P. (ed.) (1991). *Irish Peatlands, The Critical Decade. International Mire Conservation Group Excursion & Symposium Proceedings, Ireland 1990.* Irish Peatland Conservation Council, Dublin.

Fox, A.D. (1986a). The breeding teal *(Anas crecca)* of a coastal raised mire in central West Wales. *Bird Study,* **33**, 18–23.

Fox, A.D. (1986b). Effects of ditch-blockage on adult Odonata at a coastal raised mire site in central west Wales, United Kingdom. *Odonatologica,* **15** (3), 327–334.

Fox, A.D. & Stroud, D.A. (1986). The Greenland White-fronted Goose in Wales. *Nature in Wales,* **4**, 20–26.

Fuller, R.J. (1982). *Bird Habitats in Britain.* Poyser, London.

Galvin, L.F. (1976). Physical properties of Irish peat soils. *Irish Journal of Agricultural Research,* **15**, 207–221.

Gilham, C.A., Leech, P.K. & Eggleston, H.S. (1992). *UK Emissions of Air Pollutants 1970–1990.* Warren Spring Laboratory, Stevenage.

Giller, K.E. & Wheeler, B.D. (1986). Past peat cutting and present vegetation patterns in an undrained fen in the Norfolk Broadland. *Journal of Ecology,* **74**, 219–244.

Giller, K.E, Wheeler, B.D. (1988). Acidification and succession in a flood plain mire in the Norfolk Broadland, U.K. *Journal of Ecology,* **76**, 849–866.

Glaser, P.H. (1987). The ecology of patterned boreal peatlands of northern Minnesota: a community profile. *U.S. Fish and Wildlife Service,* **85**, 98pp.

Glaser, P.H., Janssens, J.A. & Siegel, D.I. (1990). The response of vegetation to chemical and hydrological gradients in the Lost River peatland, Northern Minnesota. *Journal of Ecology,* **78**, 1021–1049.

Goldsmith, F.B. (ed.) (1991). *Monitoring for Conservation and Ecology.* Chapman & Hall, London.

Goodman, G.T. & Perkins, D.F. (1959) Mineral uptake and retention in cotton grass (*Eriophorum vaginatum L.*). *Nature,* **184**, 467–468.

Goodwillie, R. (1980). *European Peatlands.* Nature and Environment Series No. 19. Council of Europe, Strasbourg.

Gore, A.J.P. (1983a). *Ecosystems of the World 4A: Mires: Swamp, Bog Fen and Moor, General Studies.* Elsevier, Amsterdam.

Gore, A.J.P. (1983b). *Ecosystems of the World, 4B: Mires, Swamp, Bog, Fen and Moor. Regional Studies.* Elsevier, Amsterdam.

Gorham, E. (1949). Some chemical aspects of a peat profile.

Journal of Ecology, **37**, 24–27.

Gorham, E. (1956). The ionic composition of some bog and fen waters in the English Lake District. *Journal of Ecology*, **44**, 142–152

Grime, J.P., Hodgson, J.G. & Hunt, R. (1988). *Comparative Plant Ecology*, Unwin Hyman, London.

Grosvernier, Ph., Matthey, Y. & Buttler, A. (1995). Micro-climate and physical properties of peat: new clues to the understanding of bog restoration processes. *Restoration of Temperate Wetlands* (eds B.D. Wheeler, S.C. Shaw, W.J. Fojt & R.A. Robertson), Wiley, Chichester, *in press.*

Hammer, D.A. (1992). *Creating Freshwater Wetlands.* Lewis, London.

Hancock, C.G. (1991). *Somerset Levels Reclamation and Management.* Evidence to the Plantlife Commission of Inquiry into Peat and Peatlands. November 1991.

Harris, R.W. (1979). Peat and engineering, the sponge effect. *Soil and Water*, **15**, 27–28.

Hayward, P.M. & Clymo, R.S. (1983). The growth of *Sphagnum* – experiments on, and simulation of, some effects of light flux and water table depth. *Journal of Ecology*, **71**, 845–863.

Heathwaite, L. (1995). Problems in the hydrological management of cut-over raised mires – with special reference to Thorne Moors, South Yorkshire. *Restoration of Temperate Wetlands* (eds B.D. Wheeler, S.C. Shaw, W.J. Fojt & R.A. Robertson). Wiley, Chichester, *in press.*

Heathwaite, L. & Göttlich K.H. (1993). *Mires: Process, Exploitation, Conservation.* Wiley, Chichester.

Heaver, D. & Eversham, B. (1991). *Thorne and Hatfield Moors Invertebrate Survey:* Final Report.

Heikurainen, L. & Seppälä, K. (1963). Kuivatuksen tehokkuus ja turpeen lämpötalous. Summary: The effect of drainage degree on temperature conditions of peat. *Acta Forestalia Fennica*, **76(4)**, 33pp.

Heil, G.W. & Bruggink, M. (1987). Competition for nutrients between *Calluna vulgaris* (L.) Hull and *Molinia caerulea* (L.) Moench. *Oecologia*, **73**, 105–107.

Heinselmann, M.L. (1963). Forest sites, bog processes and peatland types in the glacial Lake Agassiz region, Minnesota. *Ecological Monographs*, **33**, 327–374.

Higgs, A.J. (1981). Island biogeographic theory and the nature reserve design. *Journal of Biogeography*, **8**, 117–124.

Hill, M.O., Preston, C.D. & Smith, A.J.E (1991) (eds). *Atlas of the Bryophytes of Britain and Ireland, I. Liverworts (Hepaticae and Anthocerotae).* Harley Books, Colchester.

Hill, M.O., Preston, C.D. & Smith, A.J.E (1992) (eds). *Atlas of the Bryophytes of Britain and Ireland, II. Mosses (except Diplolepidae).* Harley Books, Colchester.

Hobbs, N.B. (1986). Mire morphology and the properties and behaviour of some British and foreign peats. *Quarterly Journal of Engineering Geology*, **19**, 7–80.

Holmes, P.R., Boyce, D.C. & Reed, D.K. (1993a). The ground beetle (Coleoptera: Carabidae) fauna of Welsh peatland biotopes: factors influencing the distribution of ground beetles and conservation implications. *Biological Conservation*, **63**, 153–161.

Holmes, P.R., Fowles, A.P., Boyce, D.C. & Reed, D.K. (1993b). The ground beetle (Coleoptera: Carabidae) fauna of Welsh peatland biotopes: species assemblages in relation to peatland habitats and management. *Biological Conservation*, **65**, 61–67.

Humphreys, W.E. & Kitchener, D.J. (1982). The effect of

habitat utilization on species area curves: implications for optimal reserve area. *Journal of Biogeography*, **9**, 391–396.

Hutchinson, J.N. (1980). The record of peat wastage in the East Anglian Fenlands at Holme Post 1848–1978 A.D. *Journal of Ecology*, **68**, 229–245.

Hyman, P.S. (Updated by M S. Parsons) (1992). *A Review of the Scarce and Threatened Coleoptera of Great Britain.* Part 1. UK Nature Conservation Reviews, No. 3. Joint Nature Conservation Council.

Ingram, H.A.P. (1982). Size and shape in raised mire ecosystems: a geophysical model. *Nature*, **297**, 300–303.

Ingram, H.A.P. & Bragg, O.M. (1984). The diplotelmic mire: some hydrological consequences reviewed. *Proceedings of the 7th International Peat Congress, Dublin, June, 1984. Irish National Peat Committee, for the International Peat Society*, **1**, 220–234.

Ivanov, K.E. (1981). *Water Movement in Mirelands (Vodoobmen v bolotnykh landshaftakh).* Academic Press, London. (Translated by A. Thomson & H.A.P. Ingram).

Jonasson, S. & Chapin, F.S. III. (1985). Significance of sequential leaf development for nutrient balance of the cotton sedge, *Eriophorum vaginatum* L. *Oecologia (Berlin)*, **67**, 511–518.

Joosten, J.H.J. (1992). Bog regeneration in the Netherlands: a review. *Peatland Ecosystems and Man: An Impact Assessment.* (eds O.M. Bragg, P.D. Hulme, H.A.P. Ingram, R.A. Robertson). pp. 367–373. International Peat Society / Department of Biological Sciences, University of Dundee, Dundee.

Joosten, H. (1993). Denken wie ein Hochmoor: Hydrologische Selbstregulation von Hochmooren und deren Bedeutung für Wiedervernässung und Restauration. *Telma*, **23**, 95–115.

Joosten, H.J. (1995). Time to regenerate: long-term perspectives of raised bog regeneration with special emphasis on palaeoecological studies. *Restoration of Temperate Wetlands* (eds B.D. Wheeler, S.C. Shaw, W.J. Fojt & R.A. Robertson). Wiley, Chichester, *in press.*

Joosten, J.H.J. & Bakker, T.W.M. (1987). *De Groote Peel in verleden, heden en toekomst.* Rapport 88-4, 291pp. Staatsbosbeheer, Utrecht.

Jortay, A.u. & Schumacker, R. (1989). Zustand, Erhaltung und Regeneration der Hochmoore im Hohen Venn (Belgien). *Telma*, **B2**, 279–294.

Karlin, E.F. & Bliss, L.C. (1984). Variation in substrate chemistry along microtopographical and water chemistry gradients in peatlands. *Canadian Journal of Botany*, **62**, 142–153.

Key, R.S. (1991). Peat cutting and the invertebrate fauna of lowland peatland; Thorne and Hatfield Moors in a national context. *Thorne & Hatfield Moors Papers*, **2**, 19–24.

Kirby, P. (1992a). *A Review of the Scarce and Threatened Hemiptera of Great Britain.* UK Nature Conservation Review, No. 2. Joint Nature Conservation Council. Peterborough.

Kirby, P. (1992b). *A Review of the Scarcer Neuroptera of Great Britain.* Research and Survey in Nature Conservation, No. 34. Nature Conservancy Council / Joint Nature Conservation Council. Peterborough.

Kirby, P. (1992c). *Habitat Management for Invertebrates.* Royal Society for the Protection of Birds, Sandy.

Kneale, P.E. (1987). Sensitivity of the groundwater mound

model for predicting mire topography. *Nordic Hydrology,* **18**, 193–202.

König, A. (1992). Die Libellenfauna im Abbaugebiet Haidauer Ried des Wurzacher Riedes. *Telma,* **22**, 109–122.

Kulczynski, S. (1949). *Peat Bogs of Polesie.* Mémoires de l'Académie Polonaise des Sciences et des Lettres, Cracovie; Classe des Sciences Mathematiques et Naturelles; Serie B: Sciences Naturelles: **15**, 1–336.

Kuntze, H. & Eggelsmann, R. (1981). Zur Schutzfähigkeit nordwestdeutscher Moore. *Telma,* **11**, 197–212.

Kuntze, H., & Eggelsmann, R. (1982). Zur Schutzfähigkeit nordwestdeutscher Moore. *Informationem zu Naturschutz und Landschaftspflege in Nordwestdeutschland,* **3**, 3–111.

Limbert, M. (1987). Some notes on the landscape history of Thorne Moors. *Thorne Moors Papers,* (ed. M. Limbert), pp. 31–51. Doncaster Naturalists' Society, Doncaster.

Limbert, M., Mitchell, R.D. & Rhodes, R.J. (1986). *Thorne Moors, Birds and Man.* Doncaster & District Ornithological Society. Doncaster.

Lindholm, T. & Vasander, H. (1990). Production of eight species of *Sphagnum* at Suurisuo mire, southern Finland. *Annales Botanici Fennici,* **27**, 145–157.

Lindroth, C.H. (1985). The Carabidae (Coleoptera) of Fennoscandia and Denmark. *Fauna Entomologica Scandinavia.* **15 (2)**, 226–495.

Lindsay, R.A. (1993). Peatland conservation – from cinders to Cinderella. *Biodiversity and Conservation,* **2**, 528–540.

Lindsay, R.A., Charman, D.J., Everingham, F., O'Reilly. R.M., Palmer, M.A., Rowell, T.A., & Stroud, D.A. (1988). *The Flow Country. The Peatlands of Caithness and Sutherland.* Nature Conservancy Council, Peterborough.

Lindsay, R.A. *et al* (in prep). *The National Peatland Resource Inventory.*

Lugo, A.E., Brinson, M. & Brown, S. (eds) (1990). *Ecosystems of the World 15. – Forested Ecosystems.* Elsevier, Amsterdam.

Luken, J.O. (1985). Zonation of *Sphagnum* mosses: interaction among shoot growth, growth form and water balance. *The Bryologist,* **88**, 374–379.

Madden, B. (1987). The fauna of bogs. *The IPCC Guide to Irish Peatlands,* (ed. C. O'Connell), pp. 23–25. Irish Peatland Conservation Council, Dublin.

Mallik, A.U. (1989). Small-scale succession towards fen on floating mat of a *Typha* marsh in Atlantic Canada. *Canadian Journal of Botany,* **67**, 1309–1316.

Malmer, N. (1986). Vegetation gradients in relation to environmental conditions in northwestern European mires. *Canadian Journal of Botany,* **64**, 375–383.

Malmer, N. (1988). Patterns in the growth and the accumulation of inorganic constituents in the *Sphagnum* cover on ombrotrophic bogs in Scandinavia. *Oikos,* **53**, 105–120.

Markert, B., Steinbeck, R., Nick, K-J., & Bernhardt, K. G. (1990). A contribution to the distribution of some chemical elements in *Molinia caerulea* and *Eriophorum vaginatum* during reinstatement of the Leegmoor, Emsland, FRG. *Environmental Geochemistry and Health,* **12**, 239–244.

Masing, V. (1976). The influence of man on the bog ecosystems in the Estonian SSR. *Proceedings of the 5th International Peat Congress, Poland.* Vol. 1. 169–173.

Mawby, F.J. (1995). Effects of damming peat cuttings on Glasson Moss and Wedholme Flow, two lowland raised bogs in North West England. *Restoration of Temperate Wetlands* (eds B.D. Wheeler, S.C. Shaw, W.J. Fojt & R.A. Robertson). Wiley, Chichester, *in press.*

May, R.M. (1975). Island biogeography and the design of nature reserves. *Nature,* **254**, 177–178.

McGraw, J.B. (1987). Seed bank properties of an Appalachian *Sphagnum* bog and a model of the depth distribution of viable seeds. *Canadian Journal of Botany,* **65**, 2028–2035.

Meade, R.M. (1992). Some early changes following the rewetting of a vegetated cutover peatland surface at Danes Moss, Cheshire, UK, and their relevance to conservation management. *Biological Conservation,* **61**, 31–40.

Meharg, M.J., Montgomery, W.I., McFerran, D. (1992). Potential damage to peatland ecosystems by mechanised peat extraction. *Peatland Ecosystems and Man: An Impact Assessment.* (eds O.M. Bragg, P.D. Hulme, H A.P. Ingram, R.A. Robertson) pp. 23–30. International Peat Society / Department of Biological Sciences, University of Dundee, Dundee.

Middleton, R. (1990–1992) (ed.). *North West Wetlands Survey, Annual Reports.* Lancaster University Archaeological Unit, Lancaster.

Money, R.P. (1994). *Restoration of lowland raised bogs damaged by peat extraction – with particular emphasis on* Sphagnum *regeneration.* PhD Thesis, University of Sheffield.

Money, R.P. (1995). Re-establishment of a *Sphagnum*-dominated flora on cut-over lowland raised mires. *Restoration of Temperate Wetlands* (eds B.D. Wheeler, S.C. Shaw, W.J. Fojt & R.A. Robertson), Wiley, Chichester, *in press.*

Montag, A. (1989). Erfahrung mit Hochmoor-Renaturierungsprojekten im Solling. *Telma,* **B2**, 265–278.

Moore, P.D. (1982). How to reproduce in bogs and fens. *New Scientist,* 5 August 1982, 369–371.

Moore, P.D. (1990). Soils and ecology: temperate wetlands. *Wetlands: a Threatened Landscape.* (ed. M. Williams), pp. 95–114. Blackwell, Oxford

Moore, P.D. & Bellamy, D.J. (1974). *Peatlands.* Elek Science, London.

Mossakowski, D. (1970). Ökologische Untersuchungen an epigischen Coleopteran atlantischer Moor und Heidestandorte. *Z. Miss. Zool.* **181**, 233–316.

Müller, K. (1976). Zur Frage der "Mineralbodenwasserzeiger" auf ombrogenen Moorkomplexen. *Beitrag Biol. Pflanzen,* **52**, 311–318.

Müller, K. (1980). Versuche zur Regeneration von Hochmoor. *Telma,* **10**, 197–204.

Nature Conservancy Council (1990). *Handbook for Phase I Habitat Survey. A Technique for Environmental Audit.* Nature Conservancy Council, Peterborough.

Nelson, J.M. (1983/4). Some insects from a portion of East Flanders Moss, Central Region. *Forth Naturalist and Historian,* **8**, 55–63.

Nick, K-J. (1985). Wiedervernäßung von industriell abgebauten Schwarztorfflächen. *Natur und Landschaft,* **61**, 48–50.

Nick, K-J. (1993) (ed.). Beiträge zur Wiedervernäßung abgebauter Schwaztorfflächen. *Naturschutz und Landschaftspflege in Niedersachsen,* **29**, 1–127.

Nilsson, H.D., Famous, N.C. & Spencer, M.P. (1990). *Harvested Peatland Reclamation – Harvesting Impacts, Case Studies and Reclamation Options.* Unpublished report to Down East Peat L.P., Maine.

Ohlson, M. & Malmer, N. (1990). Total nutrient accumulation and seasonal variation in resource allocation in the bog plant *Rhynchospora alba*. *Oikos*, **58**, 100–108.

Orford, N. (1973). Breeding distribution of the Twite in Central Britain. *Bird Study*, **20**, 50–62.

Paffen, B.G.P. & Roelofs, J.G.M. (1991). Impact of carbon dioxide and ammonium on the growth of submerged *Sphagnum cuspidatum*. *Aquatic Botany*, **40**, 61–71.

Paje, F. & Mossakowski, D. (1984). pH preferences and habitat selection in carabid species. *Oecologia*, **64**, 41–46.

Pedersen, A. (1975). Growth measurements of five *Sphagnum* species in south Norway. *Norwegian Journal of Botany*, **22**, 277–284.

Perring, F.H. & Walters, S.M. (1962). *Atlas of the British Flora*. Nelson, London & Edinburgh.

Peus, F. (1932). *Die Tierwelt der Moore*. Handbuch der Moorkunde, **3**. Berlin.

Pfadenhauer, J. (1989). Renaturierung von Torfabbauflächen in Hochmooren des Alpenvorlands. *Telma*, **B2**, 313–330.

Pigott, C.D. & Pigott, M.E. (1959). Stratigraphy and pollen analysis of Malham Tarn and Tarn Moss. *Field Studies*, **1**, 84–101.

Poelman, A. & Joosten, J.H.J. (1992). On the identification of hydrological interaction zones for bog reserves. *Peatland Ecosystems and Man: An Impact Assessment*. (eds O.M. Bragg, P.D. Hulme, H.A.P. Ingram, R.A. Robertson), pp. 141–148. International Peat Society / Department of Biological Sciences, University of Dundee, Dundee.

Pollard, D.F.W. & Walters-Davies, P. (1968). A preliminary study of the feeding of the Greenland White-fronted Goose *Anser albifrons flavirostris* in Cardiganshire. *Wildfowl*, **19**, 106–116.

Pons, L.J. (1992). Holocene peat formation in the lower parts of The Netherlands. *Fens and Bogs in The Netherlands* (ed. J.T.A. Verhoeven), pp. 7–80. Kluwer Academic Publishers, Dordrecht.

Poore, M.E.D. (1956). The ecology of Woodwalton Fen. *Journal of Ecology*, **44**, 455–492.

Poschlod, P. (1988). Vegetationsentwicklung ehemaliger Torfabbaugebiete in Hochmooren des bayrischen Alpenvorlandes. *Tuxenia*, **8**. 31–53.

Poschlod, P. (1989). Untersuchungen zur Diasporenbank der Bunkerde am Beispiel der Kollerfilze (Rosenheimer Becken; Alpentorfwerke, Raubling). *Telma*, **B2**, 295–312.

Poschlod, P. (1990). Vegetationsentwicklung in abgetorften Hochmooren des bayrischen Alpenvorlandes unter besonderer Berücksichtigung standortskundlicher und populationsbiologischer Faktoren. *Dissertations Botanicae*, **15**. J. Cramer, Stuttgart.

Poschlod, P. (1992). Development of vegetation in peat-mined areas in some bogs in the foothills of the Alps. *Peatland Ecosystems and Man: An Impact Assessment*. (eds O.M. Bragg, P.D. Hulme, H.A.P. Ingram, R.A. Robertson). pp. 287–290. International Peat Society / Department of Biological Sciences, University of Dundee, Dundee.

Poschlod, P. (1995). Diaspore rain and diaspore bank in raised bogs and its implication for the restoration of peat mined sites. *Restoration of Temperate Wetlands* (eds B.D. Wheeler, S.C. Shaw, W.J. Fojt & R.A. Robertson), Wiley, Chichester, *in press*.

Poschlod, P. & Pfadenhauer, J. (1989). Regeneration veget-

ativer Sprossteilchen von Torfmoosen – Eine vergleichende Studie an neun *Sphagnum*-Arten. *Telma*, **19**, 77–88.

Press, M.C., Woodin, S.J. & Lee, J.A. (1986). The potential importance of an increased atmospheric nitrogen supply to the growth of ombrotrophic *Sphagnum* spp. *New Phytologist*, **103**, 45–55.

Proctor, M.C.F. (1992). Regional and local variation in the chemical composition of ombrogenous mire waters in Britain and Ireland. *Journal of Ecology*, **80**, 719–736.

Proctor, M.C.F. (1995). The ombrogenous bog environment. *Restoration of Temperate Wetlands* (eds B.D. Wheeler, S.C. Shaw, W.J. Fojt & R.A. Robertson), Wiley, Chichester, *in press*.

Ratcliffe, D.A. (1964). Mires and Bogs. *The Vegetation of Scotland*, (ed. J.H. Burnett), pp. 426–478. Oliver & Boyd, Edinburgh.

Ratcliffe, D.A. (ed) (1977). *A Nature Conservation Review*. Cambridge University Press, Cambridge.

Ratcliffe, D.A. & Walker, D. (1958). The Silver Flowe, Galloway, Scotland. *Journal of Ecology*, **46**, 407–445.

Reinikainen, A., Vasander, H. & Lindholm, T. (1984). Plant biomass and primary production of southern boreal mire-ecosystems in Finland. *Proceedings of the 7th International Peat Congress, Dublin, Ireland, 1984*. Vol. IV, 1–19.

Reynolds, W.D., Brown, D.A., Mathur, S.P. & Overend, R.P. (1992). Effect of *in-situ* gas accumulation on the hydraulic conductivity of peat. *Soil Science*, **153**, 397–408.

Richards, J.R.A. Wheeler, B.D. & Willis, A.J. (1995). The growth and value of *Eriophorum angustifolium* Honck. in relation to the re-vegetation of eroding blanket peat. *Restoration of Temperate Wetlands* (eds B.D. Wheeler, S.C. Shaw, W.J. Fojt & R.A. Robertson). Wiley, Chichester, *in press*.

Robinson, M., Blackie, J., Bromley, J., Biggin, D., Crane, S., O'Hara, J. & Bragg, O. (1992) *Additional hydrological investigtion for Thorne Moors SSSI*. Institute of Hydrology.

Rochefort, L., Gauthier, R. & Lequéré D. (1995). *Sphagnum* regeneration – toward an optimisation of bog restoration. *Restoration of Temperate Wetlands* (eds B.D. Wheeler, S.C. Shaw, W.J. Fojt & R.A. Robertson). Wiley, Chichester, *in press*.

Rochefort, L., Vitt, D.H. & Bayley, S.E. (1990). Growth, production and decomposition dynamics of *Sphagnum* under natural and experimentally acidified conditions. *Ecology*, **71**, 1986-2000.

Roderfeld, H. (1992). Erste Ergebnisse zur Bewertung von Bunkerde für die Hochmoorregeneration. *Telma*, **22**, 217–233.

Rodwell, J.S. (ed) (1991). *British Plant Communities Vol. 2. Mires and Heaths*. Cambridge University Press, Cambridge.

Rodwell, J.S. (ed) (in press). *British Plant Communities. Swamps & Tall-herb Fens*. Cambridge University Press, Cambridge.

Romanov, V.V. (1968). *Evaporation from Bogs in the European Territory of the USSR*. (N. Kaner, translator; Heimann editor). Israel programme for scientific translations, Jerusalem.

Rowell, N.T. (1988). *The Peatland Management Handbook*. Research and Survey in Nature Conservation, No 14, Nature Conservancy Council, Peterborough.

Roworth, P.C. (1992). A common bird census on Thorne Moors National Nature Reserve, South Yorkshire – a relic cut-over raised mire. *The Naturalist*, **117**, 5–18.

Royal Society for the Protection of Birds. (1983). *Survey of the Ornithological Value of the Remnant Mosslands of GMC and Merseyside.* RSPB North West Regional Office, Huddersfield. (unpublished).

Ruckley, B. & Doar, N. (1991). *Peatland management and conservation on Scottish Wildlife Trust's raised mire reserves.* Evidence to the Plantlife Commission of Inquiry into Peat and Peatlands. November 1991.

Rudolf, H. & Voight, J.U. (1986). Effects of NH_4^+-N and NO_3^--N on growth and metabolism of *Sphagnum magellanicum. Physiologia Plantarum*, **66**, 339–343.

Ruttledge, R. F. & Ogilvie, M. A. (1979). The past and current status of the Greenland White-fronted Goose in Ireland and Britain. *Irish Birds*, **1**, 293–313.

Sabotka, D. (1976). Regeneration and vegetative propagation of *Sphagnum palustre* as a factor of population stability. *Acta Societalis Botanicum Poloniae*, **45**, 357–367

Salonen, V. (1987a). Revegetation of an area of Mustasuo-Mire after clearing for peat harvesting. *Suo*, **38 (1)**, 1–3.

Salonen, V. (1987b). Relationship between the seed-rain and the establishment of vegetation in 2 areas abandoned after peat harvesting. *Holarctic Ecology*, **10**, 171–174.

Salonen, V. (1992). Effects of artificial plant cover on plant colonization of a bare peat surface. *Journal of Vegetation Science*, **3 (1)**, 109–117.

Schneebeli, M. (1989). Zusammenhänge zwischen Moorwachstum und hydrologischer Durchlässigkeit und ihre Anwendung auf den Regenerations prozeß. *Telma*, **B2**, 257–264.

Schouwenaars, J.M. (1982). Massnahmen im Wasserhashalt der niederlandischen Hochmoorreste – zur Kenntnis der Anforderungen fur eine Hochmoorregeneration. *Telma*, **12**, 219–234.

Schouwenaars, J.M. (1988). The impact of water management upon groundwater fluctuations in a disturbed bog relict. *Agricultural Water Management*, **14**, 439–449.

Schouwenaars, J.M. (1990). A study on the evapotranspiration of *Molinia caerulea* and *Sphagnum papillosum* using small, weighable lysimeters. *Problem Oriented Studies on Plant-Soil-Water Relations.* Thesis, Agricultural University Wageningen.

Schouwenaars, J.M. (1992). Hydrological characteristics of bog relicts in the Engbertsdijksvenen after peat-cutting and rewetting. *Peatland Ecosystems and Man: An Impact Assessment.* (eds O.M. Bragg, P.D. Hulme, H.A.P. Ingram, R.A. Robertson). pp. 125–132. International Peat Society / Department of Biological Sciences, University of Dundee, Dundee.

Schouwenaars, J.M. (1993). Möglichkeiten für die Wiedervernässung van Hochmooren in Abhängigkeit von der Torfmächtigkeit. *Telma*, **23**, 117–123.

Schouwenaars, J.M. (1995). The selection of internal and external water management options for bog restoration. *Restoration of Temperate Wetlands* (eds B.D. Wheeler, S.C. Shaw, W.J. Fojt & R.A. Robertson). Wiley, Chichester, *in press.*

Schouwenaars, J.M. & Vink, J.P.M. (1992). Hydrophysical properties of peat relicts in a former bog and perspectives for *Sphagnum* regrowth. *International Peat Journal*, **4**, 15–28.

Schouwenaars, J.M., Amerongen, F. & Booltink, M. (1992). Hydraulic resistance of peat layers and downward seepage in bog relicts. *International Peat Journal*, **4**, 65–76.

Segal, S. (1966). Ecological studies of peat-bog vegetation in the North-western part of the province of Overijsel (The Netherlands). *Wentia*, **15**, 109–141.

Shaw, S.C. & Wheeler, B.D. (1990). *Comparative Survey of Habitat Conditions and Management Characteristics of Herbaceous Poor-fen Vegetation-types.* Contract Surveys, No. 129. Nature Conservancy Council, Peterborough.

Shaw, S.C. & Wheeler, B.D. (1991). *A Review of the Habitat Conditions and Management Characteristics of Herbaceous Fen Vegetation Types in Lowland Britain.* Unpublished report to Nature Conservancy Council, Peterborough.

Shirt, D.B. (ed) (1987). *British Red Data Books, Vol. 2. Insects.* Nature Conservancy Council, Peterborough.

Sjörs, J. (1950). On the relation between vegetation and electrolytes in North Swedish mire waters. *Oikos*, **2**, 241–258.

Skidmore, P. (1991). *Phaonia jaroschewskii* Schnabl (Diptera; Muscidae), 'The Hairy Canary'. *Naturalist*, **116**, 69–71.

Slater, F.M. (1976). Contributions to the ecology of Borth Bog, Wales. II. Human influence. *Proceedings of the 5th International Peat Congress, Poznan, Poland.* Vol. 1. 174–182.

Smart, P.J., Wheeler, B.D. & Willis, A.J. (1986). Plants and peat cuttings: historical ecology of a much exploited peatland – Thorne Waste, Yorkshire, UK. *New Phytologist*, **104**, 731–748.

Smart, P.J., Wheeler, B. D., & Willis, A. J. (1989). Revegetation of peat excavations in a derelict raised bog. *New Phytologist*, **111**, 733–748.

Smith, A.J.E. (1978). *The Moss Flora of Britain and Ireland.* Cambridge University Press, Cambridge.

Smith, A.J.E. (1991). *The Liverworts of Britain and Ireland.* Cambridge University Press, Cambridge.

Smith, L.P. (1976). *The Agricultural Climate of England and Wales.* MAFF Technical Bulletin 35, HMSO, London.

Soeffing, K. & Kazda, J. (1993). Die Bedeutung der Mykobakterien im Torfmoosrasen bei der Entwicklung von Libellen in Moorgewässern. *Telma*, **23**, 261–269.

Southwood, T.R.E. (1978). *Ecological Methods.* London, Chapman & Hall.

Sparling, J.H. (1967). The occurrence of *Schoenus nigricans* L. in blanket bogs. I. Environmental conditions affecting the growth of *S. nigricans* in blanket bog. *Journal of Ecology*, **55**, 1–13.

Stead, I.M., Bourke, J.B. & Brothwell, D. (1986) (eds). *Lindow Man, the Body in the Bog.* London

Sternberg, K. (1982). Libellenfauna (Odonata) in Hochmooren des Sudschwarzwaldes. *Telma*, **12**, 99–112.

Streefkerk, J.G. & Casparie, W.A. (1989). *The Hydrology of Bog Ecosystems – Guidelines for Management.* Staatsbosbeheer.

Stroud, D.A. (1989). Birds of raised and cut-over raised mires. *Cut-over Lowland Raised Mires.* (eds W. Fojt & R. Meade), pp. 22–31. Nature Conservancy Council, Peterborough.

Succow, M. & Lange, E. (1984). The mire types of the German Democratic Republic. *European Mires* (ed. P.D. Moore) pp. 149–175. Academic Press, London.

Tallis, J.H. (1973). The terrestrialization of lake basins in north Cheshire, with special reference to the development of a 'schwingmoor' structure. *Journal of Ecology*, **61**, 537–567.

Tallis, J.H. & Yalden, D.W. (1983). *Peak District Moorland Restoration Project. Phase 2 Report: Revegetation trials.* Peak Park Joint Planning Board, Bakewell.

Tamm, C.O. (1954). Some observations on the nutrient turnover in a bog community dominated by *Eriophorum vaginatum* L. *Oikos*, **5**, 189–194.

Tansley, A.G. (1939). *The British Islands and their Vegetation.* Cambridge University Press, Cambridge.

Thiele, H. U. (1977). *Carabid Beetles in their Environments.* Springer, Berlin.

Treweek, J.R. (ed.). (1993). *Wetland Restoration: Techniques for an Integrated Approach.* Phase II Report to MAFF. Institute of Terrestrial Ecology, Monks Wood.

Turchenek, L.W., Tedder, W.S. & Krzanowski, R. (1993). *Mapping and Characterization of Cutover Peatlands for Reclamation Planning.* Alberta Conservation and Reclamation Council, Report No. RRTAC 93-6.

Tüxen, J. (1976). Uber die Regeneration von Hochmooren. *Telma*, **6**, 219–239.

Twenhöven, F.L. (1992). Competition between two *Sphagnum* species under different deposition levels. *Journal of Bryology*, **17**, 71–80.

UKRGAR (1990). *Acid Deposition in the United Kingdom 1986 – 1988.* Third report of the United Kingdom Review Group on Acid Rain. Department of the Environment, London.

Usher, M.B. (1991). Scientific requirements of a monitoring programme. *Monitoring for Conservation and Ecology.* (ed. F.B. Goldsmith), pp. 15–32. Chapman & Hall, London.

van der Molen, W.H. (1981). Über die Breite hydrologischer Schutzzonen um Naturschutzgebiete in Mooren. *Telma*, **11**, 213–220.

van der Schaaf, S., van't Hullenaar, J. W., Kate, J. R. & van der Molen, W.H. (1992). *In situ* measurement of acrotelm transmissivity. *Proceedings of the 9th International Peat Congress, Uppsala, Sweden, July, 1992*, 227–228.

van Walsum, P.E.V. (1992). Water management in the Groote Peel bog reserve and surrounding agricultural area; simulation and optimization. *Report* **49**, DLO Winand Staring Centre, Wageningen.

van Wirdum, G. (1991). *Vegetation and Hydrology of Floating Rich-fens.* Academisch Proefschrift, Universiteit van Amsterdam.

van Wirdum, G. (1995). The regeneration of fens in abandoned peat pits below sea level in The Netherlands. *Restoration of Temperate Wetlands* (eds B.D. Wheeler, S.C. Shaw, W.J. Fojt & R.A. Robertson). Wiley, Chichester, *in press*.

van Wirdum, G, den Held, A.J. & Schmitz, M. (1992). Terrestrializing fen vegetation in former turbaries in The Netherlands. *Fens and Bogs in The Netherlands* (ed. J.T.A. Verhoeven), pp. 323–360. Kluwer Academic Publishers, Dordrecht.

Vitt, D.H., Crum, H. & Snider, J.A. (1975). The vertical zonation of *Sphagnum* species in hummock-hollow complexes in northern Michigan. *Michigan Botanist*, **14**, 190–200.

von der Heide, A. (1991). Zum Auftreten von Stechimmen in stillgeleten Abtorfungsflächen eines Hochmoores bei Oldenburg i.o. (Hymenoptera: Aculeata). *Drosera*, **91**, 57–84.

von Post, L. & Granlund E. (1926). Sodra Sveriges tortillangar I. *Sveriges Geol. Unders.*, **C335**, 127pp.

Walker, D. (1970). Direction and rate in some British postglacial hydroseres. *Studies in the Vegetational History of the British Isles,* (eds D. Walker & R.G. West) pp. 117–139. Cambridge University Press, Cambridge.

Wallace, I.D. (1991). *A Review of the Trichoptera of Great Britain.* Research and Survey in Nature Conservation, No. 32. Nature Conservancy Council, Peterborough.

Wallén, B, Falkengren-Grerup, U. & Malmer, N. (1988). Biomas productivity and relative rate of photosynthesis of *Sphagnum* at different water levels on a South Swedish peat bog. *Holarctic Ecology*, **11**, 70–76.

Ward, D.E., Hirons, G.J. & Self, M.J. (1995). Planning for the Restoration of Peat Wetlands for Birds. *Restoration of Temperate Wetlands* (eds B.D. Wheeler, S.C. Shaw, W.J. Fojt & R.A. Robertson). Wiley, Chichester, *in press*.

Warren, S.M., Fox, A.D., Walsh, A.J., Merne, O.J. & Wilson, H.J. (1992). Wintering site interchange amongst Greenland White-fronted Geese *Anser albifrons flavirostris* captured at Wexford Slobs, Ireland. *Bird Study*, **39**, 186–194.

Waughman, G.J. (1980). Chemical aspects of the ecology of some South German peatlands. *Journal of Ecology*, **68**, 1025–1046.

Weber, C.A. (1908). Aufbau und Vegetation der Moore Norddeutschlands. *Engler, Botanischen Jahrbüchern*, **90**, 19–34.

Wheeler, B.D. (1984). British fens: a review. *European Mires* (ed. P.D. Moore), pp. 237–281. Academic Press, London.

Wheeler, B.D. (1988). Species richness, species rarity and conservation evaluation of rich-fen vegetation in lowland England and Wales. *Journal of Applied Ecology*, **25**, 331–353.

Wheeler, B.D. (1993). Botanical diversity in British mires. *Biodiversity and Conservation*, **2**, 490–512.

Wheeler, B.D. (1995). Introduction – restoration and wetlands. *Restoration of Temperate Wetlands* (eds B.D. Wheeler, S.C. Shaw, W.J. Fojt & R.A. Robertson), Wiley, Chichester, *in press*.

Wheeler, B. D. & Shaw, S. C. (1991). Above-ground crop mass and species-richness of the principal types of herbaceous rich-fen vegetation of lowland England and Wales. *Journal of Ecology*, **79**, 285-301.

Wheeler, B.D. & Shaw, S.C. (1995). A focus on fens. *Restoration of Temperate Wetlands* (eds B.D. Wheeler, S.C. Shaw, W.J. Fojt & R.A. Robertson). Wiley, Chichester, *in press*.

White, J.M. (1930). Re-colonisation after peat cutting. *Royal Irish Academy Proceedings*, Series B, **39**, 453–476.

Woodin, S.J. Parsons, A. & Mackenzie, S. (1991). The implications of acid deposition for upland vegetation in Wales. *Proceedings of Acid Deposition in Gwynedd Conference* (ed. R.H. Gritten), pp. 169–175. Snowdonia National Park Authority.

Wynne D. & O'Donnell, T. (1993). Conservation challenge: conservation of iron age roadway and associated peatlands at Corlea, Co. Longford. *The Engineers Journal*, **46**(3), 44–47.

Appendix 1

Glossary of terms

Acrotelm	The term 'acrotelm' refers to the surface layer of a peatland that is above the limit of permanent saturation (*cf.* catotelm). In a little-damaged raised bog, it refers to the uppermost, 'active layer' [see Box 1.4], comprising the living plant cover passing downwards into recently-dead plant material and thence to fresh peat. It forms the largely oxygenated surface layer with high hydraulic conductivity, within which the water table fluctuates and the main water movement occurs. Strictly speaking, cut-over bogs also have an acrotelm, but this lacks some of the distinctive features of the acrotelm layer of a little-damaged bog surface, such as its apparent capacity for hydrological self-regulation. In this report, unless qualified, the term 'acrotelm' is restricted to refer to the 'fully-functional' surface layers such as characterise little-damaged bogs.
Active porosity	Tenacity with which water movement occurs within the peat matrix (comprises the amount of loosely-bound inter-particle (interstitial) water).
Allochthonous	Of imported origin *(cf.* autochthonous). (*e.g.* allochthonous deposits are those formed from material brought in from outside, such as inwashed silts).
Allogenic	Caused by external factors (*cf.* autogenic).
Anoxic	Lacking oxygen.
Aquifer	Water-bearing substratum, at full moisture capacity.
Autochthonous	Formed *in situ* (*cf.* allochthonous).
Autogenic	'Self-made'. [caused by reactions of organisms themselves,] (*cf.* allogenic).
Baulks	Upstanding blocks of peat between peat cuttings or fields.
Block-cutting	Method of peat extraction in which the peat is cut in blocks from a vertical face [2.3.1]
Bog	General term for ombrotrophic mires (but sometimes used colloquially for other types of wetland).
Bog species	Any species typically found on bogs. [Many of these also occur in fens or other habitats.]
Bog vegetation	Refers to any species / vegetation-type typical of, or closely resembling, that found on little-damaged raised bogs.
Bog-*Sphagnum* vegetation	This category accommodates vegetation in which 'bog-*Sphagnum*' species are prominent, often dominant, components. It includes *NVC* mire expanse community M18 and the bog-pool communities M2 and M3. These latter may occur as a mosaic with M18 vegetation, forming the so-called 'regeneration complex'. This vegetation is particularly characteristic of the surface of little-damaged raised bogs.
Borrow pit	A pit from which 'construction' material (*e.g.* peat) is removed.
Bulk density	The amount of solid material per unit volume.
Bund	Used here to mean an embankment used to pond back water, to a greater extent than a dam, which in this context has been confined to use for structures built to block linear water courses. Elsewhere, such structures have been variously referred to as dams, embankments and dykes.
Bunkerde	There is no standard definition of 'bunkerde' – it is a German term for the surface layer of vegetation and peat which is removed prior to peat cutting, at each cutting phase, and subsequently returned to the peat cuttings / fields. [see 9.6]

Catotelm	The lower 'inert' layer of the peat of an undamaged raised bog [see Figure 1.1]. The catotelm underlies the <u>acrotelm</u>, and is permanently saturated, mainly <u>anoxic</u> and of low <u>hydraulic conductivity</u>.
Climax ecosystem	The mature or stabilised stage in a successional series of communities
Cut-over surfaces	General term used to refer to the peat surface remaining after extraction (by any extraction method).
Depression	Effectively refers to areas that have been cut for peat and which form hollows or flat surfaces *in relation to adjoining blocks.* They tend to have an overall *concave* or *water holding* profile. [*cf.* <u>massif</u>]. [2.1]
Diaspore	Any spore, seed fruit, or other portion of a plant when being dispersed and able to produce a new plant.
Diplotelmic	'Two-layered'. In raised bogs, this refers to the typical occurrence of an uppermost 'active layer' (the <u>acrotelm</u>) and lower 'inert layer' (the <u>catotelm</u>) [1.7].
Draw-down	Refers to the fall in water level caused by a steepened <u>hydraulic gradient</u>, for example as a result of water movement to drains or ditches.
Edge effects	Effects associated with the transition between habitat types; for example, the tendency to have greater variety and density of organisms in the boundary zone between communities or habitats.
Ericoid / ericaceous	Pertaining to plant species of the Heath family (Ericaceae).
Eurytopic	Used to refer to invertebrates having a wide range of geographical distribution (*cf.* <u>stenotopic</u>).
Eutrophic	Nutrient-enriched (not necessarily base-rich).
Evapotranspiration	Loss of water from the soil by evaporation from the surface and by transpiration from the plants growing thereon; the volume of water lost in this way.
Feeder tank	Lagoon constructed to help soak adjoining baulks of peat.
Fen	General term for <u>minerotrophic</u> mires.
Flats	The base of the peat cuttings, in a block-cut system.
Flooding	Inundation of the peat surface, with water levels usually at least $> + 10$ cm.
Flux density	Flow per unit area per unit time.
Forb	A non-graminoid <u>herb</u> [an herbaceous plant, other than a grass or grass-like plant].
Gradient feeding	The gravity flow of water through a system of lagoons constructed across a slope.
Growth lagoon	Lagoon constructed primarily for direct plant colonisation.
Guanotrophication	Nutrient enrichment owing to bird droppings.
Haplotelmic	A <u>diplotelmic</u> mire from which the upper surface layer (<u>acrotelm</u>) has been removed or otherwise destroyed.
Herb	A vascular plant with a green, non-woody stem.
Humification (von Post scale)	Degree of decomposition (of peat) [production of humus from the decay of organic matter as a result of microbial action] [see Table 1.3].
Hydraulic conductivity $[K; K_{sat}]$	The rate at which water moves through a material. K_{sat} denotes saturated hydraulic conductivity – *i.e.* the rate at which water moves through a saturated material.
Hydraulic gradient	The change in hydraulic head or water surface elevation over a given distance.
Hydraulic head	The difference in pressure-head between two hydraulically-connected points.
Hydrosere (hydroseral)	<u>Autogenic</u> terrestrialisation of open water.
Hydrostatic pressure	The pressure created by the weight of water acting upon itself.

Lagg	Swedish term for the outer margin of a raised bog, typically with a water course and / or fen (usually poor fen or fen woodland), into which water from the bog drains. [Few 'natural' examples remain in the UK as most sites have suffered at least some degree of marginal damage].
Levelling (levelled)	(a) Measurement of the surface topography using surveying equipment. (b) Configuration of the peat surface to even-out topographical variations.
Macrofossils	Plant or animal remains preserved in peat which can be identified without the use of a high-powered microscope (*e.g.* stems, leaves and roots but not pollen grains).
Massif	Used as a relative term to refer to any upstanding block of peat within a peat-cutting complex. A massif may have been cut for peat, either across its entire surface or as plots within it. [*cf.* depression] [2.1]
Meteoric water	Water derived from precipitation.
Milling	Modern method of peat extraction in which the bare peat surface is milled to a depth of 15–50 mm and harrowed to promote drying, prior to collection [2.3.1]
Mineralisation	The oxidative breakdown of organic matter into its constituent inorganic components and carbon dioxide, thereby making nutrients (*e.g.* nitrate, phosphate) available to plants. [2.3.3]
Minerotrophic	Fed by groundwater.
Minerotrophic mire	Mire whose surface is irrigated both by precipitation and groundwater.
Mire	A general term applied to peat-producing ecosystems which develop in sites of abundant water supply. Some workers also include some mineral-based wet land within the compass of 'mire'.
Mire macrotope	Mire complex which has been formed by the fusion of isolated mire mesotopes which originated from separate centres of mire formation.
Mire mesotope	Mire system developed from one original centre of peat formation. May join together into a macrotope.
Mire microtope	Small-scale topographical features associated with the mire surface, for example a regular arrangement of ridges and hollows.
Monophagous	Used to refer to invertebrates restricted to a very narrow range of food plants.
Niedersachsen	Lower Saxony (North Germany).
Oligophagous	Used to refer to invertebrates restricted to a single order, family or genus of food plant.
Oligotrophic	Nutrient poor (not necessarily base-poor).
Ombrotrophic	Supplied solely by water derived from the atmosphere (rain, snow, fog *etc.*).
Ombrotrophic bog	Bog whose surface is irrigated more-or-less exclusively by precipitation inputs.
Palaeoecology	The study of the relationship between past organisms and the environment in which they lived.
Paludification (paludosere)	The development of wetland directly over mineral ground due to waterlogging through impeded drainage and / or increase in water supply.
Para-bog vegetation	This category is used to refer to vegetation with broad similarities to 'bog-*Sphagnum*' vegetation, but which differs either in not containing all of the species typical of the latter, or in having them but not with the same proportions or structure. Ericaceous species or *Eriophorum vaginatum* typically dominate (rarely *Molinia caerulea*). *Sphagnum* species are often sparse or represented mainly by taxa characteristic of the drier microsites within bogs (*e.g. S. capillifolium*), but in some (relatively species-rich) examples it is possible to find most of the characteristic species of 'bog-*Sphagnum*' vegetation. Various additional species, particularly taxa associated with drier conditions may also occur. It includes some examples of *NVC* communities M15, M20, M25a. Such vegetation may be indicative of partial damage to a bog surface (*e.g.* burning or drainage) but it may possibly also be a natural constituent of some little-damaged bogs, as on the drier slopes of a rand or as part of a 'still-stand' condition.

Peat cuttings	Generally used to refer to areas from which peat has been extracted using methods other than milling (*i.e.* mainly hand or machine block cutting).
Peat field	Used for the areas between the open drains in the <u>milling</u> system of peat extraction.
Peat workings	General term for areas from which peat has been extracted using any method.
Perched water mound	Refers to the water mound developed within a raised bog as a result of impeded drainage and storage of water derived solely from precipitation (*i.e. perched* above the level of regional groundwater tables). [1.7]
Permeability	The capacity of a porous medium for transmitting water.
Poor fen	<u>Minerotrophic</u> mire, typically of pH less than *c.* 5.5.
Porosity (pore space)	That portion of the soil occupied by air and water, usually expressed as a percentage of the total volume.
Precipitation	Deposition of water on the earth's surface by rain, snow, mist, frost, condensation *etc.*; the quantity of water so deposited.
Rafting	Used here to refer to the growth of plants and vegetation, floating in or on (sometimes shallow) supra-surface water.
Rand	The outward-sloping margins of a raised bog (Swedish) [see Figure 1.1].
Recharge	Water supply.
Regeneration	The *de novo* accumulation of peat.
Remnant	Used to refer to a block of peat within a peat-cutting complex which has been received little, if any, direct damage by peat extraction, but which may have become damaged indirectly.
Renaturation	The redevelopment of an appropriate <u>ombrotrophic</u> vegetation.
Rewetting	The restoration of surface-wet conditions.
Rich fen	<u>Minerotrophic</u> mire, typically of pH more than *c.* 5.5.
Runoff	The (amount of) water leaving a peatland (or specified area) and entering drains or water courses due to gravity.
Schwingmoor	Floating vegetation mat / raft (German).
Seed / diaspore bank	The reservoir of seeds / <u>diaspores</u> which do not germinate immediately, but remain dormant and become incorporated into the soil.
Sere	Plant succession.
Shoeing	The return of the upper, unusable, layer of peat plus vegetation into the peat cutting.
Soaking	The rewetting of peat in which the water table is brought close to the surface of the peat, but remains essentially sub-surface.
Stenotopic	Having a restricted range of geographical distribution (*cf.* <u>eurytopic</u>).
(Peat) stratigraphy	Description of the layering within a peat deposit based on the composition and character of the peat and mineral content.
Surface configuration / conformation	Topographical disposition of the peat fields *etc*. Also used to refer to the manipulation of the micro- or macro-topography, usually by moving the surface peat around.
Telluric	Used to refer to water derived from the earth.
Vagility	The ability of an organism or group of organisms to disperse, or be dispersed in a given environment.
Water storage	Volume of water present in a given volume of soil (*e.g.* litres of water per m^3 soil). Also used for the volume of water above a given reference level (*i.e.* can include open water).
Water storage capacity	The total amount of water that can be held in a given volume of soil. (*e.g.* 900 litres of water per m^3 soil $\equiv$ water storage capacity of 90%).

Water storage coefficient	The ratio between the change in water volume (cm^3 cm^{-2}) and the change in water level depth (cm). [A measure of the amount of water that is removed (added) from a peat profile when the water table is lowered (raised) – the storage coefficient of open water is 100%.]
Water table	Level at which the porewater pressure is equal to atmospheric pressure, forming the junction between saturated and unsaturated conditions.
Xerophyte	Plant adapted to conditions of low water supply.

Appendix 2

Legislation relating to peat extraction and restoration options

1.1 Introduction

Formulation of an appropriate restoration strategy for any site must take full cognisance of any relevant international, national and local legislation. The most important aspects to be considered concern planning, conservation and water resources, the main relevant legislation for which is briefly outlined in Chapter 7 and considered in more detail below.

1.2 Mineral planning and environmental assessment legislation

Peat, when cut and sold commercially, is classed as a mineral under UK planning law and is subject to the same planning requirements as any other extracted mineral. Responsibility for implementation of mineral planning legislation lies with the mineral planning authority (MPA), generally the County Council, or Unitary Authority (*e.g.* Metropolitan District Council) in England and Wales. In Scotland, control of mineral extraction and related operations is the responsibility of the development control authority, which is the District Authority or, where only one tier of local government operates, the Regional or Island council. In Northern Ireland, the responsibility lies with the Department of the Environment (Northern Ireland).

For the purposes of discussion in this document the term 'mineral planning authority' (MPA) is used for all development control authorities in the UK.

The Town and Country Planning Act 1990 represents the primary legislation in England and Wales covering planning procedures for the winning and working of minerals. In Scotland, this is based upon the Town and Country Planning (Scotland) Act 1972. In Northern Ireland, the main legislation is the Planning (Northern Ireland) Order 1991. This basically leaves a situation similar to that in England prior to the 1981 Town and Country Planning (Minerals) Act, in that planning permission is required for extraction of peat intended

for sale – there is no provision for statutory after-care conditions, but restoration requirements can be specified.

Extraction of peat thus requires planning permission from the MPA, which, in order to exercise control over developments, may place conditions on working practices and specify after-use and after-care conditions. Planning conditions may cover factors such as phasing and methods of working, the use of imported fill materials, ongoing restoration and final contours. Restoration conditions apply to the restoration of the site after completion of extraction, by the use of subsoil, topsoil or soil-making materials. Aftercare conditions are conditions which require steps, following the initial restoration procedures, to bring the land to the standard required for a specified after-use for agriculture, forestry or amenity purposes. "Amenity" includes nature conservation.

Many planning permissions for peat extraction were granted in the early years after the first Town and Country Planning Act in 1947, before the nature conservation importance of peat areas had been fully appreciated. Many of the existing permissions thus lack planning conditions to control methods of working, restoration and aftercare. Some sites with early planning permission have subsequently been notified as SSSI / ASSI (see below), which has highlighted conflicts of interests between the peat industry and conservation.

The duty of MPA's (excluding those in N. Ireland) to review mineral working sites with existing planning permissions, and the powers to update existing permissions through particular types of orders, including the imposition of aftercare conditions, were first introduced by the Town and Country Planning (Minerals) Act 1981. These provisions have now been incorporated into the 1990 Town and Country Planning Act for England and Wales. The aftercare period can be up to a maximum of five years. Aftercare conditions can only be applied where there are restoration conditions. The latter are limited in that they can only refer to movement or use of soil or soil-forming material. Aftercare conditions can only apply to treatment of land by fertilisation, planting, cultivation, drainage *etc.*, not to the provision of items such as visitor facilities, paths, *etc.* although these can be covered by other conditions or planning obligations.

Issues such as long term maintenance and management and provision of items which are not required by aftercare or other planning conditions can be covered in a voluntary agreement or planning obligation between the mineral operator and the MPA, under Section 106 of the 1990 Act.

Certain after uses, such as those involving the construction of buildings, may require separate planning permission. In England and Wales this should be obtained from the Local Planning Authority (usually the District or Borough Council), unless the development conflicts with a restoration or aftercare condition, when it is a matter for the MPA.

The MPA has the powers to make the following orders, in suitable cases:

- *Revocation Order*   to revoke or reduce the area covered by a permission;

- *Discontinuance Order*   to discontinue use or impose conditions on a use;

- *Prohibition Order*   to prohibit resumption of working where the site is abandoned, so that restoration can be carried out;

- *Suspension Order*   where working has temporarily ceased, to deal with environmental problems;

- *Modification Order*   to modify the conditions of the planning permission.

However, use of these orders may often involve payment of compensation to the parties affected and the likely scale of compensation payable may constitute a significant disincentive for their use.

MPA's have to make decisions on planning applications for the winning and working of minerals, having regard to the development plan for the area and to any other material considerations. The Planning and Compensation Act 1991 amended the 1990 Act by introducing a presumption in favour of development which is in accordance with the development plan unless it would cause demonstrable harm to interests of acknowledged importance. Under this Act the MPA's are required to prepare or update Minerals Local Plans, and in relevant areas these plans may need to include policies on peat extraction. Changes to the development plan provisions of the 1991 Act also included, for the first time, a requirement for all plans to include policies in respect of the conservation of the natural beauty and amenity of the land. PPG 12[1]

advises on development plans. The provisions of the 1991 Act covering Scotland have not yet been introduced.

The 1991 Act (Sections 22 and Schedule 2) also introduced new procedures for dealing with permissions for the winning and working of minerals or the depositing of minerals waste, originally granted under Interim Development Orders (IDO's). They are referred to in the 1991 Act as 'old mining permissions'. MPG's 8[2] and 9[3] give advice on these procedures.

In 1992, the Department of the Environment issued a consultation paper on old mineral permissions, as part of its review of the operation of the 1981 Minerals Act. This mentioned peat working as one of the particular problems. A second consultation paper on the reform of old mineral permissions was issued in April 1994. In this, the Government proposes that all mineral planning permissions should be reviewed and planning conditions should be brought up to modern standards without compensation. It also proposes that there should be no blanket revocation of minerals permissions in Sites of Special Scientific Interest, National Parks or Areas of Outstanding Natural Beauty.

A series of Planning Policy Guidance Notes (PPG's) and Minerals Planning Guidance Notes (MPG's), published by the Department of the Environment provide guidance on national policies[4] in England and Wales. There are also a series of Regional Planning Guidance notes (RPG's) for England. General advice on planning conditions is contained in PPG 1[5] and Department of the Environment Circular 1/85 (Welsh Office 1/85)[6]. These documents set out criteria for imposition of conditions. The scope and potential coverage of conditions relating to mineral extraction are described in MPG 2[7]. MPG 7[8] deals specifically with reclamation of mineral workings to after-uses

---

[1] Department of the Environment (1992). Planning Policy Guidance (PPG)12: *Development Plans and Regional Planning Guidance.* HMSO.

[2] Department of the Environment / Welsh Office (1991). Mineral Planning Guidance (MPG)8: *Planning and Compensation Act 1991; Interim Development Order Permissions (IDO's)- Statutory Provisions and Procedures*, HMSO.

[3] Department of the Environment / Welsh Office (1992). Mineral Planning Guidance (MPG)9: *Planning and Compensation Act 1991; Interim Development Order Permissions (IDO's) - Conditions.* HMSO.

[4] Note that these do not apply in Scotland or Northern Ireland

[5] Department of the Environment / Welsh Office (1992). Planning Policy Guidance (PPG)1: *General Policy and Principles.* HMSO.

[6] Department of the Environment (1985). Circular 1/85 (Welsh Office, 1/85), *The Use of Conditions in Planning Permissions.* HMSO.

[7] Department of the Environment / Welsh Office (1988). Mineral Planning Guidance (MPG)2: *Applications, Permissions and Conditions.* HMSO.

[8] Department of the Environment / Welsh Office (1989). Mineral Planning Guidance (MPG)7: *The Reclamation of Mineral Workings.* HMSO.

including agriculture, forestry and amenity, together with definitions of restoration and aftercare conditions.

Guidance on planning policy in Scotland is contained in National Planning Policy Guidelines (NPPG's) supplemented, where necessary by Planning Advice Notes (PAN's). The recently-published NPPG 4[1] includes guidance on peat extraction.

The European Community Directive No. 85/337[2] on the assessment of the effects of certain public and private projects on the environment is implemented in England and Wales by the Town and Country Planning (Assessment of Environmental Effects) Regulations 1988, and in Scotland by the Environmental Assessment (Scotland) Regulations 1988. Guidance on the requirements of the regulations is given in a Department of the Environment Circular 15/88 (Welsh Office 23/88)[3] and, for Scotland in SDD Circular 13/88[4]. Mineral workings are listed in Schedule 2 of the regulations, so an environmental assessment is required to accompany the planning application only if the proposed operation is likely to have significant effects on the environment by virtue of factors such as nature, size and location. Northern Ireland is covered under The Planning (Assessment of Environmental Effects) Regulations, NI 1989.

In 1992, the Department of the Environment established a Working Group on peat extraction and related matters. The findings of the group have been published in a report[5] which considers a range of complex issues concerning nature conservation and mineral extraction interests affecting peatlands in Britain, and sets out suggestions for a policy approach which should be consistent with the Government policies for sustainable development and for nature conservation.

1.3 Wildlife and conservation

1.3.1 Introduction

Although one of the main aims of the restoration schemes considered in this document will be to maintain and enhance the conservation 'value' of a

site, it should be recognised that operations must be carried out with due regard to the current conservation legislation. For example, there may be certain restrictions on the work that can be carried out without consent from the statutory conservation agencies and there may be circumstances where a conflict of conservational interest needs to be resolved (for example, where a statutorily-protected species of bird occurs in an area which would be disturbed through restoration operations). It is important that the relevant agencies are consulted about these aspects before carrying out any work [see below and Chapter 7].

1.3.2 International Legislation

The *EC Wild Birds Directive* (EC Directive 79/409 on the Conservation of Wild Birds) provides for the general protection of all birds, their eggs, nests and habitats, with special conservation measures for listed, threatened or vulnerable species ('Annex 1 species') and all regularly occurring migratory species, in particular through the designation of special protection areas (SPA's). Such areas are eligible for special protection, for example to avoid pollution or deterioration of habitats or any other disturbances affecting the birds, and to ensure the protection of sufficient habitat to maintain populations at ecologically and scientifically sound levels. Annex 1 species occurring on raised-bog habitats include merlin, hen harrier, nightjar and the Greenland race of white-fronted goose. The provisions of the Directive are covered through national planning and conservation legislation for example, the Wildlife and Countryside Act (1981) [see below].

The *Ramsar Convention on Wetlands of International Importance Especially as Waterfowl Habitat* (1971), provided for the promotion of conservation of wetlands and waterfowl, in particular through the special protection of a range of wetlands of international significance, designated as 'Ramsar Sites'. In the UK, these will normally already be designated as SSSI's or ASSI's, and as for the *Birds Directive* [see above] the provisions of the Convention are implemented through national planning and conservation legislation

The *Berne Convention on the Conservation of European Wildlife and Natural Habitats* (ratified by the UK in 1982) also carries an obligation to conserve the habitats of wild plants and animals, especially those listed in the convention which are endangered or vulnerable. Local Authorities should be aware of the broad requirements of the Berne Convention, and are advised to consult the relevant bodies about any development proposals which may affect an area which may have importance as a wildlife habitat, whether or not it has been designated as a SSSI (or ASSI). In 1985, the UK also ratified the *Bonn Convention on the*

---

[1] Scottish Office Environment Department (1994). National Planning Policy Guideline (NPPG) 4: *Land for Mineral Working.*

[2] CEC (1985). 85/337/EEC. *Directive on the Assessment of the Effects of Certain Public and Private Projects on the Environment.* Official Journal of the European Communities. L175, 40-48.

[3] Department of the Environment (1988). Circular 15/88 (Welsh Office, 23/88), *Environmental Assessment.* HMSO

[4] Scottish Development Department (1988). Circular 13/88. *Environmental Assessments: implementation of EC Directive. The Environmental Assessment (Scotland) Regulations.*

[5] Department of the Environment (1994). *Report of the Working Group on Peat Extraction and Related Matters.* DoE, London.

Conservation of Migratory Species of Wild Animals.

The *EC Habitats Directive* (Council Directive on the Conservation of Natural Habitats of Wild Flora and Fauna – 92/43/EEC) aims to maintain, or restore at a favourable conservation status certain natural habitats and species that are considered endangered, rare or endemic within the Community, and require special attention. Special protection will be given to habitat types listed under Annex 1 "Natural habitat types of community interest whose conservation requires the designation of special areas of conservation". Active raised bog and degraded raised bog (still capable of natural regeneration) are both included, the former being considered a priority habitat type. Protection will also be afforded to all *Sphagnum* species under Annex V ("Animal and plant species whose taking in the wild and exploitation may be subject to management measures"). The Directive came into force in June, 1994, and regulations to transpose the requirements of the Directive into UK law came before Parliament in July 1994. A national list of sites considered to be 'Special Areas of Conservation' (SAC's) must be submitted to the Commission by June 1995, and sites of Community importance must be agreed by June 1998. Thereafter, the sites must be formally designated as soon as possible, and by 2004 at the latest. It is, as yet, unclear what bearing this piece of legislation will have on the restoration of cut-over raised-bog habitats.

Protection of wetlands is also afforded through the designation of Environmentally Sensitive Areas (ESA's). The designation is designed to ensure that traditional farming practices are continued within the area concerned, with financial incentives offered to farmers not to intensify their agricultural practices. Although this is not directly applicable to land not currently under agricultural use, this scheme has been used in such areas as the Somerset Levels to encourage farmers to raise water levels on peatlands. The concept of ESA's was introduced in E.C. Regulation 797/85 *On Improving the Efficiency of Agricultural Structures* specifically Article 19, *National Aid in Environmentally Sensitive Areas.* In the UK the designation and management of ESA's is covered under Section 18 of the Agriculture Act 1986.

1.3.3 UK Legislation

The Wildlife and Countryside Act 1981 remains the primary legislation in Britain for the protection of wildlife. The main provisions of the Act are described in Department of the Environment Circular 32/81 (Welsh Office 50/81)[1], SDD 3/82 and 31/86. The Act is generally administered by English Nature (formed

from the Nature Conservancy Council by the 1990 Environmental Protection Act), Countryside Council for Wales and Scottish Natural Heritage, together with the Countryside Commission in England.

Part I of the 1981 Act deals with the protection of individual plant and animal species. All birds, except for a few pest species are protected from being killed, injured or taken, from having their eggs destroyed or their nests destroyed while in use. Certain rare species, listed in Schedule 1, are given extra protection by special penalties. Schedule 1 species occurring on raised-bog habitats include merlin and hen harrier.

About 30 mammals, reptiles, amphibians and invertebrates, listed in Schedule 5, are given full protection under section 9 of the Act. This protection includes causing deliberate harm to a species and deliberate damage, destruction or obstruction of any structure or place used by the animal for shelter or protection and disturbance of the animal while it is occupying this structure or place. Amongst the species protected are all species of bats, otter, adder (*Vipera berus*), grass snake (*Natrix natrix*), and great crested newt (*Triturus cristatus*). Of these, adders are the most likely to be encountered on cut-over peatland sites. Badgers (*Meles meles*) may also be occasionally encountered – they are fully protected by their own legislation: The Protection of Badgers Act 1992.

Ninety two species of vascular plants are included in Schedule 8 of the Wildlife and Countryside Act. It is an offence for any person to intentionally pick, uproot or destroy any of these wild plants. These species are included in the British Red Data Book for Vascular Plants (Perring & Farrell, 1983)[2] which details all native or probably native species recorded in 15 or fewer 10 km grid squares from 1930 onwards; some 317 species or sub-species in total.

Quinquennial reviews of Schedules 5 and 8 are carried out. The review to be undertaken may advise the Secretary of State to extend protection to selected lichens and bryophytes.

Part II of the Wildlife and Countryside Act 1981 deals with the conservation of habitats. A Site of Special Scientific Interest (SSSI) is defined by Section 28 of the Act as "any area of land which (in the opinion of the conservation agency) is of special interest by reason of any of its flora, fauna, or geological or physiographical features". Under the Town and County Planning General Development Order 1988 (General Permitted Development (Scotland) Order 1992 in Scotland), MPA's, or development control authorities in Scotland, are obliged to consult the bodies administering the Wildlife and Countryside Act 1981

---

[1] Department of the Environment (1981). Circular 32/81, *Wildlife and Countryside Act.* HMSO.

[2] Perring, F.H. & Farrell, L. (1983). *British Red Data Books. I. Vascular Plants.* 2nd Edition, RSNC, Lincoln.

when considering planning proposals that are likely to impinge on an SSSI.

Protection is given to designated sites of nature conservation or wildlife value through policies in structure and local plans. Guidance on nature conservation and planning is given in DoE Circular 27/87 (Welsh Office 52/87)[1] and DoE Circular 1/92 (Welsh Office 1/92)[2] and in Scotland SOEnD Circular 13/91. A Planning Policy Guidance note which will supersede some or all of these circulars for England and Wales should be published later in 1994.

The main conservation designations for sites containing important habitats in Northern Ireland are broadly similar to those in the rest of the UK. Under the Nature Conservation and Amenity Lands Order 1985 (NCALO) there is a statutory obligation on the DoE(NI) to designate qualifying sites as Areas of Special Scientific Interest (ASSI's). The Wildlife (Northern Ireland) Order 1985 gives the species provisions equivalent to those under the Wildlife and Countryside Act 1981.

The owner of the land within an SSSI / ASSI is obliged to consult the statutory nature conservation agencies before carrying out any changes in land use and management. For each SSSI (or ASSI) there are identified a list of Potentially Damaging Operations (PDO's). The list may include: the extraction of minerals (including peat), ploughing, planting, drainage, construction *etc.* If the owner or occupier of the land wishes to carry out any of these PDO's, four months notice in writing must be given to the conservation agency. The agency may consent to the operation, or, if the operation is regarded as damaging, will approach the owner to negotiate a compromise. This may involve compensation for any profit forgone by not carrying out the PDO. It is a reasonable excuse (in any event) under the 1981 Act, for a person to carry out an operation if it was authorised by a planning permission (Section 28(8)(a)). Of course, compensation would not be negotiated where there is another impediment to carrying out the PDO, *e.g.* refusal of planning permission. Sites lying within National Nature Reserves and many County Wildlife Trust Reserves are better protected as they have management agreements in place with owners.

While there is no specific legislation covering the transplantation of material, under the Wildlife and Countryside Act, the removal of organisms from, or introduction to an SSSI / ASSI site may be considered a potentially damaging operation, for which consent is required from the statutory conservation agencies. Uprooting of any plant from the wild also requires the consent of the landowner. It is recommended that guidance on intra-site translocations of both flora and fauna is sought from these agencies, as the general guidelines are currently under review.

1.3.4 Archaeology

The Ancient Monuments and Historical Buildings Act (1979) protects major archaeological monuments and significant areas of historic landscape, with section 1 of the Act protecting those classed as particularly valuable sites. Guidance on archaeology, which includes industrial archaeology, is contained in PPG 16 on Planning and Archaeology issued in November 1990[3]. The guidance sets out advice on:

- inclusion of policies in development plans for the protection, enhancement and preservation of sites of archaeological interest and their settings;

- the need to take into account archaeological considerations from the beginning of the development control process;

- the steps of consultation, field evaluation, preservation and recording which may precede development.

In Scotland relevant guidance with respect to archaeology can now be found in PAN 42[4], NPP Guideline 4[5] and NPP Guideline 5[6].

Archaeological artefacts may be damaged directly by drainage or other works involving the lowering of water tables, and consequent drying out and decay of organic and environmental remains. Damage may also result from any earthworks carried out in association with restoration. Cut-over bogs should therefore be treated as for any other sites of archaeological value and should be subject to appropriate archaeological assessments [see Chapter 7]. If remains are to be disturbed as part of restoration they should be accurately recorded and preserved where possible. Some mires contain Scheduled Ancient Monuments and '*scheduled monument consent*' is required before work can be carried out on them. The bodies administering scheduled monuments are English Heritage, Cadw (Welsh Historic Monuments) and Historic Scotland, in England, Wales and Scotland

---

[1] Department of the Environment (1987). Circular 27/87 (Welsh Office 52/87). *Nature Conservation.* HMSO.

[2] Department of the Environment (1992). Circular 1/92, (Welsh Office 1/92). *Planning Controls over Sites of Special Scientific Interest.* HMSO.

[3] Department of the Environment (1990). Planning Policy Guidance (PPG)16: *Archaeology and Planning.* HMSO.

[4] Scottish Office (1994). Planning Advice Note (PAN)42. *Archaeology - The Planning Process and Scheduled Monument Procedures.*

[5] Scottish Office (1994). National Planning Policy Guideline (NPPG)4, *Land for Mineral Working.*

[6] Scottish Office (1994). National Planning Policy Guideline (NPPG)5, *Archaeology and Planning.*

respectively. Other bodies such as the Royal Commissions on Ancient and Historic Monuments and the Council for British Archaeology can offer advice on peatland archaeology.

1.3.5 Summary

Particular attention should be paid to conservation legislation where operations being carried out may directly or indirectly affect any of the following:

- Species specially protected under the Wildlife and Countryside Act 1981 (as updated and amended);
- National Nature Reserves (NNR);
- Sites or Areas of Special Scientific Interest (SSSI / ASSI);
- Ramsar Sites;
- Special Protection Areas (SPA); and, in future, Special Areas of Conservation (SAC)
- Environmentally Sensitive Areas (ESA);
- National Parks;
- Areas of Outstanding Natural Beauty (AONB);
- Heritage Coasts;
- Public Rights of Way;
- Scheduled Ancient Monuments (SAM);
- Listed Buildings;
- Local Nature Reserves (LNR).

Any further sites of environmental or archaeological interest such as those identified by Local Authorities and those owned or managed by the National Trust or voluntary conservation bodies.

1.4   Water resources

1.4.1 Introduction

In England and Wales, the National Rivers Authority (NRA) has a statutory responsibility for water resources management, pollution control, flood defence, fisheries, navigation, recreation and conservation. This includes the management and protection of water resources; the regulation of all water abstractions from rivers, lakes and underground; the monitoring of water quality; and the regulation of all discharges to rivers, lakes, and the sea. It is required to maintain and improve fisheries in inland waters; to conserve and protect the water environment; and to promote recreational activities relating to inland water. In certain areas, Internal Drainage Boards (IDB's) are, in turn, responsible for agricultural land drainage – the improvement and maintenance of flood defence and drainage systems. Similar statutory responsibilities are held in Scotland by the River Purification Boards and in N. Ireland by DoE (NI).

The NRA and IDB's also have statutory responsibilities for conservation. Under section 16 of the Water Resources Act 1991 and section 12 of the Land Drainage Act 1991, the NRA and the IDB's are obliged to:

- conserve and enhance the natural beauty, wildlife geology and physiographical features of special interest consistent with any enactments relating to their functions;
- protect and conserve buildings, sites, and objects of archaeological, architectural, or historical interest;
- preserve public rights of access.

Section 2(2) of the Water Resources Act 1991 imposes a duty on the NRA to promote the conservation and enhancement of the natural beauty and amenity of inland and coastal waters and of land associated with such waters, and the conservation of the flora and fauna which are dependant on an aquatic environment.

One of the major requirements of any restoration scheme involving wetlands will be the manipulation of water levels to provide suitable conditions for the flora and fauna. This may range from small-scale damming of surface ditches, to large-scale impoundments or diversions of water courses. Although the legislation concerning water resources mainly relates to the major water courses, and restoration work may be confined 'on-site', the behaviour of water 'off-site' may be influenced, for example by affecting water levels in surrounding land, regulating run-off or modifying storm discharges. It is therefore recommended that the appropriate authorities are consulted at an early stage in the planning process over the details of any restoration scheme.

There are several areas in which the water resources authorities must be specifically involved in planning and carrying out restoration measures:

1.4.2 The Reservoirs Act 1975

This Act covers England, Wales and Scotland. In Northern Ireland it is not an Act but its provisions are followed. It imposes safety provisions on reservoirs and artificial lakes that are designed to hold or are capable of holding more than 25,000 m^3 of water above the 'natural level' of any part of the adjoining land; the main intention being to limit potential danger to life or property through the sudden release of water due to the failure of the retaining structures. The provisions require that the construction or enlargement of large lakes be undertaken in accordance with the design and under the supervision of a qualified civil engineer appointed by the Secretary of State to a panel under the Act. The filling or storage of water other than in accordance with the engineers' certificates is also prohibited.

The volume of water specified is equivalent to *c*. 4.5 ha flooded to 50 cm depth. It is thus possible that parts of some restoration schemes may come under the provisions of the Act, if the intention is to create large, flooded lagoons. However, an authoritative statement on the application of the Reservoirs Act to the restoration of abandoned peat workings cannot be given as it will depend on such factors as the precise nature of the proposed works (*e.g.* size and number of lagoons, nature of the water retaining constructs), the relationship with natural land levels and potential for catastrophic failure. A practical test is to estimate whether failure would cause at least 25,000 m^3 of water to flood adjacent natural land. If so, then qualified panel engineers should be consulted. It is recommended that advice should be sought from a qualified engineer at an early stage in planning a restoration strategy.

1.4.3 Land Drainage Act 1991

Under the Land Drainage Act 1991, any works which interfere with existing drainage require *Land Drainage Consent* – this would include the building of any constructs on or adjacent to water courses, and the diversion of any streams around a bog. Details of the proposed work must be notified to the water resource bodies, who, before issuing consents, must be satisfied that either the works will not adversely affect drainage on land owned by third parties or that those third parties agree to accepting the consequences of the proposals.

1.4.4 Water abstraction and impound-ment licences

Under Section 24 of the Water Resources Act 1991 a licence is needed to abstract water from any source of supply (*e.g.* water courses or groundwater). This includes the consent of the NRA for small-scale or one-off abstractions. Section 25 covers the requirement for

an impounding licence which may be required, for example, if 'on-stream' water is impounded or an existing water course diverted. In Scotland this is covered by the Water (Scotland) Act 1980 Section 17, and in Northern Ireland it comes under the Water and Sewerage Services Act 1973 Article 11.

1.4.5 Consent to discharge

In some circumstances, it will be necessary to make provision for the discharge of water. This will usually require the issuing of a certificate giving the *consent to discharge*, unless drainage rights already exist. Situations where this may apply include the provision of specific outfalls from a bog and pumping of enriched water from a lagoon. It is necessary to provide details of the quality of the water to be discharged. Discharge licences are granted in England and Wales under the Water Resources Act 1991; in Scotland under the Control of Pollution Act 1974 and in Northern Ireland by the Northern Ireland Water Act 1972.

1.5 Miscellaneous legislation

Health and Safety at Work *etc.* Act 1974

Adherence to health and safety legislation should form part of the requirements for any work carried out in connection with restoration works.

Other

It is important that other possible legal constraints on development, such as common land, turbary rights, rights of way, riparian rights, mineral rights, shooting rights, grazing rights, location of public utilities such as gas pipes, electricity pylons *etc.* should be fully taken into consideration in any restoration schemes.

Appendix 3

Synopsis of characteristics of the main plant species associated with lowland raised bogs in Britain*

Species	Distribution in Britain	Habitats and vegetation-types	Preferences	Regeneration	Seed bank	Seed wt.	Notes
Andromeda polifolia Bog Rosemary	Mainly in NW & W England, with some outliers in S Yorks. & C. Scotland	Lowland ombrotrophic bog, occasionally upland. Rarely in wet heath and poor fen. Wider habitat range elsewhere (e.g. Fennoscandia).	Little known. Not usually found in very wet conditions.	Seeds dispersed by fauna and wind. Vegetative clonal growth	Persistent	0.166 mg	Able to tolerate a considerable degree of damage and dehydration. Can colonise suitable habitats in damaged bogs.
Betula pubescens Birch	Widespread, but local in parts of C & E England	Wide range of habitats and vegetation types. Abundance and performance regulated by vegetation management and water regimes	Tolerates wide range of pH and water conditions	Wind-dispersed with large numbers of seeds	None reported	0.12–0.18 mg	Spreads rapidly, especially onto bare peat surfaces. Invasion onto raised bogs usually considered undesirable (removal is often a major management problem), although may provide ornithological interest. Establishment may be reduced by raising water levels and removing seed sources
Calluna vulgaris Heather	Widespread, but local in C & E England	Typical of lowland heath and moorland, but also occurs in most bog communities and many poor fens. Occasionally in rich fen.	Usually found in drier microsites in wetlands; favoured by controlled burning; suppressed by over-grazing	Produces large numbers of minute, light seeds. Probably wind dispersed.	Large and persistent	0.03 mg	May be dominant in sites that have been drained or damaged. Able to rapidly colonise new areas, especially if bare. Suppressed by over-grazing.
Drosera rotundifolia Round-leaved sundew	Widespread, but rare or absent from English Midlands and parts of Eastern England	Occurs widely in mires (especially poor fens and bogs) but also wet heath and some types of wet acidic grassland. Occasionally in rich fen.	Essentially a plant of wet, acidic, low-fertility environments. Limited tolerance of shading	Produces large numbers of minute, light seeds, probably dispersed by wind and fauna. Possibly some vegetative spread from buds or regeneration of parts of moribund plants.	Yes	10–20 µg	Characteristic species of bogs. May survive short periods of drying, but typically found in permanently wet areas, and generally absent from drained sites. Field performance may be related to carnivorous success and availability of prey. Can rapidly colonise suitable substrata, including (moist) bare peat and carpets of *Sphagnum etc.*, probably mainly from seed. Can be expected to colonise suitably wet sites in cut-over sites, but may require artificial re-introduction into sites from which it has been lost through drainage *etc.*

Species	Distribution	Habitat / Ecology	Reproduction	Seed persistence	Seed weight	Notes
Erica tetralix Cross-leaved Heath	Widespread, but absent from English Midlands and scarce in E. England	Mainly found in moist or wet open habitats; widespread in bog, poor fen, wet heath and moorland. Also in acid grassland and occasionally in rich fens. Generally most vigorous in moist, rather than saturated, conditions. Restricted to acidic, low-fertility soils. Tolerant of some shading, grazing and burning.	Mainly vegetative in undisturbed, wet habitats, but also produces small seeds (probably wind-dispersed).	Yes	0.01–0.02 mg	Can survive for quite long periods on partly-drained peat, but may be constrained by competition with plants such as *Calluna*, *Molinia* and *Pteridium*. Can colonise bare peat surface quite rapidly and can establish on *Sphagnum* rafts unless inundated.
Eriophorum angustifolium Common cotton-grass	Widespread, esp. in N & W. More localised in S & E	Occurs widely in bogs, poor fens, rich fens, around pools, and sometimes in wet heath and wet grassland. Recorded from wide pH range, but restricted to soils of low fertility. Particularly favours wet conditions – not as tolerant of dry conditions as *E. vaginatum*.	Primarily vegetative, with strong rhizomatous growth. Seed germinates readily, but establishment from seed thought to be infrequent.	Possibly	0.44 mg	Widespread in bogs, both natural and damaged. Important colonist of bare peat (if sufficiently wet); can spread rapidly vegetatively once established and may help to bind the surface and prevent erosion. Particularly important as a pioneer colonist of shallow, open water, where it may help to produce floating rafts.
Eriophorum vaginatum Hare's tail cotton-grass	Widespread, but rare in lowlands of S & E	Occurs in all bog and many poor-fen vegetation-types. Typically found on acid peats, but occasionally pH >6.0. May become more abundant following drainage. Tolerant of superficial burning and grazing. Apparently tolerates some degree of atmospheric pollution.	Primarily by seed.	Persistent	1.02 mg	Widespread in bogs, including damaged examples. One of the few bog species that will readily recolonise moist peat excavations, including quite dry milled peat surfaces. Dense stands may prevent establishment of other more 'desirable' species, but sparse swards may assist *Sphagnum* establishment by providing a 'climbing frame' and improving the microclimate.
Juncus effusus Soft rush	Common throughout UK	Occurs in a wide range of vegetation-types and habitats, especially wet grassland, wet heath and poor fen, but also alongside streams and lake margins . Grows in a very wide range of pH and moisture regimes. Dominance may be related to some nutrient enrichment and disturbance. Tolerant of moderate cutting and trampling; often avoided by grazing stock.	By seed and vegetative expansion. Produces copious amounts of minute, mucilaginous seeds, dispersed by wind or animals.	Yes	0.01 mg	Not a characteristic bog species. May be an important colonist of wet, abandoned peat cuttings, but establishment often regarded as 'undesirable' and indicative of some damage or enrichment. However, may be an important primary colonist of shallow open water, and unless very dense, may help to provide a 'climbing frame' that facilitates *Sphagnum* establishment.
Molinia caerulea Purple Moor Grass	Widespread	Wide variety of habitats and vegetation-types, including wet grassland. Found in all main bog and many fen communities. Favoured by partial drainage and fluctuating water levels. Relatively high nutrient requirements	Primarily seed	Possibly–conflicting data	0.53 mg	Spreads rapidly, especially onto bare peat surfaces. Extreme abundance on bogs most usually a reflection of damage (*e.g.* drainage, burning, atmospheric pollution): usually considered undesirable, although small quantities may be beneficial as 'nurse' species for *Sphagna*. May be possible to control by ensuring permanent saturation of the peat.

contd

Species	Distribution in Britain	Habitats and vegetation-types	Preferences	Regeneration	Seed bank	Seed wt.	Notes
Narthecium ossifragum Bog Asphodel	Widespread in much of N & W, but absent from much of C, S & E England.	Occurs in a wide range of wetland habitats and mire vegetation-types. Most characteristic of some poor-fen types, but also in wet heath, wet grassland, moorland and ombrotrophic bog. Frequent in rich fen in NW.	Mainly occurs where water table is sub-surface; generally absent from dry and inundated areas. Growth apparently favoured by water movement, high redox potentials and modest supply of nutrients. Intolerant of dense shading. Tolerant of grazing and light burning.	Mainly vegetative in closed vegetation. Large clonal patches may develop. Copious, viable seed produced, but dispersal agent not known.	No data	*c.* 0.06 – 0.1 mg	Does not usually persist in drained sites or where dense scrub develops; conversely, establishment may be inhibited by water tables at or above the surface. A frequent recolonist of some abandoned peat workings.
Pteridium aquilinum Bracken	Common throughout UK	Found in numerous types of vegetation and habitat, but generally most abundant on relatively dry, acidic soils. Not a typical wetland species, but often occurs around wetlands or in drier microsites within them.	Broad ecological tolerance to many conditions, but intolerant of waterlogging.	Spores produced abundantly; widely dispersed. Once established, vegetative expansion can lead to rapid development of extensive colonies.	May have a spore bank		Presence on bogs usually indicates severe disturbance and dehydration – often occurs on baulks. Rapidly colonises bare peat surfaces and may replace some other species, *e.g. Calluna* or *E. vaginatum*. Control may be desirable in some situations.
Rhynchospora alba White-beaked sedge	Widespread, but local, mainly in S & NW England and NW Scotland. Sporadic elsewhere.	Wet, acidic situations on open peaty or skeletal mineral substratum. Mainly poor-fen, bog and wet heath communities	Little known. Manly found in wet, but not permanently inundated open, low-fertility environments, typically of low pH	Nut. Probably dispersed by birds and human disturbance	Yes	*c.* 0.4 mg	Primary colonist of bare peat, including peat cuttings if wet (but not if deeply inundated). Probably easily lost through drainage and damage.
Trichophorum cespitosum Deer grass	Widespread, particularly in N & W. Absent or local in much of C & E England	Most typical of wet heaths, moorland and blanket peat, but also widespread on raised bogs and some poor fens. Wide range of vegetation types.	Little known, but primarily associated with low fertility, low pH environments. Seems to withstand periodic burning.	Primarily by seed, probably dispersed by grazing animals and birds.		*c.* 0.42 mg	Does not appear to be a rapid recolonist of damaged peat surfaces, but has been recorded from numerous old peat cuttings.
Vaccinium oxycoccos Cranberry	Similar to, but wider than, *Andromeda polifolia* (*q.v.*)	Found frequently in bogs and poor fens; less frequently in wet heath, acid grassland and rich fens.	Little known; usually absent from areas of permanent inundation. Typically most abundant creeping over low *Sphagnum* hummocks.	Seed within berry, dispersed by birds *etc.* Creeping shoots root readily.	Yes	*c.* 0.41 mg	Important and characteristic species of many raised bogs. Probably easily eradicated by drainage. Often not a rapid colonist of bare peat surfaces, nor of very wet conditions, but does occur in revegetated peat cuttings.

Species	Distribution	Habitat	Conditions	Regeneration	Comments
Sphagnum capillifolium	Widespread, especially in N & W. Absent or local in S & E England	Found in wide range of oligotrophic to weakly minerotrophic mires – common in poor fens, bogs and wet heath; rare in rich fen.	Most common in acid, oligotrophic mires, in drier microsites. Intolerant of base-rich conditions.	Vegetative. Importance of regeneration from spores not known.	Can grow in wet microsites, but usually excluded by the more aquatic species (*e.g. S. cuspidatum*).
Sphagnum cuspidatum	Widespread, especially in N & W. Absent from much of C, S & E England	Floating or submerged in oligotrophic pools, also along pool margins, hollows and soaks in bogs and poor fens.	Generally restricted to acidic, oligotrophic conditions. Some tolerance to desiccation, but permanent wet conditions required for continued growth	Vegetative expansion may be rapid in suitable conditions. Regeneration can occur from fragments (except leaves). Importance of regeneration from spores not known	A vigorous, pioneer colonist of shallow open water, forming rafts which may be later invaded by other bog species. Often the first species to colonise wet peat cuttings and a particularly important species in bog restoration.
Sphagnum magellanicum	Most abundant in N & W, occasional in E & S England	Widespread in *Sphagnum* bogs and poor fens, forming low hummocks / carpets	Largely intolerant of base-rich conditions, and sensitive to atmospheric pollution.	Vegetative; can regenerate from fragments (except leaves). Spore capsules are rare.	One of the important 'bog-building' Sphagna in some raised bogs. Can grow well in pools, but often excluded by the more aquatic species (*e.g. S. cuspidatum*). Only occasionally found in peat cuttings – may require a permanently wet surface.
Sphagnum papillosum	Widespread, but mainly in north and west. Absent from much of S, C & E England	Common in acid, oligotrophic peatlands; often principal peat-former. Recorded from all main bog and poor-fen communities and occasional in others.	Most prolific when water tables within a few cm below capitula. Wide pH range, but mainly pH 4 – 4.5. Sensitive to acid pollutants.	Vegetative; can regenerate from fragments (except leaves). Importance of regeneration from spores not known.	Can colonise primary rafts; provides a niche for vascular plants (*e.g. Drosera* spp.). Important in hydroseral development from open water to bog communities. May tolerate mild nutrient enrichment, but sensitivity to atmospheric pollutants may affect capacity to recolonise some damaged mires. A major peat-forming species in bogs.
Sphagnum recurvum	Mostly throughout UK, but absent from much of C & E England	Found in large number of mire community-types; on ombrotrophic and minerotrophic mires (particularly poor fens), wet fields, woodlands and hillside flushes.	Tolerant of a wide range of chemical and physical conditions, but seems to favour weakly minerotrophic and flushed conditions. The most tolerant *Sphagnum* of atmospheric pollutants.	Vegetative expansion may be rapid in suitable conditions. Importance of regeneration from spores not known	One of the commonest and most widespread British *Sphagnum* species. Important colonist of wet, abandoned peat workings which exhibit some mineral enrichment, where it may proved a niche which other species can colonise. May be a particularly important recolonist in sites grossly affected by atmospheric pollution.

* Main sources include: Perring & Walters (1962); Grime *et al.* (1988); Shaw & Wheeler (1990); Rodwell (1991; in press); Money (1994); Poschlod (1995); J.G. Hodgson, unpublished data.

Appendix 4

Plant species recorded on raised bog sites in the UK

Columns: Uncut, WC (wet cuttings), DC (dry cuttings), MH (marginal habitats).

+   species recorded;   (+)   species recorded but not fully typical

Columns RF (rich fen), PF (poor fen) and B (bog) indicate occurrence in wetland habitats:

a: atypical;   p: principal (a main constituent species).

c: companion (occurs frequently, but not primarily characteristic of this wetland type);

Based on: unpublished survey information (B.D. Wheeler, S.C. Shaw, R.P. Money); Hill, Preston & Smith (1991, 1992); Smith (1978, 1991) Rodwell (1991, in press).

Table A4.1: Species characteristic of undamaged raised bog

Name	Uncut	WC	DC	MH	RF	PF	B
Andromeda polifolia	+	+	+			r	p
Aulacomnium palustre	+	+		+	a	p	p
Calliergon stramineum	+					p	p
Calypogeia neesiana	+					p	p
Calypogeia sphagnicola	+	+				p	p
Campylopus introflexus	(+)						(+)
Carex limosa	+	+			p	p	p
Carex magellanica	+					p	p
Cephalozia connivens	+					p	p
Cephalozia divaricata	+					+	+
Cephalozia hampeana	+					+	+
Cephalozia lotlesbergeri	+					p	p
Cephalozia pleniceps	+					p	p
Cephaloziella elasticha	+					p	p
Cephaloziella rubella	+					p	p
Cladopodiella fluitans	+					p	p
Cladopodiella francisci	+					p	p
Dicranum undulatum	+						p
Drepanocladus fluitans		+				p	p
Drosera anglica	+	+			p	p	p
Drosera intermedia	+	+			p	p	p
Drosera rotundifolia	+	+	+		p	p	p
Eleocharis multicaulis	(+)	+ ?			a	p	a

contd.

Table A4.1 (continued)

Name	Uncut	WC	DC	MH	RF	PF	B
Empetrum nigrum	+		+		a	p	p
Erica tetralix	+	+	+		c	*p*	*p*
Eriophorum angustifolium	+	+	(+)		p	p	p
Eriophorum vaginatum	+	+	(+)		a	p	p
Kurzia pauciflora	+	+			a	p	p
Ledum palustre[1]	(+)	+					
Menyanthes trifoliata	+	+		+	p	p	p
Molinia caerulea	+	+	+	+	p	p	p
Mylia anomala	+	+				p	p
Myrica gale	+	+	+	+	p	p	p
Narthecium ossifragum	+	+	+	+	a	p	p
Odontoschisma sphagni	+	+				p	p
Osmunda regalis	(+)	+			p	p	p
Pleurozia purpurea	(+)					p	p
Polytrichum alpestre	+	+				p	p
Rhynchospora alba	+	+			a	p	p
Rhynchospora fusca	(+)	+				p	p
Rubus chamaemorus	+						p
Scirpus cespitosus	+	+	+			p	p
Sphagnum auriculatum	+	+				p	a
Sphagnum capillifolium	+	+	+		a	p	p
Sphagnum cuspidatum	+	+				p	p
Sphagnum fimbriatum	(+)	+		+	c	p	c
Sphagnum fuscum	+				a	p	p
Sphagnum imbricatum	+					p	p
Sphagnum magellanicum	+	+				p	p
Sphagnum palustre	(+)	+		+	c	p	a
Sphagnum papillosum	+	+				p	p
Sphagnum pulchrum	+	+				p	p
Sphagnum recurvum	+	+		+	c	p	?
Sphagnum squarrosum		+		+	c	p	c
Sphagnum subnitens	+	+			p	p	p
Sphagnum subsecundum	+	+			p	p	?
Sphagnum tenellum	+	+	+			p	p
Utricularia minor	(+)	+			p	p	p
Vaccinium oxycoccos	+	+			a	p	p
Vaccinium uliginosum	(+)						

---

[1] probably not native

Table A4.2: Fen species recorded from raised bog sites

Name	Uncut	WC	DC	MH	RF	PF	B
Alnus glutinosa				+	c	c	a
Angelica sylvestris		+			p		
Calliergon cuspidatum		+			p		
Calliergon giganteum		+			p		
Caltha palustris		+	(+)		p		
Campylium stellatum		+			p	p	
Carex curta	(+)	+		+	a	p	a
Carex diandra		+			p	p	
Carex lasiocarpa		+		+	p	p	a
Carex nigra		+	+	+	p	p	a
Carex panicea		+	+	+	p	p	a
Carex paniculata		+			p	p	
Carex rostrata	(+)	+		+	p	p	a
Cicuta virosa		+			p		
Dryopteris carthusiana		+		+	p	p	a
Dryopteris dilatata			+	+	c	c	a
Eleocharis palustris		+			p		
Epilobium palustre		+		+	p	p	
Equisetum fluviatile		+			p	p	
Equisetum palustre		+		+	p	p	
Filipendula ulmaria		+		+	p		
Frangula alnus	(+)	(+)	(+)	+	p	p	a
Galium palustre				+	p	p	a
Hydrocotyle vulgaris		+		+	p	p	a
Iris pseudacorus		+			p	p	
Juncus acutiflorus	(+)	+		+	p	p	a
Lychnis flos-cuculi		+			p		
Lycopus europaeus		+			p		
Lysimachia vulgaris		+			p		
Mentha aquatica		+		+	p	p	a
Phalaris arundinacea		+			c		
Phragmites australis	(+)	+		+	p	p	a
Pinguicula vulgaris		+			p	p	c
Platanthera bifolia		+			c	p	a
Potamogeton polygonifolius	(+)	+			p	p	a
Potentilla palustris		+		+	p	p	a
Ranunculus flammula		+		+	p	p	a
Ranunculus lingua		+			p		
Salix aurita		+			r	p	a
Salix cinerea		+		+	p	p	a
Scorpidium scorpioides		+			p	p	a
Typha latifolia		+			p	p	
Valeriana officinalis		+			p	c	
Viola palustris		+			a	p	?

Table A4.3: Species for which bogs or fens are not main habitat

Name	Uncut	WC	DC	MH	RF	PF	B
Betula pendula			+	?	a	c	a
Betula pubescens	+	+	+	+	c	c	a
Calluna vulgaris	+	+	+	+	a	c	c
Calypogeia fissa	+	+	+	+	+	+	+
Campylopus atrovirens	+						p
Cephalozia bicuspidata		+					
Chamerion angustifolium			+	+	a	a	
Deschampsia cespitosa		+	+	+	c	c	
Deschampsia flexuosa	+		+	+	a	c	c
Dicranum bonjeani	(+)	+			c	p	c
Dicranum fuscescens	(+)		+				c
Dicranum polysetum	(+)		+				c
Dicranum scoparium	+						p
Dryopteris carthusiana	+				c	c	a
Dryopteris filix-mas			+	+	a	a	a
Galium saxatile	+		+	+	a	c	c
Hypnum cupressiforme	+	+	+		c	c	c
Juncus bulbosus	(+)	+			c	p	c
Juncus effusus	(+)	+		+	c	c	c
Leucobryum glaucum	+	+	+	+		c	c
Listera cordata	(+)					r	r
Lophozia ventricosa	+					?	?
Luzula multiflora		+	+	+	c	c	a
Pinus sylvestris	(+)		+		a	a	a
Pleurozium schreberi	+	+	+			c	c
Polygala serpyllifolia		+			c	c	c
Polygonum amphibium		+	+		a	a	
Polytrichum commune	+	+	+		c	p	p
Potentilla erecta	(+)	+	+		c	c	c
Pteridium aquilinum	(+)		+	+	a	a	a
Pyrola minor	(+)		+			c	a
Rhododendron ponticum[2]	+		+				a
Rumex acetosa		+			c		
Rumex acetosella		+				a	a
Sphagnum compactum	(+)		+	+		a	a
Sphagnum molle	+		+	+		a	a
Succisa pratensis		+		+	c	c	c
Vaccinium myrtillus	+	+	+	+		a	a
Vaccinium vitis-idaea	+					c	c

[2] not native

Appendix 5

Bird Species Nomenclature

The following list provides the English and Latin names of bird species mentioned in the text.

BEARDED TIT	*Panurus biamicus*
BITTERN	*Botaurus stellaris*
BLACK GROUSE	*Lyrurus tetrix*
BLACK-HEADED GULL	*Larus ridibundus*
BLACK-TAILED GODWIT	*Limosa limosa*
COOT	*Fulica atra*
CUCKOO	*Cuculus canorus*
CURLEW	*Numenius arquata*
DUNLIN	*Calidris alpina*
GOLDEN PLOVER	*Pluvialis apricaria*
GRASSHOPPER WARBLER	*Locustella naevia*
GREENLAND WHITE-FRONTED GOOSE	*Anser albifrons flavirostris*
GREYLAG GOOSE	*Anser anser*
HEN HARRIER	*Circus cyaneus*
MALLARD	*Anas platyrhynchos*
MARSH HARRIER	*Circus aeruginosus*
MEADOW PIPIT	*Anthus pratensis*
MERLIN	*Falco columbarius*
MONTAGU'S HARRIER	*Circus pygargus*
MOORHEN	*Gallinula chloropus*
NIGHTINGALE	*Luscinia megarhychos*
NIGHTJAR	*Caprimulgus europaeus*
PINK-FOOTED GOOSE	*Anser brachyrhynchus*
RED GROUSE	*Lagopus lagopus*
REDSHANK	*Tringa totanus*
REED BUNTING	*Emberiza schoeniclus*
REED WARBLER	*Acrocephalus scirpaceus*
RUFF	*Philomachus pugnax*
SEDGE WARBLER	*Acrocephalus schoenobaenus*
SHORT-EARED OWL	*Asio flammeus*
SKYLARK	*Alauda arvensis*
SNIPE	*Gallinago gallinago*
STONECHAT	*Saxicola torquata*
TEAL	*Anas crecca*
TREE PIPIT	*Anthus trivialis*
TWITE	*Carduelis flavirostris*
WATER RAIL	*Rallus aquaticus*
WHINCHAT	*Saxicola rubetra*
WILLOW WARBLER	*Phylloscopus trochilus*

Appendix 6

Summary of restoration measures implemented in selected peatland sites in lowland Britain and parts of NW Europe

The following table provides a brief summary of restoration measures taken at the sites in the UK, Ireland, The Netherlands and Germany visited in 1992 by the authors in the course of research for the current project. The main techniques used are outlined and comments given on the perceived success at the time of visiting the sites (updated where possible). Scrub control has not been specified as this forms an integral part of most management programmes. Deliberate inoculation with plant material is indicated, where known. Further details can be obtained by contacting the appropriate organisations: BnM – Bord na Mona; CCW – Countryside Council for Wales; CWT – County Wildlife Trust; EN – English Nature; NT – National Trust; PPA – member of Peat Producers Association; SNH – Scottish Natural Heritage; SWT – Scottish Wildlife Trust.

Site	Objectives	Starting conditions	Action	Materials	Date started	Comments
England and Wales						
Astley Moss, Lancs. [CWT]	Restoration of cut-over and drained site to raised bog	Mainly dominated by birch and *Molinia*	Ditch blocking	Peat dams	1988	Water held on site for longer in summer; spread of *Eriophorum angustifolium*; increase in dragonflies; die-back of *Molinia*..
Burtle Road (Somerset Levels) [PPA]	Creation of lake and reedbeds in worked out peat cuttings	Bare clay base	Surface configuration – sides bunded and islands created	Clay bunding	1990	Holding water and starting to revegetate with *Phragmites* and *Typha latifolia*.
Cors Caron (SW & NE bogs), Dyfed [CCW]	Restoration of drained bog surface and marginal peat cuttings	Cuttings mainly dominated by *Molinia* and birch	Ditch blocking and marginal bunding of cuttings	Peat dams and bunds	1988	Water levels raised by ditch blocking – possibly only locally; bunds have effectively raised levels in the cuttings; some die back of *Molinia* and birch. Water levels relatively stable throughout year.
Cors Fochno, Dyfed [CCW]	Reduction in water loss through drains and marginal peat cuttings	Non-mire plants spreading in drained and cut-over areas.	Ditch blocking and marginal bunding	Peat dams and bunds	1981. Bund in 1992	Rise in water levels locally up to 2 m. Increase in wetland fauna due to creation of 'pools' in the drains; die-back of *Molinia etc*, colonisation by Sphagna. Dampening of water-level fluctuations, particularly in area of old peat cuttings.

Site	Purpose	Site description	Measures	Materials	Date	Results / Comments
Crowle Moors, Lincs. [CWT]	Restoration of cut-over area	Probably mainly birch scrub / woodland and *Molinia* on block-cut topography.	Ditch blocking. Tramways act as bunds. Small embankment built on southern reserve.	Peat + wood	Early 1970's	Floating rafts in old peat cuttings (including *Sphagna*, *E. angustifolium*, *Vaccinium oxycoccos*). Water levels thought to have risen in recently-blocked areas. Some die-back of birch. Increase in teal population in response to increase in open water – subsequent decline as revegetation progressed.
Danes Moss, Cheshire [CWT]	Restoration of peat cuttings; control of eutrophic water.	Block-cut topography; mainly *Molinia* and birch.	Diversion of main drain; weir; ditch blocking. Some vegetation material transplanted into site.	Plywood dams (old tramway acts as a bund).	1974	55 cm water level rise within 2 years. Now extensive areas of open water in cuttings; increase in wetland fauna; die-back of *Molinia* and *Calluna*; some expansion of *Sphagna*, *Juncus effusus* and poor-fen species; floating peat particles forming colonisation surface for *Sphagna*.
Epworth Turbary, Lincs. [CWT]	Restoration of cut-over and drained site	Mainly birch scrub / woodland and *Molinia* – uneven topography.	Creation of pools using a digger		1976	Open water retained in at least one pool throughout droughts. Some colonisation of the pools by *Sphagnum*. Increase in diversity of fauna (*e.g.* dragonflies and birds) in response to increased provision of open water.
Fenns / Whixall Moss, Shropshire / Clywd [EN]	Restoration of commercial block cuttings	Recently block-cut area – bare peat or *Molinia* / birch	Surface bared and configured using a 'screw leveller'; ditch blocking	Peat dams	(1981) 1990	Early indications show rewetting and flooding. Some expansion of *Sphagna*, *E. angustifolium* and *E. vaginatum*; *Calluna* killed by flooding.
Glasson Moss, Cumbria [EN]	Restoration of marginal peat cuttings; prevention of water loss from uncut surface	Typical block-cut topography, part vegetated – mainly by *Calluna*, with *Sphagna* in wetter hollows and drains.	Ditch blocking	Peat dams ± impermeable cores	1986	Rewetting with variable success; *Sphagna*, *E. angustifolium* and *E. vaginatum* spreading; die-back of *Calluna*. Increase in dragonflies.
Risley Moss, Cheshire [Cheshire County Council]	Restoration of commercial peat cuttings	Typical block-cut topography. Much *Molinia* and scrub invasion.	Ditch blocking	Sand-bag dams; sluices; sheet metal dams;	1976	Rise in water levels up to 2.5 m, but limited effect on higher ground. *Molinia* die-back; increase in cover of *Sphagna* and *E. angustifolium*. Marked increase in wetland birds and possibly Odonata.
Roudsea Mosses, Cumbria [EN]	To rewet site following extensive drainage of uncut bog surface	Damaged bog vegetation	Ditch blocking	Peat ± plastic core	c. 1982	Water levels raised by c. 1m and more stable; *Sphagnum cuspidatum* spreading in wetter areas; increase in peatland birds and invertebrates.
Shapwick Heath, Somerset [EN]	Rewetting site following drainage and peat cutting. Preservation of ancient wooden trackway.	Mainly wooded	Water pumped onto site and distributed through pipes. Partly bunded.	Fixed pipes and clay bund.	1985	Pumping apparently successful in keeping trackway wet; but some enrichment from supplementary water supply may be detrimental; bund has been leaky.
Thorne Moors, S. Yorks. [EN]	Restoration of commercial peat cuttings	Mainly *Molinia* and birch in block-cut topography	Mainly ditch blocking and supplementary water supply	Peat dams and movable pipes / pump	1992	Results encouraging, at least in terms of water retention. Some pumping of drainage water back into abandoned cuttings also being tried.

contd

Site	Objectives	Starting conditions	Action	Materials	Date started	Outcome to date
Wedholme Flow, Cumbria [EN]	Restoration of commercial peat cuttings	Typical block-cut topography, part vegetated.	Ditch blocking	Peat dams	1990	Early indications show rewetting and flooding; *Sphagnum cuspidatum* spreading in wettest areas.
Westhay Moor: Old Westhay, Somerset Levels [CWT]	Attempt to increase *Sphagnum* cover in upstanding remnant	Mainly *Molinia* and birch	Small-scale scrapes			*Sphagnum* starting to colonise
Westhay Moor: Getty's Mire, Somerset Levels [CWT]	Experimental surface configuration of cut-over surface	Bare peat (fen / transition)	Surface profiled to fit calculated groundwater mound. Control of water levels in adjacent drains by pumping. Transplants of living bog vegetation.		1990	Water levels conformed to mound in winter, but inverted in summer. Some establishment from transplanted material.
Wicken Fen, Cambs. [NT]	To reduce loss of water from upstanding peat block	Fen vegetation	Bunding of part of margin	Clay + peat	1984/9	Apparently successful in retaining water

Scotland

Site	Objectives	Starting conditions	Action	Materials	Date started	Outcome to date
Bankhead Moss, Fife [SWT]	To allow for colonisation / regeneration by *Sphagnum* (mainly for dragonflies initially); also to provide open water habitat	Small holes within original bog surface (dug for lint retting)	Vegetation cleared from lint holes.		1984	Sphagna apparently colonising pools, but adjoining main bog surface remains fairly dry.
Bankhead Moss, Fife [SWT]	Prevention of water loss	Damaged bog vegetation – mainly dominated by *Calluna*, with patchy Sphagna.	Ditch blocking	Peat + wooden stakes	1985	At least two out of four dams considered effective in retaining water, at least locally, but effects on water levels at bog surface not known.
Blawhorn Moss, Lothian [SNH]	To rewet site following extensive drainage c. 50 years ago.	Damaged bog vegetation – mainly dominated by *Calluna*, with patchy Sphagna.	Ditch blocking	Steel sheet dams across small drains; wooden palisade dams across erosion gullies	1987	Considered generally effective in decreasing water losses – water levels thought to have gradually risen by < 10 cm.
Flanders Moss, Stirlings. [SNH/SWT]	Reduction in water loss	Partly-drained bog surface	Ditch blocking	Peat / wood / PVC dams	1990	Success thought to be limited so far. Extensive programme of scrub clearance and ditch blocking recently started by SNH.

Site	Objective	Initial condition	Measures	Structure	Date	Results
Gardrum Moss, Falkirk [PPA]	Restoration of commercially cut-over area	Bare peat	Creation of lagoons; transplants of bog vegetation	Peat bunds bulldozed into position	1991	Apparently holding water well, with some expansion of transplanted plant material.
Moine Mhor, Argyll [SNH]	Rewetting of drained site with marginal domestic peat cuttings	Damaged bog vegetation	Ditch blocking	Wooden palisade dams	1989	Some ponding back of water locally, but effect may be of limited extent.
Northern Ireland						
Peatlands Park, Armagh [DOE,NI]	Restoration of extensive commercially cut-over area	Typical block-cut topography; mainly bare peat.	Ditch blocking; surface configuration (levelling-out – peat from baulks used to infill drains)	Peat dams	1984	Much flooded in winter, but water sub-surface in summer. Revegetation with *Calluna* etc.; Sphagna mainly confined to trenches and depressions; *S. cuspidatum* forming rafts in former lake area.
Brackagh Moss, Armagh [DOE,NI]	Maintenance of diverse vegetation of extensively cut-over area; reduction of eutrophic influence; reduction in water losses	Good natural recolonisation on mainly fen peat.	Ditch carrying eutrophic water diverted; part bunded.	Peat bund (on existing trackway)	1990	Bund retaining water well – water held in cuttings. Raised baulks remain dry. Site managed to maintain habitat mosaic, particularly acid heath, fen and open water, rather than promoting restoration to raised bog.
Ireland						
Clara Bog, Offaly [Wildlife Service]	Rewetting of intensively- drained bog surface	Damaged bog vegetation	Ditch blocking	Peat dams	1986	Dams of variable quality, but mostly effective.
Corlea Bog, Longford [BnM]	Preservation of ancient wooden trackway in upstanding peat remnant	Damaged bog vegetation	Complete peripheral bunding of remnant; plus lagoons on one side.	Peat + plastic membrane; provision of moat along part of bund	1992	Visited soon after construction in 1992 – recent results not known.
Turraun Bog, Offaly [BnM]	Restoration of completely worked-out milled bog	Bare peat	Ditch blocking, bunding and inundation	Bund of peat and underlying marl. Island created in lake.	c.1990	Creation of lake; starting to revegetate with minerotrophic plant species.

contd

Site	Specific problem / objectives	Starting conditions	Action	Materials	Date started	Comments
The Netherlands						
Bargerveen – Meerstalblok (Drenthe)	Protection of small remnant adjoining extensive marginal commercial peat cuttings	Damaged bog vegetation; white peat bunkerde over black peat in block-cuttings	Ditch blocking and bunding of remnant; creation of extensive series of lagoons	Mainly black peat	1968	Remnant partly rewetted, but further bunding necessary. Lagoons flooded and holding water well; floating rafts of Sphagna establishing where bunkerde rose to form floating rafts.
Bargerveen – Amsterdamsche Veld (Drenthe)	Extensive milled peat fields	Bare peat and some white peat bunkerde	Ditch blocking / filling; narrow peat baulks	mainly white peat	1983	Formation of extensive lagoons. Raft formation by S. cuspidatum
Engbertsdijksveen (Overijssel)	Protection of small remnant, with extensive marginal commercial peat cuttings	Damaged bog vegetation; Molinia etc. ± bare peat in cuttings (no bunkerde)	Ditch blocking and bunding of remnant; creation of lakes; blocking of peat cuttings; ditch blocking	peat dams + plastic sheets; bund + plastic membrane; deep drain infilled with peat after laying plastic membrane in base.	1960's	Ditch blocking and lakes inadequate to rewet remnant, although some improvement in bog vegetation – also bunded in 1991. Peat cuttings rewetting; S. cuspidatum colonising open water; decline in Molinia and birch with increased water levels.
Fochteloёrveen (Friesland / Drenthe)	Protection of small remnant [with extensive marginal peat cuttings]	Damaged bog vegetation	Bund around remnant; ditch blocking	Bund – white peat + plastic membrane	1984	Bund holding water well, but possibly too far out to rewet centre effectively. Death of Molinia by flooding. Further 'concentric' bunding may be considered.
Germany **Lower Saxony:**						
Lichten Moor	Experimental area – block cut	Typical block-cut topography. Most trenches with < 50 cm bunkerde	Ditch blocking; weirs	Peat? Railway embankments served well as baulks.	1976	Area rewetted; surface swollen by 20 cm; water table maintained < 2 m above the groundwater table over a distance of c. 20 m. Reduction in Calluna; Sphagna have recolonised trenches.
Lichten Moor	Restoration of recently abandoned, milled fields	30 cm layer of bunkerde on black peat (< 5% vegetation cover)	Low peat walls to sub-divide area and retain water. Ditches infilled, some surface levelling	Peat walls formed by bulldozers	1988	Rapid colonisation by Molinia, Eriophorum vaginatum, E. angustifolium. S. cuspidatum in drains.
Leegmoor	Restoration of extensive area of milled peat cuttings	50–60 cm bunkerde over black peat (unvegetated)	Low peat walls to sub-divide area and retain water. Ditches infilled, some surface levelling	Peat walls formed by bulldozers	1983	First bunds washed away. Replaced with greater number and more careful positioning. Starting to revegetate with Molinia, E. angustifolium, E. vaginatum, S. cuspidatum.

Site	Aim	Condition	Measure	Material / method	Date	Results
Esterweger Dose	Restoration of commercial cuttings	Bunkerde over white peat	Lagoons created using bunds	White peat / black peat bund	1980's	White peat bund replaced by black peat because ineffective. Increase in water retention and colonisation by *E. angustifolium*. Trials indicate some beneficial effects of *bunkerde*'.
Bissendorfer Moor	Restoration of bog remnant and peat cuttings	Block-cut topography	Marginal bund; ditch blocking; small bunds	Marginal bund – peat, sods and sand; peat + PVC dams;	1976	Marginal bund ineffective in rewetting; cuttings well revegetated; increase in wetland fauna; effectiveness of damming restricted to limited area.
Neustädter Moor	Restoration of bog remnant and block peat cuttings	Mainly dominated by *Calluna, Molinia* or *E. vaginatum*, or bare peat.	Ditch blocking; creation of lagoons with bunds	Peat; sheep grazing	late 1970's	Variable results as peat cutting and drainage continue. Some birch death through flooding, and increase in *Eriophorum vaginatum–Erica tetralix* community. Possible conflict between rewetting for bog vegetation and optimal habitat conditions for golden plover.
Bavaria:						
Breitenmoos	Restoration of sloping milled-over surface.	Bare peat	Small lagoons created	Low peat walls constructed using bulldozer.	1989	Full scheme not executed due to lack of funds. Walls built, but no real attempt to reduce slope; erosion is a problem. Poor recolonisation to date – best in wettest areas.
Kendlmühlfilze	Restoration of block cut area	Bare peat (fen peat and dark peat)	Creation of small lagoons. Inoculation with transplanted material.	Small bunds of peat, bulldozed up.	1970's; 1987	Early experimental lagoons not recolonised very effectively. Some vegetative spreading of planted material in recent experimental areas. Fen species establishing on fen / transition peat. Water fluctuation of only 10–15 cm, but area has high rainfall.
Seemoos	Hand peat cuttings	Small-scale cutting, vegetation returned to cuttings	Natural recolonisation following natural occlusion of main outfall.		> 1950's	Excellent recolonisation by bog species, with *Sphagnum* mat c. 40 cm deep. Attributed to return of vegetation layer, and inundation. Actively-growing bog vegetation restricted to cuttings.
Wendlinger Filz	Restoration following drainage and domestic peat cuttings (some small-scale milling)	Bare peat slopes (from small-scale milling operations)	None			Poor recolonisation of slopes mainly attributed to erosion of peat and propagules. Signs of drying in uncut area. Fen species recolonised in cuttings exposing fen peat. Best recolonisation where cuttings wettest.
Wieninger Filz	Natural revegetation of hand peat cuttings	Small-scale cutting, vegetation returned to cuttings	None		> 1930's?	Excellent recolonisation by bog species, with *Sphagnum* mat 50–60 cm deep. Attributed to return of vegetation layer, and water levels not falling below surface in summer, inundated in winter.

Appendix 7

Useful contact addresses

Biological Records Centre
Monks Wood Experimental Station
Abbots Ripton
Huntingdon
Cambridgeshire
PE17 2LF

British Trust for Ornithology
National Centre for Ornithology
The Nunnery
Thetford
Norfolk
IP24 2PU

Cadw
Brunel House
2 Frazer Road
Cardiff
CF2 1UY

Council for British Archaeology
Bowes Morrell House
111 Walmgate
York
YO1 2UA

Council for the Protection of Rural England
Warwick House
25 Buckingham Palace Road
London
SW1W 0PP

Countryside Council for Wales
Plas Penrhos
Ffordd Penrhos
Bangor
Gwynedd
LL57 2LQ

Department of the Environment (Northern Ireland)
Environment Service
20-24 Donegal Street
Belfast
BT1 2GP

Department of the Environment (Minerals Division)
2, Marsham Street
London
SW1P 3EB

English Heritage
Fortress House
23 Saville Row
London
W1X 2HE

English Nature
Northminster House
Peterborough
Cambridgeshire
PE1 1UA

Health and Safety Executive
Broad Lane
Sheffield
S3 7HQ

Historic Scotland
Playfair House
6 Broughton Street Lane
Edinburgh
EH3 6RA

Institute of Hydrology
Maclean Building
Crowmarsh Gifford
Wallingford
Oxford
OX10 8BB

Joint Nature Conservation Committee
Monkstone House
City Road
Peterborough
Cambridgeshire
PE1 1JY

National Rivers Authority
Rivers House
Waterside Drive
Aztec West
Almondsbury
Bristol
BS12 4UD

Peat Producers Association
c/o Levington Horticulture Ltd.
Paper Mill Lane
Bramford
Ipswich
Suffolk
IP8 4BZ

Royal Commission on Historical Monuments of
Wales
Plas Creig
Aberystwyth
SY23 1NJ

Royal Commission on Historical Monuments of
England
Fortress House
23 Saville Row
LONDON
W1X 2HE

Royal Commission on Ancient & Historical
Monuments of Scotland
John Sinclair House
16 Bernard Terrace
Edinburgh
EH8 9NX

Royal Entomological Society
41, Queens Gate
London
SW7 5HU

RSNC - The Wildlife Trusts Partnership
The Green
Witham Park
Waterside South
Lincoln
LN6 7JR

Royal Society for the Protection of Birds
The Lodge
Sandy
Bedfordshire
SG19 2DL

Scottish Natural Heritage
2–5 Anderson Place
Edinburgh
EH6 5NP

Scottish Office, Environment Department
St Andrews House
Edinburgh
EH1 3DD

Scottish Wildlife Trust
Cramond House
Kirk Cramond
Cramond Glebe Rd
Edinburgh
EH4 6NS

Ulster Wildlife Trust
3 New Line
Crossgar
Down
BT30 9EP

Welsh Office
Cathays Park
Cardiff
CF1 3NQ